Composition in Context

Essays in Honor of
Donald C. Stewart

Edited by
W. Ross Winterowd and Vincent Gillespie

PE
1404
.C625
1994

SOUTHERN ILLINOIS UNIVERSITY PRESS
CARBONDALE AND EDWARDSVILLE

CAC0195

INDIANA-
PURDUE
LIBRARY
WITHDRAWN
NOV 12 1999
FORT WAYNE

Copyright © 1994 by the Board of Trustees,
Southern Illinois University
"Canonicity and the Renaissance Cicero," by Lawrence D. Green,
copyright © 1994 by Lawrence D. Green
All rights reserved
Printed in the United States of America
Designed by Jolene Faye Hamil
Production supervised by Natalia Nadraga
97 96 95 94   4 3 2 1

Library of Congress Cataloging-in-Publication Data

Composition in context : essays in honor of Donald C. Stewart / edited
  by W. Ross Winterowd and Vincent Gillespie.
      p.   cm.
    Includes bibliographical references.
    1. English language—Composition and exercises—Study and
teaching.   2. English language—Composition and exercises—Research.
3. English language—Rhetoric—Study and teaching.   4. English
language—Rhetoric—Research.   5. Rhetoric—History.   I. Winterowd,
W. Ross.   II. Gillespie, Vincent.   III. Stewart, Donald C.
PE1404.C625   1994
808'.042'07—dc20   93-15739
ISBN 0-8093-1862-8   CIP

Frontispiece: Donald C. Stewart

Jim W. Corder, "Humanism Isn't a Dirty Word," *This Is TCU* 24.2 (Nov. 1981):
10–11, reprinted by permission of the author.

The paper used in this publication meets the minimum requirements of American
National Standard for Information Sciences—Permanence of Paper for Printed
Library Materials, ANSI Z39.48-1984. ∞

Contents

Editors' Introduction

EVEN HARDCORE SKEPTICS, FROM THE DEEPEST ENTRENCHMENTS OF traditional English department humanities, would agree that there is a field of "composition," concerned not only with orthography and punctuation but also with such complex matters as sentence fragments and pronoun reference. At the same time, hardcore compositionists, from the front lines of the Conference on College Composition and Communication and the American Educational Research Association, know that even though they have won the battle, there is no home country to which they can return. In a word, the literarists who control English departments are now aware that there is a discipline named "composition" (concerned in some inexplicable way with the *Harbrace Handbook*), but compositionists reside in the literarist empire only as documented aliens, the courses they teach entitling them to green cards. The context of composition is, by and large, an institution so structured as to provide no territory for the discipline (as opposed to the practice).

This paradox—the homelessness of composition as a discipline in an academic community that prides itself on specialization—was one that bedeviled Donald C. Stewart. It was formative of his career, a constant echo in his writings, and a determinant of his major professional interests. That in part the paradox shaped *Composition in Context: Essays in Honor of Donald C. Stewart* is, hence, not accidental. In examining that paradox, the editors believed that three questions were inevitable: What is the history of the context? How does composition function within its context? How should we interpret or reinterpret the context? The questions were not intended to seek coherent, definitive answers so much as diverse viewpoints, various angles of attack, traditionalists and dissenters. Thus, the list of contributors to this volume (the result of a good deal of consulting) is an ideal mix of what one, in a futile effort to be delicate, might call "old flatulations" (e.g., Dick Young, Dick Larson, Janice Lauer) and relative youngsters (e.g., Bill Covino, Nan Johnson, Jim Berlin).

Such compositionist colleagues' contributions to a collection could have been cacophonous; the danger of dada was dire. The result, however, was fugal and polyphonic, themes contrapuntally developed in a continuous inter-weaving of voices. (Perhaps the term *contrapuntally* should be emphasized.) The seventeen important essays collected are, consequently, a unity.

Vincent Gillespie's opening essay, "Donald Charles Stewart," does more than briefly describe the colleague whom this volume honors. Gillespie reminds us that Stewart's career was illustrative of the status of composition and rhetoric in our colleges and universities. Accepted because they are forma-tive of the literate, responsible self and basic to a liberal education, they are denied the valorization demanded by specializations that depend on them, that, indeed, evolved from them. Donald Stewart, however, was exemplary and illustrative of the best of us. He could not be denied. The strength of his character and the nature of his being remind us of what the classical rhetors sought as the end of their discipline.

Constructing the Context
(What Is the History of the Context?)

It can and should be argued that composition really began in the last quarter of the eighteenth century, with two massively influential works: Campbell's *The Philosophy of Rhetoric* (1776) and Blair's *Lectures on Rhetoric and Belles Lettres* (1783). But if Campbell and Blair initiated a historical epoch, they were also the products of history. Nan Johnson's chapter, "Quintilian and the Nineteenth-Century Rhetorical Tradition," explains one crucial strand in the fabric of composition's history from the ancients through the rationalists to the nineteenth-century current-traditionalists and thence to our own age and context: the influence of Quintilian.

In "Canonicity and the Renaissance Cicero," Lawrence D. Green makes the telling point that every age uses its resources for its own ends, sometimes forgetting that in most hermeneutic enterprises, ultraliberal interpretation must be checked by strict construction else the original document is completely lost. Green might well have titled his piece with the admonitory "A Lesson in the Perils of Interpretation."

In the histories of composition, Campbell and Blair appear to stand alone, two Scots single-handedly laying the basis for nearly two centuries of dogma, doctrine, and practice, but, as Winifred Bryan Horner points out in "The Scottish-American Connection and the Emergence of Belletristic Composi-tion," appearances are just that. Horner lays out quite comprehensively how interrelated and logical were the extensive philosophic and pedagogical influ-ences that linked together the rise of composition and rhetoric instruction in

Scotland and the United States. Economic, social, and political needs forged relationships between the nations in the nineteenth century and have been strong bonds since. Horner clearly delineates those relationships in the nineteenth century and their forming influences on the varied streams of modern composition teaching.

Everyone who has been in composition for longer than forty-eight hours has sensed that the step into the field has been viewed by literary colleagues as a downward, not a lateral, move. In "Postmodernism, the College Curriculum, and Composition," James A. Berlin persuasively argues that rhetoric and composition may well be the last, best hope for English department humanities. Berlin's brief historical survey of composition's pivotal role in shaping liberal education establishes its formative influence in nineteenth- and twentieth-century society. He argues, most convincingly, that as political, social, and economic forces further shape our curricula and intensify academic and professional specialization, the changing nature of rhetorical and composition instruction may well bring such forces center stage. The demand for professional, innovative, collaborative information systems may be formative of a rhetoric that, at its best, will foster a socially moral and politically responsible ethos, one that will forward a democratic, egalitarian community.

The history of rhetoric since the romantic movement has been one of privatization. As Ralph Waldo Emerson, that archetypical American romantic, said in "Self-Reliance," "To believe your own thought, to believe that what is true for you is true for all men—that is genius. Speak your latent conviction, and it shall be the universal sense" (145). Thus, argument and persuasion are unnecessary, if one merely speaks his or her "mind" with conviction. And, in fact, as Janice Lauer demonstrates in "Persuasive Writing on Public Issues," expressive and expository writing have flourished, while argumentation and persuasion have been etherealized (deprived of both ethos and pathos) and have been relegated to obligatory brief chapters in the textbooks.

Edward P.J. Corbett asks the perennially troubling question in our history, "How Did Rhetoric Acquire the Reputation of Being the Art of Flimflam?" This historical survey traces the debasement of rhetoric from classical Greece through the present.

With remarkable brevity, Robert J. Connors offers a telling view of the profession in "Crisis and Panacea in Composition Studies: A History." Not only a historical survey of composition studies during the past 150 years, the essay is also a perceptive comment on the character of our search for answers, of our constant struggle with each new crisis and our faith in our ability to solve it. But the hallmark of our history as it is revealed in our literature is not naive faith in delivery; rather, it is our belief that the new flame is worth the candle. We continue to seek new answers to old problems because the field deals with essential public need and private fulfillment. One might argue, in fact, that the terms *crisis* and *panacea* in a sense characterize the context of composition.

Working Within the Context
(How Does Composition Function Within Its Context?)

Four or five years ago, W. Ross Winterowd asked some fifty composition teachers in a large program to write a page or two in response to this hypothetical question from a dean or other administrator: "What is the rationale for your composition course?" The first reaction of the fifty was a chorused gasp: the writing teachers were being asked to write a couple of pages! Nonetheless, most of the teachers did bite the grindstone, put their noses to the midnight oil, and burn the bullet, so that the following week thirty-five statements of rationale were duly submitted. Eagerly Winterowd started to read them, intending to sort them into the two or three categories that he predicted they would represent (e.g., writing as a way of thinking, writing as self-discovery, writing as effective communication). When he finished reading, he had thirty-five one-item piles—complete idiosyncrasy (a slight exaggeration for rhetorical effect).

In "Enlarging the Context: From Teaching Just Writing to Teaching Academic Subjects *with* Writing," Richard L. Larson shows that the experience recounted above was not totally unique. His report on a study that he did for the Ford Foundation depicts a profession—the teaching of writing—lacking in clear focus and purpose for its work. Larson is careful to qualify: not all programs (or teachers) lack focus and purpose. However, the reasons for doing what compositionists do is a major concern.

In "Impediments to Change in Writing-Across-the-Curriculum Programs," Richard Young elaborates on the theme of Richard Larson's chapter. What happens to the reforms and revolutions in composition once they become institutionalized? The image is vinegar taffy. You boil it and cool it and pull it and let it set until it's glassy-hard, then break it into alabaster pieces and leave it on the plate overnight; the next morning, you find the individual pieces have slumped together into one gooey mass. To paraphrase Richard Young, our problem with new programs is to find ways of keeping them from slumping, overnight, back into a gooey mass.

We clearly remember the debate over wheel versus travois. The wheel, it was said, needed an axle on which to turn, and that involved bearings and some kind of lubricants—complication upon complication. Just as clearly, we remember a volume by Wilbur Cross, titled something like *Bibliographic Guide to English Studies*, and we recall that we spent countless hours going through the Modern Language Association bibliographies—detailed maps of the territory of literary studies. But there was no composition; that was the territory ahead. And who can map the territory ahead? If there is a discovered territory, there must be maps.

Which is exactly Paul T. Bryant's point in "No Longer a Brand New World: The Development of Bibliographic Resources in Composition." In this essay, Bryant traces the rich development of bibliographic resources in composition and rhetoric since 1973.

Almost all scholarly fields have identity and status within the institutions of higher education; there are departments of physics, history, education, and so on. The historian can wander into the departmental coffee room and find someone who is interested in his or her work, who reads the same journals, and who attends the same conventions. There is no such coffee room for the compositionist, but there have been such institutes as the ones sponsored by the National Defense Education Act and projects such as the National Writing Project. These institutions—never on a main line in the organizational structure of universities and colleges—have given compositionists a place to gather, a locus where others of their persuasion would be available for talk and cooperation. Thus, institutes and projects have been more important for composition than are such efforts for traditional disciplines. Richard Lloyd-Jones traces the development of institutes and projects in composition, language, and rhetoric. Recognizing the pedagogical and philosophic importance of the National Writing Project, Lloyd-Jones delineates those professional influences that did much to give rise to it and to foster a sophistication that refocused our profession's understanding of its subject matter and its pedagogy. The Basic Issues Conference of 1958, the College Entrance Examination Board institutes of the 1960s, and their resulting summer programs—the NDEA Institutes, the National Endowment for the Humanities Institutes for Directors of Freshman Composition in Colleges, the Iowa Writing Project, and the Bay Area Project—are all recognized for their contributions. Their influence has been profound: the development of other such programs, the growth of regional cooperation, the source of major, germinal texts and of countless curriculum materials and publications, the involvement of other disciplines in composition and rhetoric teaching—all such concerns owe much to the development of major institutes and programs. Richard Lloyd-Jones, himself a consequential force in the evolvement, describes their history and their interrelationships with gratifying clarity in "On Institutes and Projects."

Reinterpreting the Context
(How Should We Interpret or Reinterpret the Context?)

Histories of rhetoric are, by and large, histories of the epistemologies of rhetoricians. For example, romantic theories of language, aesthetics, and rhetoric originate with the epistemology of the German idealists (Kant, Fichte, and Schelling) as transmitted through (and transmuted by) Coleridge, De Quincey, Carlyle, Pater, and others in Great Britain and Emerson, Thoreau, and others in the United States. I. A. Richards was so deeply influenced by Coleridge that to study Richards is to see Coleridge through the lens and filter of a scholar-teacher who believed profoundly in the utopian potential of science, thus paradoxically embodying the romantic belief that all knowledge is personal and subjective as well as the modernist faith in objective, empirical science.

One reason for the ghettoization of composition within the English department is the romantic legacy of values and epistemologies that prevails among literary scholars—a view of language and texts that holds teaching to be impossible and that relegates "nonimaginative" texts to a status well below that of "imaginative" texts. This strange situation alienates English department "literature" from "factual" texts that are now in the commonplace (as was the novel in the nineteenth century) and that are significant works of art (e.g., *Pilgrim at Tinker Creek*, *The Snow Leopard*, *Friendly Fire*).

Since "composition"—under whatever guise, such as "Freshman Writing," "Freshman English," "Writing Across the Curriculum," and "Business Writing"—aims to teach students to write what Comley and Scholes call "pseudononliterature" (98), it is a less noble and ennobling enterprise than "creative writing," which engenders "pseudoliterature," for the poem "permits its readers at once to cherish its creation as a closed object, one that comes to terms with itself, and to recognize its necessarily incomplete nature in its dependence on us as its readers, on literary history, on the general language system, and on the way of the world" (Krieger 540). On the other hand, a freshman theme or an advanced composition essay invites us only to mark errors and point out incoherence, lapses in reasoning, lack of sufficient evidence, and the clumsy title.

In "Phantastic Palimpsests: Thomas De Quincey and the Magical Composing Imagination," William A. Covino delineates the romantics' reassertion of the validity of the phantastic/rhetorical imagination as a mode of invention, a validity called into doubt by the Enlightenment's distrust of nonrational faculties. Focusing on De Quincey's metaphor of the creative imagination as a palimpsest, Covino shows the romantic reinvigoration of phantasy. Reflecting a modern emphasis, he discusses the arresting and provocative metaphor of the computer screen as an electronic palimpsest—as a mode of our entrance into the composing imagination.

A less-than-careful and less-than-sympathetic reading of deconstructionist doctrine might lead one to the conclusion that writing is construction and reading is deconstruction. Thus, one somehow grasps the entirety of *Middlemarch* at a glance and then begins to take it apart à la Hillis Miller or Barbara Johnson. In "Voice as Echo of Delivery, Ethos as Transforming Process," Theresa Enos develops the corrective argument that the transforming power of ethos is possible only in the movement from constructing to reconstructing, a necessary process that can only then free the reader to begin deconstructing, a form of revision after all.

Victor J. Vitanza's essay, our interpretation of it, and his response to our interpretation constitute an apt and cautionary example of the difficulties of hermeneutics in the poststructuralist age. In any case, here is our reading of "Threes":

> The zithered melody of "The Third Man Theme" still twangs in Vienna's *Rathskeller*, and the sinister Third Man or Woman lurks at the edge of all dialogues, ready to disagree and contradict, unless the talkers can exclude him or her. In "Threes," says Victor Vitanza, "a successful communication is the exclusion of the third man." If, however, one assumes the position of this demon, then one is in the position of eternally critiquing the dialogue. For Vitanza, the critique is as important as the dialogue—perhaps more so because it will transform rhetoric by making the dialogue a multi-voiced "one," a rhetor of all being-in-consciousness.

And here is Vitanza's critique of our reading:

> My sense is that your description is the absolute opposite of what I am talking about in my ms. (1) The third man (woman) does not give a "critique," which would imply the exclusive use of discursive thinking. To be sure, I employ critique but only to use it against itself, so as to bring about a contradiction (a third subject position such as an hermaphrodite). I would say, and have said, that I engage in "paracritique," which is a word that you might not want to use. (No word exists that I know of; therefore, I have to invent one!)
>
> (2) Moreover, I do not "transform rhetoric by making the dialogue a multi-voiced 'one,' a rhetor of all being-in-consciousness." This sounds like a Platonized view of what I am attempting, or at least a Burkean view. The dialogue becomes overwhelmed, or falls into *aporia*, because of *noise*, or infinite regress, or again contradiction. A Platonic "One" is shattered, or a Burkean synecdochic view is similarly exploded. I'm talking about the "delirium of the many" that cannot be systematized. Therefore, there is no "multi-voiced 'one'." Instead, there is, as I count: one, two, and *some more*, the latter signifying an irrational move, or a radical multiplicity, or what Feyerabend calls a "paratactic aggregate."
>
> "Some more" signifies, then, the so-called "threes" of the title; or, e.g., it signifies not a third man or third woman, but a third (or "some more") possibilities. Hence, my discussion toward the end of the paper on gender via Butler's book *Gender Trouble*.

From another angle, that of ecofeminism, C. Jan Swearingen and Diane Mowery also propose a revolution in composition and rhetoric. To oversimplify briefly and tentatively, and only for the sake of clarity, one might say that compositionists now fall into one of two categories: the New Romantics or the New Rhetoricians. The most significant difference between the two is that New Romantics view writing as a way of *making* or *finding* something (meaning, a poem, the writer's self) whereas New Rhetoricians view writing as a way of *doing* something (convincing, alienating, informing, consoling, elating, amusing). The way to heal this schism is, of course, to speak of "both . . . and" rather than "either . . . or." Swearingen and Mowery argue that within composition theory, feminist approaches can help restore dignity and cognitive substance to discourse models such as the expressive and the narrative that have recurrently been demeaned within composition scholarship just as composition, as a field, sustains renewed questioning within English studies.

In "Style, Invention, and Indirection: Aphorisms," George Yoos and Philip Keith reinterpret composition teaching from the standpoint of the tradition of "commonplaces" and of a contemporary theory of communication (that of Sperber and Wilson in *Relevance: Communication and Cognition*). This chapter— interpreting the tradition from the standpoint of the present—is a fitting coda for a collection that views composition in context.

Works Cited

Comley, Nancy R., and Robert Scholes. "Literature, Composition, and the Structure of English." *Composition and Literature: Bridging the Gap*. Ed. Winifred Bryan Horner. Chicago: U of Chicago P, 1983. 96–109.

Emerson, Ralph Waldo. "Self-Reliance." *The Writings of Ralph Waldo Emerson*. Ed. Brooks Atkinson. New York: Random House, 1940. 145–69.

Krieger, Murray. "An Apology for Poetics." *Critical Theory Since 1965*. Ed. Hazard Adams and Leroy Searle. Tallahassee: Florida State UP, 1986. 535–42.

Donald Charles Stewart
1930–1992

Vincent Gillespie

> *It is not true, as some writers on the art maintain, that the probity of the speaker contributes nothing to his persuasiveness; on the contrary, we might almost affirm that his character is the most potent of all the means to persuasion.*
>
> —*Aristotle*

DON DID NOT FEIGN EMBARRASSMENT WHEN I TOLD HIM WHAT I WAS doing. He knew of Ross Winterowd's plan to put together *Composition in Context* and knew, I suspect, that Ross had asked me to write an appropriate, informal profile.

So we began, quite simply, to talk about it. He was quite gracious and unselfconscious. And, although he never voiced it, I know he was pleased. He thought of himself as rather typical, as one of those who had become involved in composition and rhetoric and had achieved a measure of success. He believed that such a profile might be interesting. Admittedly, even he wondered at times why a sensible, reasonably ambitious person would choose as unpromising a path as composition-rhetoric back in the late 1950s and early 1960s. I think he talked as easily about his past as he did because he wondered about the answer.

Don Stewart did not believe in miracles—wonders, yes, but not miracles. He assumed that he might see *Composition in Context*, might get to thank those who contributed to it. He assumed that, but he knew otherwise. We both knew it. Indeed, questions and answers were considered in that light. He made only two requests—demands, really. "Don't embarrass me—don't make more than what is there." And, "Don't, for all our sakes, write an extended five-paragraph essay—just do an informal, a personal piece."

For those who knew Don, what I write will hold no surprises. Some details may be unknown, but the thrust is what one would expect. Don

Stewart was wiser than most; his integrity, always mentioned, was never questioned. He was guileless—so much so that he believed most of us were as well; he was self-effacing (though hardly ever reticent); he was incredibly fair in dealing with others—personal differences never resulted in spitefulness. He was also competitive, contemptuous of personal and professional affectation, as disciplined as time and as stubborn as stone. He was also, at times, a missionary in a heathen land. He would pursue truth until it became everyone's fact.

In traditional terms, Don Stewart's professional success can be readily summarized. A Wisconsin Ph.D. at thirty-two. Full professorship at a ranked university. Four books. Chapters in seven other books. Literary criticism enough to prove he could do such work when he felt he had something worth saying. Over sixty articles on composition and rhetoric and teaching. A dozen or so reviews. Two dozen stories and general articles (environmental concerns, music, fly fishing, sports, and whatnot). More national, regional, and state conference papers than even he would want to sit through. Kansas State University's Outstanding Teaching award. Demanding National Council of Teachers of English and Conference on College Composition and Communication editorial positions. President of the Kansas Association of Teachers of English. Service on several national NCTE committees. Almost every appointive and elective position in the CCCC, including the national chair. He was unable to participate in professional conferences after the fall of 1986.

As impressive as all that is, enough indeed for two careers, it does not sum up the Don Stewart that I and others admired, the person whom we knew.

Don wasn't a reluctant English major, not exactly, but he was surprised to find himself one when he graduated from the University of Kansas in Lawrence in May 1952. He most certainly did not know what he would do with that degree, and he accepted a GTA (graduate teaching assistantship) from KU only to give himself time to figure it out. Besides, as he put it, graduate school was only a place to go between summers spent as a ranger and naturalist at Yellowstone Park. But he really wasn't enthusiastic about graduate school. Better than a desultory student, for his pride and competitive juices saw to that, he was comfortable with the life. (Don was really made for a university or, at least, for the better parts of it—all really but its politics.) He loved the campus ("KU *is* beautiful") and avidly attended its football and basketball games. He seldom ignored a cultural event and played a consequential role in the University Symphony Orchestra. In fact, music opened KU's doors for him.

Don was an excellent violinist and as a student was provided financial assistance (much needed) by the orchestra and served as its concertmaster. He spent hours as an English graduate student practicing his violin. That love was ever part of Don. Some persons who wondered where Don was during

CCCC or NCTE convention cocktail parties and those evenings of collegial conviviality after daytime sessions ended would have been surprised to learn that he was frequently at some private home playing in a chamber music quartet. One of Don's pleasures after making convention arrangements was to utilize his membership in the Amateur Chamber Music Players Incorporated, contact fellow members (invariably strangers) in the convention city, and arrange to spend an evening in a member's home playing to his and, I'm sure, his host's hearts' content. Don's rank as a player was rather conservatively and officially just below that of "Near Professional." His enthusiasm for the music and for the experience characteristically resulted in an article in *The Christian Science Monitor*. Don wanted always to share his joys.

Don could have gone with music. He did serve as violin instructor at Baker University in nearby Baldwin City for a period of time when he held his GTA at KU. But Don felt that being a professional musician was not his career. He was not committed enough to the discipline to satisfy all the personal demands he would have made of himself. He could have gotten his music degrees and taught at a university—the College of Fine Arts certainly wanted him to—but the violin was a matter of love. Don wanted to keep it that way.

Don wasn't sure, but he assumed that as time passed he would know what he wanted to do. He didn't want to leave the university; he knew that. He enjoyed most classes, and teaching struck a responsive note for him, appealed, as he said, to the "ham" in him.

That is when I met Don. We were both beginning GTAs in the fall of 1952. We were not the closest of friends. Don was single; I was married. Don was officed in one bull pen; I was in another. Don ran with an odd assortment of personalities; I gravitated toward a more orthodox group. Don was, for many of us, that strange fellow in the building's tower office who could be heard practicing his violin at any time of day or night—literally. (What I thought quaintly aberrant was, of course, what I discovered later a significant characteristic of Don's: his need to do superlatively well any task that he became engaged in.) I remember, also, one other thing: Don had the most thorough memory one can imagine for KU sports trivia—indeed for all sports trivia, national and international, professional, Olympic. Even after forty years, he could recall the members of teams and describe in detail the moves of crucial plays and critical moments.

And 1952 was the year that Al Kitzhaber came to KU to direct its composition program. Still writing the dissertation that became a scholarly landmark in American rhetoric studies, Kitzhaber, fresh from Porter Perrin's program at the University of Washington, was to be a force consequential to Don. KU needed Kitzhaber and, to its credit, knew it. Its composition sequence—two three-hour semester courses followed by two two-hour comp and lit courses—was current-traditional with a vengeance: a theme a week, each marked, graded, revised, graded again, and abhorred by student and instructor alike, and editorial skills, drills, and exercises—a landscape of futility. We were expected to enforce a "hit list," popular at the time as yet another panacea: twenty error types, all weighted by importance, all determinative of grades (one sentence fragment = F; one comma splice = F; two dangling modifiers = D; and on and on). Don remembered his freshman comp instructor: "Any person who fails to place a comma before a pure conjunction separating the coequal parts of a compound sentence should not be taking up my or the university's time. Conscientious care is demanded." All hissed through pursed lips. The KU program needed Kitzhaber.

Don needed him, too; he just didn't know it at the time. Al Kitzhaber arrived in September, a time too late to initiate a comp syllabus and too early to attempt a philosophic overhaul. He did, however, introduce a course required of all new GTAs, a course that considered the nature of composition and its teaching and examined the core assumptions that drove most programs. He also instituted facultywide department grading sessions in which all ranks battled back and forth—marvelously rancorous meetings—to determine appropriate, realistic grades and comment standards for selected papers.

For Don and for others, that class (only the second of its kind at the time in the nation—a statement that may have been in error but was significant in being believed) and those meetings were harbingers of pedagogical grace. We hashed over, lashed over actually, the absurdities of current assumptions about writing behavior; supporters of the hit list had the opportunity to defend giving an A to an errorless, vacuous paper while failing an interesting, innovative argument mortally scarred by a comma splice and two misspellings. Some members began to realize that not every idea was expressible in a five-paragraph essay. And Kitzhaber's course had its effect. We all wrote a lengthy paper outlining our teaching philosophies; we all wished we hadn't. (I can still see his comment on mine. "You must have attended college in the 1890s. At least your pen must have.") He cleverly assigned to each a usage study. We each surveyed the linguistic data dealing with one of the items on the hit list. We all discovered that the "errors" were matters of style, levels of usage, incorrect assumptions about English, and of course, sometimes, just plain errors. But we discovered that such matters were not rabbinic pronouncement; rather, they were the features of a living language.

Don remembered his reaction to all that. Suddenly, he realized that what he had resisted teaching, what he had found inhibiting about classroom writing demands throughout high school and college, what he had intuitively realized about academic writing was, indeed, self-defeating, a thoughtless melange codified by little more than outdated institutional and social criteria. Kitzhaber was interested in invigorating writers. In Don Stewart he had enlivened a teacher. But Don didn't know that yet.

Don changed his grading and his teaching. He still took classes, still talked about KU's '52 NCAA basketball championship, still played his violin.

And he still hadn't quite decided what to do when his summers ended and he had to leave Yellowstone.

Then he met Patricia Pettepier. In the fall of 1954, Don was most impressed by a new GTA, a twenty-two-year-old Colorado M.A., one who in meeting him was not so immediately impressed. Quite suddenly, the latent drive and unfocused ambition took body. Quite suddenly, Lawrence was more than a long interlude between Yellowstones. And, though not quite so suddenly, she began to note his lack of self-absorption, his multifaceted talents (she too knew music), his omnivorous interests in all and everything, his perceptiveness, and as she puts it, his encyclopedic knowledge. She had become most impressed.

He began to contemplate, now quite seriously, what Patricia was already committed to—an academic career. That, of course, meant teaching literature and conducting complementary studies (no one considered composition and rhetoric in those days, no one who was ambitious anyhow). With their decision to marry came consequent changes. If they wanted careers at a university, Pat argued, they needed greater challenge, a different university for their Ph.D.s, for degrees with strong national reputations. Wisconsin would do it. They applied, were offered GTAs, were married, and went off to Yellowstone. Pat had to accept that—after all, he could be as stubborn as stone.

If anyone is to know Don Stewart, *My Yellowstone Years* is a must. He acknowledged the shaping force of Yellowstone in his introduction: "Other than my marriage to Pat and the birth of our children, the most important thing that ever happened to me were the thirteen summers spent in Yellowstone National Park." The book explores those summers, to be sure, but its value lies in our discovery of a Don Stewart so obvious as to be unseen.

Don revered that wondrous life, that joy in a wilderness where the loss of self is the beginning of awareness. Exploring the cycle of summer, the text uses the schema of days to celebrate dawn into sunset and the intimacy of fireside evenings. Don became an expert fly fisherman in those summers and yet kept no fish. The satisfaction was in the act. A fish once caught was gingerly unhooked, admired for its verve and beauty, and then slipped back into one of the rapids or quiet recessed pools that Don fished. He writes of the wildlife: the water life, the deer and elk, the bears. And one becomes aware of his love for the flora of the Yellowstone meadows and the mountains, for the geysers, for the near-boiling pools. But what one discovers on reflection is not Don's love of the wilderness, his sense of its strength and repose and beauty. No, what strikes one is that this work that celebrates the solitude of nature is a work teeming with people, with names of passersby and acquaintances, of strangers and fellow workers, with the presence of tourists named and unknown, with the personalities of those who, as fellow sojourners, returned each year to renew friendships.

Assuredly, *My Yellowstone Years* honors our first national park and acknowledges Don Stewart's coming of age. But more importantly, I think, it reveals a truth so central to his being that it was a defining characteristic. Don Stewart loved people, wanted to go among them, to talk endlessly to them, to help them see beyond themselves, to awaken them to the world that was a joy to him. His sought-after and then cherished position in Yellowstone was not that of the romanticized, lonely Ranger camping in the remote wilderness. What he most loved was being a Naturalist, lecturing at one of the park's tourist museums, answering questions countless times, engaging in conversations with all manner of people and—his glory—giving talks around campground firesides far into the darkness and until the tourists' energies would give out. Don Stewart couldn't help himself. He was a teacher.

So, it wasn't the ham in him, really; it was the missionary, the bringer of life. He needed to be a teacher. He just didn't know yet what kind he would be. The University of Wisconsin would help him decide.

Wisconsin, Don discovered, wasn't Kansas, and a university was not a university was not a university. The University of Kansas, a state of mind for Don, was congenial, collegial. Graduate students and faculty alike recognized a professional identity and a shared personal respect for one another. Graduate students worked together, shared notes, borrowed one another's texts, and helped those preparing for orals or written prelims. KU was for Don a universe compatible. But Wisconsin, he felt, was another matter. It was in its heyday with the likes of White, Wallerstein, Hughes, Doran—superb scholars, but faculty members who for the most part maintained a chilling distance from their students. It mattered little that Hughes would write "brilliant" on Don's Chaucer paper or that Doran would argue that he should consider a career in her field of Renaissance studies. For Don, intellectual respect was not a substitute for the warmth of personal engagement. But he could handle that. What he couldn't tolerate (and I could hear it in his voice some thirty-five years later) was the small-minded competitiveness of so many of his fellow graduate students. KU's collegiality was gone. Here was the constant reference to grades, the attempt to measure one another's B.A.s, the petty games of literary one-upmanship, the seeking of preference at another's expense. He wasn't ready for that world, and he didn't want to be.

He did his work, of course, and much better work than most. Pat, too, went on—she was actually better at it than Don, for one of her strengths has always been the ability to withstand, deflect, ward off, turn aside, however one wants to put it, the pettiness of others. But in doing his work, in passing course after course, test after test, paper after paper, Don couldn't find personal satisfaction and fulfillment.

Fortunately, he found that outside the English graduate program.

Wisconsin at the time disallowed husbands and wives both holding GTAs (Don and Pat had received their appointments before they were married), and so Don chose to accept an appointment as English instructor in Robert Pooley's

Integrated Liberal Studies Program, a two-year humanities-core sequence. The program, designed by Pooley for Wisconsin's better undergraduates, offered a superb liberal arts education to those who sought challenge. The program's faculty and students represented the university's best.

For Don the change made all the difference. Wisconsin's regular composition courses were as hoary as Kansas's had been before Kitzhaber, perhaps even more so. What was worse as far as Don was concerned was his fellow GTAs' attitudes. Composition was drudgery, was nothing beyond a stipend to enable them to carry on their literature course work. Uninterested in the work, the GTAs could only disparage it. And the program's administration championed the formal essay, the usage drills, and the efficacy of mastering editorial skills. Good manners were more important than a hearty meal.

The Integrated Liberal Studies Program and Robert Pooley were different. And Pooley, a former director of the regular comp program, was an administrator of vision and talent. A linguist by interest (he authored the NCTE's classic *Teaching English Usage*) and teacher-administrator by choice, Pooley had formed the ILS program to attract humanities students and provide them with a solid liberal arts foundation. He soon became, in effect, the second rhetoric-composition mentor who strongly influenced Don. The ILS program served about 300 of Wisconsin's undergraduates and served them well. Don's responsibilities were, at first, the teaching of a few comp sections. But Pooley's intent was refreshing to Don. Composition was not an end in itself, not a task nor a series of courses to get through; rather, composition was a means for students to realize ideas, to employ behaviors that led to discovery, to clarification, to the integration of ideas. Pooley encouraged the use of collaborative learning and cooperative action; he provided his instructors with the time and the means to employ tutorial techniques. An administrator who respected his staff and faculty and joined good judgment to personal warmth and collegiality, he gave his staff a sense of professional responsibility, a pride in their teaching, an awareness that much began in their classrooms. And Don blossomed. He became in Pooley's judgment the "best person [Pooley probably said "man"] he had ever had in the program." During both a semester sabbatical and a year's leave, Pooley turned the administration of the comp staff over to Don. Without intending to, Don moved closer to his eventual career.

He continued his graduate studies, passed the exams, and began his dissertation on Meredith. He might have chosen a different topic had the possibilities been unlimited, but one rarely wrote composition-rhetoric studies during the early 1960s. One certainly didn't, most assuredly didn't, in order to enhance one's credentials. Don was interested now in those credentials. Although her own graduate studies had been proceeding with characteristic and exceeding excellence, Pat had decided in 1958 that personal needs should put graduate work on hold. She taught briefly in high school and then for nearly three years served on the university library staff. By late 1961, Pat and Don had their first child. Don needed a full-time position.

In the spring of 1962, he was winding up the dissertation and considering options. A return to KU became possible; an opening in Ohio and another in Colorado (he admitted that the mountains were almost enough to do it) and inquiries from a few others presented possibilities. Then changes at the University of Illinois opened an unexpected path—one in comp and rhetoric. The others were literature, and though some were inviting, none was compelling. But at Illinois, the department was revamping its traditional administration of the comp program. Rather than assign the overseeing of some 130 or so GTAs to a single director, the department decided to create Ph.D. instructorships in composition and assign thirty GTAs to each for training and supervision. For Don, the position opened the door. He passed through and never looked back—well, hardly ever.

That was the moment of commitment for him, but he would, again, have to choose. In 1967, Illinois discontinued that administrative structure (Don had been promoted to assistant professor in his second year), and Don gave thought to taking a lit position or seeking another in composition and rhetoric. The fact that he had already published a few articles in composition journals suggested his course. He accepted an assistant professorship at Kansas State University in Manhattan, one that called for half-time within the comp program. But within K-State's structure, that was not the fast track, nor the most rewarding career. And I told him so.

Why, then, did he come; why take a long shot? The answer to that is the nature of the man—is, he thought, what made him typical of those who chose as he did.

Though Don published few literary studies, he certainly did not deprecate such work. He published, as I mentioned, enough to prove to himself that he could (and then only when enthusiasm carried him), but for him there was a difference between the motivations and the means that produced them and the interests that stimulated him. Too often he found literary studies to focus on the ephemeral and/or esoteric and to reflect, quite understandably, professional goals rather than teaching needs. Too often such studies, he felt, were functionally detached from the classroom and had little to do with students. But comp and rhetoric studies were different. They pointed toward helping students, became part of one's teaching, offered new approaches. Not centered on the interests of a few, they touched the needs of nearly every student. That appealed to him.

While Don was still at Illinois, he wanted to follow up some notions he had regarding freshman comp text studies and so applied for one of Illinois's then rather easily available summer stipends for younger faculty—a usual perk to encourage faculty publications. His $500 request was denied because his proposal centered on comp-rhetoric, an interest of only "peripheral interest." Lucky for him.

Believing his idea had value, he sent the proposal to the NCTE's Research Foundation in Honor of J. N. Hook. Dick Braddock at Iowa, who served the foundation's board as consultant, recognized the worth of Don's idea and took a realistic approach to its research costs. The foundation offered Don a $2,100 budget. (Don recalled his meeting with Braddock and commented that Braddock was the first professional who gave him the sense that he was doing something useful and wanted and needed by the profession.) The conference Don had with Braddock in the latter's Iowa office was notable for another reason: it was there that Don first came upon Rohman and Wlecke's *Pre-Writing: The Construction and Application of Models for Concept Formation in Writing*, a germinal work in Don's development and the philosophic basis for his own *The Authentic Voice*, his most consequential work in composition and, in James Berlin's view, the "most complete and intelligent textbook based on the work of Rohman and Wlecke" (147).

And other influences were coming together. His GTA supervisory responsibilities at Illinois had forced Don's attention to conceptual matters. He reread Kitzhaber's dissertation, "Rhetoric in American Colleges, 1850–1900," in order to discover, as he put it, "where we had come from." He found there evidence that the country had not always been that of the blind. Though many attitudes of the 1950s and 1960s could be traced to the philosophic rigidity of the "school of Bain," minor but otherwise encouragingly rich traditions offered promise—and not the least of those was that of Fred Newton Scott. (We'll come back to Scott later. Don always came back to Scott.) And Kitzhaber's *Themes, Theories, and Therapy: Teaching of Writing in College* (1963) clarified for Don both the sterility and the promise of the way in which composition was being and could be taught in our colleges.

Don was encouraged, too, by knowing that a significant segment of the academic world was involved in work that drew him. He discovered that he was not alone; he realized he was involved in a movement that emphasized his pedagogical and humane values, that could make the classroom a rich mine of satisfaction.

Kitzhaber and Pooley had been personal influences; Don was now becoming aware of the fledgling CCCC and its influence on restoring the rhetorical tradition. At Illinois, he was a stone's throw from the NCTE in Urbana. He knew, of course, of Wayne Booth's MLA paper "The Revival of Rhetoric" and his plea for a judicious balance of English department interests. And he also knew, of course, of Corbett, Winterowd, Gorrell, Burke, Kinneavy, Tate, Steinmann—his list would be embarrassing only by my omissions. For him, such voices made of the wilderness a harmony of promise.

So Don didn't worry whether comp and rhetoric was a fast track at K-State. He had found a personally rewarding world, and that would be enough. That was always what mattered to Don: he had to be involved in that which engaged purpose, that furthered his notions of service and personal fulfillment. (I would not be misunderstood. Don didn't publish all that he did, didn't devote the time and energy he was noted for, without ambition playing its role. Don wanted recognition, merit, promotion—all that he deserved and earned—but those were not the determinants of his work; they didn't shape its qualities and characteristics. They didn't provide the drive.)

Don was becoming aware that composition and rhetoric and the CCCC and the NCTE were providing more than intellectual stimulus and professional satisfaction. He found, as well, that he was rubbing elbows with and becoming engaged by people he found admirable ("I wouldn't try to mention names," he said; "I know I'd leave some of the best out.") He responded to colleagues in comp and rhetoric. He found them, he believed, characteristically, unaffected. They could and did spend their professional energies and intellectual talents on tasks that touched teaching and students most meaningfully.

(If Don had a weakness, a blind spot, and I suppose he did, it was his impatience with a near-myopic vision of those who were unsympathetic to comp and rhetoric studies. To be sure, the antagonisms that have existed between composition and the literature interests of the twentieth-century English departments nearly justified his viscerogenic reaction, but Don could be at times less than flattering to what he perceived motivated such persons. Wisconsin, and more especially Illinois, it seems, had lasting effects.

Rightly or wrongly he did perceive such persons harshly [and was occasionally privately embarrassed by his caricatures]: "They are always carrying the *New York Times Book Review* under their arms, never to be opened." "They read and argue the latest critical fad and never approach the primary text." And it didn't help his opinion that he once gave a test to a group of seventy-four secondary and college-level English teachers. Seeking to test their awareness of the field for which they were responsible [collectively they spent over 50 percent of their time on composition], he asked them to indicate their familiarity with ["had they read or did they recognize the titles of"] twenty historically consequential works in rhetoric. With a possible score of 100, Don found a median of 12.5 and an average of 16. Fifteen persons scored 2.5 or less. Perhaps he was less harsh than first opinions would suggest.

But, as Don would be quick to point out, I'm getting off the track.)

The enthusiasm for worthy service, for the personal engagement of composition instructor and student seeking each to discover, to shape, to understand self and realize humane values was, Don believed, the very centrality, the informing principle that shaped comp and rhetoric studies. He didn't reject the sometimes pejorative description of the field as a "service" course; indeed, he welcomed it.

Don was helping students in Comp 1 or 2 or Intermediate or Advanced Comp or in graduate seminars, anywhere and everywhere, to broader awareness and more insightful understanding. He insisted that writing be vital and direct, that it avoid sterility of form and substance, and not just because such would make for better reading. His argument was more classical than that. Writing was not merely expressive; writing was formative. It both reflected and shaped ethos. Writing must not be sterile and rigid, because producing such affected the writer far more consequentially than the reader.

That is where his drive came from; that was the missionary zeal. He loved that engagement. He thought everybody should. Those who didn't, those who scorned that "calling," who found it tedious and complained of the work, were for him, paradoxically, the unimaginative drones who gathered no honey and offered no sting.

And that drive stimulated his scholarship as well. Don's first major text, *The Authentic Voice*, is in large part not merely instructive. As important is its exhortatory tone. It is itself an argument for a writer's need for self-respect, and its pedagogical structure emphasizes stimulation and discovery, both means to that validity. Stewart's publications during the 1970s and 1980s frequently challenged the profession. In article after article, he argued that we must valorize composition teaching and research and that to do so, we must go beyond yesterday's perception of our profession. He felt strongly that just as a writer must seek an authentic voice, so the profession must question its academic conservatism and recognize the changing role of writing instruction and those needs that call for a greater service function. To a degree unusual, Don was aware of our profession's roots in rhetoric and felt not that contemporary rhetoric scholars were attempting to elbow their way into the lecture room but that they were reminding their colleagues that a profession, ignorant of its past, can neither understand nor resolve its present conflicts. That part intrigued Don, as his most extensive body of rhetoric studies makes clear. He was for some the most significant contemporary scholar of nineteenth-century American rhetoric studies. For all, he would be considered among the very ablest. Certainly his bibliographic work is for now definitive for nineteenth-century studies.

I asked Don the obvious question. "What professional study most satisfies you?" I emphasized "professional," for I knew *My Yellowstone Years* was on the tip of his tongue. He thought for a few moments and then said, "My work on Fred Newton Scott." When I replied, "But that's not yet finished," he was quick: "Oh, yes. It really is.

"You know, Kitzhaber identified Scott as the only original thinker among the four significant academic rhetoricians at the turn of the century—Scott at Michigan, Adams and Hill at Harvard, and Barrett Wendell at Amherst. Yes, Kitzhaber identified him, but I rescued him. I brought him back from our profession's callous indifference to its own past. So that job really is done."

His work on Scott was Don's consuming scholarly interest in the last years. He spent countless hours before his computer. He had traveled across country, spent two weeks of three summers at Michigan's Bentley Library, visited with Scott's daughter, talked or corresponded with those students of his that he could locate (Scott retired in 1927), laboriously transcribed his meticulous and at times near illegibly scripted diary, and communicated exhaustively with institutions and associations with which Scott had contact.

Don left a 1,500-page manuscript. The work is being completed by Pat—his and Paul Bryant's fellow collaborator on *The Eclectic Reader*—a task for which we will owe her much.

The immediate reason for Don's enthusiasm is obvious. Scott was an extraordinarily gifted man committed to disciplined, responsible work, an eclectic at home in the sciences and social sciences, the arts and the humanities. Holding all his degrees from Michigan, he became a full professor just three years after receiving his Ph.D. and head of the university's new Department of Rhetoric in but an additional two years. He was president of the MLA, of the North Central Association, of the American Association of Teachers of Journalism, and was the first (and only two-time) president of the NCTE. Scott wrote alone or in collaboration a total of fifteen books on rhetoric, writing, aesthetics, and literary criticism and over one hundred articles on teaching, philology, and matters of style and linguistics. Such was enough to justify anyone's enthusiasm. (And although he did not realize it at the time, Don's intellectual attraction to Scott had a touch of academic fate to it, for Scott had been the teacher-mentor of Sterling Leonard, who in turn was on the Wisconsin faculty during Pooley's years of Ph.D. study. Like Pooley, Leonard was a linguist-rhetorician of national stature. The influence of strong, germinal leaders runs deep and long, to be sure.)

Don responded not to Scott's achievement alone but to the man as well. Scott was by present standards light years ahead of his contemporaries. He recognized the behavioral component that shapes the process of writing; he deplored the preoccupation of some with pedagogically "efficacious" forms and editorial skills; he challenged the then too-prevalent notion that model imitation led to writing improvement and perfection. He recognized the validity of levels of usage; he early on appreciated what today we argue is the "student's right to his or her own language"; he saw writing as a mode of revelation and self-discovery. And, as Don did, Scott believed the comprhetoric instructor was a major formative influence in the life of the student and on the civil health of society. Don chose in forwarding the ethos of *Phaedrus* and in providing a pretextual inscription to *The Versatile Writer* a quotation from Scott: "The main purpose of training in composition is free speech, direct and sincere communion with our fellows, that swift and untrammeled exchange of opinion, feeling, and experience which is the working instrument of the social instinct and the motive power of civilization."

Such was Scott as Don saw him—the embodiment of what is best in our profession, a reminder of what we could accomplish. Don spent years with Scott's life for a simple reason: Scott was excellence personified. Don paid homage to that which he unconsciously sought within himself.

I was witness to much of that. Don and I were members of the same departments for nearly thirty of our forty professional years. He came to K-State in 1968 (our head encouraged his work in rhetoric) and began his prolific research and publishing interests. But his career mirrored the conflicts that have bedeviled the field. Though strongly supported for tenure by the faculty, he was denied by a then newly installed head whose opposition to composition-rhetoric was druidic in cast. (Before a grievance committee he denied that Don had published, and when confronted by articles and a book manuscript, he merely noted, "Oh, that's all on composition. That stuff doesn't count." The grievance committee thought otherwise and supported Don and the faculty.) Shortly after, a new head took the reins and Don came into his own. Our following three heads considered Don as properly consequential as he was. One rock in the road was bearable. Don was pleased that he came. He must have been, because he never sought to leave, though, to be sure, he could have with no difficulty.

I know I'm glad he remained. We were good friends who shared the same enthusiasms (though not the violin—Don joked that I play a mean radio). When I directed the comp program for nearly a decade, I had in Don strong informed support. When he forwarded—successfully—proposals for courses or degree programs in rhetoric and composition, he counted on my vote. When we differed on departmental matters, he invariably explained why he differed with me (doubtless out of guilt and in the knowledge that I was right).

Don was no passive go-along-to-get-along department member. He held strong views and could be unyielding when his dander was up. And he did not hold forth frequently or thoughtlessly. I can still see him and will long remember that body language and his facial gestures. When he was convinced, indeed positive, he would sit up straighter; his head would be rigid. He'd clear his throat and then begin. "I wonder if we have given sufficient consideration to an idea that I've looked closely at. . . ." We knew his explanation would be lucid, emphatic, and—let's face it—often lengthy (one colleague has said that talking with Don always required barging in between paragraphs). But he had something to say. He would say it, too, even when he knew it was a lost cause. When he would finish, he would set his lips rigid as though to say, "Well, chew on that for a while." And he was never petty. I knew better than most just whom he could abide philosophically or personally, and I was always pleased that Don could vote for an issue he was not completely sold on championed by someone he couldn't stand. He couldn't have been unfair if he had tried. More importantly, he never tried. Though he didn't advertise the fact, Don was one of the few persons in the department who carried his protests to the dean when he felt that office was improperly acting against the department or a faculty member's just interests. Don wouldn't be ignored.

I've mentioned his love for teaching, but I haven't commented upon Don as teacher. I never saw Don's student evaluations; I imagine that though they were positive overall, they were probably mixed. But student evaluations are reactions to a given instructor in a given class. They do not evaluate teachers.

I've long been familiar with Don's comp texts, and they are good when applied with the spirit in which he employed them. But they assume not merely an active student; they require a committed, dedicated teacher. (I have no idea how many of Don's students' papers I have seen that, without the slightest exaggeration, contained his comments running to greater length than the papers themselves.) He didn't address himself to the paper; rather, his comments made contact with the student. Rather than mark editing errors or underscore faults in logic or structure, Don suggested alternatives (accompanied by their advantages and disadvantages) and explained how the student's approach affected him as interested reader. Students sensed that Don worked with them because he respected the effort they were making; indeed, he was ever conscious that an insensitive or unnecessarily harsh comment could result in "schizokinetic scribophobia"—a term he took seriously, perhaps because more than most, Don believed that Zoellner's "Talk-Write" voiced a powerful truth. When one thinks about it, too, one realizes that Don's insistence upon an authentic voice from every student emphasized self-worth to them.

Don enjoyed teaching the short story, Modern British fictive prose, and the American Western novel. In doing so, he saw students not as problems but as inexperienced equals whose responses to literature were necessarily unsophisticated and personal. When I handled some of his classes, I admired how students responded. And, oh, how persistent he could be in requiring that a student substantiate his or her position. He would have exasperated Socrates. So, too, with his rhetoric course. Students learned that the ill-prepared, off-handed remark would lead to Don's terrier-like search for the student's rationale. His mind worked analytically and perceptively and swiftly; hence, students were constantly challenged. They never accused him of being easy.

Other evidence as well suggests Don's worth as teacher. Don, more than any other teacher I have known, had former students who kept in touch with him through visits, telephone calls, and most especially by lengthy correspondence. Some sought advice about teaching, some about writing and publishing, some even discussed personal problems. One, now teaching for some fifteen years in Georgia, stopped by to express his thanks for Don's making him aware of the personal element, the need of respect for and patience with students regardless of their sophistication. Once a frustrated instructor, he is now an enthusiastic and accomplished teacher of remedial students. Another wrote often simply to discuss whatever literature he was teaching or reading. A young woman, who became a bank executive in Dallas, kept up her correspondence for several years just to stay in touch with a man she respected. He was always getting that feedback—unsolicited, warm, generous, filled with respect, affection, and, frequently, unexpressed thanks for having been there to offer whatever they needed. Once while I was visiting him in the hospital during one of his many needed blood plasma transfusions, a former undergraduate student now in graduate school came by to visit. She was there, I suspect, to offer encouragement and to express her obvious concern for him. The exchange was a telling one. She was a national-class track athlete who was having some temporary difficulties with her form. They didn't talk about Don and his condition. He wouldn't give her time for that. He focused instead upon her problem, her work, her progress, her expectation. When she left, she had encouraged him by again allowing him to touch her life in the way he always had. I could see it in his response, his animation. Don simply loved people. That was the secret to his joy in teaching and his success in front of a class.

And that love for teaching was apparent even beyond the classroom. Don was once staying at a hotel where Suzuki, the internationally renowned violin teacher and developer of the acclaimed Suzuki method for teaching children, was holding a workshop. Ever curious, Don dropped by to hear the master. Ever patient and polite, Don waited until the proper moment. Ever the teacher, Don politely introduced himself to Suzuki and proceeded to explain how Suzuki's instructions for the proper handling of the bow led to movements that were necessarily physically awkward for children. Don, still ever the teacher, demonstrated a better way. I doubt if he even hesitated. Such was Don. Suzuki, I'm sure, was most polite.

That need to teach was also one major reason that he kept going on the way he did. Don's illness was debilitating and insidious—the very nature of multiple myeloma. Even with an otherwise healthy person, the condition becomes known only when it is too late. And Don was otherwise healthy. He was a lifelong physical fitness advocate—a fine high school athlete, he never once smoked, never drank, avoided caffeine and refined sugars, and was a jogger a decade and more before it became popular in the early 1980s. When he could no longer jog, he became Manhattan's first practitioner of wet-vest water walking and running; indeed, characteristically, he introduced the professionals of K-State's athletic department to its value as a conditioning and rehabilitating regimen for injured athletes. He was always in contact, always helping.

His illness was diagnosed in 1986. His oncologist's initial prognosis was necessarily conservative—perhaps no more than one year. If he responded well to chemotherapy and radiation, two, or with luck, three years. Those were the standards. Don nearly doubled that. Such is the power of will and the strength of a life lived for others. Don was neither saintly nor superhuman. He would have gladly foregone suffering, for to him, it had no ameliorating grace. And though he did not curse the darkness, he did comment on the irony that the body repaid his years of disciplined care with vicious injustice indeed.

He was frequently subjected to four- and six-hour blood plasma transfusions, periods of chemotherapy and radiation-induced illness, and as bone deterioration became pronounced, increasingly intense episodes of and eventually ceaseless pain. (Typical for Don, the magnitude of that pain was admitted only in the privacy of his personal daybook.) But he taught until the last two weeks. He taped his lectures, kept study notes, read scholarly manuscripts, and graded papers—patiently and with undiminished care—both in bed and out, at home and in the hospital. It helped keep him going, helped fix his mind on that concern for others. In that he could find some relief.

His two daughters, Ellen and Mary—themselves teachers and a source of merited pride for him—noticed how profound was his need to reach out, to communicate. As one said, "If Dad was alone on a street corner, he'd talk to the light pole." He took great joy in his family, in Pat and Ellen and Mary, and though I could comment on Don as husband and father, that would be better done by them. But one comment should be reported. When Pat, Mary, and I were shuffling through some of Don's files, searching for particular articles and essays, Mary couldn't help but remark that Don had done far more than she had ever realized. Pat agreed and then, almost as a newly remembered afterthought, said, "Yes, and the amazing thing is that he always had time for us. Whether it was to stop and answer a question, help with homework, play a game, or go with us on an errand, he would always say, 'Just let me wind up this paragraph and I'll be with you.' We were never ignored."

The fact is that we who were privileged to know Don could have all made that comment. He had life for all of us. Touching others was so very much the nature of Don. In the last few years, Don helped others who faced the difficulties he did. He offered advice and comfort to some and eased the fears and anxieties of others. One told me that she approached him as a stranger on the phone (she had called on a matter of public concern) and he spoke with her for over an hour discussing the plight of the handicapped and the despair she felt over the recent loss of her son. She responded to his warmth and concern as she had to that of few others. He mentioned in passing, she said, that he too was handicapped. She did not learn until a month later when he died how handicapped he was. His attention had been fixed on her problem. He had put his aside.

And characteristic, too, of Don was his concern for his oncologist. Don recognized the emotional burden that such a man can feel who deals constantly with those who face despair. In preparation for his periodic visits, Don would remind himself to bear up well, to have a light comment or joke ready, to carry in an appropriate cartoon. Don, quite simply, wanted his doctor to feel better for his visit.

In the last analysis, Don's need for people and the will to escape self-absorption may be the key to his involvement in composition and rhetoric. On nearly every page of his work, the insistence on authenticity, on the necessity to discover self and to present that persona honestly to others and to oneself is paramount. And rhetoric provided both a means to that discovery and a mode to vitalize the best that one may become. It both expressed and shaped the man. Don saw the means of rhetoric as a way to help everyone realize his or her potential. To do so was for him a moral imperative.

And toward the end, his reaching out was evident. I mentioned that he continued to attend classes, but I omitted the cost. In the hospital, he fought through minimum sedation and endured pain in order to tape lectures and grade papers. (When the department head thought of a substitute to ease Don's cares, he realized that that would not be acceptable to Don.) For the last year and a half Don fought. He went from walker to cane and back to walker, from periods of extreme to excruciating pain to hardly bearable agony. Pat would help him into the car, drive to the university, and help him struggle into the classroom. They became an image: Don, Pat, and the ever-present walker. He endured the pain of sitting upright (she remained in the room—just in case) for each seventy-minute class. He would continue to teach.

The correspondence kept up—the voluminous correspondence—and Norma and Ross Winterowd's CCCC tribute to Don movingly revealed both its quantity and quality. On the occasions when Don and I chatted on the phone, he commented on a letter from this or that friend or on the comments he was making on a manuscript some publisher sent. His scholarship and miscellaneous writing stepped up in pace. The Scott manuscript grew, book reviews were written, a manuscript dealing with his illness was developed, articles were sent off. During his last week, he received five acceptances.

And that was Don's way. Always doing, always reaching out, always living beyond the moment, and always for someone else. My wife, Jeane, and I last visited Don in the hospital two days before he died. It was, of course, an agonizing time. Don knew too well that he was ending. He tried his best to comfort us, to apologize, even, for the pain his passing caused. By then his sedation was heavy and he was moving in and out of consciousness, moment by moment. When we had to leave and he knew that it was for the last time, he literally reached out and touched me. I was a close friend, I know, but I know, too, that I was also a surrogate for others, for many, many others. "Don't feel so bad, buddy. I'm ready and it's not so bad now. I've had a good life, you know. Good friends helped make it that way."

When the *K-State Collegian* reported Don's passing, the article ended by quoting one of those good people. "He was a good friend, a good man." Simple. Authentic.

Works Cited

Berlin, James. *Rhetoric and Reality: Writing Instruction in American Colleges, 1900–1985*. Carbondale: Southern Illinois UP, 1987.

Stewart, Donald C. *My Yellowstone Years*. Fowlerville, MI: Wilderness Adventure Books, 1989.

Part 1
Constructing the Context

1   Quintilian and the Nineteenth-Century Rhetorical Tradition

Nan Johnson

> Generally speaking, the best and most proper expressions are those which a clear view of the subject suggests. . . . This is Quintilian's observation: "The most proper words, for the most part, adhere to the thoughts which are to be expressed by them, and may be discovered as by their own light. But we hunt after them as if they were hidden, and only to be found in a corner. Hence, instead of conceiving the words to lie near the subject, we go in quest of them to some other quarter, and endeavor to give force to the expressions we have found out."
>
> —Alexander Jamieson,
> A Grammar of Rhetoric and Polite Literature

IN CITING QUINTILIAN'S ADVICE ON THE DEVELOPMENT OF AN ELOQUENT style, Alexander Jamieson reveals a regard for classical authority, which is a distinctive characteristic of the nineteenth-century tradition. Although nineteenth-century theorists frequently recontextualized classical advice within the epistemological and belletristic contexts of their philosophical and pedagogical interests, a debt to classical wisdom is a noticeable component in influential nineteenth-century treatises throughout the century.[1] Often quoted and frequently acknowledged along with Cicero, Aristotle, and Horace under the title "the ancients," Quintilian emerges within the nineteenth-century tradition as a noteworthy voice on the nature and practice of rhetoric, particularly with regard to canonical guidelines and definitions of rhetoric as an art. In addition to Jamieson, Henry N. Day, Adams Sherman Hill, Merritt Caldwell, and prominent homiletician John A. Broadus were just a few of the well-known nineteenth-century rhetoricians who referred to Quintilian's teachings in their analyses of the canons and discussions of the responsibilities of the speaker.

Acknowledgment of the authority of "ancients" by the nineteenth-century

3

tradition is largely a consequence of the influence of the major architects of the New Rhetoric, George Campbell, Hugh Blair, and Richard Whately. Campbell's *The Philosophy of Rhetoric* (1776), Blair's *Lectures on Rhetoric and Belles Lettres* (1783), and Whately's *Elements of Rhetoric* (1828) provided the most powerful models for the development of nineteenth-century theory.[2] In theoretical terms, the nineteenth-century tradition can be understood as executing a refined synthesis of the major theoretical commitments of the New Rhetoric: a philosophical approach to rhetoric that examined the nature and aims of rhetoric in terms of the processes of the mental faculties; the view that the study of rhetoric applied to all major forms of communication, oral and written; an aesthetic/ethical commitment to the study of criticism and the development of taste; and a neoclassical approach to rhetoric as the art of adapting discourse to purpose, audience, and occasion. The New Rhetoricians repositioned classical tenets within the epistemological and belletristic rationales that dominated their efforts to reconcile traditional rhetoric with the theories of the mind, logic, language, and aesthetics that emerged from the Baconian-Lockian tradition. Campbell, Blair, and Whately incorporated a number of significant classical principles in the combined scope of their treatises, including treatments of the canons of invention, arrangement, style, and delivery and analyses of the nature and contexts of the major rhetorical genres. In addition to preserving these systemic features of classical rhetorical theory, Campbell, Blair, and Whately gave consistent attention to the strategic importance of audience analysis and the considerations that an orator or writer must keep in mind when adjusting the canons to subject and context. Often quoting Quintilian, Cicero, and Aristotle on these issues, the New Rhetoricians reinscribed classical maxims regarding rhetorical practice and cited classical authorities regarding the importance of the speaker's moral character and centrality of rhetoric as a cultural art.

The debt of the New Rhetoric to classical influence was reincorporated by the nineteenth-century tradition that preserved many of the features of the New Rhetoric, including a respect for classical wisdom. Such nineteenth-century theorists as Day, David J. Hill, Adams Sherman Hill, and John Franklin Genung drew upon these major strands of the New Rhetoric to develop a hybrid theoretical base that combined the major interests of Campbell, Blair, and Whately. The resulting synthesis typically conflated Campbell's epistemological revision of the dynamics of rhetoric with Blair's belletristic interests in the function of rhetoric in the development of taste and criticism and Whately's analysis of the nature of argumentation in oratory and composition. Neoclassical features of this synthesis included treatment of the canons of rhetoric as well as the major rhetorical genres; the assumption that effective rhetoric proceeds from a thorough understanding of purpose, subject, audience, and occasion; and the assumption that the study of theory and diligent practice are crucial to acquiring rhetorical skills. Like their influential predecessors, nineteenth-century rhetoricians frequently cited classical advice on topics ranging from the stylistic use of the figures to the nature of rhetoric as an art. Such frequent acknowledgment of classical figures, including Quintilian, indicates the extent to which nineteenth-century rhetoricians followed the lead of the New Rhetoricians in confirming the relevance of classical rhetoric to their own enterprise.

Nineteenth-century rhetoricians were influenced by the New Rhetoricians' habit of reiterating certain classical principles and repositioning others in order to strengthen their own theoretical interests. On many occasions throughout his lectures, Blair reiterates classical wisdom he wants his reader to regard as the last word on a technique. At other times, however, he coopts a familiar classical adage to further his analysis of how the rhetor must anticipate the responses of the imagination and the passions (the aesthetically sensitive faculties of the mind that Blair believes play a crucial part in persuasion). For example, Blair cites a number of classical pronouncements in his analysis of harmony in sentence structure, reinscribing advice from both Cicero and Quintilian alongside his own pronouncements on the importance of appealing to the taste of the imagination. Although Blair quotes Quintilian's caution that "nothing can enter into the affections, which stumbles at the threshold by offending the ear," he uses this adage to draw attention to the special responses of the imagination, which he insists "revolts" whenever it hears disagreeable sounds (134).[3] Campbell and Whately employ similar methods—at times they reinscribe classical wisdom directly, and at other times they coopt the authority of classical maxims in the service of what the New Rhetoricians and nineteenth-century rhetoricians alike often refer to as as a more "modern" understanding of the dynamics of rhetoric. Nineteenth-century rhetoricians adopt this same method of selective citation and quotation to reinscribe the complete authority of selected pronouncements of the "ancient writers" and revise others in the light of the epistemological and belletristic points of view that permeate the nineteenth-century synthesis. Unlike Whately, who tended to favor Aristotle over other classical authorities, Campbell and Blair cite from a range of classical sources, including frequent quotation from Quintilian.[4] A closer examination of how Campbell and Blair construct the authority of classical rhetoric in general, and the status of Quintilian in particular, can provide insight into the methodology that nineteenth-century theorists imitated in their incorporation of Quintilian's advice.

Campbell revises or shifts the slant of classical advice by recontextualizing classical rules in terms of how rhetorical technique is to be reconciled with the functions of the mental faculties. In his discussions of how arguments are to be adapted to audience and how the speaker is to present his character (71, 96), Campbell reiterates the classical maxim that the rhetorician must adapt subject to audience and occasion; however, he also revises the classical concept of what strategic appeal to audience involves by shifting the theoretical emphasis away from a consideration of audience type to an emphasis on epistemological circumstances. Campbell clearly reinscribes the utility of pathetic appeal when he observes that "rhetoric . . . not only considers the subject, but also the hearers and the speaker" and when he insists that the emotional sense of any idea advanced must fall within the hearer's "sphere" of knowledge (71). However, he recontextualizes pathos in a new theoretical context when he argues that the emotions or passions must engage the imagination through content and style that create a sense of presence (73). Campbell stresses that appealing to the hearer's frame of mind depends largely on qualities of language (vivacity, beauty, sublimity, and novelty) that simulate empirical veracity. Campbell validates the general classical principle regarding the necessity of appealing to the hearer's frame of mind; however, he does so in the service of explaining how the faculties of the mind can best be engaged.

Campbell combines the methods of reinscription and revision again in his discussion of ethos, treated under the topic "Of the consideration the speaker should have of himself" (96). Campbell reiterates familiar maxims in his discussion of the speaker's obligation to generate sympathy, or the positive regard of the hearers: "Sympathy in the hearers to the speaker may be lessened several ways chiefly by these two; by a low opinion of his intellectual abilities, and by a bad opinion of his morals. The latter is the more prejudicial of the two. Men generally will think themselves in less danger of being seduced by a man of weak understanding, but of distinguished probity, than by a man of the best understanding who is of a profligate life. So much more powerfully do the qualities of the heart attach us, than those of the head" (97). Campbell goes on to remind the reader of the "common" advice that the speaker must project goodwill and authority in order to be heard with attention, but he does so in order to stress that sympathy has its "foundation in human nature" (97). Campbell defines the gaining of sympathy as a necessary step in affecting the passions, which in turn engage the will. Although Campbell's discussion of sympathy reinscribes a classical emphasis on the role of the speaker's charac-ter in persuasion, Campbell's central interest is to extend his analysis of how the speaker exerts influence over the faculties of the mind. He defines sympathy as a mandatory epistemological connection that must be secured to initiate the reactions of the interdependent mental faculties. From Campbell's point of view, sympathy is not a mode of argument that may or may not be suited to subject or occasion but rather "one main engine by which the orator operates on the passions" (96).

Campbell revises classical principles within an epistemological context far more often than he reinscribes classical authorities as fundamental authorities; however, his references to classical precepts and sources are frequent enough to make it clear that he chooses to coopt classical tenets rather than discredit them. Quintilian's influence on Campbell is obvious from the outset. Camp-bell adopts Quintilian's definition of rhetoric as his definition of eloquence in the very first paragraph of his treatise, quoting Quintilian's definition of ora-tory as "that art or talent by which the discourse is adapted to its end" (1). Having first drawn upon Quintilian's authority, Campbell characteristically moves to reposition Quintilian's definition in support of a faculty psychology view of the mind, using Quintilian's maxim to confirm his own dominant premise that "the ends of speaking are reducible to four . . . to enlighten the understanding, to please the imagination, to move the passions, or to influence the will" (1). Campbell's persistent revisionist stance toward classical advice is observable in several other allusions to Quintilian's authority, including his frequent citations of Quintilian's advice on style. For example, Campbell coopts Quintilian's advice that custom, not grammatical rules, should be the standard for speech to support the epistemological observation that the listening mind processes ideas in terms of conventional associations among sounds, signs, and things (139; Quintilian 1.1. c. 6). Campbell also claims Quintilian's definition of clarity or perspicuity as "the first essential of a good style" to support his own definition of perspicuity as the most essential quality of style because all ideas, first and foremost, must be intelligible to the understanding (Quintilian 8.2.19–23). As Campbell's own comments reveal, his notion of clarity incorporates Quintilian's under a more complex concern for how the faculty of the understanding must be engaged: "If he [the speaker] does not propose to convey certain sentiments into the minds of his hearers, by the aid of signs intelligible to them, he may as well declaim before them in an unknown tongue. . . . Every sentence ought to be perspicuous. . . . This being to the understanding what light is to the eye, ought to be diffused over the whole performance" (216).

Campbell's treatment of Quintilian is representative of a characteristic tendency among the New Rhetoricians to recast classical advice continuously in a new light. Blair also puts the wisdom of Quintilian and Cicero to the service of his own arguments about rhetorical practice; however, he reinscribes classical advice more often than Campbell (or Whately), especially in his treatments of the canons. In his analysis of arrangement or "the conduct of a discourse," Blair reinscribes classical definitions of the parts of an oration and their functions by citing classical advice and examples at regular intervals (156–202). To read Blair's discussion of the parts of the oration is to be reminded of various classical rules on arrangement: "This is, or ought to be the main scope of an Introduction. Accordingly, Cicero and Quintilian mention three ends, to one or other of which it should be subservient 'Reddere auditores benevolos, attentos, dociles.' . . . Ancient Critics distinguish two kinds of Introductions, which they call 'Principium,' and 'Infinuatio' " (158–59); "Cicero is very remarkable for his talent of Narration; and from the examples of his Orations much may be learned" (176); "When our Arguments are doubtful, and only of the presumptive kind, it is safer to throw them together in a crowd, and to run them into one another . . . as Quintilian speaks" (186). Blair cites Quintilian frequently to reinforce several traditional rules for structuring the speech and uses examples from Cicero's speeches to illustrate many of the rules he suggests.

Blair often justifies the importance of a particular canon or principle by appealing to the authority of the classical tradition, as he does in his justification of the study of delivery: "How much stress was laid upon this by the most eloquent of all Orators, Demosthenes, appears from a noted saying of his, related both by Cicero and Quintilian; when being asked, What was the first point in Oratory? he answered, Delivery; and being asked What was the second? and afterwards, What was the third? he still answered, Delivery" (203). Blair is given to more quotation of classical authorities than Campbell, and he frequently quotes at length from Quintilian's *Institutio Oratoria*. For example, in his treatment of "Eloquence of the Bar," Blair quotes from Quintilian's "many excellent rules" regarding a lawyer's methods, recalling Quintilian's advice regarding the importance of dignity of character in the speaker and the necessity for the speaker to have a thorough knowledge of the cause pleaded for (79–85).

Blair's willingness to reinscribe classical advice extends to broader issues than matters of technique. He calls the ancients to mind again and again in his discussions of how eloquence may be acquired and what qualifications an effective speaker and writer must have: "Nothing is more necessary than to be a virtuous man. This was a favorite position among the ancient Rhetoricians"; "Next to moral qualifications, what, in the second place, is most necessary to an Orator, is a fund of knowledge. Much is this inculcated by Cicero and Quintilian" (226–45). Using citations such as these in combination with extensive analysis of classical orations as exemplary models of arrangement, argumentative force, and effective style, Blair establishes a strong profile for the authority of classical sources throughout his lectures.

Blair refers to Quintilian as the "most instructive, and most useful" of all the ancient writers (244). Although he relies on Quintilian's advice more extensively than does Campbell, Blair's general treatment of Quintilian does not differ significantly from Campbell's in that he cites Quintilian's rules most often on the topics of style, argumentation, arrangement, and virtue in the speaker. In his discussions of arrangement and style, Blair's habit of recasting classical advice to support his own theoretical interests is evident in how he adapts Quintilian's maxims to his own purposes. For example, in his discussion of the pathetic part of an oration, Blair cites Quintilian's advice that the speaker must enter into those passions he wants to excite in others: "Quintilian, who discourses upon this subject with much good sense, takes pains to inform us of the method which he used, when he was a Public Speaker, for entering into those passions which he wanted to excite in others; setting before his own imagination what he calls 'Phantasiae' and 'Visiones' " (194). Although Blair highlights Quintilian's advice, his real interest is in using Quintilian's position to support the epistemological argument that the speaker can only arouse the appropriate passions by engaging the faculty of the imagination first. Blair insists that the orator must engage his own imagination in recalling vivid images that will, in turn, engage the appropriate passions he needs to feel. In this state of mind, the speaker can present the circumstances of the case in such a way that the "lustre and steadiness resemble those of Sensation and Remembrance," qualities that allow hearers to respond in terms of their own empirical experience (193–94).

That Blair is inserting Quintilian's view in a different philosophical context is evident when we note that Quintilian's discussion of how the speaker can generate the proper emotions is actually quite a pragmatic one. Quintilian argues that the audience's sense of the speaker as a person of good character can be impaired if the speaker doesn't seem to be sincere. "Consequently, if we wish to give our words the appearance of sincerity, we must assimilate ourselves to the emotions of those who are genuinely so affected, and our eloquence must spring from the same feelings that we desire to produce in the mind of the judge. . . . But how are we to generate these emotions in ourselves, since emotion is not in our own power?" (6.2.27–29). When Quintilian advises the speaker to engage the power of the imagination, he is not assuming, as Blair does, that the imagination is a discrete faculty of the mind that must be engaged in order for the subsequent faculty of the passions to respond. Quintilian's use of the term *imagination* is equivalent to what he calls a person's capacity for "fantastic hopes or daydreams," and he is interested primarily in how "it may be possible to turn this form of hallucination to some profit" (6.2.30–31). For Blair, the "imagination" is of a much higher order of epistemological significance. He assumes that the imagination allows the mind to apprehend aspects of truth that cannot be perceived directly by the understanding or faculty of reason. All of Blair's recommendations regarding the imagination are governed by the philosophical viewpoint that the imagination has innate perceptual sensitivities that can be accessed only through vivid language. Blair's use of Quintilian's advice regarding the use of vivid images is typical of how he and Campbell both reposition certain classical tenets, slanting theoretical implications in the direction of their views of how rhetoric must adapt to natural mental processes.[5]

Whether in the form of revised treatments of classical advice or reinscribed classical maxims, Blair's and Campbell's acknowledgment of the authority and relevance of classical insights is a persistent theoretical thread in their treatises. Nineteenth-century rhetoricians continue the same methodological practice of reinscribing selected classical precepts and recasting others.[6] They also confirm Campbell's and Blair's high regard for Quintilian by calling attention to Quintilian as a major classical writer, often reiterating many of the references made by Campbell and Blair in their discussions of the canons. Several nineteenth-century rhetoricians cite Quintilian, along with Cicero and Aristotle, in their treatments of style, arrangement, argument, and the virtues of the speaker. The authority of Quintilian on the canons is predisposed by a general recognition of Quintilian's importance as an authority on the nature of rhetoric and its status as an art. Two influential nineteenth-century theorists, Alfred H. Welsh, author of *Complete Rhetoric* (1885), and John A. Broadus, author of *A Treatise on the Preparation and Delivery of Sermons* (1889), begin their discussions of rhetoric with homage to Quintilian's authority: Welsh cites Quintilian's definition of what a complete theory of rhetoric ought to offer and his notion that "bare bones" treatises of rules ought to be covered with theoretical flesh (vi); Broadus lists Quintilian, along with Aristotle and Cicero, as a theorist he is "chiefly indebted to," later praising Quintilian's work as a "systematic treatise on grammar and rhetoric, abounding in good sense, and more valuable than those of Cicero" (x, 31). Such deference to Quintilian's authority often results in reinscription of one or more of Quintilian's maxims on the nature of rhetoric. Merritt Caldwell, whose manual on elocution, *A Practical Manual of Elocution* (1845), was widely circulated in colleges and to the general public at midcentury, relies on one of Quintilian's principles in the introduction to his text in which he argues that the best rhetorical technique is drawn from observed practice: "This is the origin given of the principles of the orator's art by Quintilian, who says 'As in physic, men, by seeing that some things promote health and others destroy it, formed the art upon those observations; in like manner by perceiving that some things in discourse are said to advantage, and others not, they accordingly marked those things, in order to imitate the one and avoid the other' " (26). Such reinscriptions of Quintilian's advice reveal that many nineteenth-century theorists shared Blair's evaluation of Quintilian as the most instructive and most useful of the ancient writers.[7] Even those rhetoricians who consider Cicero to be a higher authority feel compelled to acknowledge Quintilian's status. For example, Joshua Hall McIlvaine acknowledges Quintilian in his roll call of "the opinions of the great orators and rhetoricians [who] are strongly in favor of the importance of a good delivery": "Quintilian also teaches us that 'it is not of so much importance what our thoughts are, as it is in what manner they are delivered; since those who we address are moved only as they hear.' We need not subscribe to this statement in its utmost force, yet the authority is a very high one" (6).

In addition to reinscribing Quintilian's "high" authority on rhetoric, several nineteenth-century theorists reiterate his advice on various aspects of style, arrangement, argumentation, and the relationship between the speaker's moral character and the ability to persuade (all issues linked to Quintilian by Blair and Campbell). A typical example is Adams Sherman Hill's reinscription of Quintilian's advice on unity in his discussion of arrangement. Quoting Quintilian's adage that every composition should be " 'a body, not a mere collection of members,' a living body," Hill emphasizes the point that unity does not come from perfection but from the conception of a discourse as a whole (246). Hill draws an exact connection between what Quintilian defines as the cohesive linking of thoughts and what he calls "harmonious arrangement of the parts" (Quintilian 7.10.13–17). Hill's adherence to Quintilian's principle of unity is even more obvious when he argues that the ability to employ unity comes "from natural qualities" and the study of good examples, an observation faithful to Quintilian's point that to possess the gift of unity, "our orator will require all the resources of nature, learning, and industrous study" (7.10.13–17).

Day, Welsh, and Franz Theremin also reinscribe Quintilian's opinions regarding the canons. Day quotes Quintilian frequently along with Cicero on invention and style. His restatement of Quintilian's distinction between thesis or cause from question illustrates how Day uses Quintilian's authority to further his theoretical distinctions: "The ancient rhetoricians carefully distinguished between the general subject or theme of the discourse, the particular question discussed arising out of the theme; and the point on which the question turned. Quintilian, thus, in his work *de Institutione Oratora*, Book Third, distinguishes the *thesis or causa* from the *quaestio* and both from *status causae*. Common language recognizes a like distinction. We speak of the *subject of discussion, the question raised,* and the *point at issue*" (89–90). Using Quintilian as a spokesman for "the ancient rhetoricians," Day confirms that the classical position supports current understandings of the structure of arguments. Welsh also reiterates Quintilian's advice on arguments by reminding his reader of Quintilian's rule that the proper arrangement of a refutation requires that the opponent's argument be replied to first, "lest," as Quintilian says, "if this is in the mind of the hearers they may think it unanswerable until it is answered" (207). Like Day and Welsh, Theremin quotes from more than one classical source, citing Cicero and Aristotle along with Quintilian in his discussions of argument, the species of rhetoric, and the ethos of the speaker. In his discussion of the important characteristics of the orator, Theremin reinscribes Quintilian's view on the character of the speaker as the ultimate classical pronouncement, citing Quintilian's definition of the orator as "an upright man who understands speaking" as "indisputably the best that has come down to us from antiquity" (126). Other theorists note Quintilian's view on the character of the speaker, including C. W. Barden, who makes reference to Quintilian's maxim that the speaker must be of excellent moral character in his discussion of the importance of sincerity in eloquence (263). Day also recalls Quintilian's advice on the relationship between character and the impact of oratory in his discussion of "the expression of right sentiments" in which he once again cites Quintilian as a representative of the "ancients": "It was on good grounds that the ancients urged so earnestly the importance of character to success in oratory; for, as Quintilian reasons, 'discourse reveals character and discloses the secret disposition and temper; and not without reason did the Greeks teach that as a man lived so he would speak' " (287).

Of all the topics on which Quintilian's advice is reiterated, his rules regarding style—including the use of custom as a guide to usage, the importance of the economic use of figures, and the nature of perspicuity or clarity—are quoted the most frequently by nineteenth-century theorists. Influenced by the fact that both Campbell and Blair cite Quintilian's observation that the clarity of style must be undeniable, nineteenth-century rhetoricians cite Quintilian's rule regarding perspicuity so frequently that it achieves an authority unrivaled by any other single classical pronouncement on style. There are obvious similarities between Campbell's and Blair's quotations of the relevant passage and nineteenth-century references to the same passage:

> "By perspicuity," as Quintilian justly observes, "care is taken, not that the hearer *may* understand, if he will; but that he *must* understand, whether he will or not." (Campbell 216)

> Discourse ought always to be obvious, even to the most careless and negligent hearer: so that the sense shall strike his mind, as the light of the sun does our eyes, though they are not directed upwards to it. We must study not only that every hearer may understand us, but that it shall be impossible for him not to understand us. (Blair 10.102, 1831 ed.)

> Clearness requires, according to Quintilian, "not that the reader *may* understand if he will, but that he *must* understand whether he will or not." (Quackenbos 284)

> "Discourse," says Quintilian, "ought always to be obvious, so that the sense shall enter the mind as sunlight the eyes, even though they are not directed upwards to the source." We should take pains not only that the meaning be understood, but that it must be understood. (Welsh 62)

> As Quintilian says, the expression should be so clear that the hearer not only *may* but *must* understand. (D. Hill 54)

> One cannot expect, as Quintilian already remarks, "that the hearer will be so intent upon understanding as to cast upon the darkness of the speech a light from his own intelligence. What we may say must be made so clear that it will pour into his mind as the sun pours into the eyes, even when they are not directed toward it. We must take care, not that it shall be possible for him to understand, but that it shall be impossible for him not to understand." (Broadus 341)

Quackenbos and Hill adopt Campbell's version of Quintilian's maxim while Welsh and Broadus favor Blair's fuller rendering of the reference. Varied renditions of Quintilian's "may-must" maxim are reinscribed as well by Adams Sherman Hill, Day, Broadus, and Genung, all of whom stress the relationship between sense and style that clarity ensures. The frequent reiteration of this particular Quintilian maxim points not only to the intimate relationship between nineteenth-century theory and the New Rhetoric but also to the fact that nineteenth-century rhetoricians used classical precepts in the same fashion as their influential predecessors—they both reinscribed and recontextualized Quintilian's advice. For example, although Broadus reinscribes Quintilian's maxim on clarity, he later puts that advice in an epistemological context by stressing the importance of the preacher's appeal to the faculty of the understanding. Like Campbell and Blair, Broadus makes the point that the speaker cannot hope to influence his listeners if they cannot associate what he is talking about to their own experience or sense of reality. However, as a homiletician, Broadus is concerned not only with the epistemological aspect of style but also with the moral ramifications of Quintilian's "may-must" maxim. Broadus links perspicuity to the preacher's ability to influence his audience to "do good." "It is a mournful thing to think of, but one of not infrequent occurrence, that men should so misunderstand us, as to take what we meant for medicine and convert it into poison. As we love men's souls we must strive to prevent so dreadful a result" (341). By enlisting Quintilian's authority in his argument that the preacher must be concerned with how style serves his overall aim of motivating moral conduct, Broadus expands the application of Quintilian's advice to the sphere of ethical intention. In so doing, Broadus offers an innovative adaptation of Quintilian's advice while still preserving Campbell's and Blair's concern for the orator's obligation to please the faculty of the understanding through perspicuity.

Nineteenth-century theorists often put Quintilian's advice on style in new contexts, most typically in discussions of the figures and the relationship between style and occasion. For example, James De Mille uses Quintilian's definition of the figure of climax to draw attention to how the mind processes information presented in this particular construction. De Mille recalls Quintilian's definition of climax as the disposition of statements that "go on increasing in importance by successive stages, but at every stage of the ascent a new statement is compared with the previous one, and formally elevated above it" (165). De Mille quotes Quintilian as saying that climax "recurs to what has been said, and takes a rest, as it were, on something that precedes, before it passes on to anything else" (165). Although De Mille acknowledges the common sense of this definition, he urges his reader to see climax as a figure that functions in a broader epistemological context, having more to do with "statements arranged in an ascending series, the final being the most important." Thus, through the use of climax, De Mille argues, "thoughts thus presented fall upon the mind as though with successive blows, the final one having the greatest force" and making the strongest impression on the understanding (165). De Mille's revision of Quintilian's advice is typical of how nineteenth-century revisions of Quintilian's rules typically work—the classical definition is not refuted but turned to the advantage of another perspective, in this case, an insight into how the faculty of the understanding responds to an ascending series of ideas.[8]

Reinscriptions and revisions of Quintilian's precepts on style, arrangement, and invention and his opinions about the nature of rhetoric and the character of the speaker by such theorists as De Mille, Theremin, Day, Adams Sherman Hill, and Broadus preserved Quintilian's theoretical presence in academic rhetoric throughout the nineteenth century. Quintilian was cited in successful academic treatises circulating as late as 1900, and his name was frequently evoked in the roll call of the "ancients" by critics wanting to honor the history of rhetoric and the contribution made by Quintilian in establishing rhetoric as "a science" (Coppee 26). Like the New Rhetoricians, nineteenth-century rhetoricians were well aware of the long tradition that preceded them and of the status of Quintilian and other "ancients" in that tradition. Far from attempting to overthrow the influence of the ancients in any aggressive sense, many nineteenth-century rhetoricians actively promoted the longevity of classical influence by reiterating key classical commonplaces, such as Quintilian's assumption that only the person of good character can aspire to true eloquence. It is crucial to understand that specific acknowledgment of Quintilian by nineteenth-century rhetoricians was made within a theoretical climate that was already deeply permeated by classical assumptions, including the principle that effective rhetoric proceeds from a thorough understanding of purpose, subject, audience, and occasion and the assumption that rhetorical skills depend upon the study of the canons. To observe the respect that many nineteenth-century rhetoricians held for Quintilian is to observe a specific manifestation of this general indebtedness, an indebtedness inspired by Campbell, Blair, and Whately who wove the force of classical rhetoric throughout their theories of rhetoric for a new age. Similarly challenged with the task of articulating a theory of rhetorical practice in the face of changing times, nineteenth-century rhetoricians generally held to the powerful example of the New Rhetoricians— they reviewed the past for its relevant wisdom and used it to best advantage.

Notes

1. My argument in this chapter, that nineteenth-century rhetoric was strongly influenced by classical authorities and presumptions, confronts the position argued most recently by James A. Berlin that classical influence had been "overthrown" by epistemological and belletristic philosophies by 1800 (4–8). In *Nineteenth-Century Rhetoric in North America,* I argue at length against this interpretation of the theoretical and pedagogical interests of the nineteenth-century tradition, offering instead the view I reiterate in this chapter—that nineteenth-century theory was a hybrid of epistemological, belletristic, and classical principles.

2. I discuss the disposition of nineteenth-century theory in "Nineteenth-Century Rhetorical Theory: Legacy and Synthesis" in *Nineteenth-Century Rhetoric in North America* (65–111).

3. All Blair references are to the 1965 Harding edition unless otherwise noted.

4. Whately also uses classical authorities but tends to take a rather persistent revisionist stance when referring to classical sources. Whately favors Aristotle above all other classical "writers on Rhetoric," arguing that Aristotle's treatment is more systematic than either Cicero's or Quintilian's works. Although he credits Cicero's "excellent practical remarks" and Quintilian's "good sense" and "many valuable maxims" (7–8), Whately rarely refers to either Cicero or Quintilian in his text, preferring to quote and paraphrase frequently from Aristotle's rhetoric. Although Whately makes frequent references to Aristotle's advice, he does so only when it seems to support his theoretical interest in giving advice on the "management" of the faculties in argumentation. As in the case with

Campbell's and Blair's treatments of Quintilian, Whately's treatment of Aristotle reveals both his desire to rely on classical advice and his impulse to recontextualize it. See Whately's reinscriptive citation to Aristotle on the definition of rhetoric as an art and Whately's repositioning of Aristotle's advice on style in his discussion of energy (14, 283).

5. Even when seeming to recommend Quintilian unreservedly, Blair and Campbell often do so to support their respective interests in the cultivation of taste and function of rhetoric in appealing to the faculties of the mind. Blair leaves no doubt as to his high regard for Quintilian when he refers to Quintilian as the "most instructive, and most useful" of the the ancient writers on rhetoric. Even in this seemingly unqualified accolade, Blair turns Quintilian's authority to the service of his own enterprise by stressing Quintilian's taste and critical judgment: "I know few books which abound more with good sense, and discover a greater degree of just and accurate taste, than Quintilian's *Institutions*. Almost all the principles of good Criticism are to be found in them. He has digested into excellent order all the ancient ideas concerning Rhetoric, and is, at the same time, himself an eloquent Writer" (244–45).

6. Nineteenth-century dependence on classical sources is more pronounced between 1800 and 1875; in the last decades of the century, rhetoricians cited classical figures less often than they did the pronouncements of Campbell, Blair, and Whately and influential nineteenth-century theorists such as as Henry N. Day, Alexander Bain, and Adams Sherman Hill.

7. Some criticize Quintilian's definition of rhetoric as the art of speaking as being incorrect, either because it is too broad or because it does not take in the scope of rhetoric as an art of oral and written communication that also concerns itself with criticism. See Coppee, 25–26, or De Mille, 13–14.

8. For another example of recontextualization see C. W. Barden's use of Quintilian's advice on descriptive language (156). Barden quotes one of Whately's few citations of Quintilian's advice that to "tell the whole . . . is by no means to tell everything" to support his point that detail and expansion are required in order to impact on the feelings and allow the understanding "to form vivid and distinct ideas."

Works Cited

Barden, C. W. *A Shorter Course in Rhetoric*. New York: American Book, 1885.

Berlin, James. *Writing Instruction in Nineteenth-Century American Colleges*. Carbondale: Southern Illinois UP, 1984.

Blair, Hugh. *Lectures on Rhetoric and Belles Lettres*. 1783. Ed. Harold F. Harding. Carbondale: Southern Illinois UP, 1965.

———. *Lectures on Rhetoric and Belles Lettres*. New York: G. & C. & H. Carvill, 1831.

Broadus, John A. *A Treatise on the Preparation and Delivery of Sermons*. New York: Armstrong, 1889.

Caldwell, Merritt. *A Practical Manual of Elocution: Embracing Voice and Gesture*. Philadelphia: Sorin and Ball, 1845.

Campbell, George. *The Philosophy of Rhetoric*. 1776. Ed. Lloyd F. Bitzer. Carbondale: Southern Illinois UP, 1988.

Coppee, Henry. *Elements of Rhetoric*. Philadelphia: E. H. Butler, 1860.

Day, Henry N. *Elements of the Art of Rhetoric*. New York: Barnes and Burr, 1866.

De Mille, James. *The Elements of Rhetoric*. New York: Harper, 1878.

Genung, John Franklin. *The Working Principles of Rhetoric*. Boston: Ginn, 1886.

Hill, Adams Sherman. *The Principles of Rhetoric*. New York: American Book, 1895.

Hill, David J. *The Elements of Rhetoric*. New York: Sheldon, 1878.

Jamieson, Alexander. *A Grammar of Rhetoric and Polite Literature*. New Haven: A. H. Maltby, 1844.

Johnson, Nan. *Nineteenth-Century Rhetoric in North America*. Carondale: Southern Illinois UP, 1991.

McIlvaine, Joshua Hall. *Elocution: The Sources and Elements of Its Power*. New York: Scribners, 1870.

Quackenbos, G. P. *Advanced Course of Composition and Rhetoric*. New York: American Book, 1884.

Quintilian. *The Institutio Oratoria*. Trans. H. E. Butler. Cambridge: Harvard UP, 1976.

Theremin, Franz. *Eloquence a Virtue*. Trans. William G. T. Shedd. Philadelphia: Smith, English, 1859.

Welsh, Alfred H. *Complete Rhetoric*. New York: Silver, Burdett, 1885.

Whately, Richard. *Elements of Rhetoric*. 1828. Ed. Douglas Ehninger. Carbondale: Southern Illinois UP, 1963.

2 Canonicity and the Renaissance Cicero

Lawrence D. Green

During the Renaissance, the discourse that was most extensively analyzed and criticized was not the vernacular literature of the period that so commands our attention today.[1] Outside of the Bible, the body of discourse most analyzed and most criticized were the works of Cicero and, in particular, the oratory of Cicero. The amount of material is enormous. Cicero's orations provided what Renaissance readers might have understood as their literary canon; the texts were shared property, they were studied and written about in every country in Europe, and they provided a shared background for literate discussions for several centuries.

The Renaissance debates about Cicero are no longer a live issue for us today, but the very distance between Renaissance concerns and our modern concerns makes it possible to look more dispassionately at the dynamics of interpreting canons and canon formation. It is a truism that the context we create for a writer determines how we understand that writer, but the more we are caught up in the immediacy of the debates about a given writer—say, Kenneth Burke—the more difficult it is to understand the processes by which we create those contexts. In the present chapter I am interested in how the knowledge of a shared literature is shaped, first by the theoretical understandings and second by the interpretive intentions that critics bring to bear on that literature. For the case of Cicero in the Renaissance, those concerns can be phrased as two seemingly paradoxical questions: To what extent did the various commentators' own skills with Ciceronian rhetorical theory interfere with their criticism of Cicero's speeches? And to what extent did the humanists' purposes in composing commentaries interfere with their understanding of Cicero's speeches?

As a canonical body of discourse, Cicero's orations exceeded even the giant masterworks revived from antiquity, and for several reasons. First, the major lines of rhetorical education in the Renaissance were derived from Cicero, even when filtered through Quintilian. Cicero's orations were re-garded as the praxis for his theory, even when critics disagreed about both the theory and the praxis.[2] Second, Cicero's orations were taught during the early years of schooling, often alongside the graduated series of schoolroom exercises known as the *progymnasmata*; a speech would be analyzed in chunks and then studied in its entirety.[3] Third, we find a constant drumbeat of Cice-ronian reference in the critical studies of other classical authors, but only rarely is the process reversed, and only rarely do we find attempts to explicate Cicero by reference to other writers (the notable exception, of course, is the recourse to Demosthenes, due in large part to the pairing of the two orators in Plutarch's *Parallel Lives*).[4]

Perhaps all these same reasons explain why it is that when we today look back upon this enormous enterprise we see a monolithic enterprise. All those teachers, all those books, all those students, all of them focused for so long upon what are, finally, just a very few speeches, give us the distinct impression that when you've seen one analysis you've seen them all. This impression is all the stronger for us when we filter this critical enterprise through the polemical Renaissance arguments over "Ciceronianism" made by Erasmus, Scaliger, Ramus, Harvey, and many others. But there was nothing monolithic about it. Between 1400 and 1700 there were major intellectual shifts in the Renaissance criticism of Cicero, with marked differences north and south of the Alps, and over time the emergent national perspectives also affected this body of criticism. In this chapter I want to examine one of the earliest Renais-sance analyses of Cicero, contrast it with a relatively late analysis, and then close with a brief survey of the variety of rhetorical approaches and interpretive intentions that developed in the course of the sixteenth century.

I. Early Italian Renaissance

The Quattrocento interest in the revival of a Ciceronian rhetoric for what has been called "civic humanism" is widely recognized. But how, exactly, did this work? Antonio Loschi (Antonius Luschus de Vicentinus, Antoine Losco; 1368–1441) was the first of the Renaissance commentators on Cicero's speeches, and his *Inquisitio super XI orationes Ciceronis* (1392–1396) provides a clear illustra-tion of the interest of the early humanists.[5] His lengthy commentary was widely distributed in manuscript form before being appended to the first edition of Asconius Pedianus's histories of the Ciceronian speeches in 1477, and it was reprinted throughout the sixteenth century, both with and without Asconius.[6] Loschi was a student of the humanist leader Collucio Salutati (1331–1406), who was the chancellor of Florence, and Loschi himself worked in the chancery for many years before succeeding to the secretaryship at Milan. And the rhetorician Gasparino Barzizza of Bergamo (1360–1430) delivered a famous series of lectures in the 1420s on Cicero's speeches, based largely on unattributed borrowings from Loschi.[7] What were Loschi's procedures?

Loschi establishes six categories that he tries to use for each of the eleven speeches he examines. He starts with an *argumentum*, a summary with background material. Next he establishes the kind of oratory, whether judicial, demonstrative, or deliberative. Third, he determines the stasis of the question at issue, according to its kind of oratory—in general, this is the point in a judicial speech where the prosecution and the defense join battle. Fourth, Loschi discusses the *dispositio* of the speech, its parts, and the arrangement of those parts. The fifth category is particularly detailed, since it is here that Loschi discusses each of the parts in detail and lists the various commonplaces Cicero uses. The sixth category is called *elocutio*, but rather than being a discussion of style it merely lists the figures of thought and sentence throughout the speech, with no attempt to be methodical or inclusive.

The actual execution of this design is nowhere near as neat as the design itself, as we can see with Loschi's analysis of Cicero's *Pro Milone* (*Inquisitio* sigs. b5ʳ–d6ʳ). The story concerns two Roman gangsters whose gangland families bumped into one another one dark night on a road outside of Rome. In the melee that followed, the godfather of one of the families was rubbed out, and the godfather of the other family, Annius Milo, had to stand trial for murder. Since both mobsters had their fingers into politics as well as every other kind of racket, the trial also took on political dimensions. Cicero was Milo's mouthpiece.

Antonio Loschi provides most of this background within his *argumentum*, and much of it is taken without attribution directly from Asconius Pedianus, including the wording.[8] But the second category, the determination of the kind of speech (*genus causae in quo haec habetur oratio*), is much more problematic. Each kind of speech has its own particular end, as Aristotle points out, so it is important for Loschi to know the end of the *Pro Milone*. Cicero's speech is, of course, judicial. But it is a judicial speech given in a political context, and Cicero intends to use the welfare of the Roman state as part of the judicial defense of Milo. Moreover, Loschi discerns a great deal of demonstrative oratory in the *Pro Milone*, since Cicero heaps abuse upon the victim while praising Milo (*nam summe hic vituperatur Clodius. Milo laudatur*). Having come this far, Loschi then despairs of making sense of any of it, and simply declares that the speech really is primarily judicial, and that courtrooms always have a great deal of praise and blame.

The third category of Loschi's analysis deals with the stasis of the question (*constitutio causae in qua haec habetur oratio*), and almost all of it is borrowed without attribution from Martianus Capella's *Marriage of Philology and Mercury* (ca. 410–439). It now becomes clearer what Loschi is trying to do. Martianus Capella, in his own treatise, does not discuss the *Pro Milone* for the sake of analyzing the speech but rather for discussing the convolutions of stasis theory as it stood in late antiquity.[9] Martianus merely uses the *Pro Milone* as an exemplar for his theoretical discussion. And the case is nearly the same with Loschi's wholesale borrowing from Martianus. Loschi is analyzing Cicero's orations not to understand them as productions in their own right but as a vehicle for teaching rhetorical theory "on the fly," by showing how it worked in action. Thus the problem of how to determine the stasis for the *Pro Milone* becomes an opportunity in Martianus for a complete discussion of all aspects of stasis theory, including parts that are clearly irrelevant.[10]

This interest in theory over instantiation carries into the remaining categories of Loschi's analysis. The parts of the *Pro Milone* are interesting to him primarily because they violate the canonical form of a classical oration and show how a speech can be accommodated to the situation at hand. The normal order would be to offer a narration of events followed by a confirmation of positive proofs and then a refutation of the opposing arguments. Cicero's problem in the *Pro Milone* is to counteract the general sense of revulsion about his client Milo, and so he begins with a *refutatio*, which comes before even the *narratio*, much less the *confirmatio*. The procedure that Loschi then uses to analyze the *confutatio* will stand for his analysis of all the remaining parts. Cicero argues the justice of the killing of Clodius, based on the commonplace of the lesser and the greater evil. Cicero argues the justice of killing persons dangerous to the commonweal. Cicero argues from the Roman Twelve Tables and from the commonplace of self-defense. Cicero argues from equity, from nature, from common sense, and so on.

Let me return briefly to one of the questions with which I started: to what extent did the commentators' own skill with Ciceronian theory interfere with their criticism of Cicero's speeches? In the case of Antonio Loschi, and of many others who followed him, the answer might be "a great deal." When we finish Loschi's very long and detailed commentary on the *Pro Milone*, almost no sense of Cicero's dynamic speech survives. What instead emerges is an elaborate Ciceronian theory of speaking combined with a Quattrocento theory of governing. In the words of one recent critic, "The themes that appear in Loschi's commentary reflect clearly the emphases of Florentine humanism from Brunetto Latini to Salutati, Vergerio, and Bruni, as well as the school of Chrysoloras and the new connection established there between Cicero and Plato: the connection between the art of speaking and the art of governing, between the laws of nature and a state based on reason" (Rabil 1:238).

II. Late Northern Renaissance

I now jump ahead to a figure who is far more familiar to us today, Petrus Ramus (Pierre de la Ramée, 1515–1572). Like the Quattrocento humanists south of the Alps, Ramus also was interested in joining eloquence to philosophy. As Ramus saw it, the greatest impediment to meaningful discourse was ambiguity, and so he elaborated logical procedures that would be as useful in the analysis of discourse as they would be in the generation of discourse. By analyzing discourse, one could come to acquire the necessary skills for one's own discourse, in a kind of imitation, albeit not the *imitatio* of the early humanists. Thus Ramus can look at Cicero's *Pro Milone* and see it in a very different light than did Antonio Loschi. In an interesting parallel with today's critical procedure of *déconstruire*, Ramus proposed the critical procedure of *retexere*, of "unraveling."[11] When Ramus unravels the *Pro Milone*, he finds within it one, and only one, "dialectical ratiocination":

> It is permissible to kill a criminal;
> But Clodius was a horrible criminal;
> Thus, it is permissible for Milo to kill Clodius. [12]

And that is all that Ramus finds when he unravels the *Pro Milone*. Everything else in the speech, that is, all the other syllogisms (and many of them are "concealed"), all the amplifications, and all the ornamental elocution, all this needs to be stripped away from the speech, and then the underlying syllogism will stand out clearly. The point of such unraveling was not to promote intellectual bankruptcy, nor was the point of it to destroy Western civilization, although both charges were levied against Ramus (e.g., by Jean Riolan). The point was to develop faculties in everyone sufficient to attain truth, defend it, and use it. Part of his program was to demonstrate how language and thought worked, not to diminish them but to make available their power.

My comments about Ramus's deconstructive unweaving of the *Pro Milone* come from the *Dialecticae institutiones*, since Ramus did not live to complete the full commentary he intended for the *Pro Milone*. But the procedure that he uses in his complete Ciceronian analyses is consistent with what I have said here. When he looks, for example, at Cicero's *Catilinarian* orations, he, like Loschi with the *Pro Milone*, starts with an *argumentum*, but unlike Loschi, he then explains the logical procedures and the rhetorical figures without worrying about the traditional questions of genus or stasis or the number of parts of an oration.[13] It is not necessary to spend time on the theory of these things, as Ramus explains in his commentary on Cicero's second *Agrarian* speech, because a properly executed unraveling will make all of these intuitively clear to an alert person.[14] Instead, what the critic needs to do is unravel the central syllogism; in this case,

> Perniciosi cives sunt morte multandi:
> Catilina perniciosus est civis:
> Catilina igitur morte multandus. (*Praelectiones* 26)[15]

And this says roughly what the syllogism on the *Pro Milone* said. As for the category of *elocutio*, where earlier Antonio Loschi had provided a random listing of rhetorical figures, Ramus instead provides a tabulation of figures by classification: "There are nearly eighty metaphors, forty metonymies, twenty synecdoches, and six ironies" (*Praelectiones* 49).[16]

III. Cross-Currents

Antonio Loschi and Petrus Ramus do not represent the only possibilities for rhetorical criticism of Cicero's speeches. They do not even represent something as simple as two ends of a spectrum. Joachim Classen has argued that Ciceronian commentary in Italy came in two different waves. The initial interests ranged from humanist concerns for political rhetoric, scholastic studies of style, and historical linguistics to antiquarian book-collecting and textual criticism. The second wave concentrated much more narrowly on linguistic and stylistic matters and contributed much to the development of Italian.[17] In Spain the study of Cicero's oratory was oriented toward education in grammar, linguistics, and the cultivation of both oratory and philosophy, but most of all it was oriented toward immediate service to the state and to the propagation of the Faith.[18] In France the story was more complicated. There was intense study by a relatively small group of people gathered around the royal court who had literary interests, but there was no sustained study at the university and little interest outside Paris. The work was largely that of private, self-taught men interested in immediate application to political and judicial rhetoric and Protestant, but not Catholic, preaching.[19]

The material conditions of Ciceronian studies in German-speaking lands differed from those of other countries. Unlike the situation in Italy, study of Cicero's speeches did not begin until after the advent of printing, so that from the outset relatively inexpensive editions were widely available, and it was possible to study Cicero without the presence of a learned professor. Unlike the situation in France, there was no center of intellectual life such as Paris, so that competing approaches could develop in different universities in response to different needs and interests. And unlike the situation in Spain, humanistic studies were not constrained by the needs and authority of the Catholic church.[20] Let me list some of the other Renaissance possibilities for rhetorical approaches to Cicero's speeches, drawing on Classen's several studies.[21]

Bartholomaeus Latomus (Barthélemy Henrici, Bartholomäus Steinmetz; 1485–1570) was a teacher of rhetoric in Cologne who wrote manuals and redacted the manuals of others and served as professor of Latin eloquence at the Collège de France. In 1528, the same year that Erasmus published his scathing *Ciceronianus*, Latomus produced a massive commentary on the *Pro Milone* in which he paid extraordinary attention to the details of grammar, phrase, sentence, and figure. Where Antonio Loschi a century earlier was interested primarily in the larger rhetorical and structural questions, Latomus focused on detail. The purpose of studying the *Pro Milone* was to develop good grammar and good taste, to make students able to participate in civic life.

Philipp Melancthon (1497–1560) lectured at Tübingen and Wittenberg, published widely on theological and humanistic issues, taught rhetoric, and published manuals of rhetoric. He wrote his commentaries on Cicero at about the same time as Latomus. Melancthon's approach, unlike that of Latomus, was to stress structural concerns in Cicero's speeches, and this approach is consistent with the perspectives of Rudolf Agricola, whose disciple Melancthon was. After analyzing a speech, students would discuss how it was put together, how each part related to every other part, and then try their hands at manipulating those parts, making the speeches shorter or longer. By such practice, Melancthon's students would make Cicero's structural principles become their own structural principles and be able to apply them in their own letters and orations.

Johann Sturm (Joannes Sturmius, Jean Sturm; 1507–1589) was an enormously influential educator and reformer who taught rhetoric in Paris (Ramus was one of his students) and classical languages in Strassburg. Sturm seemed to have some of the same goals as Melancthon, but his procedures for both analysis and *imitatio* were very different. Where Melancthon analyzed Cicero's speeches for underlying structural principles, Sturm, writing in the 1570s, instead analyzed the speeches for local features of text and texture. Students would then accumulate vast *copia* of Ciceronian words, phrases, and figures and categorize them through enormous systems in the hope of being able to use these in their own writing. Sturm also had a strong religious interest in the ethos proper to a Christian writer, and so he focused on Cicero's own *ethopoiia*.

Joachim Camerarius (1500–1574) was a friend of Melancthon and Luther, and the prolific author of more than 150 treatises. He was a professor of classical Greek, a major voice in reforming university education, and taught at Nuremberg, Tübingen, and Leipzig. Camerarius produced editions and commentaries on Cicero's work and directly challenged Erasmus's ideas on Ciceronianism by proposing that *imitatio* had what we might today call a heuristic function in self-realization. The struggle of students was to learn for themselves how words could lead them to their own thoughts, and *imitatio* of Cicero's speeches was a discipline in exploring the heuristic power of words.

I have bypassed a great number of other Renaissance rhetorical critics and rhetorical approaches in this chapter, but some observations about canonical aspects of Cicero are still in order, and I return to my initial concerns and questions. To what extent did the rhetorical skills of the various commentators interfere with their criticism of Cicero? Greatly. If the early analyses of Cicero tend to be deterministic, the later analyses are sophisticated to a fault, and even precious, finding applications of Ciceronian theory in the speeches that would astound even Cicero. The criticism of the speeches is more in keeping with the spirit of the early *De inventione* (and the *Ad Herennium*) than the later *Orator* and *De oratore*, despite the fact that Cicero wrote those later treatises precisely because his career in oratory made him dissatisfied with his immature work. Renaissance commentators, working without an arena for the kinds of speaking that most concerned Cicero, looked at his speeches and saw mostly the bare bones of his theory.

To what extent did the intentions of the commentators interfere with the understanding of Cicero? Greatly. To speak of only the commentators mentioned in this last section, all of their pedagogical approaches have a familiar ring to them. Latomus trained students to participate in elite political and social strata. Melancthon wanted to develop adepts of the structures of rational argument. Sturm realized that ethos rests in the details and minutiae of discourse, and control of ethos depends upon control of massive amounts of detail. And Camerarius encouraged a kind of imitative role-playing to help students discover their own ideas. In each case, the pedagogical procedures declared a slightly different reading of the Ciceronian canon for the students schooled in those procedures.

All of these goals could have been pursued, and were pursued, in terms of other authors. But Cicero's speeches were known and acclaimed throughout Europe, and educators took for granted that a theory of careful reading was coordinate with a theory of careful composition. From our modern vantage point today, Cicero's speeches provide a stable test case with which to compare Renaissance procedures and power, with which to measure changes, and by which to calibrate intellectual revolutions and even social revolutions. Renaissance writers provided the diversity, and Cicero provided the fixed point of reference. And perhaps, in times of critical ferment, that is one of the functions of what we now call a canon.

Notes

1. This essay was originally delivered at a meeting of the Modern Language Association in San Francisco, December 29, 1991.

2. See, for example, the massive Aldine volume *In omnes de arte rhetorica M. Tvllii Ciceronis libros, item in eos ad C.Herennivm scriptos, doctissimorvm virorvm commentaria* (Venice, 1551), which gathers together numerous studies on Cicero's theoretical works by sixteen different commentators, illustrated copiously by Cicero's speeches.

3. Richard Sherry (fl. 1550) provides an example familiar to English readers in *A Treatise of the Figures of Grammar and Rhetoric, profitable for al that be studious of Eloquence, and in especiall for such as in Grammer scholes doe reade moste eloquent Poetes and Oratours: Whereunto is ioyned the oration which Cicero made to Cesar, geuing thankes vnto him for pardonyng, and restoring again of that noble man Marcus Marcellus* (London, 1555).

4. An interesting example is found in Guillaume Du Vair (1556–1621), *De*

L'eloqvence françoise, & des raisons pourquoy elle est demeuree si basse. Edition nouuelle, reneue & augmentee (Paris, 1600), which after the first 49 pages of theory spends the remaining 362 pages comparing speeches by Demosthenes and Cicero, with a speech by Aeschines and an imagined speech by "Clodius" thrown in for good measure.

5. *Inquisitio super XI orationes Ciceronis* (Venice, 1477), published with Asconius Pedianus, *Commentarii in orationes Ciceronis*, Secco [Xicho] Polenton (1370–1463), *Argumenta XII super aliquot invectivis et orationibus Ciceronis* [1414], and George of Trebizond (Georgius Trapezuntius, 1396–1486), *De artificio Ciceronianae orationis*, a commentary on Cicero's *Pro Ligario*.

6. See Monfasani, 3:188.

7. See Pigman, 130–31.

8. Where Asconius writes, "Miloni & Clodio summae erant inimiciae: quae & Milo Ciceronis erat amicissimus" (*Commentarii* sig. A10ʳ), Loschi writes, "Cicero ergo Milonis amicissimus inimicissimus Clodiis pro Milone orationem hanc habuit insignem atque notabilem" (*Inquisitio* sig. b6ʳ). On the other hand, Poggio Bracciolini is usually credited with the rediscovery of Asconius Pedianus a full decade after Loschi's commentaries; see Monfasani, 3:188.

9. Martianus Capella (Marcianus Minucius Felix, fl. 470), sect. 451–58.

10. In some instances Martianus Capella and Cicero actually are found together, as in the volume from the library of the Benedictine Monastery of St. Peter at Salzburg, in which are bound both Martianus's *De nuptiis philologiae et mercurii* (Modena, 1500) and Cicero's *Orationes* (Venice, 1499).

11. Ong translates Ramus's *retexere* as "unweaving" or "disentangling" and argues that Ramus intentionally deviates from the usual Latin translation of ἀναλύειν as *resolvere* or "analyze" (191).

12. *Dialecticae institutiones* (Paris, 1543), 48: "Sic miloniana Cic. in vnum dialecticae ratiocinationis vinculum est inclusa: Sceleratum hominem licet interficere. . . . At P. Clodius homo sceleratus insidiarum vim parauit. . . . Iure igitur caesus est Clodius: hoc modo Cicero Milonis defensionem disposuit."

13. *Praelectiones in Ciceronis orationes octo consulares* (Basel, 1575), 25–122.

14. "Haec secundae est ἀπόδειξις, ex qua praeterea & Rhetoricae & Logicae non solum sensum, sed vsum faciliorem habebis. Nam si nullam vnquam Rhetoricam & Logicam artem ante didicisses, tamen haec Aristotelis ἐπαγωγῇ καὶ ἱστορίᾳ ita retextis & rhetoricae elocutionis & topicae inuentionis, & analyticae dispositionis partibus magnam tibi vtriusque artis informationem afferrent, cum in nobili praestantique exemplo omnium fere & Rhetoricam & Logicarum virtutum tantam frequentiam, tamque gratam videres. Cicero ait orationem Caesari in legem Caepionis sibi a pueritia magistram fuisse: Credo, in qua nempe omnes has rhetoricas & logicas laudes studiose contemplatus esset, imo meditatus & aemulatus esset. Quid igitur prohibet, quin vnam Ciceronis orationem magistram habeamus, & dum Ciceronis studium imitamur, fructum quoque consequamur?" (*Praelectiones* 238–39).

15. Ramus analyzes this syllogism again on page 44. Along the way, he unravels numerous subsidiary syllogisms, many of them in the form of Stoic hypotheticals rather than Aristotelian categoricals, for example, "Si suspectus & insensus es, abi in exilium: Sed primum: Secundum igitur" (*Praelectiones* 35).

16. "Metaphora locis fere octoginta apparebit, Metonymia quinquaginta, Synecdoche viginti, Ironia sex." Ramus's further tabulation characterizes this *Catilinarian* by comparing it with Cicero's *Agrarian* speeches: "In figuris verborum,

epizeuxis quater est, quae in Agrarijs nulla fuit; Anaphora vicies, Epistrophe semel, Symploce vt Epanalepsis, & Gradatio nulla. Epanodos semel, Anadiplosis ter, vt Paronomasia: Polyptoton vero bis & vicies" (*Praelectiones* 49).

17. "Nach dem politisch-rhetorischen, dem schulmäßig-stilistischen, dem historisch-sprachlichen, dem antiquarischen und dem textkritischen Studium Ciceros beginnt damit die zweite Welle eines engherzigen, sprachlich-stilistischen Studiums der Reden Ciceros, die vor allem dadurch fruchtbar wirkt, daß sie zur Entfaltung der Muttersprache beiträgt" (Classen, "Cicerostudien" 217).

18. "Nirgendwo wird in Spanien das Studium der Antike um seiner selbst willen betrieben, überall steht es unmittelbar im Dienst der Erziehung: des grammatischen Unterrichts, der sprachlichen Schulung und der rednerischen— und philosophischen—Ausbildung; die Erziehung aber steht im Dienst der Festigung und Ausbreitung des christlichen Glaubens" (Classen, "Cicerostudien" 228).

19. "In fast ungebrochener Tradition bleibt in Frankreich das Interesse an der Antike, speziell der antiken Rhetorik spürbar, das zeitweilig von einem kleinen Kreis königlicher Sekretäre (neben einigen Dichtern) stärker belebt wird; und bei ihnen, den königlichen Beamten und Diplomaten, den Parlamentariern und Juristen erhält es sich, während die Universitäten abseits stehen, mit Ausnahme der lecteurs royaux. Es fehlt die Kontinuität und Stabilität, die der Universitätsunterricht schafft, es fehlt der Ansporn, der durch den Wettstreit mehrerer Akademien und kleiner Höfe (wie in Italien) garantiert ist; es fehlt auch die weltferne, künstliche Übertreibung der 'Ciceronianer' Italiens. Vielmehr sind die Franzosen oft Einzelgänger, Autodidakten, unmittelbar an der Sache interessiert und ihr hingegeben, daher bemüht, die Texte selbst zu klären in dem Bestreben, deren Gehalt nutzbar zu machen, das juristische Wissen, die rhetorischen Erkenntnisse, die sprachlichen Möglichkeiten—im Hinblick auf die eigene Sprache wie auf das Lateinische. Und ausgenutzt werden diese neugewonnenen Schätze im Bereich der Politik und der forensischen Beredsamkeit, doch—da die Theologen Zurückhaltung üben—nicht wie in Spanien in der Predigt oder richtiger nur in der Predigt der Protestanten" (Classen, "Cicerostudien" 241–42).

20. "(1) Anders als in Italien erwacht das Interesse an der Antike erst eigentlich nach der Erfindung der Buchdruckerkunst; damit ist von vornherein die Möglichkeit der verhältnismäßig raschen und weiträumigen, zugleich preiswerten Verbreitung einzelner Schriften gegeben, während die Vermittlung durch Lehrende zurücktritt. (2) Anders als in Frankreich gibt es kein Zentrum geistigen Lebens, das Paris vergleichbar wäre. (3) Anders als in Spanien wenden sich viele Humanisten dieses Raumes von den Traditionen der katholischen Kirche ab" (Classen, "Cicero Orator" 81).

21. To those listed above, add Classen, "Cicero Orator Inter Germanos Redivivus, II," 157–76, for the following summary of Latomus, Melancthon, Sturm, and Camerarius, as well as for bibliographical details on these commentators.

Works Cited

Asconius Pedianus, Quintus. *Commentarii in orationes Ciceronis.* Venice, 1477.

Capella, Martianus. *The Marriage of Philosophy and Mercury.* Ed. and trans. William Harris Stahl and Richard Johnson, with E. L. Burge. *Martianus Capella and the Seven Liberal Arts,* 2 vols. New York: Columbia UP, 1971. Vol.2.

Classen, C. Joachim. "Cicero Orator Inter Germanos Redivivus." *Humanistica Lovaniensia* 37 (1988): 79–114.

———. "Cicero Orator Inter Germanos Redivivus, II." *Humanistica Lovaniensia* 39 (1990): 157–76.

———. "Cicerostudien in der Romania im 15. und 16. Jahrhundert." *Cicero: ein Mensch seiner Zeit*. Ed. Gerhard Radke. Berlin: Walter de Gruyter & Co., 1968. 198–245.

Du Vair, Guillaume. *De L'eloqvence françoise, & des raisons pourquoy elle est demeuree si basse. Edition nouuelle, reneue & augmentee*. Paris, 1600.

In omnes de arte rhetorica M. Tvllii Ciceronis libros, item in eos ad C.Herennivm scriptos, doctissimorvm virorvm commentaria. Venice, 1551.

Loschi, Antonio. *Inquisitio super XI orationes Ciceronis*. Venice, 1477.

Monfasani, John. "Humanism and Rhetoric." *Renaissance Humanism: Foundations, Forms, and Legacy*. Ed. Albert Rabil, Jr. 3 vols. Philadelphia: U of Pennsylvania P, 1988. 3:171–235.

Ong, Walter J., S.J. *Ramus: Method, and the Decay of Dialogue*. Cambridge: Harvard UP, 1958.

Pigman, G. W., III. "Barzizza's Studies of Cicero." *Rinascimento: Revista dell'istituto nazionale di studi sul rinascimento* 2d ser. 32 (1981): 123–63.

Rabil, Albert, Jr. "Humanism in Milan." *Renaissance Humanism: Foundations, Forms, and Legacy*. Ed. Albert Rabil, Jr. 3 vols. Philadelphia: U of Pennsylvania P, 1988. 1:235–63.

Ramus, Petrus. *Dialecticae institutiones*. Paris, 1543; rpt. Stuttgart: Friedrich Frommann, 1964.

———. *Praelectiones in Ciceronis orationes octo consulares*. Basel, 1575.

Sherry, Richard. *A Treatise of the Figures of Grammar and Rhetoric, profitable for al that be studious of Eloquence, and in especiall for such as in Grammer scholes doe reade moste eloquent Poetes and Oratours: Whereunto is ioyned the oration which Cicero made to Cesar, geuing thankes vnto him for pardonyng, and restoring again of that noble man Marcus Marcellus*. London, 1555.

3   The Scottish-American Connection and the Emergence of Belletristic Composition

Winifred Bryan Horner

IN THE LITERATURE ON THE HISTORY OF WESTERN RHETORIC, THE EIGH-
teenth and nineteenth centuries are generally considered a period of decay.[1]
Professors James L. Golden and Edward P.J. Corbett speak of the "incipient
decline of traditional rhetoric"(1). George Kennedy concludes his study *Classical Rhetoric and Its Christian and Secular Tradition from Ancient to Modern Times*
with only a very brief look at the eighteenth century and Hugh Blair. James
Murphy in an address to the International Society for the History of Rhetoric
in 1979 speculated about the reasons for the "decay of rhetoric" in the nineteenth and twentieth centuries.[2] At one time I argued that this belief was
incorrect and that rhetoric survived in spirit if not in name. Today I am not
so certain. In this chapter I shall argue that instead of itself surviving, rhetoric
spawned a number of offspring that do survive and thrive today. Today,
English language studies, in the form of literature, criticism, and composition,
can be traced within the rhetoric and logic courses at the eighteenth- and
nineteenth-century Scottish universities.

The term *English language studies* itself presents difficulties, especially during the nineteenth century. Today we might consider composition, literature,
and criticism under such a rubric, three studies that in the eighteenth and early
nineteenth century were synonymous with rhetoric. Before the eighteenth
century, with very few exceptions, English was not studied at the universities
in England, Scotland, or the United States. Latin was the language of learning,

and the study of literature was the study of Greek and Roman classics. English literature and history and English composition were considered the province of any educated person, and one did not attend a university in order to learn the "vernacular·language" or the "folk literature." University lectures were in Latin, and students learned English by translating their Latin. And even after professors began lecturing in English in the eighteenth century, as Thomas Miller points out, "they were lecturing in English before they were lecturing on it. . . . English was not the object of study" (52).

What we see in early nineteenth-century Scotland is a break of the traditional educational mold that was failing to fulfill the needs of a people. There is a similar break in the American tradition, but because of eighteenth-century Scottish influences on American rhetoric, that break resulted in a different tradition in English studies in the United States, particularly in the composition course. It is the connections between those two traditions and the different outcomes that are traced here.

The Roots of Scottish and American Education

In 1750, before the Revolution, the American colony was supporting eight colleges: Harvard, William and Mary, New Jersey, King's, Philadelphia, Rhode Island, Queens, and Dartmouth. At the same time, England had only two institutions, and Scotland had five. Among the basic needs of the colonists, together with shelter and food, was the desire for schools. As the anonymous author of an early colonial treatise put it, "One of the . . . things we longed for, and looked after, was to advance *Learning* and perpetuate it to Posterity" (*New England* 12). In his history of Harvard University, Samuel Eliot Morrison states that "the two cardinal principles of English Puritanism which most profoundly affected the social development of New England and the United States were not religious tenets, but educational ideals: a learned clergy, and a lettered people" (45).

Many of these early American schools were little more than log cabins and dreams in the minds of their founders. Frederick Rudolph, the author of one of the definitive histories of American higher education, described those colleges: "Often when a college had a building, it had no students. If it had students, frequently it had no building. If it had either, then perhaps it had no money, perhaps no professors; if professors, then no president, if a president, then no professors" (47).

There were great difficulties in the new country. In 1619, the Crown had allocated 9,000 acres in Virginia for the foundation of a college, but an Indian massacre in 1622 eliminated most of the institution's supporters. In 1693, the Crown had granted a college charter to the state for "the saving of souls," but their Majesties' attorney general reacted with the comment, "Souls! Damn your souls! Raise tobacco!" (11–15).

While the American universities were struggling for their existence, the

29

Scottish universities were well established with a long history. The universities of St. Andrews and Glasgow and two colleges at Aberdeen, Kings and Marischal, had been founded in the fifteenth century; the University of Edinburgh had been founded in the seventeenth. There were no log cabins in the Scottish universities.

As early as the seventeenth century, education in Scotland was already considered both the right and the responsibility of every citizen. The educational system was built on a strong preparatory program of parish schools in the country and burgh schools in the cities. Despite the country's poverty, every burgh and town provided for some instruction in Latin. For a relatively poor country, Scotland had a well-established system of education. In the colonies, on the other hand, up until the Revolution in 1776, there was no provision for elementary education. Wealthier colonists provided tutors for their children, often Scottish tutors, but for the most part instruction in reading, writing, and arithmetic was the responsibility of the parents who had little time or energy for such pursuits in the hard life of the early colonies.

With the widespread revival of religion in eighteenth-century America and the Great Awakening, congregations and churches split into a number of factions, including conservatives and liberals. The Congregationalists founded their own college, Dartmouth, and the Baptists and the Dutch Reformed followed suit. However, education in the colonies was still limited to the few, largely because it was considered unnecessary for material success or religious salvation. In 1775, it was estimated that only one out of every thousand colonists had been to college, and most of those did not complete a full course. At the year of the Revolution, there were only 3,000 living college graduates in the United States, many of whom became political leaders in the forming of the Constitution. Although some middle- and lower-class families sent their sons to college, the "overwhelming majority of their sons stayed home, farmed, went West, or became—without benefit of a college education—Benjamin Franklin or Patrick Henry" (Rudolph 21–22).

In the eighteenth century, the American universities were still struggling. The historians of education tell harrowing tales of their early years.

> On a cold drizzly day in January 1795, a two-story empty brick building that called itself the University of North Carolina was opened to the public. An unsightly landscape of tree stumps, rough lumber, scarred clay, and a bitter wind greeted the governor, who had wanted to be on hand for this important event. He was also met by the faculty which consisted of one professor doubling as president. A month later the first applicant for admission knocked at the door. In the same year, far to the north the founders of a college that would be called Bowdoin were offering the entirety of a township in Maine to any contractor who would build them a four-story building. They could find no takers. (Rudolph 47)

The history of Miami University, now one of the prestigious state universities of Ohio, tells the story of the Reverend John W. Brown and his efforts to raise money for the fledgling college. Then president of the United States James Madison offered no assistance, but in Delaware Brown raised $22, the president of Princeton gave him $5, and John Adams, in his retirement, gave him two books and $10. Altogether his efforts brought a wagonload of books and $700 for the new college. Life was hazardous for the traveler in those days, and soon after his return he slipped and drowned in the Little Miami River (44–45).

Fire took its toll on the early log buildings. Nassau Hall at Princeton burned, as did the first building erected at Dickinson College the following year. At Ohio University, the only structure was hit by lightning and was saved from total destruction by torrential rains (45). But the spirit persisted. In 1842, eight French priests, barely able to speak English, walked into northern Indiana and founded the college that would become Notre Dame.

In spite of hardships, fires, and dissension, Americans never abandoned their dream of education. Between 1750 and 1800, twenty-seven American colleges were founded. By 1875 there were 250, of which 182 still survive.

There were only seven universities in the British Isles from 1591 to 1828, and Scotland had four of them. At the same time, more than seventy universities were founded in the United States that still survive. In the third quarter of the nineteenth century, in the red-brick explosion, the number of British universities doubled; during the same period in the United States, college enrollments also doubled.

Two events occurred in the nineteenth century that affected the North American universities. The first was the amassing of great fortunes by the robber barons, who in turn salved their consciences and perpetuated their names by founding colleges. Thus Vassar, Smith, Johns Hopkins, Stanford, Chicago, and Wellesley were all founded by single donors. Although the states were unable to underwrite the number of private denominational institutions that had grown up, they were often able to give them land, of which there was still plenty in the nineteenth century. In most cases sectarianism cut off state support and emphasized the private nature of these institutions. Increasingly they looked to private donors for their support, as they still do today.

The second event of the nineteenth century that greatly affected the American institutions was the Land Grant College Act of 1862. Congressman Justin Morrill of Vermont, the man behind the legislation, suggested as early as 1848 that American colleges might well "lop off a portion of the studies established centuries ago as the mark of European scholarship and replace the vacancy—if it is a vacancy—by those of a less antique and more practical value" (Rudolph 249). Morrill introduced a bill in 1857 incorporating provisions for a technical and scientific education, particularly in the case of agriculture, that would deal effectively with the necessity of saving the resources of the land from erosion and soil depletion. The act, passed in 1862, provided for a college in each state with studies related to agriculture and engineering, "without excluding other scientific or classical studies" (252). This act provided support for the state universities, some of which grew out of the small denominational colleges, some of which were combined with the private institutions as at Cornell and Rutgers, and some of which were founded from the act. Out of this act came the great state universities of Michigan, Illinois, Ohio, Indiana, California, and Minnesota, all of which now number well over 50,000 students, and many of which, like California, have grown into huge state systems of ten or twelve institutions.

There was a similar development in Scotland in the establishment of evening classes in Glasgow in 1800 for working mechanics and artisans. In 1886, the various institutions that had arisen to provide technical education during the century were amalgamated into a single institution called Glasgow and West Scotland Technical College. In 1886, an agricultural department was added, but it was not until 1964 that it merged with the Royal College of Science and Technology to become the University of Strathclyde. In 1966, Heriot-Watt University was established in Edinburgh as an amalgamation of a number of technical and scientific colleges. It was out of the same impulse toward a technical, mechanical, and agricultural education that these institutions came into being and out of which the later universities developed. However, the movement was far less strong in Scotland and slower to develop than in the United States.

While the American universities in the nineteenth century were moving toward expansion to serve their population in an upwardly mobile society that now equated a college degree with material success, the Scottish universities were embarked on reform. They were investigated by two Royal Commissions appointed in 1826 and 1876. (Reports of these investigations were later published.) After the Act of Union in 1707, Scotland had maintained its own democratic system of education, but in 1858 the universities were nationalized. Standards were raised and entrance exams were instituted, and thus the Scottish universities lost their distinctive thrust and became, in effect, English. The ensuing acts of 1872 and 1889 completed the metamorphosis.

The Eighteenth Century: Scottish Influence on America

In the eighteenth century, in contrast to the struggling American universities, the Scottish universities were thriving. Free from the religious restrictions of the universities in England and Ireland, they attracted students from America, where their influence was broad, and the Continent as well as from England. Edinburgh's well-known medical school brought many students from outside of Scotland. Moreover, it was at the Scottish universities rather than at Oxbridge that innovations took place. There, English literature as an academic study was introduced, and agriculture and Newtonian theories were added to the curriculum.

After the Act of Union in 1707, Scotland, freed of trade restrictions, prospered, and in the Age of Enlightenment, her universities prospered as well. Oxford and Cambridge, on the other hand, were a preserve for the "idle and rich." They were expensive and elistist and offered little that was new for the well-prepared student.

There were a number of reasons for the strong Scottish influence on the philosophy, political thinking, and educational practices in the United States. Like the Americans, the Scots had always placed a high priority on education and believed in a practical education for their farmers and merchants. With certain deep philosophical beliefs in common, it was only natural that the early founders of the American universities looked to the Scottish universities for their inspiration and for their leaders. Scotsman Hugh Blair's *Lectures* dominated English rhetoric in the first part of the nineteenth century and was the most widely used textbook in American colleges during that time (see Johnson, Kitzhaber).

The Scots, like the Americans, suffered from a colonial inferiority complex. The emphasis on education in both countries and their ready acceptance of the concept of taste, as popularized by Hugh Blair, can be seen as an attempt to rid themselves of Scottish and American "rusticisms" and to become more "English." Both peoples spoke a "nonstandard" dialect, in that London English was the standard, and the rise of elocution in both countries was a reflection of this lack of confidence not only in their own speech but also in themselves as provincials. Elocution teachers were abundant in eighteenth-century Edinburgh, and they thrived on offering lessons in "proper English." Along with this desire, there was the wish to understand literature—the entertainment of the upper classes before television and VCRs. Reading aloud was an important part of elocutionary training since it was considered a tasteful activity and a decorous way for the well-bred family to pass their leisure.

At the same time, both Scotland and the United States experienced a revival in nationalism—Scotland in fear of losing its identity while taking on an English identity and the United States as a struggling new nation in a new world. Both countries were seeking a voice. Consequently, the United States was in many ways a fertile ground for Scottish influence during the eighteenth century. The skepticism of Berkeley and Hume had left the individual open to an unknown fate, and the Scottish Common Sense philosophy was attractive to Americans in restoring their faith. In addition, Scotland and America shared a philosophy of government and education and a deep democratic bond that permeated their thinking and their actions. As a result, the exchange of peoples and ideas between Scotland and the United States proliferated. As Americans attended the world-renowned Scottish universities, Scots came in a steady stream to settle and work in the New World.

Many of the well-educated Scots came to the United States and established churches and presbyteries. They were much in demand as the colonists sought education, which was exactly what many of the Scots had to offer. A number found a place in religious institutions, medicine, or higher education. Others became schoolmasters or tutors. This migration was largely to the southern United States—Virginia, Maryland, South Carolina, and Georgia. Some, however, went to Pennsylvania, particularly Philadelphia, and a few to northern New York. Only a very few emigrated to New England. By 1790 there were between 200,000 and 250,000 people of Scottish birth or descent in the United States (Turnbull 137). William R. Brock demonstrates the difficulty of tracing Scottish Enlightenment thought in America, asserting that it may well be through the influence of these "hundreds of forgotten ministers, schoolmasters, tutors, and merchants" that Scottish ideas affected American thought, a fact that can be "neither measured nor ignored" (171).

Scottish educational philosophy permeated the early thinking in American politics and education. There was a deep philosophical bond between the Scots and the writers of the Declaration of Independence and the makers of the Constitution of the United States. Four of the signers of the Declaration were native-born Scots—Benjamin Rush, John Witherspoon, James Madison, and James Wilson. Archie Turnbull argues convincingly

> that the spirit that infuses many of the central doctrines of Congress, from 1774 to 1787, is in peculiar harmony with the legal, philosophical and moral teachings of Hutcheson, Reid and Kames; whose views in turn reflect the historical and constitutional inheritance of Scotland itself. Directly through their books, and as mediated by their disciples in the American colleges the ideas of these three men were familiar to all the most eminent statesmen, Franklin, John Adams, Dickinson and Jefferson among them. (149)

In his *Idea of a Perfect Commonwealth*, Hume suggests that "areas be divided into communities of such a size that electors and representatives remained mutually aware of each other's needs and responses." (qtd. in Turnbull). Turnbull points out the striking similarity between Hume's ideas and the formation of the United States (149). He also emphasizes that Madison studied under John Witherspoon, who himself studied at Aberdeen, and Witherspoon's influence went far beyond his own students. He was active in the political issues of the day and was the only Christian minister to sign the Declaration of Independence. One of his colleagues during the 1777 Congress remarked about Witherspoon: "He can't bear anything which reflects on Scotland. The Dr says that Scotland has manifested the greatest spirit for liberty as a nation, in that their history is full of their calling Kings to account and dethroning them when arbitrary or tyrannical" (qtd. in Turnbull 144). This spirit infused the thinking in the early colonies and influenced political and educational decisions. In addition, the many Americans who went abroad to study at the highly respected Scottish universities returned to become statesmen and educational leaders, bringing with them the Scottish democratic philosophy.

By far the most influence exerted by the Scots on the new nation was in education. Harvard College was founded in 1636, but the second college to be established in the New World was William and Mary in 1693. Its first president was James Blair, who attended the grammar school of Marischal College in Aberdeen and went to the University of Edinburgh at the age of fifteen. He graduated from the arts program and then studied for the ministry. His Scottish career came to an end, however, when he refused to take the religious oath required by the Test Act of 1681 (Scott 205). On the founding of William and Mary College in 1694, he was appointed president for life. James Blair's heavy Scottish influence was evidenced in the model he set up—a grammar school or preparatory section based on his own Aberdeen experience and a philosophically grounded arts curriculum followed by training in divinity. Students were accepted at an early age as they had been in Scotland. He instituted the specialized professorships, which were identical to those at Marischal and in direct contrast to the regenting system in operation at Harvard at the time (Sloan 20–21). Blair appointed many of his fellow Scots to positions in the college. Mungo Ingles, head of the grammar school, and Alexander Irvine, professor of natural philosophy and mathematics, were both Edinburgh graduates. He also appointed Dr. William Small from Marischal. Thomas Jefferson, the drafter of the Declaration of Independence, was one of Small's students and wrote admiringly in his *Autobiography* of his lectures on ethics, rhetoric, and belles lettres and the "habitual conversations" to which "I owed much instruction" (qtd. in Turnbull 140).

Francis Alison is a relatively neglected figure in the story of Scottish influence on American education (see McAllister and Turnbull). He studied under Hutcheson, one of the early Common Sense philosophers, at Glasgow, and student transcripts of Alison's lectures, which he gave at what would later become the University of Pennsylvania, were "Hutcheson *verbatim*" (Turnbull 140). William Smith, a graduate of King's College, Aberdeen, like Alison came first to America as a tutor to the children of a New York family. In a series of pamphlets, he urged the founding of a college there that would eventually become Columbia University. In 1754, he took a position teaching ethics, rhetoric, logic, and natural philosophy also at the college that later became the University of Pennsylvania.

John Witherspoon, unlike Alison and Smith, came to New Jersey at the height of his career. He was 45 years old and well known for his leadership in church affairs. He had written a number of religious pamphlets supporting the conservative cause, although he was primarily a mediator between opposing elements in the church. His concern for unity in the church was attractive to the Americans who recruited him for the presidency of the College of New Jersey. He set up a curriculum with four classes that carried the English names of freshman, sophomore, junior, and senior but a sequence of courses that was modeled after the Scottish universities. He introduced the Scottish method of dictating lectures, which were then used as a basic text. He lectured, continued as president for the college that was to become Princeton University, and maintained an active role in the political affairs of his day. He combined piety, politics, and rhetoric in his own career, but he is probably best known for his role in the American Revolution and as a signer of the Declaration of Independence. He brought to his career the rhetorical concept of the good man who is a good citizen. Michael Halloran speculates how different English studies might have been if Witherspoon's lectures had had the wide circulation that Hugh Blair's *Lectures* had. Witherspoon's rhetoric was "a political art in the tradition of Aristotle and Cicero, an art of confronting civic issues" (7).

The influence of these Scotsmen in the new colleges in America was strong and has been well documented, but the influence of hundreds of tutors and schoolmasters, though undocumented in the literature, may well have been equally strong. These individuals exerted an influence on the young people in the New World that was bound to have effects that long outlasted their own lifetimes.

In addition to this direct kind of influence, the indirect influence on American students exerted by the heavy use of textbooks written by eighteenth-century Scotsmen was substantial and remarkably long-lasting. Hugh Blair's lectures were published in Scotland in 1783 and were adopted as a textbook at Yale in 1785, at Harvard in 1788, and at Dartmouth in 1822. There were 130 editions of his *Lectures* in England and America, the last in 1911. Harvard still has on its shelves no fewer than twenty-six separate printings of the *Lectures* issued between 1789 and 1832. In 1850 it was used in twenty of forty-three American colleges and was in use at Yale and Williams until 1850 and at Notre Dame as late as 1880 (Kitzhaber 50). George Campbell and Richard Whately's texts were also heavily used. Nan Johnson demonstrates the important influence of Blair, Campbell, and Whately. The American universities were greatly influenced by the Scots both directly through their teachers and educational leaders and indirectly through their reading until the middle of the nineteenth century. It was not until then that America began to produce its own educational leaders and textbooks, and even during the second half of the nineteenth century Bain's *English Composition and Rhetoric* was the most widely used textbook in American college English.

The Nineteenth-Century Connection

In the first half of the nineteenth century, the Scottish and American universities were similar in many ways. The American universities were still heavily influenced by the Scottish model. In the second half of the century, however, Scottish and American education took very different directions. Both were influenced by the German models in becoming graduate and research institutions; the American universities, like the English, felt the influence more than the Scottish. Johns Hopkins University was opened in 1876, and graduate education was launched. The Scottish universities embarked on a series of so-called reforms in the second half of the century, and by 1900, as the American universities expanded, the Scottish universities adopted the English model, abandoning, in large part, their centuries-old philosophically based education that had served the country so well.[3]

During the nineteenth century in Scotland, there were three distinct developments in the rhetoric courses, led by three outstanding educators at three quite different institutions—Edinburgh, Aberdeen, and Glasgow. In the case of Edinburgh, the development almost exactly paralleled the developments that were taking place at American universities. At Aberdeen, Alexander Bain developed a course very specifically designed to improve the writing and speaking skills of the northern Scots, and his work was highly influential in the United States. In Glasgow, George Jardine prefigured many of the most important composition theories of the second half of the twentieth century in North America, but during the nineteenth century, he had little or no influence beyond his own university.

When William Edmondstoune Aytoun took over the chair of rhetoric and belles lettres at Edinburgh, the tradition of belles lettres was already well established. John Stevenson in the early part of the eighteenth century had lectured on English literature in his course in logic, metaphysics, and rhetoric. One of his students was Hugh Blair, who in 1759 took over the popular lecture series initiated by Adam Smith and Robert Watson in the city of Edinburgh. When the lectures were moved to the university, the chair of rhetoric and belles lettres was established. Aytoun held the chair from 1845 to 1865 and concentrated more and more on literature rather than on rhetoric. At the beginning, examples from English literature were used to demonstrate principles of rhetoric, but gradually the analysis of literature became the focus of the course, an emphasis vastly preferred by both the professor and his students. In the manuscript of Aytoun's introductory lecture, the line "I would much rather sit in this chair as professor of English literature" is written over with the words "I am happy to sit in this chair as Professor of English Literature" (National Library of Scotland Ms. 4897). In 1860, he received the title. At approximately the same time, Francis Child at Harvard initiated the study of English literature in the United States. It was first designated as a field of study in 1868–69, and the trend at Harvard was fairly typical of what happened at other schools in the United States (Kitzhaber 33). It is interesting that Child and Aytoun, the first professors of English literature at the universities, are both best known today as collectors of English ballads. Although they apparently did not know each other, they shared a love of their native expression in story and song. There are no direct influences in this case, but the close parallels are striking.

Largely because of the success of Aytoun's course at Edinburgh, the Royal Commission in 1861 recommended that the study of English be instituted at all of the Scottish universities. But for the students in the north, the study of English, under Alexander Bain, was not the study of literature; it was the study of grammar and composition. Compared to his English course, his psychology class was vibrant and exciting. His psychology students idolized him; his English students abhorred his course. His *English Composition and Rhetoric* initiated the idea of the paragraph as an important division of discourse marked by unity, coherence, and emphasis and introduced the topic sentence, the thesis, and other concepts still familiar to millions of American students. The book was the most widely-used text in North American universities in the second half of the nineteenth century (Johnson, appendix). It was written by Bain to improve the grammatical correctness of the students who came to the Scottish northern universities ill-prepared in the niceties of the English language, and it found a ready home in the United States.

Bain exerted a direct influence on the American composition course during the second half of the nineteenth century and the first half of the twentieth. He has been vilified by the composition theorists who attribute to him the worst of the current traditional rhetoric practices. He deserves more study to exonerate him from these largely undeserved charges. Bain, in fact, takes much of the blame for didactic rules established by the later text writers who adapted his work. The fact remains, however, that Alexander Bain, through his textbook, exerted a strong and direct influence on the American composition course.

While Bain's small textbook had approximately 23 printings between 1866 and 1910, George Jardine's book *Outlines of Philosophical Education,* first published in 1818, was reprinted only once, in 1825. Bain's ideas were eagerly adopted in both Scotland and the United States, while Jardine was largely ignored after his own lifetime in spite of the fact that his pedagogical theories are surprisingly similar to the work of contemporary compositionists. He used what today we call peer evaluations, sequencing of theme assignments, collaborative learning, and class discussions. He suggested encouragement for the beginning writer and overlooking "first faults" and saw writing as process and discovery. Even the terms in which he couched his theories sound amazingly like the compositionist theorists of the 1960s and early 1970s—Kenneth Bruffee, Mina Shaughnessy, Donald Murray, and Peter Elbow. Still, we can only look to his work as prefiguring what is happening in twentieth-century composition theory. It failed to influence the American universities of the nineteenth century either directly or indirectly, and his work remains largely unknown to this day.

The only direct influence on American composition from nineteenth-century Scotland was the strong and pervasive influence of Alexander Bain. English literature as a discipline coupled with criticism developed at the same time and in much the same way in both Scotland and North America. One did not influence the other. Nor did the work of Jardine influence American composition. However, this particular mix of influences and connections combined to shape and form composition as it is taught today in American universities.

Conclusion: Literature and Belletristic Composition

No one will argue with the idea that communication skills as they are taught today in North American colleges are vastly different from what Aristotle taught his students. To begin with, the langauge is different, even though scholars and students stuck to Latin well into the eighteenth century, only then breaking with tradition and allowing the vernacular languages to invade the universities.

In addition, the medium is writing instead of speech, a change that came slowly over the years but was virtually complete in the nineteenth century. Rhetoric and the ancient principles still held their place during that period in those courses having to do with oratory or homiletics. Rhetoric also survived in the North American speech departments that broke off from English in the early twentieth century until they, too, abandoned the old precepts in favor of more modern critical and linguistic principles.

But by far the most fundamental changes in English language studies in North America in the nineteenth and twentieth centuries were in the development of the study of English literature and criticism and the belletristic emphasis in composition courses within the large and powerful twentieth-century English departments. When speech departments abandoned rhetoric, English departments took it up to legitimize their composition programs. In the United States, rhetoric has been revived and has found new life. The composition course itself is often called rhetoric/composition as its professors seek to establish its roots in the tradition of Aristotle, Plato, and Cicero. Graduate programs are almost always named rhetoric/composition, even though their connections to the old tradition are tenuous at best. But composition, as it is taught today in North America, is not rooted in the ancient rhetorical precepts. Rather than rhetoric/composition, the modern course is in fact a belletristic composition with deep roots in the Scottish tradition of the eighteenth and nineteenth centuries.

Belletristic composition, that composition which emphasizes voice and discovery and allows and encourages such forms as the personal essay, is currently firmly established in English departments. Alexander Bain's rhetoric of mechanical correctness held sway in the American universities after the middle of the nineteenth century and well into the twentieth, and his principles are still widely taught today by teachers working with basic writers. The paragraph, topic sentence, and thesis statement have, by no means, been abandoned in twentieth century composition courses. The *Harbrace Handbook*, the best-selling college textbook, still emphasizes such basics simply because that is what many composition teachers still teach. But many more compositionists have adopted a belletristic composition. The reasons are many for this evolution from classical rhetoric as public discourse that grappled with civic issues and sought informed judgments by the good citizen within a community to a personal, largely interior search for meaning and identity by the individual in an alien society. These reasons are deeply rooted in the eighteenth- and nineteenth-century Scottish/American tradition, and the evolution is clearly evident in this study. In addition, the development of belletristic composition has been firmly reinforced by philosophic, political, and economic factors in the twentieth-century American university.

The study of English literature developed within the rhetoric course simultaneously in Scotland and the United States primarily during the nineteenth century. Before this period, literature was Greek and Roman; however, classical literature was never investigated in the same way that English literature is today. It was used as an accompaniment to rhetoric, providing examples of rhetorical principles. The term *literature,* as the study of the writings of a certain period (eighteenth-century literature) or of a certain nation or geographic location (French literature), did not come into use, according to the *Oxford English Dictionary*, in either French or English until the beginning of the nineteenth century. The study of literature as practiced today was a new concept in the 1800s.

This new and eagerly adopted idea in the Scottish and American universities was, however, eschewed by the English universities until well into the twentieth century. This fact is easy to understand against the social and political backdrop of Scotland and America. Students from these countries, so recently provincials, felt that they were basically second-rate and spoke a "nonstandard" dialect inferior to the London standard. In order to become more "English," they wanted to know and understand the literature of England and speak and write the London standard. Their English courses, which included both composition and rhetoric, were a way to reach this goal.

The concept of taste reinforced this attitude. Originating in France, it was popularized by eighteenth- and nineteenth-century Scottish rhetoricians and transferred to the United States through their texts. Hugh Blair's concept of taste was zealously adopted by the provincials: "Taste . . . is ultimately founded on an internal sense of beauty, which is natural to men, and which in its application to particular objects, is capable of being guided and enlightened by reason" (Lecture II, "Taste"). It was natural that the concept should have been warmly received in Scotland, a land that was trying to establish its legitimacy within the English world. For the same reasons it was even more natural that the concept was readily adopted in the United States and was part of every student's college training for nearly a hundred years. Both nations suffered from a colonial mentality. Taste, as Blair defined it, was inborn, but more importantly it could be guided and enlightened. In other words, students from the provinces who felt that they were in some ways subordinate could train their inborn sense of taste to appreciate English literature.[4]

Another reason for the study of English literature in Scotland was the idea that literature fostered a sense of national pride, and in both Scotland and the United States it furnished a moral vision of the world. This idea recurs over and over again in the course notes in this study. In 1828, Thomas Dale describes his purpose in all his lectures on "that glorious and inexhaustible subject the LITERATURE of our country—I shall esteem it my duty . . . to inculcate lessons of virtue, through the medium of the masters of our language" (qtd. in Palmer 20). In the eighteenth century, the universities were largely staffed by ministers who were there for the purpose of teaching ministers, a fact that did not change until well into the nineteenth century. A strong sense of nationalism and morality and the idea that good literature was morally uplifting survived well into the twentieth century.

The importance of science in the nineteenth century also encouraged the study of literature. In the notes annotated in this study, the term *science* comes up again and again as humanists and rhetoricians sought to legitimize their subject by connecting it with the new science: "Rhetoric is the art of effective writing and speaking; the Science of the laws which relate thought to expression; the science of the style, and principles of Literature; the Science of Literature" (Masson, Edinburgh University Library Ms. Gen. 1401–03 vol 3, 1). The syllogism that starts with known truths comes more and more heavily under attack as known truths in a scientific world become less reliable. The new inductive science depends on observable physical data on which to build, and literature becomes the data for the science of rhetoric.

The first literature courses were broad in their scope. David Masson divides the authors of a period "according to the field of literature in which they chose to exhibit their talents." The fields included history, science and philosophy, oratory and exposition, and imagination and poetry, in which he included novelists, dramatists, and poets (Edinburgh University Library Ms. Gen. 1401–03). When "English" was introduced into all the Scottish universities by fiat of the Royal Commission in 1858, the field was broadly conceived. English included some history, a little geography, and a literature that encompassed essays in history, science, and philosophy. Today literature has narrowed its scope to include only what David Masson considered "literature of the imagination." Scientific and historical essays were once part of the canon, but today such essays find their place only occasionally in the freshman composition course. The literary canon is restricted to works of the imagination, which made up only a quarter of what Masson called literature.

One obvious change that is apparent throughout the nineteenth-century courses is the shift of rhetoric as a generative, creative act to rhetoric as an interpretive, analytical act. Over and over again in these course notes we find rhetoric being defined as "criticism." Robert Eden Scott asserts that the "science" of rhetoric is "also sometimes denominated Criticism, Eloquence, or the Belles Lettres" (Aberdeen University Library K190, 1).

The same kind of mental shift took place in music and the other arts as scholars interpreted and criticized music, art, and literature rather than produced it. The reasons for this reformation are open to conjecture. It is easier and far more pleasant to criticize than to create, as anyone who has put pen to paper or brush to canvas can attest. Certainly the rise of the universities during this period further encouraged this shift as a canon of English literature was established and scholars sought new ways to look at an ever-narrowing body of material.

The shift from a generative rhetoric to an interpretive rhetoric was never completed in the nineteenth century, so that professors of English maintained their interest in and emphasis on composition while they concentrated their efforts, with the exception of Alexander Bain, on literature. In the nineteenth century, rhetoric, literature, and composition were bound together for better or for worse.

The wedding between composition and literature was consummated by economic factors in the second half of the nineteenth century when the German influence ushered in the large graduate programs that dominated the American and British universities for the next century. It proved to be a happy economic union for composition and literature in the North American universities but an increasingly unhappy philosophic one. Composition courses were turned over to graduate students. Professors were relieved of the onerous duty of teaching writing and reading themes and could devote their time to the study of literature. Literary scholarship thrived; rhetoric and composition scholarship at the university level languished. Only education schools maintained any interest in composition theory or pedagogy.

For North American administrators, the arrangement was economically advantageous. The largest course in the university, the only required course for every student, was taught by graduate students, cheap and efficient labor. Once established, there was no way to reverse the situation without a large outlay of money. For English professors, the situation was even more propitious. The composition course supported their Ph.D. students who, in turn, filled their Milton and Shakespeare seminars so that they could continue to teach the subjects that interested them. Graduate students, however, found teaching composition a burden and only vaguely related to their study of literature. Sometimes it was made tolerable for them by the introduction of some literature. Or they sneaked in a bit of *Sartor Resartus* in their freshman course since they had just covered it in their graduate seminar. The graduate students in the 1940s and 1950s, forced to teach writing while pursuing their studies in literature, came to despise it. When they graduated and found jobs, they thankfully took up teaching in their literary specialty, gratefully turning over composition to graduate students, vowing never to teach it again if they could help it. One of the lures to attract promising new faculty was the promise that they would never have to teach composition.

The unhappy union of composition and literature continues to the present day. Even the flooding of the market with English literature Ph.Ds unable to acquire positions fails to alter a situation too firmly entrenched and too satisfying to administrators and by now senior tenured English literature professors. In the 1970s and 1980s, graduate programs in rhetoric/composition came into existence—within English departments—more as an answer to the job market than as a philosophic change. Research in rhetoric and composition is still considered second-class in tenure decisions, and textbooks are not considered at all in such deliberations. One wonders if Aristotle would have been given tenure on the basis of his *Rhetoric,* which was basically a collection of lecture notes for his students. Most English programs still emphasize literature either through required course work or through the shape of the comprehensive exams. English professors still want to fill their Milton seminars.

Belletristic composition, as conceived by Hugh Blair, as reinforced in the 1960s by the expressive school of Peter Elbow, Donald Murray, and Ken Macrorie, as locked in for financial reasons in the twentieth century, is firmly in place by the end of the twentieth century. Because of the job market, graduate programs in rhetoric/comp attract students, many of whom in reality vastly prefer studying literature. Students in literature programs display rhetoric prominently in the titles of their dissertations in order to enhance their chances in the ever-tightening job market. As a result, composition texts, for the most part, are strongly belletristic, encouraging students to find a voice, to search for an identity, to explore meaning, and to write in metaphor and simile. The so-called scientific essays of Joan Didion and Loren Eisely are, in fact, only slightly disguised literary works comfortably within the tradition of the humanities. Students are urged to read and write literature, and more and more the composition course is losing its classical basis in a rhetoric that explores public issues and encourages informed opinions. The belletristic trend was introduced in the nineteenth century and continues in the twentieth encouraged by irreversible economic and political factors.

Today in British and American universities, English literature and criticism are firmly ensconced in large and powerful departments. Composition, historically linked to English literature through their common ancestor, rhetoric, fails to develop in the British and European universities, which in the nineteenth century delegated that onerous task to the lower schools. However, since British universities still have limited enrollments, classes are small, and students are expected to write in all courses. All professors consider the improvement of student writing as part of their responsibility.

In the United States, on the other hand, with a basically democratic form of education, the composition course continues to thrive. The fact that composition has been taught and its pedagogy researched by scholars trained in literature and criticism has produced in American institutions a belletristic rhetoric much more connected with the eighteenth- and nineteenth-century belletristic movement than with traditional classical rhetoric. Much as we may try to connect ourselves in the rhetoric/composition course to the great philosophers, the traditional public rhetoric of the good citizen, which deals with civic issues encountered in our daily lives, is with us no longer. In its place is a belletristic composition, a direct result, I believe, of North American composition having grown up and shared its youth with literature, criticism, and psychology in the house of eighteenth- and nineteenth-century Scottish logic and rhetoric.

Notes

1. A version of this chapter appears in my book *Nineteenth-Century Scottish Rhetoric: The American Connection* (Carbondale: Southern Illinois UP, 1993).

2. Donald Stewart is one of the few reliable interpreters who has brought to us his rich research on Fred Newton Scott and nineteenth-century American rhetoric.

3. George Elder Davie, in *The Democratic Intellect: Scotland and her Universities in the Nineteenth Century*, gives an account of this change during the nineteenth century. He defends the Scottish philosophy-based university education and regards the visits by the Royal Commissions as "assaults" on Scottish education. It was this book that originally piqued my interest in the Scottish/American connection during this period. R. D. Anderson's later book *Education and Opportunity in Victorian Scotland: Schools and Universities*, offers a clear, well-documented view of what he calls the Scottish universities' adaptation "to the changing conditions of the nineteenth century" (361).

It was, of course, almost always *English* literature. Scottish and American literature did not enter the academy as legitimate studies until well into the twentieth century. It proved as difficult for these literatures to find their places in the universities as it had been for English literature.

Works Cited

Anderson, R. D. *Education and Opportunity in Victorian Scotland: Schools and Universities.* Oxford: Clarendon, 1983.

Bain, Alexander. *English Composition and Rhetoric, A Manual.* London, 1866.

Blair, Hugh. *Lectures on Rhetoric and Belles Lettres.* 1783. Ed. Michael Halloran and Greg Clark. Carbondale: Southern Illinois UP, 1992.

Brock, William R. *Scotus Americanus: A Survey of the Sources for Links between Scotland and America in the Eighteenth Century.* Edinburgh: Edinburgh UP, 1982.

Davie, George Elder. *The Democratic Intellect: Scotland and Her Universities in the Nineteenth Century.* Edinburgh: Edinburgh UP, 1961.

Golden, James L., and Edward P.J. Corbett. *The Rhetoric of Blair, Campbell, and Whately.* New York: Holt, 1968.

Halloran, Michael. "Rhetoric and the English Department." *Rhetoric Society Quarterly* 17 (Winter 1987): 3–10.

Jardine, George. *Outlines of Philosophical Education Illustrated by the Method of Teaching the Logic, or First Class of Philosophy in the University of Glasgow.* Glasgow, 1818.

Johnson, Nan. *Nineteenth-Century Rhetoric in North America.* Carbondale: Southern Illinois UP, 1991.

Kennedy, George A. *Classical Rhetoric and Its Christian and Secular Tradition from Ancient to Modern Times.* Chapel Hill: U of North Carolina P, 1986.

Kitzhaber, Alfred. *Rhetoric in American Colleges.* Dallas: Southern Methodist UP, 1990.

McAllister, James L., Jr. "Francis Alison and John Witherspoon: Political Philosophers and Revolutionaries." *Journal of Presbyterian History* 54 (Spring 1976): 33–60.

Miller, Thomas P. "Where Did College English Studies Come From?" *Rhetoric Review* 9 (Fall 1990): 50–69.

Morrison, Samuel Eliot. *The Founding of Harvard College.* Cambridge: Cambridge UP, 1935.

New England First Fruits. London, 1643.

Palmer, D. J. *The Rise of English Studies: An Account of the Study of English Language and Literature from Its Origins to the Making of the Oxford English School.* London: Oxford UP, 1965.

Royal Commissioners Appointed to Visit the Universities and Colleges of Scotland: General Report. October 1830.

Rudolph, Frederick. *The American College and University.* New York: Vintage Books, 1962.

Scott, P. G. "An Edinburgh Graduate in Virginia: The Educational Influence of James Blair." *University of Edinburgh Journal* 27 (1975–1976): 205–8.

Sloan, Douglas. *The Scottish Enlightenment and the American College Ideal.* New York: Columbia Teachers College Press, 1971.

Turnbull, Archie. "Scotland and America, 1730–90." *A Hotbed of Genius: The Scottish Enlightenment.* Ed. David Daiches, Jean Jones, and Peter Jones. Edinburgh: Edinburgh UP, 1986. 137–52.

4   Postmodernism, the College Curriculum, and Composition

James A. Berlin

A COLLEGE CURRICULUM IS A DEVICE FOR ENCOURAGING THE PRODUCTION of a certain kind of graduate, in effect, a certain kind of person. In directing what courses will be taken and in what order, the curriculum undertakes the creation of consciousness. The curriculum does not do this on its own, free of outside influence. It instead occupies a position between the conditions of the larger society it is serving—the economic, political, and cultural sectors—and the work of teacher-scholars within the institution. The students themselves are of course involved in this circle of influence, but, unfortunately, their impact has recently been limited as conservative forces have succeeded in all but silencing them. The curriculum thus serves as a mediator between the demands of those outside the institution (employers, government agencies, political groups) and those within it (primarily faculty and the disciplines they serve). The response of the curriculum to the exigencies of its historical moment is thus a negotiation among forces both outside and inside the institution.

I want here to examine the changes within the larger society and the changes within certain academic disciplines that are together arguing for a new kind of liberal arts curriculum—shifts that are being discussed under the heading of the *postmodern*. I wish to examine the tensions and conflicts the curriculum is undergoing and suggest some possible responses. The center of my concern will be the role rhetoric and composition will play in these curricular revisions. In making my case, I will rely first on a historical approach. Thus, before examining the postmodern and its influences inside and outside the college, I will take a brief look at the nineteenth-century college curriculum and the curriculum of the modern university in order to demonstrate how each responded to its own historical moment. I will then turn to the radical transformations that are being encountered today in the economic, social, and cultural spheres and in the disciplines of the human sciences, tracing the consequences of both for the liberal arts and for rhetoric courses.

The Nineteenth-Century College

The college curriculum in the U.S. in the nineteenth century was relatively uniform and monolithic throughout the country. The college was intended to prepare students—overwhelmingly male until late in the century—for law, the ministry, and politics, and it was assumed that a single liberal arts curriculum based on classical texts served all professions equally well. Higher education was by and large meant primarily for those already financially secure who were getting ready to take their rightful roles as professionals and community leaders. The key to upward mobility in this period of competitive capitalism was through business, mainly the entrepreneurial venture. But colleges ignored the needs of commerce and manufacturing, arguing that its mission was to prepare moral and civic leaders (most colleges were church schools), not technicians. Practical scientific training was acquired in the world of work, after the college experience (Rudolph ch. 6). The center of the curriculum was three to four years of rhetoric, where the students brought to bear the products of their learning in public performances and written essays (Wozniak 29–67). Study in most colleges was finally capped by the senior-year course in moral philosophy taught by the college president.

The Modern University

Frederick Rudolph has detailed the tradition of complaint that surrounded the old liberal arts college. Attempts to introduce new scientific courses were limited at most schools. Furthermore, those that provided an alternative science curriculum commonly treated the students enrolled in it as less than full-fledged members of the college community (Rudolph 221–33). But dramatic, quick, and widespread changes in the curriculum took place during the last twenty-five years of the nineteenth century. The major cause of the change involved the shift from entrepreneurial to corporate capitalism. The college was now regarded as an institution designed to serve the economic and social needs of the larger society, or at least the needs of newly emerged power bases. The small liberal arts college was gradually replaced by the research university. This reformed institution was to conduct empirical study in the useful sciences, improving the techniques of farming, mining, manufacturing, and commerce. It was also to train the professionals who were to take their specialized training into the larger society, providing both increased profits for businesses and an improved standard of living for all (for example, through new techniques in health care and urban management). This effort is found in the new land-grant colleges, but private schools, notably Harvard and Johns Hopkins, and other state schools—Michigan, Wisconsin, Cornell—actually led the way (Veysey ch. 2).

Colleges today are to provide graduates with the expertise to solve practical problems as well as serve as leaders, thereby combining the objectives of the old curriculum with the new. A college education becomes the means of assured upward mobility at a time when the possibilities of entrepreneurial ventures are severely limited. The professional middle class is created—a newly formed group composed of managers and technicians who are to rationalize all features of daily life. (Today, of course, this group has become central to the operation of our society as people of all classes routinely seek out the appropriate professional for whatever ails them, from sick children to sick marriages to sick office spaces.) For most of the twentieth century, a college degree has been a ticket to prosperity as the corporation and other businesses have increased their profits through an application of the skills of trained professionals and as government agencies have looked to educated experts to fulfill progressive social policies (Carroll and Noble 350–54).

The elective system was created so that students could select the curriculum appropriate to their career ambitions. This meant that the common core curriculum was abandoned. At Harvard, for example, the only requirement for all students by 1897 was one year of freshman composition. Later, in an attempt to provide students with a common intellectual and cultural orientation, general education requirements and core studies were introduced to counter this excessive move to specialization. Unfortunately, these core courses were commonly taught by isolated experts from different disciplines who rarely communicated with one another. Thus, at most schools the only genuinely common and unifying experience in the curriculum was freshman composition. At times this course did try to bring an organizing force to bear, proposing a sense of common values along with instruction in writing (Berlin, *Rhetoric and Reality* ch. 3–4). This, however, was difficult to do within the frame of one or two semesters. Teachers, furthermore, were rewarded for being specialists, disseminating knowledge that constituted their range of expertise, not liberal thinkers who discussed the value of their disciplines to society as a whole.

There was for the most part no great concern about the fragmented curriculum. The Enlightenment conception of the unified, autonomous subject and confidence in the coherent metanarrative of progress governing the unfolding of historical events argued that the individual could make sense of the fragmented elective curriculum. It was left to the student to organize the smatterings of knowledge gathered from different departments. All of these would, taken together, finally provide a coherent formulation, because the universe was an organized whole and the disciplines simply studied the various parts of this unified structure. In fact, this system did work well throughout most of the twentieth century as graduates called on their specialized knowledge in the disciplines and their generalist courses in writing and speaking to serve the needs of the corporate work place.

The Postmodern

Today there is uncertainty about the value of this modernist curriculum to students and society alike as the economic and social conditions of our moment and the forms of the academic disciplines undergo change. These alterations have been commonly discussed under the rubric of the postmodern. In considering the conditions of this historical development, I will rely primarily on David Harvey's *The Condition of Postmodernity*. The first concern will be an assessment of the economic conditions for which we are preparing our students.

Today there is a shift from a Fordist mode of production (marked by the large-scale mass production of homogeneous goods, a process usually concentrated in a centralized locale within a single nation) to the "regime of flexible accumulation," or post-Fordism. The differences in the new mode fall into three general categories. First, production becomes an international process made possible by the compression of time and space as a result of rapid travel and communication. Today a company might have its assembly plant in one country, its work force and parts production in two or three countries, and its markets in all of these and still others. Communication and the movement of technical experts, parts, and products among these various divisions are made possible by advances in electronics technology and modes of rapid transportation.

Second, there is a turn to small-batch production of a variety of goods rather than the mass production of homogeneous products. While corporations are larger, productions operations are smaller and responsive to demand, not, as in the Fordist mode, to resources, the means of production, and the work force. Subcontractors are more common, and they now share the risks of overproduction and underdemand, saving the larger corporations manufacturing capital.

Third, the internationalization of corporations, the decentering of operations, is accompanied by the decentralizing of urban areas. Regional industrial zones and inner cities are abandoned in favor of "green sites" that come with tax concessions and promises of a better quality of life. And, once again, all of this is encouraged by the rapid means of communication and transportation provided by the technological compression of time and space. Clearly, the managers in this system must then display extraordinary ability in communicating in written form, and to a degree greater than ever before (a matter to be considered in greater detail later).

The effects of these developments on the work force are considerable. Workers are expected to perform multiple tasks, train on the job, and work well with others—all requiring at once more adaptability and responsibility than under the Fordist mode. The work force has been radically restructured. At the center is the core group of full-time managers. They enjoy greater job security, good promotions and re-skilling prospects, and relatively generous pensions, insurance, and other fringe benefits. In return, they are expected to be adaptable, flexible, and geographically mobile. This is the group made up primarily of college graduates. Its numbers are kept small, however, and many companies even subcontract management tasks that under Fordism they performed themselves—for example, advertising. The competition for these jobs is becoming more and more intense so that today a college degree provides only a permit to compete for one of them, not a voucher for a guaranteed position.

Thus, in contrast to the modernist era, a college degree does not automatically promise upward mobility. This is seen more clearly when we consider the periphery of the new employment pattern, a sector consisting of two groups. The first is made up of clerical, secretarial, and routine and lesser-skilled manual work. Since these jobs offer few career opportunities, there is a great turnover, and so their numbers are easily controlled. The second group is made up of even less-secure part-timers, casuals, temporaries, and public trainees. These jobs are the most unstable and offer the least compensation.

One of the most obvious features of the employment picture today is the decreasing number of jobs in manufacturing and the increasing number in the service sector. One important reason is that accelerating turnover time in production requires accelerating turnover time in consumption. The result is the growth of workers—especially educated workers—who are in the business of producing the artifices of need inducement: advertising, public relations, and the like. The media through advertising and other means have encouraged "a postmodernist aesthetic that celebrates difference, ephemerality, spectacle, fashion, and the commodification of cultural forms" (Harvey 156). Other service jobs have been created by the new information industries as the organizations' need for data to coordinate their decentered operations as well as up-to-date analyses of market trends and possibilities increase. In flexible accumulation, markets are as much created as they are identified, and so "control over information flow and over the vehicles for propagation of public taste and culture have likewise become vital weapons in competitive struggle" (Harvey 160).

So far we have seen that the managerial job market that our students wish to enter values employees who are expert communicators, are capable of performing multiple tasks, can train quickly on the job, and can work collaboratively with others. In sum, workers must combine greater flexibility and cooperation with greater intelligence and communicative ability.

Any consideration of the postmodern must also examine its social and cultural manifestations. These, I would argue, are largely the response to the changing economic forces I have just discussed, representing especially the results of space/time compression. Thus, we are told we live in a decentered world, a realm of fragmentation, incoherence, and the absence of a center or foundation for experience. Cities are without a central core, except for the shopping mall and the industrial corridor, neither of which is any longer at the center of anything but itself. Our national culture seems decentered as we see more differences among our members than similarities, manifested, for example, in the lament for the lost Anglo-Saxon ideal (in the form of the literary canon, for example). We daily encounter the internationalization of our cities and experience other cultures on television and in other media. Space has been compressed as the geographical borders of the U.S. no longer provide the security and simple-minded insularity they once did. (I might also mention in passing that one result of this has been the acceptance of hopelessly infantile and fantastic narratives about the special place of the U.S. in the world order, offered at the very time that the primacy of military strength—the U.S.'s strong suit—is being superseded by the importance of the economic, a realm in which its relative position is clearly on the decline. For a more detailed discussion of these narratives, see my "Literacy, Pedagogy, and English Studies: Postmodern Connections.")

We also experience time compression in a world of fast foods, fast cars, and fast fads. Ours is declared the age of the image and spectacle, and we are daily bombarded by a variety of sensory assaults—from the shopping center to the TV. Manners, modes, and styles are constantly in flux. This compression extends to history as styles of the past in clothing, architecture, and art are appropriated indiscriminately, merging the past and the present in the "pastiche" (see Jameson). This is even seen in shopping as the products of different societies of the past and present are arbitrarily presented to us. The culture of the "simulacrum," the cultivated image and spectacle of other times and places, is celebrated as the opportunity to live from one intense experience to another (see Baudrillard). For those with the means and time, experience becomes one manufactured event after another, a simulacrum of the past or future, the end being the detachment of life from the concrete material and social conditions of one's own historical moment. One defeats time and space in the manufactured public performance.

All of this, I would argue, is made possible by the regime of flexible accumulation. The decentering of the city is the response to the international economy and its time and space compression. The constant bombardment by images is a result of the need to create new demands and new desires in order to sell products. There is nothing that advertisers will not exploit to sell commodities—from classical music to high art to canonical drama. Advertisements are continually creating realities they would have us enter. On the other hand, this process of decentering and fragmentation has indeed shaken the foundations of our experience. Our faith in the universal laws of reason and the centrality of the Western cultural heritage in the larger world is questioned. Indeed, much of U.S. chauvinism and the nostalgia for traditional forms of art and experience may be nothing more than an elaborate reaction formation.

The larger point I want to make here is that I think our colleges, even in their outmoded curricula, are much better equipped to prepare workers for the new job market than they are to prepare citizens and consumers for the conditions of our new economy. In other words, our students are much more likely to acquire the abilities and dispositions that will enable them to be successful workers than they will the abilities and dispositions to make sense of the age of the image and the spectacle. When it comes to understanding the creation and fulfillment of desire through the use of the media, our students are infants. Indeed, they are media–illiterate, all but defenseless in the face of attempts to manipulate them. Most importantly, when it comes to responding to the images that occupy the center of politics today, our students display few resources for critique, for a genuinely resistant response. To most students, images are always either accurate representations of realities or they are distortions of experiences, and they believe the two kinds are easily distinguishable. The notion that images may construct convincing but dangerous realities seems impossible to them.

Certainly learning about representation, the relation of signifiers to signifieds, must be an important part of a student's education. This leads to a consideration of developments within the university that must be taken into account in considering a revised college curriculum. Postmodernism within the academy has been manifested most conspicuously through the influence of poststructuralism, sometimes referred to as the language division of postmodernism. Poststructuralism has had its greatest impact in the humanities, particularly in language departments, but its presence has been felt from the margins of sociology, psychology, and other disciplines. Even the physical sciences have not been totally immune.

Poststructuralism can be described as a set of concerns revolving around three central tenets: the loss of the unified, coherent, autonomous, and rational subject of the Enlightenment; the centrality of signification in the formation of self and society; and the abandonment of totalizing metanarratives that attempt to account for economic, social, and political events of the past or present. From one perspective, these are the theoretical conclusions intellectuals have come to as a result of their experience of postmodern conditions. I will briefly consider each.

The unified, coherent, autonomous, self-present subject of the Enlightenment has been the centerpiece of liberal humanism. From this perspective, the subject is a transcendent consciousness that stands apart from the social and material conditions of experience. In this autonomous sphere, it acts as a free and a rational agent, adjudicating competing claims for action. This perception has been challenged by the postmodern conception of the subject as the product of social and material conditions, more specifically, the effect of the signifying practices of a given historical moment (see, for example, Benveniste, Barthes, Foucault). Rather than acting as a transcendent free agent, the subject is figured as a product of its experience. The subject is thus conflicted and contradictory, heterogeneously made up of various competing discourses, signifying practices, that render consciousness anything but unified, coherent, and self-present.

Signifying practices then are central to the formation of subjectivity. The perception of these practices is itself, however, radically altered in postmodern discussions. Language is no longer taken to be a transparent medium that transmits an externally present thing-in-itself, that is, a simple signal system that stands for and corresponds to the realities that authorize it. Language instead is taken to be a complex system of signifying practices that constructs realities rather than simply re-presents them. Our conceptions of material and social conditions then are fabrications of language, the products of culturally coded linguistic acts. Language does not reflect experience; it constitutes it. Saussure has demonstrated the ways language functions as a set of differences. Signifiers are meaningful not in relation to signifieds, external referents, but in relation to other signifiers, the semiotic system in which they are operating. A sign thus has meaning by virtue of its relation to other signs, not to objects external to it. Barthes has demonstrated the ways human behavior in the cultural sphere duplicates the semiosis of texts: the principles of coded difference found in language are seen to operate in social and material experience as well. Foucault has revealed the ways in which "discursive regimes" forge power/knowledge formations that govern attitude and action historically. Signifying practices then shape the subject, the social, and the material—the perceiver and the perceived.

These antifoundational, antiessentialist assaults on Enlightenment conceptions of the subjects and objects of experience are extended to conceptions of the narratives found in historical explanations. Jean-François Lyotard has been the central figure in denying the possibility of any grand metanarrative that might account for human conditions in the past or the present. Renouncing the totalizing discourse of such schemes as Hegelianism and Marxism, Lyotard refuses the possibility of any set of master propositions that would provide a comprehensive explanation for the myriad events of human history. All such efforts are depicted as inherently partial and interested, intended to endorse particular relations of power and to privilege certain groups in historical struggles. Against this effort, some postmodernists argue for a plurality of micronarratives, limited and localized accounts that attempt to explore features of experience that the grand narratives typically exclude. The focus is moved to such categories as class, race, gender, and ethnicity in the unfolding play of historical events. This is often history from the bottom up, telling the stories of those people and events commonly absent from totalizing accounts, whether of the right or left.

I want to interject immediately that I do not agree with those who take these propositions to mean that we live in a radically indeterminate world, a world of free-floating signifiers without anchors of any sort. Although there is not space to argue the point here, I do side with those who maintain that, despite the social construction of the subject, agency is possible. To say that the self is a multiple formation of signifying practices is not to say that it is incapable of acting for change. I would also insist that signifying practices are not all equal. Despite the lack of sure foundations for truth and value, human beings do devise means for measuring the worth of different economic, social, and political arrangements. Signifying practices always mediate our relations to the material and social, but it is possible, to invoke Barbara Herrnstein Smith, to arrive at value judgments without relying on any notion of absolute truth value. The important consideration is that decisions are made democratically in an environment that allows for open and free debate, with the final awareness that truths are always contingent and interested and never universal and eternal. They must always display their tentative status, serving as the basis for action but not without constant reevaluation. Finally, the absence of master narratives does not mean we can have no narratives whatsoever. It is not the case that there is simply no relationship among the economic, social, political, and cultural. Without some larger cognitive map of our experience, we could not act at all. Our narratives, like all of our "truths," must be provisional and continually open to revision, but we must work to devise them if we are not to be overwhelmed by blooming, buzzing confusion or the totalitarian and closed narratives of certain narrow essentialist schemes.

And now at long last I am ready to address the lessons of the postmodern condition for the curriculum in general and composition in particular. Recall that I said that economic conditions would require us to provide graduates who are excellent communicators, adept collaborators, and flexible and quick learners. The social, political, and cultural elements of our day would demand that our students understand the workings of the image and the spectacle in consciousness formation. Both of these concerns are closely related to the poststructuralist emphasis on the importance of signifying practices, of language, in the formation of individuals and social arrangements.

We obviously need an effort to achieve the objectives of the general education movement, an effort that has never been altogether absent from higher education since early in the century. The elective system provides our students with multiple subjectivities—that is, a way of looking at the world in the manner of a sociologist, a psychologist, a historian, a literary critic, a biologist, and on and on. Nowhere, however, do the contradictions created by these different subject positions get addressed. A set of cross-disciplinary courses is needed to address the different conceptions of truth—indeed, of experiencing the world—coded in each discipline. Unfortunately, all attempts to set up such courses have ended in failure. The attempt to achieve cross-disciplinarity is invariably defeated by the university's commitment to specialization. After all, the reward system in most colleges and universities is de-

signed to recognize the work of specialists, not cross-disciplinary achieve-
ments. We simply have no models for genuinely liberal and liberating work
that cuts across the narrow concerns of the disciplines. For example, an effort
at my own university to introduce a new set of general education requirements
for liberal arts students that will be especially attentive to multiculturalism
has been before the faculty for two years. The new program was given the
name "Curriculum 2000," and after months and months of turf battles over
"indispensable" courses, all of which are to remain in departmental domains,
some faculty are calling the effort "Curriculum 2100" or even "Curriculum
3000." Even after these squabbles are behind us, however, the new requirements will still be taught by experts who will find it difficult not to foreground
their own disciplinary concerns.

I would propose that rhetoric courses be returned to the role they played
in the nineteenth-century U.S. college. Students would take at least one of
these courses each year of their four-year degree program. Since many (and
perhaps most) schools now require a two-semester freshman composition
sequence and another writing course during the junior or senior year, this
plan would require only one additional course. The concern of these courses
would be the examination of signifying practices in the formation of subjectivities within concrete economic, social, and political conditions. In other words,
their work would be the study of the production and interpretation of the
different terministic screens students encounter in and out of college, with
particular attention to the effects of these screens on students and the society
in which they live. (I am of course calling on the language of Kenneth Burke
here, language that, as Frank Lentricchia has demonstrated, in myriad ways
anticipated the work of poststructuralism.) These courses would concentrate
on the various master narratives students encounter that are intended to make
sense of their personal and social experience. The narratives considered would
cut across the curriculum as well as across the political spectrum, considering
the varieties of competing and complementary formulations students meet in
school and in society.

The study of the production and interpretation of these grand narratives
must take place at several levels. Students must understand the working out
of economic, social, and political arrangements in our everyday lives. It is
difficult to deny the relevance of these larger formations for all of us as the
effects of international economic competition are played out daily in even
the most superficial news coverage. Students must learn that the concrete
experiences of their lives are intimately involved in global economics and
politics. They must encounter narratives that enable them to understand their
position in the larger scheme of society and of the place of their society in
international affairs. This requires the examination of class, race, and gender
codes—all central elements in the narratives that form them. By looking at
themselves in terms of these larger structural patterns, they begin to understand
how they have become what they are—how certain cultural codes about

nationhood, region, ethnicity, race, class, gender, age, and the like have entered into forming them. Central to this examination, of course, will be a consideration of the narratives of academic disciplines.

A disciplinary formation is organized around a set of signifying practices, a set of linguistic mediations interposed between the investigator and the external world. This has been explored in the sciences by Thomas Kuhn and Paul Feyerabend, both philosophers of science, by Donna Haraway, a biologist, by Donald McCloskey, an economist, and by Greg Myers and Charles Bazerman, both students of rhetoric. All argue that the sciences are social constructions of reality, formulations that are true because the scientific community has agreed about the standards of truth and the discoveries that have measured up to these standards. This is to say that this agreement has come as a result of examining the world in a particular way, through a particular set of terministic screens, screens that, as Kuhn has demonstrated, form research paradigms that change over time. Students should study these scientific narratives and their historical changes. Most importantly, they should consider the responsibility of science to serve the interests of society, as distinct, for example, from science serving the careers of scientists or the profits of particular economic groups. Students should thus look at the kind of research that gets funded and the kind that does not. They should examine the sources of funding and the interests these sources represent. The central problem is the determination of the principal beneficiaries of scientific research.

If the putatively "objective" sciences can be shown to be organized around social processes, then the human sciences cannot remain exempt from a corresponding investigation. The purpose of these probes is finally to forward an argument about the place of the disciplines in a democratic society. Knowledge is here regarded as a good that ought to serve the interests of individuals and the larger community. It must be situated, once again, in relation to larger economic and cultural considerations. Students must learn to locate the beneficiaries and the victims of knowledge, exerting their rights as citizens in a democracy to criticize freely those in power. I realize that after twelve years of reactionary administrations in which the end of education has been declared to be the making of money for large corporations, this proposal sounds vaguely subversive. (Recall that Bush portrayed the American Civil Liberties Union and the liberals—the "l" word—of the Democratic party as suspiciously un-American.) It is, however, in keeping with one of the oldest notions of education we in the U.S. possess, eloquently proclaimed in the American pragmatist philosophy of John Dewey. Here, the interests of the larger community and the integrity of the individual must be paramount, and this is true whether we are discussing the activities of government or large corporations. This educational scheme is designed to make human beings and their life in a community the measure of all things. In short, public education exists to encourage intelligent, articulate, and responsible citizens who understand their responsibility and their right to insist that economic, social, and political power be exerted in the best interests of the people as a whole. To use the term proffered by Henry Giroux, this is critical literacy at its best.

The rhetoric class must accordingly consider a broad range of writing and reading practices. In keeping with the comprehensive definition of textuality provided by poststructuralist speculation, students must study the production and interpretation of the media in its various forms as well as writing and speaking, reading and listening. If they are to be responsible citizens, students must study television, film, and popular forms of print. They must learn to analyze and critique the attempts to control and manipulate them, to create desire so that it may be satisfied for profit, that is so much a part of their daily experience. And students should undertake this study by becoming both producers and consumers of various media forms. Thus, just as students can best learn to be good readers by writing, they can learn to be good critics of the media by making their own media presentations. All messages are always already interpretations, whether offered in the form of print, radio, film, or television, and students will learn in the rhetoric course to decode these culturally conditioned messages.

The interdisciplinary area of study called cultural studies is today being forwarded in the university in a form that includes many of the recommendations I am making. In "Composition Studies and Cultural Studies: Collapsing the Boundaries," I explore the congruence in the projects of cultural studies as pursued by the Birmingham Center for Contemporary Cultural Studies in England and by rhetoric and composition studies in the U.S. There I make clear a point I want to emphasize here. While there are similarities in what we do, cultural studies has as much to learn from composition as composition has to learn from cultural studies. Furthermore, since the rhetoric course is a long-standing site of the juncture of theory and practice in a pedagogy committed to the production of a critical literacy, it has a secure institutional location in which it can carry out its important work. In other words, the best hope for cultural studies in the university at the present may come through its influence in rhetoric and composition programs where, unlike its status in mainstream literary studies, it is looked upon as a welcome ally.

The mention of pedagogy brings me to my next consideration. The rhetoric classes I describe require a revised course of study, but this effort cannot be successful without a revised mode of teaching. In "Composition and Cultural Studies" and in "Poststructuralism, Cultural Studies, and the Composition Classroom," I have discussed this pedagogy in detail. Here I wish to consider its most prominent elements and the ways in which they serve the purposes of critical literacy. I should first reiterate the objectives of these courses. We are, once again, striving to produce workers who can perform multiple tasks, train on the job, and work collaboratively. They must at once display more intelligence and responsibility and more initiative. At the same time, they must be first and foremost critical citizens who evaluate the consequences of their actions for the larger community and its individual members. (Readers who are beginning to suspect these two intentions may conflict in the actual conditions of work today are asked to suspend disbelief for the moment; this issue will be taken up presently.)

The model for the rhetoric classroom is found in the examples of Paulo Freire and Ira Shor. Students should not be regarded as receptacles to be filled with the expert knowledge of the teacher, a scheme Freire calls the banking model. They must instead be made active agents of knowledge acquisition. This means that teachers and students engage in dialogue. Teachers should as much as possible turn over the learning process to students. Instead of serving as the fountain of knowledge, the teacher can become an expert collaborator. This does not mean that teachers will abdicate their responsibilities. It is still their role to set learning objectives and standards. They ought, however, to allow students choices in meeting these objectives and standards. This means the classroom is marked by dialogue. Students must be encouraged to ask questions, to pose problems, and then to devise their own means of addressing them. They should engage in a variety of tasks—individual reports, group reports, strategy sessions, library investigations, ethnographic study and other field work, and the like. Again, this should involve a variety of media, including audio and video recordings and presentations. They must work collaboratively, learning to negotiate with each other in the completion of projects. As is becoming increasingly clear, collaborative learning at any level of education improves learning for all students, regardless of their background (see Jackson). Indeed, those familiar with school programs for the gifted and honors programs at colleges are aware that the learning activities I am describing are common. The point I want to make is that they should appear in all rhetoric courses, for all students.

As has been emphasized throughout, knowledge is a signifying practice, a language that enables us to experience the world in a particular way. This is why writing is now seen to be so important a device in learning. Writing involves the working out of the signifying practices that are at stake in the issue under investigation, regardless of the nature of the issue. And although it may seem strange to say, it is worth emphasizing that writing should be a daily presence in the rhetoric course, even when considering interpretations of written texts and other media. Reading can never substitute for writing.

All study in the rhetoric course, once again, must be related to larger economic and social conditions. Knowledge is always found in relation, and students must learn to locate the relevant contexts of the matters they are considering. This does not mean that the everyday experience of the student should be ignored. Indeed, I am arguing for quite the contrary. The student's own experience is always the start of any investigation, but it must not stop in the analysis of the private and the subjective. Since no incident in our lives is without its relations in larger circles of significance, the details of daily life must be considered in ascending contextual orders. The college experience and its complex web of power/knowledge formations and social relations, the immediate environment of the student, will then be at the beginning of any study. The individual is always responding to larger cultural codes, codes of race, class, gender, age, ethnicity, and the like, and these must form part of the cognitive map that the student calls upon in making sense of personal experience. This investigation, furthermore, cannot stop until it reaches the larger contexts of the economic and the political in both national and international terms. The aim of all investigation, as has repeatedly been emphasized, is critique. As Donald Morton and Mas'ud Zavarzadeh explain, this "critique (not to be confused with criticism) is an investigation of the enabling conditions of discursive practices" (7). Students must locate the sources of the multitude of cultural codes that are shaping them and strive to arrive at an understanding of the place of these codes in power relations.

It is also important to emphasize that methods of evaluation must also be devised collaboratively with students. The pressure-packed testing situation in which weeks of effort are to be measured by the performance on a teacher-devised written test of an hour or two simply does not make much sense. For example, how would writing teachers like to have their skill as writers measured by a sample elicited in a twenty-minute composing situation, as the National Assessment of Educational Progress Report does for schoolchildren? Students and teachers must together devise more fair and reasonable devices for evaluating performance.

It is now necessary to consider the obvious conflict that is at the heart of my recommendations. During his tenure in the White House, George Bush, the "education president," proposed a number of changes in the nation's schools. His emissary to higher eduction, the National Endowment for the Humanities' Lynne Cheney, carried the ball for him in English studies. Bush spoke for business interests and Cheney for a certain ethnocentric educational tradition. At the same time, Bush's widely heralded education summit of 1989 said nothing of citizenship education for a democracy, and Cheney's canonical approach ignored the realities of a multicultural society and the international character of our current economic and political ties. The claims of both for the egalitarian effects of the Western cultural heritage were hard to take seriously. At the most obvious level, democracy did indeed appear in ancient Athens in the fourth and fifth centuries B.C.E., but it was another 2,000 years before it again became an actual political practice.

The contradiction in the proposals of the right is that they call for educated workers who are independent, self-motivated, enterprising, innovational, and creative and at the same time are obedient, subservient, respectful of existing power arrangements, and team players. The contradiction of proposals from the left (like mine) are no less pronounced. On the one hand, they call for graduates who are better equipped to enter the upper level of an inequitable multiple-tiered hierarchy of workers in a post-Fordist economy. On the other, they insist on a disposition for critique that will encourage graduates to protest the very injustices of the system they are being trained to enter. In the end,

I think, the two sets of contradictions are probably closely related. The right cannot use the schools to produce the kinds of energetic and productive workers it wants without also encouraging workers who will find it difficult to conform to the system. The left cannot produce the kind of critical graduates it calls for without encouraging workers who will find it difficult to accept the system's patent inequities.

The important difference between the two proposals is that the left is prepared to acknowledge its contradictions and to welcome them. In other words, I realize that to encourage a critical and creative work force responsive to the demands of post-Fordism will mean a work force that is not likely to accept the injustices of a system that allocates the fruits of labor so unfairly, for example, the inequitable distribution of income, secure jobs, health care, housing, food, child care, and on and on (for documentation, read almost any daily newspaper). But this resistance, from my perspective, is a wholly salutary outcome. Indeed, it would be difficult to create a critically literate democratic citizenry that did not feel compelled to address the cruelties of the present economic and political system. The right, on the other hand, acts as if its contradictions do not exist. And so it continues to insist upon standardized tests that reduce education to a mechanical process of thoughtlessly filling in prepackaged answers in response to inconsequential questions while demanding a work force that is aggressively innovative, responsive to change, and eager to identify and solve problems.

Finally, the proposal I offer here asks that reading and writing teachers at all levels become transformative intellectuals. It is no longer enough simply to impart limited skills in producing and interpreting texts. The international and national crises of our time indicate that language teachers must assume a greater role in the debates on the curriculum that are being waged all around us. Teachers are, after all, at least as well equipped to decide on the preparation of students for their roles in work in a democratic society as are business leaders and political appointees, many of whom try to conceal their ideological agendas by hiding behind platitudes about prosperity and parochial notions about great books and cultural literacy. Teachers are important contributors to any curriculum, and it is time to put forth our case for better schools and a better body politic.

Works Cited

Barthes, Roland. *Mythologies*. Trans. Annette Lavers. New York: Hill and Wang, 1972.

Baudrillard, Jean. *Simulations*. Trans. Paul Foss, Paul Patton, and Philip Beitchman. New York: Semiotext(e), 1983.

Bazerman, Charles. *Shaping Written Knowledge: The Genre and Activity of the Experimental Article in Science*. Madison: U of Wisconsin P, 1988.

Benveniste, Emil. *Problems in General Linguistics*. Trans. Mary Elizabeth Meek. Coral Gables, FL: U of Miami P, 1971.

Berlin, James A. "Composition and Cultural Studies." *Composition and Resistance.* Ed. Mark Hurlbert and Michael Blitz. Portsmouth, NH: Heinemann–Boynton/Cook, 1991.

———. "Composition Studies and Cultural Studies: Collapsing the Boundaries." *Into the Field: Sites of Composition Studies.* Ed. Anne Ruggles Gere. New York: MLA, 1993.

———. "Literacy, Pedagogy, and English Studies: Postmodern Connections." *Critical Literacy: Radical and Postmodern Perspectives.* Ed. Peter McLaren and Colin Lankshear. Albany, NY: SUNY P, 1993.

———. "Poststructuralism, Cultural Studies, and the Composition Classroom: Postmodern Theory in Practice." *Rhetoric Review* 11.1 (1992): 16–33.

———. *Rhetoric and Reality: Writing Instruction in American Colleges, 1900–1985.* Carbondale: Southern Illinois UP, 1987.

Carroll, Peter N., and David W. Noble. *The Restless Centuries: A History of the American People.* 2d ed. Minneapolis: Burgess, 1979.

Feyerabend, Paul. *Against Method.* London: Verso, 1978.

Foucault, Michel. *Power/Knowledge: Selected Interviews and Other Writings.* Ed. Colin Gordon. Trans. Colin Gordon et al. New York: Pantheon, 1980.

Freire, Paulo. *Pedagogy of the Oppressed.* New York: Continuum, 1970.

Giroux, Henry A. *Schooling and the Struggle for Public Life: Critical Pedagogy in the Modern Age.* Minneapolis: U of Minnesota P, 1988.

Haraway, Donna J. *Primate Visions: Gender, Race, and Nature in the World of Modern Science.* London: Routledge, 1990.

Harvey, David. *The Condition of Postmodernity.* Oxford: Basil Blackwell, 1989.

Jackson, Allyn. "Minorities in Mathematics: A Focus on Excellence, Not Remediation." *American Educator* 13.1 (Spring, 1989): 22–27.

Jameson, Fredric. *Postmodernism, or, The Cultural Logic of Late Capitalism.* Durham, NC: Duke UP, 1991.

Kuhn, Thomas S. *The Structure of Scientific Revolution.* 2d ed. Chicago: U of Chicago P, 1970.

Lentricchia, Frank. *After the New Criticism.* Chicago: U of Chicago P, 1980.

McCloskey, Donald. *If You're So Smart: The Narrative of Economic Expertise.* Chicago: U of Chicago P, 1990.

Morton, Donald, and Mas'ud Zavarzadeh. *Theory/Pedagogy/Politics: Texts for Change.* Urbana: U of Illinois P, 1991.

Myers, Greg. *Writing Biology: Texts in the Social Construction of Scientific Knowledge.* Madison: U of Wisconsin P, 1989.

Rudolph, Frederick. *The American College and University: A History.* New York: Vintage, 1962.

Saussure, Ferdinand de. *Course in General Linguistics.* Ed. Charles Bally and Albert Sechehaye in collaboration with Albert Reidlinger. Trans. Wade Baskin. New York: The Philosophical Library, 1959.

Shor, Ira. *Critical Teaching and Everyday Life.* 3rd prtg. Chicago: U of Chicago P, 1987.

Smith, Barbara Herrnstein. *Contingencies of Value: Alternative Perspectives for Critical Theory.* Cambridge: Harvard UP, 1988.

Veysey, Laurence R. *The Emergence of the American University.* Chicago: U of Chicago P, 1965.

Wozniak, John Michael. *English Composition in Eastern Colleges.* Washington: UP of America, 1978.

5 Persuasive Writing on Public Issues

Janice M. Lauer

COMPOSITION AND LITERARY THEORISTS HAVE BEEN ARGUING FOR SOME time that English studies—both literature and composition—should exercise social responsibility through discourse practices. Such rhetorical historians as John Gage, Susan Jarratt, and James Kinneavy have pointed out that composition instruction has important lessons to learn from classical rhetoric about political power and obligations. Despite slavery, disenfranchised women, and increasing imperialism (which kept classical rhetoric's social ideals from being fully realized), rhetorical instruction for public life remained for centuries the pinnacle of education of the citizen. And during that time rhetoricians learned a thing or two about how to wield power. James Kinneavy has argued for years that persuasive writing in public contexts is essential for all students, pointing out that they have been disenfranchised by political illiteracy and an undeveloped rhetorical way of knowing. Richard Ohmann has long lamented the role of English studies in the hegemonic process. In *English in America* and his more recent *The Politics of Letters,* he blames English teachers for having contributed to the continuance of a ruling class and its ideology. He accuses William J. Bennett and E. D. Hirsch of succumbing to the mesmerizing idea that culture or English or the Great Books can stand off from the clash of purposes and interests—to serve some higher power of their own in a politically neutral way. He advocates instead that we exercise our inevitable role in power structures by working for equality, self-actualization, and the empowerment of the powerless (*Politics* 6).

In another vein, Jasper Neel castigates private discourse as weak and untested in the arena of public life, urging instead the teaching of public discourse, a strong discourse he sees as deriving its strength from its ability to withstand the scrutiny of public life. He valorizes this kind of writing as the lifeblood of democracy, contrasting it also with antiwriting, in which students demonstrate a mastery of syntax, patterns of organization, and types of writing (208).

James Berlin has become a champion for social epistemic rhetoric through which students exercise responsibility as citizens and later as experts serving the community, as writers who understand their historicity, revise themselves, and engage in situated critique. He decries preparing students exclusively for professional careers and failing to teach them to analyze contesting ideologies and values in order to become active agents of historical change ("Rhetoric").

Many literary theorists voice these same concerns. For example, Terry Eagleton maintains that writing and speaking are not textual acts to be aesthetically contemplated or endlessly deconstructed but rather are acts inseparable from the wider social relations between writers and readers. Frank Lentricchia uses Kenneth Burke's work to argue for criticism as the production of knowledge to the ends of power and social change. He cites Burke's 1935 speech to the American Writers Congress in which Burke contended that right social action is primarily grounded in rhetorical textures, strategies, and structures of discourse (26). These literary theorists, rhetoricians, and increasing numbers in composition (see Bullock and Trimbur, Cooper and Holtzman, Faigley, and Harkin and Schilb) have clearly taken the political turn. This move, however, has not been categorically embraced in composition studies (see Hairston). Writing persuasively about issues in the public world has marginal status in many composition classes both in high school and college today. Recent national and international assessments support this assertion. The 1990 Writing Report Card from the National Assessment of Educational Progress concludes that "a vast majority of high-school juniors could not write a persuasive paper that was judged adequate to influence others or move them to action" (Applebee et al. 40). Only 1 percent of the students wrote elaborated persuasive papers.

The International Educational Association reached a similar conclusion in its study of written composition in seventeen countries. One of the types they examined was the argumentative/persuasive essay (Gorman, Purves, and Degenhart). Ulla Connor and I analyzed the persuasive essays from this study written by sixteen-year-olds in three countries—New Zealand, Great Britain, and the U.S.—randomly selecting fifty compositions from each country. A holistic scoring of these essays revealed a mean for all three countries of only 2.18 on a scale of 1 to 5. The U.S. students scored significantly lower (.01) than the other two groups combined (151). We also did a Persuasive Appeals Analysis of the students' use of rational (logos), credibility (ethos), and affective (pathos) appeals. On rational appeals, the U.S. compositions scored significantly lower than New Zealand's; on the credibility and affective appeals, the U.S. students scored lower than both New Zealand and Great Britain's students (153). A common weakness in all the papers was a vague sense of audience. Overall these students were writing ineffective persuasive discourse.

The marginalization of persuasive writing stems from complex circumstances, which have been explained elsewhere. Let me briefly draw into the discussion here some historical developments. As we know from studies of Berlin, Connors, Crowley, D'Angelo, and others, the modes—description, narration, exposition, and argumentation (from which persuasion was expunged)—have dominated a large segment of composition instruction since the nineteenth century, even though the faculty psychology on which they are based has been discredited. Many writing textbooks are still organized around these modes, and many instructors stress their mastery as a goal— writing a good descriptive paper, a good narrative, and so forth.

A single mode—expository writing—has claimed the lion's share of instruction. Many of our entering freshmen expect their composition course to teach expository writing to prepare them for college and a job. Some writing-across-the-curriculum approaches further this expository emphasis in an effort to acculturate students in academic fields. Expressive writing has also edged its way into high school and college courses through the work of people like Britton, Elbow, Kinneavy, and Macrorie and the efforts of the National Writing Project. College and high school expressive textbooks have multiplied. Some of our freshmen now bring to college only expressive writing experience. This expressive/expository binary opposition devalues persuasive discourse, if not by design then certainly by default.

In many colleges and universities, the closest that freshman composition comes to persuasive writing is the teaching of argumentation. An important question to ask, then, is whether the textbook treatments of argumentation foster socially responsible writing. My investigation indicates that many do not. They appear to be caught up in explaining formal or informal reasoning strategies and the avoidance of fallacies. They pay little attention to features that are central to the kind of persuasive writing about public issues that I am discussing here. First, they do not situate argumentation in the context of public issues; in fact, they often do not situate it at all. Second, they don't show students how to relate argumentative strategies to specific audiences. Third, they neglect or minimize ethos and pathos. Fourth, they do not view argumentation as inquiry or critique. Jasper Neel describes the typical treatment of argumentation as sophistry—teaching the ability to argue rather than a concern for what is argued (81–82). Let me test these claims by looking at the treatment of argumentation in three widely used composition textbooks—*The Random House Handbook, Writing with a Purpose,* and *The St. Martin's Guide.*

The third edition of *The Random House Handbook* boasts an eighteen-page chapter on argumentation with sixteen pages devoted to logical strategies: reasoning, avoiding fallacies, conceding and refuting, and providing facts, figures, and quotations. It illustrates these strategies with a model essay, "Protecting the Rights of Non-smokers," but it identifies no audience for this essay. The chapter ignores ethos; it also condemns pathos in a section called "Avoiding Emotionalism."

The sixth edition of *The Random House Handbook* presents its discussion in four chapters: "Strategies of Analysis and Argument," "Planning an Essay," "Supporting a Thesis," and "Collaborating and Revising." Argument is defined as "the use of persuasive reasoning to convince others that a certain position on an issue is justified" (33). The strategies discussed include definition, division, illustration, reasons, causes and effects, comparison and contrast, process, and analogy (34–49). The strategies are exemplified by excerpts from a range of publications: *BASIS, The Blind Watchmaker, Silent Spring, New Republic, New York Times Magazine, Los Angeles Times, Atlantic, Zen and the Art of Motorcycle Maintenance, Dissent, Yachting, Chevron World,* and from five student essays. While the examples help to explain the strategies, the brief discussion of each is decontextualized: Nowhere does the text explain how and why these strategies work for the readers of these publications. Nowhere does the text help the student to learn the discursive practices of these complex and sophisticated readerships. No audiences are mentioned for the student essays (33–50).

In the chapter "Planning an Essay," no consideration of discourse community or intended readers appears. The writer is instructed to formulate a thesis acontextually (53–76). In the chapter "Supporting a Thesis," the text discusses and exemplifies the use of syllogisms, facts, authorities, quotations, and personal experience, but none of the examples is analyzed in terms of the context (92–102). The student is advised to avoid emotionalism (102–4). An occasional reference to the "reader" paints a generic picture of common sense, reasonableness, and openness to being interested. In the chapter "Collaborating and Revising," a Peer Editing Worksheet is provided to guide revision. Students are directed to question twelve aspects of their essays, including thesis, tone, support, order, paragraph development, introduction, conclusion, conventions, spelling, and title. No mention is made of a reader, audience, or discourse community. The student paper at the end of the chapter addresses the issue of a lottery, but no reference is made to the intended readers. Although one might assume that the instructor and /or students in the class were the intended readers, the textbook does not show the student writers attempting to analyze their knowledge, experience, values, subject formations, or attitudes in relation to lotteries. By not doing so, the text leaves the impression that all instructors and members of a class hold similar views.

The eighth and ninth editions of *Writing with a Purpose* do better. In the eighth edition, the chapter "Persuasion" starts by talking about changing readers' minds. But the concept of readers remains generic. Students are given five directives: have specific readers, identify with these readers, be careful about tone, provide evidence, and maintain readability. So far so good. But the text provides no strategies or advice about how to accomplish these difficult directives or how to do so with public discourse communities. Forty of the forty-eight pages in the chapter explain the logical appeals with no reference to audience. In two passages, for example, the text illustrates the use of two analogies—impeaching a president as major surgery and supporting equal opportunity as creeping parasitism. Students are asked to judge the effectiveness of these analogies—but for whom? They are not told (343–65). They learn that establishing ethos means presenting the subject knowledgeably and fairly (333–38), and for pathos, they are advised to use a dramatic example, which is given three illustrations: the essay "I Want a Wife," an ad for a polio vaccine depicting a pathetic child, and a vivid paragraph in "A Letter from Jail" from the book *We Are Chicanos*. But the students are never told whose emotions, attitudes, and values were being invoked in these examples (338–43).

In the ninth edition of *Writing with a Purpose*, the chapter "Argument" opens with statements about rules of evidence and logical reasoning. The authors provide an example of an older student, Matt, whose composing process is traced throughout the chapter. This student chose to write about drug testing in the workplace. Fourteen potential audiences for his writing are identified, but his ultimate selection is never revealed. The text suggests that students write a draft from the perspective of "the opposition," a collection of opposing points of views but not of any specific group of readers. An audience guide offers general directives to choose a specific group of readers and to answer questions designed to help students identify with readers and to establish their identity. They are further advised to provide appropriate evidence and readable arguments, but the example, Matt's final draft, is not analyzed for the suitability of its arguments and evidence for the intended (unknown) audience.

The text also discusses the appeals (emotional, ethical, and logical) in general terms. In the two paragraphs on the emotional appeal, one sentence attests to its effectiveness; another mentions the use of dramatic examples, concrete images, and connotative language but does not illustrate these strategies except by presenting a picture (which does not show students how to construct this appeal in words). The rest of the section warns of the dangers of the emotional appeal (131–53).

The treatment of the ethical appeal is similar. The section mentions citing authority and using evidence competently and refers to an included essay by Anna Quindlen, for which no context, including an audience, is provided. Much of this section consists of cautions about the ethical appeal (144–45, 153–55). Although the ninth edition includes more aspects of persuasion than the previous texts—considering opposing views, using an audience guide, and including the ethical, emotional, and logical appeals—it doesn't go far enough in specifically contextualizing this advice.

The third text, *The St. Martin's Guide*, treats persuasion in a chapter entitled "Taking a Position." The text provides four contextualized models: an article in the *Harvard Crimson* by a staff writer explaining the paper's decision not to run a *Playboy* ad; an essay in *Newsweek* on abortion written by a theological student and mother; an essay in *Science 81* by a biology professor discussing animal experimentation; and an essay on Gary Hart written by a student for the freshman class. Each essay has at least one exercise question directing students' attention to audience. For example: "Because the essay was published in *The Crimson*, we know that Goss was writing specifically for her fellow Harvard students. What assumptions do you think she made about her audience? Specifically what values does she assume they share with her?" (184). That sounds audience sensitive, doesn't it? But what does it assume? That students already know how to analyze discourse communities such as the readers of a campus newspaper. Nowhere else does the chapter give any advice about probing the conventions and expectations of such an audience. The questions also assume that students anywhere can figure out the Harvard readership, that what's good for the *Harvard Crimson* is good for the *Local Campus News*. The second example takes for granted that students are astute assessors of the readers of *Newsweek*, a tricky community indeed. For the biology essay, students are asked to judge its effectiveness as if they were the intended readers. Finally, questions on the student essay on Gary Hart leave the impression that all classes are similar, needing no analysis, that peers everywhere know each other's values, beliefs, and practices.

In each of these texts—*The Random House Handbook, Writing with a Purpose,* and *The St. Martin's Guide*—I wonder what the examples lead students to conclude about the kinds of public discourse communities they are being prepared to write in. And I question whether these examples will convince students that persuasive writing wields power. The texts do not disclose the impact of their sample essays on their readers: what worked and why; what changes were effected. Moreover, none of these texts gives a nod to persuasive writing as inquiry and critique.

But what would such a conception of persuasive writing entail? To answer that question we need to better understand the challenges of persuasive writing in at least three areas: the nature of public discourse communities, the demands of inquiry and critique, and the impediments posed by current cultural and educational practices. In the remainder of this essay, I will explore some of the unknowns and problems in these areas.

Public Discourse Communities

A discourse community, as characterized by Porter, is a group bound by common interests who communicate through approved channels and whose discourse is regulated. The community stipulates what can be discussed, what constitutes evidence, and what conventions are followed, governing who can speak—what ethos is required in terms of knowledge and expertise (38). As a field, we have been getting a sharper sense of two kinds of communities: the academic and the professional. Composition specialists such as Bazerman and Paradis, Maimon, Odell and Goswami, and Spilka have described academic and workplace communities. But who is studying public discourse communities? What communities are instructors now using in writing courses that engage students in persuasive writing about public issues? Let's take a look at the advantages and disadvantages of three public discourse communities used in classrooms.

The first is the class as public community. Students write for and with their peers about issues of campus life, local political situations, and national affairs affecting their lives. Here peers can be analyzed, can collaborate, and can dialogue. But is this a representative public community? Would students under any other circumstances write to each other about issues? Does this captive group have a stake in these issues? Is there a textual record with conventions and expectations for evidence that can be studied? Will these groups prepare or motivate students to write in their future public worlds? Will writing within a community of peers empower students to participate as citizens in broader public communities?

Giroux argues for public audiences, for a counterdisciplinary practice— writing in public spheres both within and outside the university. He does not, however, discuss the features of such spheres and their inherent communities. This second alternative, actual public communities, allows students to write within groups to which they already belong or wish to enter—for example, environmental groups, Young Democrats, or Students Against Drunk Driving. These groups offer opportunities for students to analyze actual discursive practices, to teach the teacher about them, and to develop strategies and understandings inductively. The advantage is that students gain experience in gleaning the conventions and expectations of communities in which they can continue and with whom they can dialogue. But the undergraduates I know find it tough to analyze discourse conventions independently, while many teachers find it difficult to offer guidance about communities unfamiliar to them.

A third alternative is the case method in which all students in a class work on the same public issue (either assigned or class-selected) with a specified outside discourse community. Here the instructor can guide the community analysis and writing. Shared authorship is also feasible. A disadvantage may be artificiality: some students may never write in the selected community or may find the assigned issue uncompelling.

Each of these alternatives entails an audience of "real social beings," as Marilyn Cooper advocates in her model of the ecology of writing. Having real readers, however, is not the entire solution. She posits such questions that need to be studied as, "What kinds of interactions do writers and readers engage in? What is the nature of the various roles readers play in the activity of writing?" (11). Giroux similarly argues that critical literacy entails "presenting students with the knowledge and skills necessary for them to understand and analyze their own historically constructed voices and experiences as part of a project of self and social empowerment" (34).

Inquiry and Critique

We also need to know more about inquiry and critique in persuasive writing about public issues. I am referring here to inquiry as I have discussed elsewhere—the process of seeking new understanding, a process initiated by questions and resonant with exploratory discourse ("Writing as Inquiry"). Critique is discussed by James Berlin in his essays on cultural studies and social epistemic writing. Critique engages students in examining "the signifying practices in the formation of subjectivities within concrete material, social, and political conditions" ("Collapsing Boundaries" 6). They study the cultural codes or discursive formations that give directions about their "behavior, scripts that have to do with such categories as race, class, and gender" (10). Such writing, Berlin maintains, prepares students for citizenship in a democratic society ("Rhetoric").

Inquiry does not always entail cultural critique. A biologist may initiate inquiry by noticing a disparity between two theories. An engineer may seek a solution to a detected design weakness. A literary theorist may be motivated by two apparently contradictory interpretations. In persuasive inquiry about public issues, however, a writer begins with cultural critique, probing dissonances, gaps, problems, or anomalies in the political and social realm, uncovering dominant and often problematic practices and beliefs that marginalize groups and reproduce the ideological forces that perpetuate economic and social inequity. But inquiry does not end there; it goes beyond to create new social formations. Inquirers not only problematize their public experience but also seek to construct new codes, judgments, and courses of action to disrupt the processes of ideological reproduction. Such writing participates in what Giroux terms "an emancipatory form of citizenship [which] not only would aim at eliminating oppressive social practices, but would also constitute itself as a new movement for moral reawakening" (6).

In contrast to treating persuasive writing as inquiry and critique, textbook depictions of argumentation still commonly represent it as a task of "putting across" a thesis already in hand, a much debated characterization of classical rhetoric (Lauer, "Issues"). These books assume that students already possess judgments and need only deploy argumentative techniques to elaborate their positions. This view of argumentation is radically different from persuasive writing as inquiry and critique, which encourages students to avoid subjects about which they have entrenched judgments (often unexamined), and to tackle puzzling issues, raising questions (for example, see Lauer et al. *Four Worlds of Writing*). They are advised to withhold premature judgment, to symbolize alternatives, taking different perspectives, welcoming heteroglossia, entering the dialogue already under way.

In persuasion as inquiry and critique, students use ethical, affective, and logical strategies to interrogate and persuade themselves within the community. Ethos becomes an expression of their own imbrication in the cultural practices under scrutiny and their commitment to challenges required by new formations. Pathos engages communal values, attitudes, and feelings entwined in practices. Logos elaborates both the shared ideologies under critique as well as the changes being socially constructed.

Educational Attitudes

This conception of persuasive writing, as inquiry and critique guided by redirected rhetorical strategies, poses challenges for instructors and obstacles for students. One obstacle is an attitude that education has continually fostered: most students have been rewarded from the first grade on for being right, for accepting existing codes and norms. Teachers often have penalized as disruptive the questions students raise about cultural practices and values. As Lentricchia explains, education has been an effort to prepare the minds of the young to maintain the principles of the dominant group (1). These students have gradually learned the "appropriate" behavior—to squelch questions as signs of weakness. They have learned how to prepare for tests, which reward correct answers, not good questions. As writers they have learned to begin with a thesis, not discover one through inquiry and critique.

Another problem for harried students is that inquiry and critique demand time, mental energy, and change. Persuasive inquiry about social issues cannot be dashed off the night before a paper is due. For the student who expects a writing course to be a lightweight experience in a heavy schedule of math and physics, the intellectual, social, and affective demands will be not only unexpected but also unwelcome. Many students resist examining cultural codes; they shrink from noticing racial or gender inequities. Instead, they want to prepare for a job. They find themselves off-balance without their most reliable technique—finding out and doing what the teacher wants. They are inexperienced at meeting the expectations of broader and more diverse public communities.

Inquiry and critique are risky undertakings. Writers tackle problems over which they do not have control. They face the possibility of exposing contradictory cultural practices and beliefs that they daily enact without reaching new judgments, practices, or attitudes. They fear the changes in their lives that alternative understandings may require. The danger of this undertaking is heightened in the English class, which has been for many students an enterprise in correct grammar, five-paragraph form, and the creation of the well-crafted essay. Students wonder whether "it" (inquiry and critique) will be worth it after all, if the teacher ends up saying, "You had weak transitions, three missing commas, and awkward sentence constructions: C."

Both we and our students are torn between two conflicting views of education, the one authoritative, the other liberating. As Freire explains, "One of the radical differences between education as a dominating and dehumanizing task and education as a humanistic and liberating task is that the former is a pure act of transference of knowledge, whereas the latter is an act of knowledge and power" (114). The first view is known and safe; the second is ill-understood and dangerous. But if we exclude persuasive writing as inquiry and critique, where will students gain the power to question and transform their public worlds?

Works Cited

Applebee, Arthur, Judith Langer, Ina Mullis, and Lynn Jenkins. *The Writing Report Card 1984–88*. The National Assessment for Educational Progress. Princeton: Educational Testing Service, 1990.

Axelrod, Rise B., and Charles Cooper. *The St. Martin's Guide to Writing*. 2d ed. New York: St. Martin's, 1988.

Bazerman, Charles, and James Paradis, eds. *Textual Dynamics of the Professions*. Madison: U of Wisconsin P, 1991.

Berlin, James. "Composition Studies and Cultural Studies: Collapsing Boundaries." *Into the Field: Sites of Composition Studies*. Ed. Anne Gere. New York: MLA, 1993. 99–116.

———. "Rhetoric and Ideology in the Writing Class." *College English* 50 (1988): 477–94.

———. *Writing Instruction in Nineteenth-Century American Colleges*. Carbondale: Southern Illinois UP, 1984.

Britton, James, et al. *The Development of Writing Abilities (11–18)*. London: Macmillan, 1975.

Bullock, Richard, and John Trimbur, eds. *The Politics of Writing Instruction: Postsecondary*. Portsmouth, NH: Boynton/Cook, 1991.

Connor, Ulla, and Janice Lauer. "Cross-Cultural Variation in Persuasive Student Writing." *Writing Across Languages and Cultures*. Ed. Alan C. Purves. Written Communication Annual. Beverly Hills: Sage Publications, 1988. 2:139–59.

Connors, Robert. "The Rise and Fall of the Modes of Discourse." *CCC* 32(1981): 444–55.

Cooper, Marilyn. "The Ecology of Writing." *Writing as Social Action*. Marilyn Cooper and Michael Holtzman. Portsmouth, NH: Boynton/Cook, 1989. 1–13.

Cooper, Marilyn, and Michael Holtzman. *Writing as Social Action*. Portsmouth, NY: Boynton/Cook, 1989.

Crews, Frederick. *The Random House Handbook*. 3rd ed. New York : Random House, 1980.

———. *The Random House Handbook*. 6th ed. New York: Random House, 1992.

Crowley, Sharon. *The Methodical Memory*. Carbondale: Southern Illinois UP, 1990.

D'Angelo, Frank. "Nineteenth-Century Forms/Modes of Discourse: A Critical Inquiry." *CCC* 35 (1984): 31–42.

Eagleton, Terry. *Literary Theory: An Introduction*. Minneapolis: U of Minnesota P, 1983.

Elbow, Peter. *Writing Without Teachers*. New York: Oxford UP, 1975.

Faigley, Lester. "Competing Theories of Process." *College English* 48 (1986): 527–41.

———. *Fragments of Rationality: Postmodernity and the Subject of Composition*. Pittsburgh: U of Pittsburgh P, 1992.

Freire, Paulo. *The Politics of Education*. Trans. Donaldo Macedo. South Hadley, MA: Bergin & Garvey, 1985.

Gage, John. "An Adequate Epistemology for Composition: Classical and Modern Perspectives." *Essays on Classical Rhetoric and Modern Discourse*. Ed. Robert Connors, Lisa Ede, and Andrea Lunsford. Carbondale: Southern Illinois UP, 1984. 152–69, 281–84.

Giroux, Henry. *Schooling and the Struggle for Public Life: Critical Pedagogy in the Modern Age*. Minneapolis: U of Minnesota P, 1988.

Gorman, T. P., Alan Purves, and R. E. Degenhart, eds. *The IEA Study of Written Composition I: The International Writing Tasks and Scoring Scales*. Oxford: Pergamon, 1988.

Hairston, Maxine. "Diversity, Ideology, and Teaching Writing." *CCC* 43 (1992): 179–93.

Harkin, Patricia, and John Schilb, eds. *Contending with Words*. New York: MLA, 1991.

Jarratt, Susan. "The First Sophists and the Uses of History." *Rhetoric Review* 6 (1987): 67–78.

Kinneavy, James. "Kairos: A Neglected Concept in Classical Rhetoric." *Rhetoric and Praxis*. Ed. Jean Moss. Washington, DC: The Catholic University of America, 1986. 79–106.

———. *A Theory of Discourse*. New York: Norton, 1980.

Lauer, Janice. "Issues in Rhetorical Invention." *Essays on Classical Rhetoric and Modern Discourse*. Ed. Robert Connors, Lisa Ede, and Andrea Lunsford. Carbondale: Southern Illinois UP, 1984. 127–39; 227–80.

———. "Writing as Inquiry: Some Questions for Teachers." *CCC* 33 (1982): 89–93.

Lauer, Janice, Gene Montague, Andrea Lunsford, and Janet Emig. *Four Worlds of Writing*. 3rd ed. New York: HarperCollins, 1991.

Lentricchia, Frank. *Criticism and Social Change*. Chicago: U of Chicago P, 1983.

McCrimmon, James, Joseph Trimmer, and Nancy Sommers. *Writing with a Purpose*. 8th ed. Boston: Houghton, 1984.

Macrorie, Ken. *Telling Writing*. Rochelle Park, NJ: Hayden, 1970.

Maimon, Elaine, et al. *Writing in the Arts and Sciences*. Boston: Little Brown, 1982.

Neel, Jasper. *Plato, Derrida, and Writing*. Carbondale: Southern Illinois UP, 1988.

Odell, Lee, and Dixie Goswami, eds. *Writing in Nonacademic Settings*. New York: Guilford, 1985.

Ohmann, Richard. *English in America*. New York: Oxford UP, 1976.

———. *The Politics of Letters*. Middletown, CT: Wesleyan UP, 1987.

Porter, James. "Intertextuality and the Discourse Community." *Rhetoric Review* 5 (1986): 34–47.

Spilka, Rachel, ed. *Writing in the Workplace: New Research Perspectives*. Carbondale: Southern Illinois UP, 1993.

Trimmer, Joseph, and James McCrimmon. *Writing with a Purpose*. 9th ed. Boston: Houghton, 1988.

6 How Did Rhetoric Acquire the Reputation of Being the Art of Flimflam?

Edward P.J. Corbett

DESPITE ITS LONG AND ILLUSTRIOUS HISTORY AS A KEYSTONE DISCIPLINE in the curricula of the schools of the Western world, rhetoric conjures up unsavory images and connotations in the minds of many people. That unsavory reputation is reflected in such familiar expressions as "beware of his rhetoric" and "we can discount the mere rhetoric of that statement." If the practitioner of rhetoric is not actually ostracized from our society, he or she is certainly suspect and is often classified surreptitiously with such other esteemed citizens of the community as the quack, the swindler, the huckster, and the prestidigitator. Usually at the first meeting of my graduate seminar in rhetoric, I have my students spend fifteen or twenty minues writing out what they know about rhetoric. Invariably, no matter what else they say about the subject, they confess that they are aware of the bad press that rhetoric has had in our society and that they themselves are skittish about it. I once had a student who confessed in a spasm of candor, "I took this course because I wanted to find out whether rhetoric was really as bad as I had always heard it was." Nor have editors, reporters, broadcasters, and columnists, who in a very real sense are themselves practicing rhetoricians, done much to rehabilitate the reputation of rhetoric. In fact, most of them will use the word *rhetoric* in a distinctly derogatory sense.

How did rhetoric acquire its prevailing reputation as the art of flimflam? As a notorious United States senator used to say, "Where there's smoke, there's fire." Aristotle, who once talked about signs as being one of the bases of probable arguments, would have applauded the aptness of that bit of folk wisdom—although he probably would have deplored the senator's suggestion that when people act furtively, they must be Communists. But Aristotle would have conceded that if a particular activity is regarded suspiciously by a great many people, there must be a reason—there must be a cause, to use the more likely Aristotelian term—for that suspicion. One cause that Aristotle might have assigned for that effect was the bad-mouthing that rhetoric got from his own teacher, Socrates. (I should remark here that when I point out some view that Socrates or some other participant in the dialogues makes, I may really be pointing out the views of Plato, the author of the dialogues, rather than the views of some character in the dialogue.)

Anyone who has studied the history of rhetoric knows that it almost got sabotaged right at its inception in fifth-century Athens. Schools of rhetoric in that society became threatening rivals of the reigning schools of philosophies. Certainly the most influential opponent of the schools of rhetoric was Socrates, the guru of the academy in Athens. (Again, maybe I should be designating Plato, rather than Socrates, as the prime opponent of rhetoric.) We discover the grounds for the antipathy to rhetoric in the two Platonic dialogues bearing the titles of *Gorgias* and *Phaedrus*. It is instructive to examine the objections leveled against rhetoric, because although contemporary opponents of it do not voice their objections to the discipline in Socrates' terms, much of the modern suspicion of it is ultimately grounded on the Socratic strictures.

In the *Gorgias*, Socrates denies that rhetoric can be considered an art at all. It is rather a knack, a contrived skill acquired through experience or practice. Along with such other skills as cookery, cosmetics, and sophistic argument, rhetoric could be classified as a species of flattery. One translator of the Greek word *kolakeia*, which is often rendered as the English word *flattery*, probably gives a more accurate sense of Socrates' animus against rhetoric by translating the term as *pandering* (*Gorgias* 44). Just as cookery panders to one of the corporal human appetites, so rhetoric, with its tendency to gratify its listeners rather than to improve them intellectually or spiritually, panders to their lower appetites. This notion that rhetoric appeals to people's appetite for pleasure nourishes a good deal of the suspicion against rhetoric that persists today. It is part and parcel with all those puritanical objections down through the ages to people's indulgence in the concupiscent pleasures of the theater, the dance hall, and the music concert.

Maybe a more fundamental objection that Socrates had to rhetoric is the one expressed in the *Phaedrus*: that rhetoric was concerned not so much with what was true as with what was merely probable or believable. Indeed, rhetoricians based their arguments not on what was verifiably true or even factual but on what seemed to be probable or plausible. For Socrates, who believed that a true art should be based on solid knowledge, rhetoric, which was content with the merely probable, led people to make crucial decisions on the basis of opinion—and worst of all, on the opinion of the many rather than on the rational conclusions of the one. For Socrates, the lover of wisdom, it was not fitting for a rational animal to be guided by the opinions of fallible creatures.

At the end of the *Phaedrus*, Socrates presented his blueprint for a respectable art of rhetoric, but the conditions that he laid down for this ideal art were so unrealistic that no one could meet his standards. Just as Socrates never succeeded in banishing poetry from any society, let alone from his utopian republic, so he failed at banishing rhetoric from the Athenian society or from any other community in the classical world. Isocrates flourished as a teacher of rhetoric (he was the Dale Carnegie of his day), and Aristotle went on to write his *Rhetoric*, which became the fountainhead of all subsequent classical rhetorics. But Socrates' (or Plato's) legacy was to create a durable suspicion in people's minds about the legitimacy of rhetorical theory and practice. All subsequent objections to rhetoric are epitomized in the view that rhetoric is a shoddy art practiced by shoddy people for shoddy purposes.

Later developments in rhetoric tended to reinforce the impression that it was a shoddy art. The grandiloquent orations of the later sophists created the impression that the ideal to strive for was not substance of thought but precious verbosity—the "sound and fury signifying nothing" that Shakespeare was referring to in *Macbeth*. This admiration for the glitter of form rather than for the solidity of the matter led to the establishment of those schools of rhetoric that concentrated on the development of the students' stylistic virtuosity. The full-blown rhetoric that had come down from Aristotle dealt with the five canons of the art: invention, arrangement, style, memory, and delivery. But the word-mongering rhetors of the sophistic schools singled out style from the canon and concentrated the efforts of their pupils on the acquisition of verbal finesse. When the cultivation of style became not just the predominant but the exclusive concern of the schools of rhetoric, the way was opened to the development of empty bombast. And indeed one of the derogatory connotations that rhetoric has for many people today is the notion of discourse characterized by pretentious words and arty structures.

It is amazing how the stereotypes that exist in the public mind about such mountebanks as the con artist, the impostor, the double-dealer, and the seducer all imply the person who uses words facilely and deviously. An image is conjured up in the public mind of the word-magicians who spellbind their victims with their "abracadabra" and then joyously fleece their entranced dupes. I suppose there lurks in everyone's subconscious an almost archetypal apprehension of the mesmerizing power of scintillating words. After all, the first seducer with words was the serpent in the Garden of Eden. So those schools of rhetoric that trained their students in the manipulation of the enchanting powers of language unwittingly contributed to the suspicions that arose in people's minds about the glib rhetorician.

But it was not just that rhetoricians duped their victims by means of skill in handling the language. There was also the suspicion that they were somehow corrupted by the power that their verbal skill gave them. If one learns all the tricks to be used in persuading people, one ultimately cannot resist the temptation to use that power to subdue or agitate others. "Power corrupts," Lord Acton once said, "and absolute power corrupts absolutely." The hedge against the corruptive potential of word power is, of course, virtue, but even when they are virtuous, skilled orators have to struggle constantly against the contrary tensions between their moral disposition and their aggressive ambitions. The force that wins out in this struggle determines whether rhetorical skills are used for good or for evil purposes.

Because of the belief that virtue was the safeguard against the unscrupulous uses of the power that rhetoric gave the orator over audiences, some teachers of rhetoric assumed responsibility not only for the intellectual formation of their pupils but also for their ethical training. There is a hint of that double obligation in Plato's *Gorgias*. The major thesis of that Platonic dialogue is that "doing wrong is worse than suffering wrong" (59) and that, as a consequence, "the supreme object of a man's efforts in public and private life must be the reality, rather than the appearance, of goodness" (148).

Quintilian, however, was the chief advocate among the classical rhetoricians of the need for an orthodox moral disposition in the orator. He adopted Marcus Cato's definition of the ideal orator as being "a good man skilled in speaking" (*vir bonus dicendi peritus*, 12.1.1.355).[1] "If the powers of eloquence," Quintilian goes on to say, "serve only to lend arms to crime, there can be nothing more pernicious than eloquence to public and private welfare alike." Firmly believing that vice was antithetical to the formation of intellectual excellence, he preached not only "that the ideal orator should be a good man" but also "that no man can be an orator unless he is a good man" (*nisi virum bonum*, 12.1.3.357). Although virtue could be acquired partly by obeying the dictates of one's natural impulses, one still had to consciously pursue and cultivate habitual rectitude. The orator, Quintilian maintained, "must above all things devote his attention to the formation of moral character and must acquire a complete knowledge of all that is just and honorable. . . . For without this knowledge," he went on to say, "no one can be either a good man or skilled in speaking" (12.2.1.381, 383).

The notion that one cannot be a consummate artist unless one is a morally good person has been much debated down through the ages, but because Quintilian espoused that notion so unequivocally, his rhetoric text was enthusiastically adopted by the schoolmasters in English and American schools. Until well into the twentieth century, most English and American schools were church related, and the schoolmasters were, for the most part, ministers of Christian churches. It was reassuring to these schoolmasters to have such an esteemed rhetorician sanction the official school policy whereby their teachers were responsible for both the intellectual and the moral formation of their pupils.

Rather surprisingly, Saint Augustine did not feel that moral rectitude was

absolutely essential if the preacher was to be effective in influencing the attitudes and the actions of his congregation. In the fourth book of *De Doctrina
Christiana*, Augustine's contribution to rhetoric, he did acknowledge that "the
life of the speaker has greater weight in determining whether he is obediently
heard than any grandness of eloquence" (4.27.59.164). But he went on to say
that "he who speaks wisely and eloquently, but lives wickedly, may benefit
many students." In Augustine's view, the word of God was so potent that it
could exert its saving properties despite the flawed moral disposition of the
one who preached the word.

The fact that rhetoric, throughout most of its history, had the stamp of
approval of the established authorities in the schools, in the churches, and
even in the government assured its protected status in society and helped to
allay the suspicions of it that many people had. In societies where a policy of
separation of church and state is not decreed by constitutional law, the schools
can legally assume responsibility for cultivating the moral character of those
who will later exert their political leadership through oratory or published
writings. But in our society, where the moral formation of the children in
our state-supported schools is reserved by constitutional law for the church
and the family, how can we prevent the cultivation of budding demagogues?
Maybe we cannot really prevent that sprouting. Maybe we have to rely on
whatever natural inclination there is in people to ethical conduct. On the other
hand, maybe our safety lies in the providence of the democratic masses. Our
electoral system and our system of checks and balances allow us to throw the
rascals out. We are all aware that a surprising number of high government
officials went to jail over the Watergate affair.

But what about the rhetoricians themselves? Did they offer any defense
against the charges leveled against their craft or any safeguards against the
seductions of unscrupulous demagogues? Gorgias, a participant in the Platonic
dialogue of the same name, attempted to exculpate teachers whose pupils
abused the skills they had acquired through training in the schools. Resorting
to an analogy, Gorgias said that if a trained boxer or fencer struck his parents
or some other relation or friend, "it does not follow that the teachers are
criminal or the art which they teach culpable and wicked; the fault rests with
those who do not make proper use of it" (35). Likewise, if an orator abused
the power which the art of rhetoric conferred on him, we should not blame
the teacher. "His instruction," Gorgias said, "was given to be employed for
good ends, and if the pupil uses it for the opposite, it is he, not the man who
taught him, who deserves detestation and banishment and death" (35).

It is questionable whether the public would repeatedly excuse the teacher
whose pupils regularly abused their acquired skills. We would no more expect
that kind of tolerance of a mentor for the sins of his or her charges than alumni
would tolerate the coach whose teams keep coming up with losing seasons.
Normally, we expect the teacher to inculcate in the students a sense of responsibility along with the skill.

But did any of the rhetoricians preach that the art itself provided safeguards against the irresponsible uses of it? It is clear from the first three chapters of Book 1 of his *Rhetoric* that Aristotle is fully aware of the charges of shoddiness that his former mentor Plato brought against the art of rhetoric. Not only is Aristotle intent on showing that rhetoric is not just a knack that can be acquired through trial-and-error experience, but he is also intent on counteracting the charge made by Plato that rhetoric is basically training in the art of pandering. To clear teachers and rhetoric itself of blame for the misuse of oratorical skills inculcated into the students, Aristotle also resorts to an analogical argument, the one about the doctor who uses his medical knowledge for evil purposes. He makes much the same point with his analogy as Gorgias did: "that is a charge which may be made in common against all good things. . . . A man can confer the greatest of benefits by a right use of them," he said, "and inflict the greatest injuries by using them wrongly" (1.1.23).

Aristotle is not content, however, to rest his defense of rhetoric on such a flimsy argument. He wants a more solid grounding for his defense. He finds that, I think, in his doctrine of the ethical appeal.

It is well known to those who have studied the history of rhetoric that Aristotle originated the notion that in the persuasive process, the orator relies on three different classes of arguments or "proofs": the rational appeal (logos), the emotional appeal (pathos), and the ethical appeal (ethos). This is not the place for me to give even a brief summary of Aristotle's disquisition on all three of those appeals. What is pertinent here, however, is a short review of his highly original notions about the ethical appeal. Aristotle says in the second chapter of the *Rhetoric*: "Persuasion is achieved by the speaker's personal character when the speech is so spoken as to make us think him credible. We believe good men more fully and more readily than others; this is true generally, whatever the question is, and absolutely true where exact certainty is impossible and opinions are divided. This kind of persuasion, like the others, should be achieved by what the speaker says, not by what people think of his character before he begins to speak" (1.2.25).

There are two things to note about what Aristotle says in that quotation. First of all, Aristotle designated those occasions or circumstances where we are likely to rely on the ethos of the speaker or writer. Whereas in discussions of things in particular we tend to make our judgments on the basis of the facts that are presented, in discussions of things in general we tend to rely more on the ethos of the person making the pronouncements. And in cases where the exact truth cannot be ascertained, we rely exclusively on the ethos of the person making the pronouncements. The other thing to note about the quotation is that Aristotle insists that our trust in the character of the speaker should be elicited by what is said in the speech rather than by the antecedent reputation of the speaker. Aristotle certainly recognized that the speaker's reputation frequently disposes an audience to trust the speaker, but he emphasizes here that the speech itself is the ultimate determinant of the audience's trust because, realist as he is, he is aware that sometimes reputedly brilliant people say very foolish things.

In the same passage in which this quotation appeared, Aristotle went on to say that the ethos of the speaker is probably "the most effective means of persuasion he possesses." That judgment puts a very high premium indeed on the ethical appeal, but here again Aristotle shows himself to be the supreme realist. He recognizes that even the most skillfully managed appeals to reason and to emotion could fall on deaf ears if the audience mistrusted the speaker.

What must the speaker do in the speech to ensure that this most potent of the persuasive appeals will function at its highest level of effectiveness? Aristotle maintains that an audience's trust will be elicited if they perceive from what is said in the speech that the speaker is a person of "good sense, good moral character, and goodwill" (*Rhetoric* 2.1.91). "Good sense," "good moral character," and "goodwill" are the words that the translator W. Rhys Roberts uses to approximate what is comprehended in the relatively precise Greek words *phronēsis*, *aretē*, and *eunoia*. Since a good deal of the built-in safeguards that Aristotle proposes against the irresponsible uses of the power of rhetoric is implicit in these constituents of the ethical appeal, I will spend a moment explaining the meaning of these precise Greek words.

Eunoia could almost literally be translated as "good thoughts" but is more accurately translated by the basic meaning of our Latin-derived word *benevolence*—"wishing well to." A speaker or writer will convey an impression of *eunoia* if he or she projects the image of someone genuinely concerned about the welfare of others.

The word *aretē* is one of the words that the Athenian Greeks used in the sense of our word *virtue*, but its more general sense was "goodness or excellence" of any kind. This is the word embedded in our word *aristocracy*—literally, "rule by the best people." The speaker or writer creates an impression of being possessed of *aretē* if he or she comes across to the audience as a morally good person, especially as a person of honesty and integrity.

Phronēsis is the most pregnant word in the triad that constitutes the Aristotelian ethos. W. Rhys Roberts translates the word as "good sense," but the phrase "practical wisdom" or the word *prudence* comes closer to catching the Greek sense of the word. *Phronēsis* is the intellectual virtue that guides a person in making judicious decisions or choices in the practical affairs of everyday life. In common parlance, the phrase "a person of common sense" would connote what is implicit in the Greek word *phronimos*—"a man characteristically displaying *phronēsis*."

I have taken the trouble to elucidate the import of the three constituents of the ethical appeal because a clear understanding of the terms might help us to see that Aristotle is not totally indifferent, as he has sometimes been accused of being, to the moral dimensions of the rhetorical act. There is ample evidence in the *Rhetoric* itself that Aristotle regards rhetoric as being, at worst, an amoral art. But he is sensitive to the suspicions of his peers about the ostensible immorality of the rhetorical act. In the very first chapter of his book, he points out that rhetoric, like dialectic, can be used to argue on both sides of a question—"not," he hastens to add, "in order that we may in practice employ it in both ways (for we must not make people believe what is wrong), but in order that we may see clearly what the facts are, and that, if another man argues unfairly, we on our part may be able to confute him" (1.1.23). There is here a clear condemnation of the use of rhetoric for evil purposes, but many people find that in other parts of the *Rhetoric*, Aristotle seems to be ambivalent about the means that can be used to effect persuasion. But it seems to me that the safeguard built right into the art of rhetoric is Aristotle's insistence that the speaker must establish and maintain in every speech an ethical stance.

If speakers or writers manifest a deficiency in any one or all of the constituents of the Aristotelian ethos, they will diminish, if not entirely destroy, their credibility and consequently their effectiveness with the audience. The crucial condition, of course, is that they must manifest, or the audience must detect, the deficiency. Clever speakers and writers might be able to conceal their malevolence or their moral depravity or their stupidity for a considerable period of time—and historically, some of them have succeeded extravagantly. But maybe our ultimate protection against the duplicity of the clever rascal rests in that fact of life best expressed by Abraham Lincoln: "You may fool all of the people some of the time; you can even fool some of the people all the time; but you can't fool all of the people all the time." And once charlatans reveal who they really are and what their true intentions are, their ethos is destroyed, and their effectiveness as persuaders is forever nullified. We all could cite an example or two from life or from legend of one who was finally exposed and permanently silenced.

If, as I have been arguing, Aristotle fitted the legacy of his rhetorical formulations with its own set of built-in safeguards, how did rhetoric fare in successive ages and cultures? Did it continue to suffer the slings and arrows of outrageous aspersions? Or did the built-in safeguards rehabilitate its shaky fortunes and its shady reputation?

As that legacy was inherited and developed by the Roman rhetoricians, it seemed to be improved. Both Cicero and Quintilian made rhetoric the keystone discipline in a liberal arts curriculum, and that humane kind of education tended to produce more responsible, more altruistic, practitioners of the craft. And we have already seen that Quintilian further rectified rhetoric's course by insisting that the teacher of rhetoric be responsible for the moral formation of the pupils as well as for their intellectual cultivation. The Roman respect for law also tended to keep rhetoricians on the straight and narrow path and made the penalties of malfeasance much more certain and severe than they had been. Still, as we learn from Cicero's rhetoric texts and from his real-life orations, the senate chambers and the courtrooms of ancient Rome were perilous places indeed, and autocratic emperors, who could order a summary decapitation with the flick of an eyebrow, often inhibited crusading orators from speaking the truth or the whole truth.

The practice of declamation, however, which the Romans had inherited from the rhetors of the Second Sophistic period, set rhetoric off in a direction that did not enhance its reputation. Requiring students to compose pro and con speeches for mock court trials, called *controversiae*, or mock political situations, *suasoriae*, established the tradition of the debate, which has persisted in the educational system of the Western world right down to the present day. But these practices also aroused suspicions about rhetorical training in the schools. The demand that students work up a case for the two sides of an issue elicited the same kind of objections about indifference to the truth that Socrates had once leveled against rhetoricians in his *Gorgias* and *Phaedrus*.

Does the reputation of rhetoric improve when it moves into the medieval period? From one point of view, it does, for rhetoric became a part of the trivium in the undergraduate curriculum of the medieval universities. It is well known, however, that although rhetoric occupied a privileged position in the curriculum, along with grammar and logic, it was overshadowed by logic. The main contributions that rhetoric made to university education in the Middle Ages were two new forms of persuasive discourse: the art of preaching (*ars praedicandi*) and the art of letter writing (*ars dictaminis*). Both of these arts were of special value to clerics, who constituted the largest segment of the student population of the universities at the time. Because rhetorical skills were largely used to conduct ecclesiastical affairs, a good deal of the stigma that had existed in the public's mind about rhetoric disappeared. After all, if the preacher was dispensing instruction or guidance based on the word of God as that was revealed in the Scriptures, the congregation was not likely to regard the preacher as a flimflam artist. The ethos of the speaker was established almost as an automatic concomitant of ordination to the priestly ranks, and the message he transmitted to his listeners was certified by the authority of the church that dispensed the canonical interpretations of the Holy Scriptures. Undoubtedly, there were rascally abbots and monks and friars in those days, but Christ's promise to his disciples, in the very last words of Matthew's gospel, "I am with you always, to the end of time" (Matt. 28:20), seemed to assure the laity that even fraudulent clerics could not seriously jeopardize the mission that Christ had delegated to his followers: "Go forth therefore and make all nations my disciples" (Matt. 28:19).

Two of the interests that the medieval church of the Western world appropriated from the Roman Empire were the interest in law and the interest in civil administration. The clerical interest in law manifested itself in the formulation of the church's canon law, and the clerical interest in civil administration manifested itself in the episcopal supervision of the widely scattered branches of the universal or "catholic" church, with its center in Rome. The dispensation of the rulings of canon law and the execution of the managerial aspects of the church's affairs were exercised, to a great extent, through the medium of the written letter. Even in Aristotle's time, persuasive discourse appeared in both spoken and written forms, but in the Middle Ages, when the province of Holy Mother the Church extended beyond the boundaries of a single state or country, much of its business had to be conducted through the formal letter. So there was a great demand for secretaries who could compose those letters, and the medieval schools responded to that demand by setting up courses in which the strategies of classical rhetoric were applied to letter writing. Even though most of those letters were written by clerics, we are not to suppose that none of those letter writers were flimflam artists. But these clerical sharpies seem not to have been prominent enough or prevalent enough to have given the rhetoric of letter writing a bad name in the Middle Ages. Moreover, since these business letters were usually read in the quiet of one's study and were detached, sometimes by thousands of miles, from the person who wrote them, readers were less susceptible to being bamboozled by the artifices of the letter writer.

The art of preaching and the art of letter writing continued to be a prominent part of rhetorical training in the Renaissance schools. Preaching, of course, was confined to the province of the clergy, but letter writing extended its purview to include the diplomatic affairs of state and the monetary transactions of merchants and bankers. Since the writers of the epistles that dealt with secular matters lacked the authoritative aura that usually attended ecclesiastical letters, those writers had to be more skilled at effecting persuasion. At the same time, they were likely to be less scrupulous than the clerical scribes in the means they used to effect persuasion. Professional letter writers set up shop to serve those who could not write at all or who could not write well enough to succeed at what they were after. And those who could not afford to hire a professional letter writer bought one of the formulary handbooks of letter writing and wrote their letters, as it were, by the numbers. These and other circumstances of the time opened the gates to abuses of the epistolary art, with the result that the reputation of rhetoric was once again tarnished.

The invention of printing, of course, considerably extended the range and even the effectiveness of the rhetorician's communications. Father Walter Ong and Marshall McLuhan have told us, in a number of books and articles, about the consequences of Gutenberg's technology. One of the consequences was that the printed book made possible the transmission of an author's message to a much larger and more dispersed audience. An orator could deliver a common message to a large number of listeners, but those listeners had to be physically present within ear-range when the speech was orally enunciated; the printed book, however, could deliver a uniform text to readers thousands of miles beyond the range of the author's voice and ultimately to readers who lived hundreds of years after the author died. In a manuscript culture, a handwritten letter could deliver the author's message to readers who existed outside the space and time dimension of the author, but if more than one copy of that message was produced, the likelihood was that the text, in its various copies, would no longer be uniform. In our time, of course, carbon paper and the xerox machine have made it possible for several uniform copies of a typed or handwritten text to be produced, but as early as the last quarter of the fifteenth century, the invention of movable type provided the technology by which multiple copies of a uniform text could be produced, and once the technology for producing paper cheaply was invented, hundreds of people could afford to buy a handy, durable copy of the uniform text.

The electronic revolution of our age has immeasurably extended the range and effectiveness of the rhetorician's efforts at communication. In the first stage of the electronic revolution, new technologies for delivering a message to distant places made use of the medium of sound—the telegraph, the telephone, and the radio. Then we got the wonderful inventions that for the first time in the history of the world made possible the preservation of the sounds of the actual words uttered by a speaker—the vinyl record and later the tape recorder. Since the end of World War II, there has been a veritable explosion of new electronic devices for transmitting messages—the teletype machine, the television set, the videotape recorder, the fax machine, and finally the computer, which has in turn spawned maybe the most marvelous of all the verbal machines, the word processor. It is too early now to tell just how extensively the word processor will revolutionize the writing process and product, but the door is wide open now for some Quintilian to come along and compose the definitive rhetoric for this wondrous facilitator.

The exercise of rhetoric is now more pervasive and dominant in our society than it has ever been, and now the rhetorician's message can reach every nook and corner of the global village. The potential of the rhetorician's craft for good or for evil is awesome. The effectiveness of the dominant rhetoricians in our society, the Madison Avenue designers of ad copy, is a pertinent example of the persuasive potential of the spoken and the written words. I do not perceive that the reputation of rhetoric as the art of flimflam has faded in our time. There are lots of people who are not aware that rhetoric is the craft behind all those ubiquitous advertising messages that constantly bombard their consciousness, but for many of those who are aware of rhetoric, even vaguely, rhetoric is a dirty word.

Rhetoric got off to a bad start. Socrates (or Plato), one of the most prestigious and influential teachers of fifth-century Athens, bad-mouthed rhetoric while it was a flourishing enterprise in his society, and Aristotle, who tried to rescue rhetoric's reputation, increased rather than diminished people's suspicions of it because of his ambivalent pronouncements. Aristotle's defense of rhetoric on the score of its ethical posture was based primarily on the proposition that rhetoric, like any other art, was an amoral pursuit, but throughout his *Rhetoric*, he tended to undermine that premise by suggesting that certain strategies or arguments used to defend a certain position could be flip-flopped to attack the same position. Even modern students of the *Rhetoric* sometimes find it hard to defend Aristotle against the charge of double-speaking.

The sophistic emphasis on the stylistic elegance of a discourse did not serve rhetoric's reputation well, either. The common epithet "mere rhetoric" stems primarily, I think, from this emphasis on style rather than on substance. And of course down through the ages, rhetoric's name has been badly tarnished by demagogues who used their eloquence to deceive people or lead them astray. Gorgias's argument that teachers cannot be blamed for what their pupils do with the skills acquired through instruction has never been very convincing for many people. They hold more to the old adage that something is to be judged by the company it keeps.

Why rhetoric has always been judged in relation to its evil practitioners rather than its noble practitioners has always puzzled me. I am aware, of course, that scoundrels usually get more coverage from the media than saints do, but I am still puzzled that rhetoric rarely gets judged on the records of those practitioners who used their verbal skills to benefit society. It is safe to assert that there have been more beneficial writers and speakers than there have been destructive writers and speakers. Some of the most glorious literature of a nation is recorded in the discourses of its citizens who used words to change the attitudes or affect the actions of their fellow citizens. Each of us could nominate our own favorite utterances if we were asked to do so. Two examples that come readily to my own mind are a written piece and a spoken piece composed by the same man in our own time: Martin Luther King's "Letter from Birmingham Jail" and "I Have a Dream." Why do we not associate rhetoric with noble utterances like those rather than with *Mein Kampf?* Noble utterances make us proud to be a part of the human race. They send tingles racing up and down our spines, and they often put lumps in our throats. They certainly make us stand up straighter and dauntlessly face what we have to face.

Still, you should not forget that this defense of rhetoric is being dispensed by a rhetorician. What assurance have you that this rhetorician is any more trustworthy than the flimflam artists you have known? What I will say finally on this score is that if you had learned well the lessons that rhetoric has to teach, you would be able to discriminate the deceiver from the truth-sayer. You would be able to make a reliable judgment about whether I am, in the medieval sense, a charlatan or a soothsayer.

Note

1. Quotations from Quintilian and Saint Augustine are documented by book, chapter, section, and page number. Quotations from Aristotle are documented by book, chapter, and page number.

Works Cited

Aristotle. *The Rhetoric and Poetics of Aristotle. Rhetoric.* Trans. W. Rhys Roberts. *Poetics.* Trans. Ingram Bywater. New York: Random House, 1984.

Augustine. *De Doctrina Christiana (On Christian Doctrine).* Trans. D. W. Robertson, Jr. Indianapolis, IN: Bobbs-Merrill, 1958.

Kennedy, George. *Classical Rhetoric and Its Christian and Secular Tradition from Ancient to Modern Times.* Chapel Hill: U of North Carolina P, 1980.

McLuhan, Marshall. *Understanding Media: The Extensions of Man.* New York: McGraw-Hill, 1964.

Murphy, James J. *Rhetoric in the Middle Ages: A History of Rhetorical Theory from St. Augustine to the Renaissance.* Berkeley: U of California P, 1974.

Ong, Walter J., S.J. *Rhetoric, Romance, and Technology: Studies in the Interaction of Expression and Culture.* Ithaca, NY: Cornell UP, 1971.

Plato. *Gorgias.* Trans. W. Hamilton. Baltimore, MD: Penguin, 1960.

———. *Phaedrus.* Trans. W. C. Helmbold and W. G. Rabinowitz. Indianapolis, IN: Bobbs-Merrill, 1956.

Quintilian. *Institutio Oratoria.* Trans. H. E. Butler. 4 vols. Cambridge, MA: Harvard UP, 1920–1922.

7   **Crisis and Panacea in
     Composition Studies**
     A History

Robert J. Connors

The professional literature of the field of composition studies
is in many ways a rich lode for the historian. It begins long before the actual
establishment of the discipline, in the earlier field of oral rhetoric, and allows
us to examine closely the forces that go into the creation and development of
an academic field. In the 1850s, with the beginnings of an American educational
establishment and the attendant growth of its literature, we can see concern
for written as well as oral English growing in the culture. Then, as "education"
became its own field in the 1880s and 1890s, there was an explosion of interest;
educational journals proliferated, then English journals were founded, and by
1911 there were numerous specialized sources that could provide the historian
with more material than she could easily assimilate.

Much of this historical material is, however, very different from contem-
poraneous scholarly materials in other nineteenth-century academic disciplines. There is a real qualitative difference between rhetorical and composition
materials and those in the sciences, the social sciences, and even those in
philology, history, and the other humanities. Examining them, we become
aware that composition scholarship throughout most of its history has been
concerned not with proposing, testing, or extending new theories, or with
arguing for new research, as most other professional literature does. Instead,
the historian finds a tremendous amount of the literature devoted to the cultural
and professional conditions within the field: forensic bows to what has come

before, deliberative discourses on what must or should be done, and especially epideictic praise or blame of the conditions described. This praise or blame all proceeds from a profoundly melioristic attitude in the field that dates back to its beginnings. In this era of dialogics and social construction, examination of this issue of meliorism in our professional literature may be useful and may help to situate us in the present.

Let me suggest that the history of the field of composition may be seen as having two central vectors. First, it is the story of a series of crises, cultural and professional, and attempts to resolve them. Second, it is the story of a series of enthusiasms and of attempts to diffuse and popularize the pedagogies that grew out of them. Crisis and panacea have been the two great gestures of the discipline, and it is to these recurring phenomena that the historian finds herself applying again and again when researching the history of both theory and techniques. They are the systole and diastole of our profession, and almost anything that has ever happened in the field can be related to a continuing backdrop of either crisis or panacea.

How have these attitudes shaped themselves? Almost as far back as we can document, there seems to have been a cultural crisis involving language learning. Through the 1840s, 1850s, and 1860s there is evidence that the developing class system in America was based on linguistic as well as economic criteria. America was developing a native gentry, and gentry were increasingly expected to speak and write with propriety as well as dress with elegance and shoot with skill.[1] The burden of this socialization was taken up by a number of novel and specialized agencies: the preparatory schools for boys, the finishing schools for girls, and, finally, the colleges. In addition to their traditional roles of preparing men for pulpit and bar, colleges after 1850 began taking on the burden of creating gentlemen and scholars—in that order.

The linguistic crisis of that early day was most clearly expressed in the great usage war of the 1860s and 1870s. American linguistic insecurity had been created by the suspicion-fostering "false syntax" exercises of post-Revolutionary grammar schools that asked students to find and correct ungrammaticality in example sentences. It was underwritten by the rise of a new intellectual culture in Eastern cities, which made propriety in language socially desirable. In 1864 this growing paranoia about usage was heightened by a book written by a supercilious Englishman, Henry Alford. Alford was dean of Westminster Cathedral, and his work, *The Queen's English*, attacked bad usage generally but singled out American usage for particular opprobrium: "The national mind is reflected in the national speech. If the way in which men express their thoughts is slipshod and mean, it will be very difficult for their thoughts themselves to escape being the same. . . . Every important feature in a people's language is reflected in its character and history. Look, to take one familiar example, at the process of deterioration which our Queen's English has undergone at the hands of the Americans" (5). Alford then went on to savage American speech and writing habits.

Defenders of America answered the dean—now-forgotten champions such as George Washington Moon and Richard S. Gould—and for two decades book after article after rejoinder appeared attacking or defending minor points of English usage and writing propriety. These salvos had only one thing in common: they assumed that correctness in writing and speaking were of the highest priority for true gentry. As Richard Meade Bache put it in 1869,

> Many persons, though they have not enjoyed advantages early in life, have, through merit combined with the unrivalled opportunities which this country presents, risen to station in society. Few of them, it must be thought, even if unaware of the extent of their deficiency in knowledge of their language, are so obtuse as not to perceive their deficiency at all, and not to know that it often presents them in an unfavorable light in their association with the more favored children of fortune. Few, it must be believed, would not from one motive or the other, from desire of knowledge, or from dread of ridicule, not gladly avail themselves of opportunities for instruction. (i)

Gradually this position spread from the popular magazines where it was argued out to the entire burgeoning intellectual culture, and it became accepted wisdom; one either spoke and wrote correctly, or one was judged a bumpkin.

Colleges, meanwhile, had been attempting to meet the challenge of this cultural demand for correctness with various adaptations of rhetorical theory, both ancient and modern. College courses had included some writing since the 1820s, but after the Civil War the written component of rhetoric separated from the oral component almost completely; oratory and "eloquence" went one way (a way of increasing technical sterility and even empty hucksterism), while rhetoric and "composition" went another. Rhetorical study up to that point had presupposed a knowledge of correctness of expression—this was, after all, the responsibility of the grammar schools—but now American college professors began to notice a change. With the hubbub of the usage debate in full cry, they were beginning to pay more attention to correctness than they had been, and students began to seem less capable than they should have been. Many, in fact, seemed unable to write with any facility at all. As Adams S. Hill complained in 1879, after having been in charge of the Harvard entrance examination for several years,

> Those of us who have been doomed to read manuscript written in an examination room—whether at a grammar school, a high school, or a college—have found the work of even good scholars disfigured by bad spelling, confusing punctuation, ungrammatical, obscure, ambiguous, or inelegant expressions. Every one who has had much to do with the graduating classes of our best colleges, has known men who could not write a letter describing their own

Commencement without making blunders which would disgrace a boy twelve years old. ("An Answer" 6)

All over the country, Hill's and Harvard's anguished cry fell on sympathetic professorial ears. Articles decrying the "illiteracy of American boys" (American girls and their literacy were not considered a serious issue) began to appear in many of the popular magazines.

Thus began the first great media-driven crisis in American college composition—indeed, the crisis that can be said to have begun college composition as we know it today. Make no mistake: this was a genuine disaster in the minds of Americans, especially educated Americans. The idea that the best American prep schools, and even the best American colleges, were turning out "illiterates" deeply shocked our increasingly nationalistic sensibilities.

The response to the crisis that followed was characteristically American: it was strident, melioristic, immediate, action-oriented, blame-bestowing. There was a crisis; "American boys" were "illiterate." This could not be borne. It was the fault of the schools. The schools must do something. Secondary education must be renovated. Meanwhile, the colleges must create a stopgap solution to the problem, enforce standards, create courses, study the problem, harass the secondary schools, pressure their teachers, establish curricula, promulgate teachable theory.

Between 1870 and 1895 this is exactly what happened. In 1874 Harvard introduced an entrance examination in writing; more than half of the students taking it did not pass. Hill, the Boylston Professor of Rhetoric, had argued for years that a required freshman course in composition be instituted, and he won his point in 1884, when Harvard put a course called English A on its books.[2] This "remedial" course, designed to cure the ills left by inadequate secondary instruction, was seen as a temporary measure, necessary until the high schools could pull their standards up. Once established, however, it took on a life of its own and became the prototypical freshman composition course.

Here, then, is our first panacea: freshman English itself. From the beginning it was generally assumed that English A, though detested, would "solve the problem" of "illiteracy." Certainly any attack on student deficiencies by trained college teachers would put things right quickly and prepare the young man for the remainder of his education. Now that Harvard was on the scene, could illiteracy persist? The Harvard Report of 1892 was the best-known klaxon of crisis, but it was also among the last of the great cries for reform of the secondary curriculum. Following in Harvard's footsteps, most colleges and universities instituted a freshman English course, staffing it with the youngest and least influential members of the English department.

Did the panacea work? According to the articles published, it seemed to. By the 1890s the note of crisis in the media reports of literacy issues began to be supplemented, and then replaced, by one of self-congratulation. Pedagogical essays began to demand that the freshman course be more oriented toward culture, toward literature, away from the brute facts of grammar and composition. The to-do over youthful illiteracy persisted in muted tones until the late 1890s, but as more and more schools adopted Harvard's entrance requirements, the hard crisis was damped down. With the private publication in 1896 of *Twenty Years of School and College English*, Harvard reviewed its positions throughout the debate and tacitly patted itself on the back for having solved the problem.[3] By 1900 the first "literacy crisis" had run its course.

I need to make clear here that although this first literacy crisis provoked the panacea of freshman English, this neat problem/solution model is by no means paradigmatic—or clear. Most crises and panaceas in composition have no direct relationships, and the relationship between the advent of freshman composition and the passing of the literacy crisis may be much more apparent than real. Certainly there were no direct claims from Harvard or anywhere else that English A and its imitators had "solved" the literacy crisis. The clamor over it went away largely because secondary schools had, indeed, slowly changed their curricula to include writing—and because educational writers discovered other and more intriguing fish to fry. The media-driven crisis, as they are wont to do, ran its course and became tiresome. The panacea attracted some interest, was widely written about, became institutionalized, and, its original "temporary and remedial" nature forgotten, was soon an accepted part of college life, a given of the freshman year. As we shall see, some panaceas, like freshman English, survive, while others have their day in the sun and perish like mayflies.

Between 1890 and 1900, English in American universities was defining itself; it was a period of extraordinary change and innovation in which self-congratulation about the end of the "literacy crisis" and "viewing with alarm" the problems inherent in teaching the vernacular course coexisted uneasily. No one was completely sure what college English courses should look like or do, and there were as many opinions as there were definitions of "English." Some were quite sanguine; in 1896, for instance, T. W. Hunt vigorously trumpeted the good work done in English, the present status of which was, he said, "justly praiseworthy and full of educational promise. The courses in English . . . will justify, I am sure, a close and critical examination, both as to their variety and educational quality" (142). But Fred Newton Scott, the most perspicacious theorist of his time, disagreed powerfully with Hunt's sunny view of the profession: "I think I speak for the majority of such investigators [of the field of English] when I say that the most characteristic thing about English teaching at the present time is its unsettledness. It is fuller of unsolved problems than any other subject that can be mentioned. It is a kind of pedagogical porcupine" (292).

Whence came these differing positions? Hunt's view was largely based on his interests in literary study, which was burgeoning, and reflects the optimism of a member of the rising classes. Scott, on the other hand, was an old composition man who saw clearly how many problems remained unsolved—and indeed, increasingly ignored and swept under the rug by many of the more literary-minded departments. Hunt's and Scott's views were united, however, in being essentially melioristic; both felt that the discipline should be the agent of cultural good, and their main disagreement concerned the length of the road left to travel and directions for getting to the Great Good Place. Hunt's view became the "official" view of the English literary establishment after 1900, not because the questions Scott brought up were answered but because literature courses blossomed, because new literary specialists were trained and hired, and because nonliterary "service" teaching and its problems stopped being considered worth serious discussion in most general English publications.

The period 1900 to 1910 was quiet in the field of composition. There was a sense in some quarters that the important problems confronting the teaching of writing had been solved,[4] but we cannot ignore the fact that with the literacy crisis put to sleep, there seemed to be little to write about for composition teachers. The primary journals in the field of English—*PMLA*, *The Journal of English and Germanic Philology*—stopped covering pedagogical issues as they moved toward an essentially literary definition of the field. More and more, the Ph.D. was a necessary prerequisite for being hired by an English department, and no Ph.D. specialties in composition issues existed in America except for Fred Scott's Michigan department. Without the sense of overwhelming problems or the impetus of novel techniques, the subject was simply not the hot item it had been in the 1880s and 1890s, and college writing disappeared from the pages of the popular magazines and even most educational journals. Composition teachers debated minor issues such as literature versus expository writing and continued to beat old horses like the college entrance exams, but the fever of interest was gone, and the literature languished. At least to many administrators, the panacea of freshman composition seemed to be working, and their primary interest was in how to keep it working most cheaply.

To teach the required composition course with the least expense, untrained beginners had to be used—graduate students, new instructors. But they could not simply be shoved into the classroom with no assistance. Educational technology was needed, and in the first decade of this century a search was on for the "teacher-proof textbook"—the composition text that any idiot could teach, whatever level of knowledge or writing skill he or she had. During the early nineteenth century there had been textbooks, of course, but they had been imperfect; they had needed to be taught and applied by a teacher. Books like Samuel Newman's *Practical System of Rhetoric* of 1827 or Richard Whately's *Elements of Rhetoric* of 1828 had been tools, adjuncts—not entire writing courses in miniature. The composition textbook genre did not really hit its stride until after 1890, producing books so simple and complete that a teacher only needed to act as a grading assistant to the all-controlling textbook curriculum.

Although the movement toward simpler exercise-based texts was not smooth or uniform, it did proceed. Each new textbook was cried up as the solution to all a teacher's problems; in fact, the publishing houses' most essential job was to produce panaceas to order. I have examined this phenomenon in some detail elsewhere,[5] and for now a short sketch of publishers' solutions to the problem will suffice. English textbooks themselves had been invented during the nineteenth century to aid in the teaching of a subject that was, as a college subject, absolutely novel. Beginning with elementary grammar texts that included composition and writing as elements, textbook publishers had expanded by 1850 to secondary and college texts concerned only with structuring classroom time spent on rhetoric and composition.

The primary textbook panacea was the "rhetoric text" itself, which solved for teachers the problem of how to spend the classroom time of a nonlecture writing course. Richard Green Parker's *Aids to English Composition* of 1844 was the first college text proceeding inductively and atomistically through series of short lessons based on the lessons in elementary texts. Each short chapter includes a "lesson" that is explained in abstract terms, an example of the lesson as illustration, and exercises that ask the student to practice the lesson using given materials. *Aids* was very popular, remaining in print for more than thirty years and seeing at least twenty-one printings. Other similar books appeared, such as James R. Boyd's *Elements of Rhetoric and Literary Criticism* (1844) and George Quackenbos's *Advanced Course of Rhetoric and English Composition* (1855), which also used a lesson-illustration-exercises approach.

Teachers who had had little rhetorical training could merely assign such textbooks and follow along themselves; by 1895, even the task of creating the order and structure of practice exercises had been taken from the teacher and assumed by the text author. Radically simplified textbooks in composition like William Williams's *Composition and Rhetoric by Practice* were the legacy of the literacy crisis of the 1880s. In addition, many publishers offered simpler books often written by the same stable of authors whose more "advanced" rhetoric texts were used in upper-division classes. These books, like Adams S. Hill's *Beginnings of Rhetoric and Composition* and John Genung's *Outlines of Composition*, contained grammar drills, capitalization and punctuation exercises, syntax practice, and the like. They were supposed to "remedy" the "deficiencies" of the "illiterate," and their authors were not shy in prefaces about proclaiming their works the answer to the problem. Rhetoric texts proliferated and soon mutated from a panacea to a tradition—largely a tradition of continual advertisement and proclamation of panacea.

By the turn of the century, an outcry about overwork and "conditions" that would eventuate in the Hopkins Report of 1912 had begun; teachers simply had too many papers to grade. This problem was so onerous that it called forth a new sort of text: the handbook, which boiled down all of the conventions of written discourse into a simple set of finite rules. This was a brilliant stroke, and the publication of Edwin Woolley's *Handbook of Composition* in 1907 ushered in a whole new era of theme correction. No longer did teachers have painstakingly to read and respond to student writing; instead they could skim it for error, sprinkle it with red rule numbers, and consider their work done. This was a panacea indeed, and soon all publishers had a handbook. The next logical step in this direction was a book that would remove all but the most mechanical responsibilities from the teacher: the workbook or drillbook of composition. The first college workbook was Charles H. Ward's *M. O. S. (Maintenance of Skills) Book* of 1926, and it was so popular that by 1935 every other textbook publisher had a workbook as well.

These three genres of composition text—rhetorics, handbooks, and workbooks—grew up and flourished because publishers saw a pedagogical need and rushed to fill it. Here once again we see the meliorism of the field—a commercially-based meliorism, of course, but no less real for that. With each new textbook type the author was staking a claim that *this* book could solve the discipline's problems more effectively than before, could create a new learning climate, could add to the advancement of the field. The textbook market is always profoundly optimistic about each new product, and by 1926 they had introduced the genres that would, they claimed, make all composition teaching successful.

After 1910, the institutional realities of the emerging English departments in the United States became clearer, particularly the reality of the two-tier hierarchy, with literature on top and composition on the bottom. A small group of dissatisfied teachers emerged, determined to show that the freshman composition system was not working—or that if it was, it was upon the broken and bleeding bodies of overworked instructors. This new crisis was precipitated by a committee organized by the English Round Table of the National Education Association in 1910. This committee, originally founded to look into the familiar problem of entrance exams, found multiple problems in teaching writing so severe that it recommended the formation of a national association of English teachers that would, as James T. Hosic said, "reflect and render effective the will of the various local associations and of individual teachers, and, by securing concert of action, greatly improve the conditions surrounding English work" (Letter 31). This term, *conditions*, was to become a watchword in the years to come, and the organization that Hosic and others formed in 1911 to deal with these conditions became the National Council of Teachers of English.

The NCTE was at first quite a radical group, simply because its leaders formed it out of dissatisfaction with existing conditions. Hosic and his colleagues were certain that the discipline was in the grip of crises, and although the members differed on what these crises were, all agreed they were serious. Eastern high school teachers desperately wanted relief from the uniform college entrance requirements that were the atrophied and sterile legacy of the Harvard exams that had started thirty-five years earlier. Midwestern college teachers were claiming that the entire organization of the discipline was hopeless since it led to grotesque overwork. Edwin M. Hopkins wrote that "under present conditions, composition teachers have from two and a half to three times as many pupils as they should . . . the average of the total labor devolving upon English composition teachers is apparently between 50 and 100 percent more than the average total of that of any other class of teachers whatever" ("Can Good Composition Teaching" 4).[6] Two other serious problems to be addressed by the council were the arguments between the advocates of composition as culture training and those who advocated vocational training and the continuing question of what place (if any) grammar study had in composition (Hopkins, "Four Problems" 49). Viewed together, claimed the founders of the NCTE, these problems created a serious crisis in English teaching, one that could be addressed only by a national council.

What I'd like to note here is the relative lack of concentration by the founders of the NCTE on the development of a body of knowledge. Because of the preoccupation with professional problems that motivated its founding, the NCTE was not much concerned with developing knowledge, with "research" per se. Instead, the organization was from its earliest point socially and professionally melioristic, devoted to addressing its crises and winning through to a better day. Hosic noted that "the movement is distinctly spirited, optimistic, and progressive. In the addresses and resolutions of the initial meeting, the feeling of desire and determination to secure greater effectiveness and better conditions in which to work is unmistakable" ("Significance" 47). This was typical of the tone of the early *English Journal*, which as the first genuine composition periodical set the tone for all subsequent publications.

That tone was melioristic, concerned with crises in the profession and with potential solutions for them. By far the most common sorts of articles in the early *EJ* were those that viewed the English situation with alarm ("Wanted—A Higher Standard of Speech" [1912], "Can Good Composition Teaching Be Done Under Present Conditions?" [1912], "Need of Improvement in Conditions Surrounding Composition Teaching" [1912], "Why College English Fails" [1914], "Some Ways in Which Our Teaching of College Composition Is Ineffective" [1914], "Lost Motion in the Teaching of English" [1915]) and those that proposed various solutions to the problems ("Vocational and Moral Guidance Through English Composition" [1912], "Culture and Efficiency Through Composition" [1912], "An Attempt to Make Oral Composition Effective" [1912], "The Study of English Composition as a Means to Fuller Living" [1915], "The Use of the Magazine in English" [1916], "The Notebook System of Theme Correcting" [1917], "The Ideal Course in English for Vocational Students" [1918]).

As the professional literature developed, it became apparent that the tendency was for authors to choose a problem or a solution and group around it in alarm or support. Thus problems and solutions tended to turn into crises and panaceas as a result of the bandwagon effect. Unlike the professional journals of other fields, which were filled with theoretical extensions and reports of content investigations, the *English Journal* from the beginning devoted the majority of its pages to reports on the field itself and its conditions and needs and to essays touting this or that pedagogical technique. Different contributors had different ideas about what was wrong, of course, but whatever the problem, complaint, or suggestion, a constant analysis of "the state of English" filled the *EJ*. Over 45 percent of all the articles in the first three volumes of the journal were field-concerned rather than theoretical or pedagogical. Since the beginning we have liked to look at ourselves just as much as at a body of knowledge.[7]

While the *EJ* was often preoccupied by the crises of English, a variety of panaceas kept coming as well. A key genre in the journal was pedagogical reports, often fairly shameless promotions for this or that teaching technique, untested except intuitively, which, the authors claimed, would solve many of the continuing problems. "The Round Table" section of the *EJ* was filled with short essays like "An Unorthodox Experiment" (using only Woolley's *Handbook* and Huxley's *Essays* in a freshman class) or "An Experiment in Oral English" or "A New Way of Approaching Grammar." Several authors in any given issue would be certain to offer solutions to the profession's crises—sometimes even the same crises being decried by other authors. There were certain recurring themes in these solutions and suggestions: better writing through "oral English," use of techniques of "laboratory work," new systems of paper correction, use of the novel Hillegas rating system for compositions. These small-scale panaceas had their adherents and detractors and came and went in what can only be called a series of fads.

It was not until the mid-1910s that the great panacea of the era appeared in the field: the concept of teaching English as a part of a student's social aims and duties. The idea was that composition had failed because theretofore it had merely tried to make the student "a better writer," ignoring the necessity of fitting him out for life as a citizen of a democracy. This "social aims" approach was based, of course, on the work of John Dewey, and between 1915 and 1930 the concept of English as a course in socialization and life experience gained more and more power, eventually becoming the organizational focus of the NCTE. Sterling Leonard's *English Composition as a Social Problem* of 1916 was based directly on his reading of Dewey's *School and Society* of 1899 and *The Child and the Curriculum* of 1902 and on the perceptions of composition teaching he had learned at Michigan from Fred Newton Scott, who was a personal friend of Dewey's. With Hosic, Leonard, W. Wilbur Hatfield, and other influential NCTE writers all in favor of socialized learning, the method became popular first in schools and then in colleges.[8]

Between 1920 and 1940, the "socialized," "life-skills," or "experience" approach to teaching writing was the primary theoretical panacea. Instead of sterile "practice periods," teachers were called upon to create for students "vitalized human situations providing for responses to all communications and favorable to the use of the social motives as one writes" (Thompson 111). Scores of impassioned arguments for the Deweyite method are found in the literature of this period, along with methods pieces, explanations of effects, and even comparative tests of life-skills methods versus Brand X. As time went on, the NCTE supported the socialized method more and more strongly, and in 1935 the organization published *An Experience Curriculum in English*, which was both a complete socialized curriculum and an impassioned plea for its adoption.

It is not too strong to say that in English, socialized or "experience" teaching was the primary panacea of the first half of this century. Up until World War II there was no pedagogical movement to rival it, and it waxed strong throughout the late 1930s. After 1940, however, the pipeline of books and articles on "socialized teaching" shut off with an almost audible clank. For reasons that are not completely clear, the experience method ceased gathering support; even the NCTE stopped touting it. Unlike scientific theories or methods, which die out because they are disproved, experience teaching simply faded away. Like most panaceas in English studies, it died of inanition and not defeat.[9]

By 1940, the discipline of composition studies as we know it today was beginning to coalesce. The NCTE was finally attracting enough numbers to represent the profession widely. Linguistic research was on the rise. World War II was shaking the pedagogical establishment, moving it from "experience" education to "American" education. It was time for another crisis. This one came with the assertion that the educational tradition was becoming too specialized, too vocational, too much oriented toward electives. (Does this sound familiar?) College curricula were perceived as fragmented, artificially divided up into disciplines and departments. Colleges were producing narrow specialists. Something needed to be done.

In 1939, a consortium of colleges established the Cooperative Study in General Education, whose goal was nothing less than a complete reevaluation of college programs in the humanities. From the time of the study's first report in 1944 through the mid-1950s, General Education was the watchword of the entire education establishment. Supported by an enlarged and active federal government, the General Ed movement gained such power that by 1952 T. R. McConnell observed that it was "a movement which began as a re-examination of the nature and purposes of liberal education and which is leading toward a revitalization of the liberal arts, and perhaps to a complete reconsideration of the nature of the learning process" (1).

One of the prime interests of the General Education movement was, as might be imagined, freshman English, that ancient bugbear. As a unifying, synthetic movement, General Education wished to heal the split between Speech and English, disciplines that had been separated for four decades, and thus was born our next great panacea: the Communications Skills movement.

The communications movement emphasized not merely writing but all four of the communications skills—writing, reading, speaking, and listening. As the Intercollegiate Committee on Communications Objectives put it,

> As an integral part of the general education movement, numerous courses have been developed to replace the customary offerings of rhetoric or freshman composition. . . . They are based on the conception that students should be adept in all of the principal skills of communication—not just a restricted one of writing or speaking or reading. The precise methods by which the skills of reading, writing, listening, and speaking are developed range from treating each in a separate course at one extreme, to attempts to provide a completely unified or integrated course including all skills. (Dressel and Mayhew 68)

During the late 1940s, over two hundred American colleges converted their freshman composition courses to communications courses (Kitzhaber 26). These courses continued to proliferate through the mid-1950s, and a great deal was written about them in professional journals. Many in composition studies today are not aware of it, but we owe our primary organization to the communications movement. By 1949 the movement had become powerful and vital enough to evolve its own professional group, the Conference on College Composition and Communication, whose journal, *College Composition and Communication*, documented many of the early moves to introduce the four communications skills into theretofore all-writing programs. As with all panaceas, the claims made for a communications approach were inflated, but to many teachers, the move away from isolated writing courses into concern with all the communications skills seemed to presage a new and better era. As Francis Shoemaker put it in 1948, "Through such explicit and sustained emphasis on self-realization in general education we may look forward to more and more individuals consciously and confidently entering into the evolutionary process of democracy" (244). Brave words, which, if they sound a bit ironic now, do strike a tone familiar to any historian of education.

The 1940s and 1950s also saw several other panaceas, which, although not so widespread or popular as communications, still gained some attention. General semantics was a movement based loosely on the ideas that Count Alfred Korzybski had advanced in his opaque *Science and Sanity* of 1933. Korzybski's ideas were explicated and popularized by Stuart Chase, Wendell Johnson, and especially by S. I. Hayakawa, whose *Language in Action* appeared in 1939 (and is still around, as the toned-down *Language in Thought and Action*). Hayakawa adapted Korzybski's paranoid theories about the abuse of linguistic symbolism to pedagogical ends, coming up with a small book that proposed a new way of thinking about the uses of language. "What this book hopes to do," he wrote in the preface to *Language in Action*, "is to offer a general system for clearing the mind of harmful obstructions." The concept of words as symbols was at the heart of general semantics—their abstraction, the problem inherent in mistaking the symbol for the thing it symbolized, the tendency to freight words with incorrect connotations. General semantics was perhaps the most messianic of the composition panaceas of this century; it proposed to do nothing less than cure the insanity of the modern world by pointing out how thought must be restructured by changing people's attitudes toward language.

The other panacea of the 1950s was structural linguistics. Since the 1930s, when descriptive linguistics became a mature discipline in America, some teachers had been seeking applications of this nontraditional grammatical knowledge to writing problems, and in the mid-1950s a number of enthusiasts began to proclaim that adaptation of structural linguistic principles was the only hope for composition. Old grammar bad, new grammar good. *College English* devoted several issues in the latter part of the decade to this controversy, and such linguists as Harry Warfel and Paul Roberts were loud in their support of linguistically based composition teaching. [10]

Once more, however, bright promises faded. The communications movement was another panacea which came to grief on the hard shoals of pedagogical reality. Its idealistic liberal education purposes were seriously questioned in the wake of the "more science" furor following Sputnik in 1957, and the uneasy coalition between Speech departments and English departments that it patched together could not often survive institutional disagreements and departmental squabbling. By 1960, communications was defunct as a movement. "Today their vogue has largely passed," wrote Albert Kitzhaber of communications courses in 1963, noting that of the hundreds that had once existed, his survey of colleges had found only six (26). Semantics petered out a bit before communications—around 1952 or 1953—when it failed to deliver on the revolutionary promise implicit in it. Structural linguistics, although critiqued as a bad pedagogy by some, was not done to death by criticism or by the fact that its parent discipline was superseded by transformational-generative grammar. It died because it was too arcane a field for most teachers to learn to master and because people lost interest in the argument for it.

These three panaceas are like many in composition history—they were proposed, gained high visibility, were argued for and about, seemed to promise a great change for the better, and then retreated back into obscurity. What is telling about these panaceas of the postwar era, however, is their number and power. They represent the beginning of a veritable barrage of new ideas in the field of composition, ideas constantly being introduced, replacing each other, fighting for adherents, for acceptance, for preeminence.

I have perhaps seemed a bit disrespectful toward these movements, calling them panaceas and reporting on their popularity and demise as if they had no lasting consequences. Their failures, however, do not make them unimportant. Although in retrospect the claims of linguistics-based composition or general semantics or communications may seem inflated and their mortality easy to predict, taken together these movements show a discipline in development—indeed, a discipline in formation: the modern discipline of composition studies. Their enthusiasms mark the beginning of the end of blind reliance on derivative tradition in the teaching of writing. After 1940 we see panacea after panacea *because* the questions and problems of composition were being widely considered for the first time in centuries. A class of composition experts was springing up, and a genuine academic discipline was on its way. That these specialists coalesced around movements that did not follow through on their sometimes inflated promises is less important than the fact that purposeful professional movements existed at all. For the first time, the inchoate meliorism of composition teachers was being addressed in large and increasingly institutionalized ways.

The thoughtful members of this new class of composition specialists realized during the late 1950s what they faced: a discipline in a chaos of ferment, scores of good ideas but no real certainty about which were important, a field with a long history of inertia and very little professional respect. Turning composition teaching into composition studies was not going to be easy. As Kitzhaber put it in 1963, most freshman teachers "are still doing business at the same old stand. Freshman English at the nation's colleges and universities is now so confused, so clearly in need of radical and sweeping reforms, that college English departments can continue to ignore the situation only at their peril" (26). Composition studies was being born at a historical point when the writing abilities of freshman students were improving to the extent that many literary scholars began to call for the abolition of freshman composition as unnecessary. The crisis of the early 1960s was a crisis of self-definition—a sense that composition teaching must either come alive or degrade, perhaps irremediably.

The awakening came in 1963. All of the failed panaceas and minor crises since the late 1940s moved the field toward the beginning of a resolution of the 1963 CCCC meeting, a conference at which, say those who attended, there was actually a different feeling in the air, a sense that the field had changed, grown. The "god term," as Richard Weaver would call it, was "rhetoric." The first series of important rhetorical papers was given at this conference by Wayne Booth, Francis Christensen, and Edward P.J. Corbett. The revival of rhetoric in composition theory and teaching had begun. On one hand, of course, this revival was an outgrowth of the communications movement, but more importantly it was the fruit of a new generation of composition scholarship, determined to apply the lessons of the past and the serious research of the present to pedagogical questions.

Many composition scholars know the literature of the last three decades well and know that the rhetorical revolution was the most profoundly melioristic period in our history. After 1963 you could not turn around without bumping into a claim that someone's rhetoric—Burke's or Young's or Rohmann's or Weathers's or Christensen's or Toulmin's—would, if applied correctly, vastly improve the teaching of writing. Large claims were made and supported by theorists and disciples. A Rhetoric Society sprang up. New journals were founded. Theory proliferated.

The Rhetorical Revolution of the 1960s was an important development for the discipline, but from this vantage point, almost three decades later, we can also see that rhetoric—important though it is—was also another in the long line of panaceas that make up the history of composition. From 1963 through 1975 or so we can see that the various forms of rhetorical theory and practice proposed—notably classical rhetoric, Christensen's generative rhetoric, tagmemic rhetoric, stylistic rhetoric, the varied inventional rhetorics and syntactic rhetorics—were all put forward as Solutions to the Problem. Francis Christensen wrote that "we need a rhetoric . . . that will do more than combine the ideas of primer sentences. We need one that will *generate* ideas" (26). That generative rhetoric, of course, the rhetoric that would make students sentence acrobats, better readers, more vital humans, was Christensen's own. While not all the new rhetoricians' claims were quite as messianic as Christensen's, his is the authentic tone of the Rhetorical Revolution. Things had been bad; now they would be put right by Rhetoric—the True Stuff. Many had the sense that a great leap forward was at hand.

And yet, in the midst of this festival of panaceas, a new crisis impinged: 1970, open admissions at CUNY; 1976, Johnny Can't Write. In an eerie replay of the literacy crisis of the 1880s, the culture at large studied, analyzed, and agonized over the deficiencies of student writers. And in a similar replay, the profession reacted. The panacea mill ground into even more feverish action, and we were given the "Back to Basics" movement, sentence combining, controlled composition. On a more fundamental level a whole new subset of the discipline, basic writing studies, was born out of the new literacy crisis. And, as crises are wont to do, this new swivet came and went in a few years, disappearing not because its problems had been solved but because funding disappeared or people got tired of talking about it.

This, then, was our recent history: the familiar systole-diastole of crisis and panacea. While it is true that the period 1963 to 1977 represents a genuine turning point in the discipline, a new professionalization of composition studies, at the same time these years were just a reiteration, writ large, of cultural and disciplinary response/stimulus systems that date back to the 1850s.

And what of current conditions? Things get more complex here, because in the last two decades composition teaching has finally produced a genuine scholarly discipline devoted to studying its issues, and the world of composition studies is very different from the world of everyday teaching. What we see today is the moving apart of the worlds of pedagogy and theory in composition that has marked the world of literary studies for the past century, and the crises and panaceas generated by the two diverging worlds are not always closely related.

The "process writing" movement gives us a key illustration of this growing gap between practice and theory. A crisis of confidence in presentational teaching methods during the late 1960s produced the panacea variously called "the third way," "the Garrison method," or simply the "process writing" movement. Led by such practitioner-heroes as Ken Macrorie, Donald Murray, Peter Elbow, and Roger Garrison, the process movement was intensely practical and student-oriented. Process-based teaching chugged through the 1970s and into the 1980s, making many converts among the mass of nonspecialist composition teachers Stephen North calls "practitioners." Adoption of process techniques—conferencing, workshop groups, student-chosen topics—was often a kind of conversion experience, and thousands sought that experience. The process movement changed teaching methods more than almost any other movement during this century—and yet it was almost completely ignored by the great majority of composition theorists working between 1970 and 1985.

What was going on over in composition studies, among the growing numbers of scholars whose Ph.D.s were actually in composition, was very different from the process action on the teaching side. While the Rhetorical Revolution was occurring during the formation of composition studies, another strand was taking shape among specialists: the research strand. Goaded by the assertion made by Braddock, Lloyd-Jones, and Schoer in 1963 that "today's research in composition, taken as a whole, may be compared to chemical research as it emerged from the period of alchemy" (5), some scholars declared that empirical research was the future and solution to composition's issues. What followed was increasingly intensive work in positivistic and behaviorist veins until by the early 1980s the research strand was the most intellectually vital element in composition scholarship. The work of Kellogg Hunt, Frank O'Hare, Stephen Witte, Lester Faigley, Janice Lauer, and many others moved gradually from interest in classroom issues and simple horse-race experiments toward interest in the psychological and cognitive makeup of the writing process itself. The ground-breaking protocol analyses of writers done in the late 1970s by Linda Flower and John Hayes were in some ways the capstone of this research effort.

Does this research effort qualify as a "panacea" in the sense we have been using the word? In a rather abstract sense, yes, because even at their most analytical and methodologically oriented, nearly all of the members of the composition research community have had issues of practical teaching somewhere in mind. In this sense, research into the meaning of T-units can be seen as somehow in the long term giving teachers techniques to use in teaching writing, as earlier T-unit research had resulted in the intensely hyped classroom panacea of sentence combining.

But pragmatic pedagogical issues can increasingly get lost as composition studies borrows more and more of its issues from philosophy and social science. Today's panaceas come from an elite world, and they have more and more tangential relations to daily problems of pedagogy. The scholarly practitioners of composition studies happily take any crisis as grist for their mills, but the crises and panaceas of today's scholarly world are more apt to have to do with philosophical or interpretive issues than with quotidian problems of teaching writing. During the late 1980s, the burgeoning research strand in comp studies was brought up short by a set of serious philosophical and interpretive critiques leveled by a group that has since become known as the "social constructionists." Experimentalism automatically decontextualizes, claimed this group, and thus the research strand was examining phenomena in a vacuum (as well as being hopelessly clogged with unexamined positivism). The solution: train students to understand how all human knowledge is a product of collaboration and group development of meaning—how, in other words, discourse communities are established.

The discipline right now seems to be evolving a new form, one that institutionalizes the two-tier hierarchy between composition scholars and composition teachers just as English departments long ago rigidified into their older hierarchy of literature and composition. This graduation to success for most composition Ph.D.s has really changed the conditions of work; most importantly, it has changed the nature of the crises that have for so long defined the field of composition. Composition scholars (as opposed to writing teachers) have no crises to goad them. Small squabbles and interpretive puzzles we have in plenty, but as scholarly specialists we are more successful than ever before, and our crises may for the nonce be the existential crises of the rising classes.

Many composition teachers, on the other hand, are still in the grip of the unsolved crises of old, and their situations seem unlikely to change as a result of more sophisticated interpretive strategies. Many panaceas have failed to improve their lot. Linguistics, which once was taken as a paradigm for discourse, has been abandoned by most composition theorists. Research, especially cognitive or quantitative research, never really tried to qualify as a true panacea of the old sort; it was also a difficult bandwagon to jump onto if you were not a trained social-science-based researcher.

Those non-social scientists who waited for the next great evangelical movement must surely have been disappointed by social construction, whose jargon is almost as dense with arcane critical and ideological terminology as the research strand was with methodological talk.[11] There is, however, one sense in which the social construction movement harks back to the older general field of composition: it is deeply melioristic. Theoretically dense though the social construction movement may be, it is essentially based on several deeply altruistic—and even idealistic—concepts. Its goal, finally, is to unite discourse communities, to give access and power in the educated community to those who have been disempowered by lacks of literacy for too long. In this sense, the point I have made throughout this chapter remains valid. We must and do believe that what we teach, investigate, and theorize about will result in a better world. Crises and our solutions to them, panaceas and the excitement of new thought, have been the motivating forces for us always, and if this is not the structure we would ideally choose for our discipline, it is at least the structure and the melioristic aims that have kept us moving, growing, striving for the past three decades.

I do not mean to criticize that meliorism. This essay may at times have seemed like a cynical reduction of our history to a series of hand-waving anxieties and petered-out educational fads, but that is only one way of looking at our past. It may not be an inspirational perspective, but it is educational, because we are always in danger of looking uncritically at the next great excitement unless we can see it as it is: one of an endless series of events and programs that will continue to shape the discipline. We can make our laudable meliorism into useful work, but only if we place ourselves historically, meet each cried-up crisis calmly, test each claimed panacea against the many that have come before it. Movement we must have, but only by understanding the future by the light of the past will we escape the bondage to temporary excitements that has made too many of our crises and panaceas into profitless exercises on the stage of a misunderstood present.

Notes

1. For more information on this increased burden of socialization, see my "Mechanical Correctness as a Focus in Composition Instruction."

2. Hill had argued since the 1870s that the sophomore rhetoric course established in 1877 was not enough, that a freshman course would shame the secondary schools into teaching better English. "Could the study [of composition] be taken up at the threshold of college life," he wrote, "the schools would be made to feel that their labors in this direction were going to tell upon a pupil's standing in college as well as upon his admission." Upper-class courses could not reach students during their more malleable years: "There are obvious obstacles in the way of [upper-class teachers] achieving results that could easily be reached with younger boys in smaller classes" (Hill 12–13). If secondary schools could not police themselves, in other words, the colleges must do it for them.

3. This was, in fact, one of those rare cases in which we might actually say that a problem *had* been defined and solved. Certainly there was little attention paid to composition in secondary schools before 1875, and there was considerable attention paid after 1895. Harvard and Adams S. Hill, in particular, were indeed responsible for this change. It may be argued, however, that while their welkin-rending cries about illiteracy woke the nation up to genuine deficiencies in secondary curricula, their college-level panacea, English A, created far more problems than it solved.

4. We should note here that some colleges during the 1890s did indeed institute important pedagogical reforms, and that even as early as this there was a powerful movement in favor of what we now call "process" teaching. The old methods of asking students to master reams of rhetorical theory was giving way to real writing practice. As Gertrude Buck put it in 1901, "The revolt against the domination of the student's writing by formal rhetorical precepts was earliest and most conspicuous. Scarcely less marked, however, tho somewhat later in time, have been the tendencies to derive subjects for writing from the student's own experience, rather than from sources foreign to his knowledge or interest;

to direct his writing toward some real audience; and, finally, to criticize his writing somewhat informally, in terms of the ultimate end of discourse" (371). Buck could not know that the process orientation she described would wither quickly within the decade.

5. See my "Textbooks and the Evolution of the Discipline."

6. This article, "Can Good Composition Teaching Be Done Under Present Conditions?," is the one whose famous first paragraph consists simply of the word "No."

7. Of course, "ourselves" gradually *became* a body of knowledge; *vide* this essay and most historical work in composition.

8. For more on this movement, see Applebee, 45–49, and Hook, 29–40. The power that the Deweyite movement was picking up in all fields is shown by the foundation of the journal *School and Society* in 1910.

9. This claim is unprovable, but it may also be that the social-experience movement decayed for political reasons. "Socialized" education sounded questionable when the great enemy was German National Socialism, and in the Red-obsessed era of the late 1940s the "social" jargon of the experience movement sounded suspiciously leftish and communal, if not communistic. It is probably no coincidence that the "American composition" movement in courses and textbooks sprang up at the same time the "experience" movement was going out of style.

10. For more detailed information on the rise and fall of structural linguistics in composition, see my "Grammar in American College Composition."

11. We are, I imagine, unlikely to see the large-scale defection from pedagogy to research or social construction that we saw from literature to rhetoric. Being returned for regrooving as a social scientist or a theory-intensive cultural critic is considerably more demanding than the regrooving most of us have already been through as we went from one humanities field, literature, into another, rhetoric and writing pedagogy.

Works Cited

Alford, Henry. *A Plea for the Queen's English*. London: Alexander Strahan, 1866.

Applebee, Arthur N. *Tradition and Reform in the Teaching of English: A History*. Urbana, IL: NCTE, 1974.

Bache, Richard Meade. *Vulgarisms and Other Errors of Speech*. Philadelphia: Claxton, Remsen, and Haffelfinger, 1869.

Braddock, Richard, Richard Lloyd-Jones, and Lowell Schoer. *Research in Written Composition*. Champaign, IL: NCTE, 1963.

Buck, Gertrude. "Recent Tendencies in the Teaching of English Composition." *Educational Review* 22 (1901): 371–82.

Christensen, Francis. "A Generative Rhetoric of the Sentence." *Notes Toward a New Rhetoric*. Ed. Bonniejean Christensen. 2 ed. New York: Harper, 1978.

Connors, Robert J. "Grammar in American College Composition." *The Territory of Language*. Ed. Donald McQuade. Carbondale: Southern Illinois UP, 1986. 3–22.

———. "Mechanical Correctness as a Focus in Composition Instruction." *College Composition and Communication* 36 (Feb. 1985): 61–72.

———. "Textbooks and the Evolution of the Discipline." *College Composition and Communication* 37 (May 1986): 178–94.

Dressel, Paul L., and Lewis B. Mayhew, eds. *General Education: Explorations in Evaluation*. Washington, DC: American Council on Education, 1954.

Hayakawa, S. I. *Language in Action*. New York: Harcourt, 1939.

Hill, Adams S. "An Answer to the Cry for More English." *Twenty Years of School and College English*. Cambridge: Harvard UP, 1896.

Hook, J. N. *A Long Way Together*. Urbana, IL: NCTE, 1979.

Hopkins, Edwin M. "Can Good Composition Teaching Be Done Under Present Conditions?" *English Journal* 1 (1912): 1–8.

———. "Four Problems for the Council." *English Journal* 1 (1912): 49.

Hosic, James F. Letter of Nov. 5, 1911, to fellow English teachers. *English Journal* 1 (1912): 31.

———. "The Significance of the Organization of the National Council." *English Journal* 1 (1912): 47–48.

Hunt, T. W. "The Study of English in American Colleges." *Educational Review* 12 (1896): 140–50.

Kitzhaber, Albert R. *Themes, Theories, and Therapy: The Teaching of Writing in College*. New York: McGraw-Hill, 1963.

McConnell, T. R. "General Education: An Analysis." *The Fifty-First Yearbook of the National Society for the Study of Education, 1952, Part I—General Education*. Chicago: U of Chicago P, 1952.

Scott, Fred Newton. "The Report on College Entrance Requirements in English." *Educational Review* 20 (1900): 289–94.

Shoemaker, Francis. "Self-Realization, Communications, and Aesthetic Experience." *Communications in General Education*. Ed. Earl James McGrath. Dubuque, IA: Wm. C. Brown, 1948.

Thompson, C. J. "A Study of the Socialized versus the Academic Method of Teaching Written Composition." *School Review* 27 (1919): 110–33.

Part 2
Working Within the Context

8   Enlarging the Context
From Teaching Just Writing, to
Teaching Academic Subjects with Writing

Richard L. Larson

IN THIS CHAPTER I OFFER, QUITE EXPLICITLY, AN ARGUMENT. I FIRST NOTE what I regard as the wide diversity in what is taught under the banner of "composition" in first-year writing courses around the country and point out the dubious messages about writing that I see being communicated to students during those courses. I observe that some of the most important acts performed by writers receive little or no attention in those writing courses. Finally, I note the inexperience of large numbers of teachers who staff these courses. My argument, quite simply, is that most colleges and universities have no moral justification for requiring students to take their first-year writing courses without requiring that they later engage in writing within the academic and professional disciplines. I will, indeed, suggest that colleges and universities in general—there are of course exceptions—have little justification for requiring the first-year writing course of all students. In the following pages I will attempt to explain, and offer evidence to support, that claim.

The investigations that led me to these conclusions began when program officers at the Ford Foundation heard of difficulties in the writing of students in college and thought that the foundation might wish to support some initiatives that would perhaps strengthen the teaching of writing in college. They invited me to meet with them for an exploratory discussion of the state of writing instruction—its emphases, work asked of students—in American colleges and universities. Later those program officers asked me to suggest initiatives that Ford might usefully support in hopes of having some positive influence on the teaching of writing. Believing that teachers of writing were, on the whole, not well prepared for that work, I had planned to suggest that Ford support the development of new approaches to preparing teachers to teach writing (both graduate students and faculty already holding positions in departments of English and other fields). But after discussions with leaders in the field of written composition, the people at Ford (whose sense of responsibility to American higher education I grew to respect greatly) became uncertain about where the "center of gravity" in our field lay and about how they could best contribute to the strengthening of our field. Still, in order to learn more about how writing is taught in American colleges, they invited me to conduct a study of trends and practices in the teaching of writing. I was to try to confirm or disconfirm my preliminary impressions of why many college writing programs might well be ineffective. With the concurrence of the people at Ford, I chose to focus on "curricula" in composition: on how students are led to view writing, on what they are asked to write, and on how they are led to produce that writing.

I give to the term *curriculum* what may be a distinctive meaning: the writing assignments that students are asked to complete, in the order and with the frequency with which they are assigned, along with the supportive activities in which students are asked to engage as part of the processes of preparing and completing those assignments. I take it, with James Moffett, that students learn to write primarily *by* writing: by moving the pen across the page, moving the typeball across the paper, placing the electronic images on the screen of the word processor. I take it, that is, that people learn to write by experiencing the sensation of seeing their thoughts and perceptions take visible form in front of them, by experiencing the dissatisfaction of sensing that what is unfolding on the page (or screen) is not "right" (i.e., by engaging in what Linda Flower and colleagues refer to as "detection," then engaging in "diagnosis"), and by struggling to reshape the ideas, structure, and language so that they are more "right," maybe more forceful.

I set out in 1986, therefore, to study the curricula in first-year writing courses primarily, in a generous sampling of two- and four-year colleges and universities across the United States. The sampling procedures, which I worked out in consultation with program officers at Ford and with experienced researchers in our profession, were not formal or strict. They included choosing every seventh name (the name typically is that of a department chair) on the Modern Language Association's listing of two- and four-year colleges arranged in order of zip code (unless the seventh name was that of someone less likely to know the details of an institution's writing program—for instance, the chair of the program in comparative literature rather than the English department chair); dropping from the list the names of schools with special emphases (beauty colleges, for instance) not likely to be helpful in the study; adding the names of all institutions designated by compilers of data in education as "historically black" (Ford had made a special commitment to assisting the development of historically black colleges); and also adding, frankly, the names of institutions described to Ford's program officers or to me as having interesting or noteworthy programs. (We are still working on the analysis of our data to see what special characteristics distinguish programs in each of the several groups.) I checked the sample to be sure that it included larger and smaller colleges and universities; institutions that grant the doctorate and institutions that do not; public and private (church-related and nonchurch-related) institutions; schools that admit both men and women; schools that admit women only; and schools that admit men only (there was only one). At least one member of each kind of institution mentioned in each of these groups was represented in the sample: not a precise stratification, but sufficient, I was told, for my purposes.

In approaching this sampling, I did not simply develop an easily answered questionnaire and send it to each institution on my list. Instead, I wrote to each, asking that a representive send to me copies of any documents—syllabi, policy statements, individual assignment sheets, memoranda to staff, internal memoranda to deans and provosts and general faculty discussing the curriculum in writing, and so on—that might show what curriculum in writing was (or what curricula were) in place at that institution. (I did not ask for copies of students' writings, though I may ask for such writings in a separate study to see what sorts of work the curricula actually evoke.) I preferred to take upon myself, and to place on the shoulders of a research assistant working with me (Keith Walters, a doctoral candidate at the CUNY Graduate Center and an adjunct lecturer at Lehman College), the task of interpreting the documents describing an institution's curriculum in writing instead of letting a faculty member at the responding institution interpret its curriculum in the course of answering the specific items on a questionnaire. I preferred raw data for another reason: we could preserve the data, and if questions we had not initially thought of came to our minds as we proceeded, we could reexamine the data for answers. Besides asking for the internal documents, we did request that respondents complete one short questionnaire about the staffing of first-year writing courses. We asked the usual questions: about percentages of teachers who are full-time and part-time, percentages of tenure-eligible and nontenure-eligible teachers, percentages of sections taught by the various groups of staff, and so on.

We sent our inquiries to chairs of departments at some 575 institutions, asking the chair to pass the inquiry on to the faculty member(s) responsible for the writing program. (All were promised that their responses would be held in confidence unless I later asked for, and received, permission to name them.) Well over 300 responded—if not to the first request, then to a second or third request. But several of these responses contained only the questionnaire with the quantitative data, and a few contained documents we could not readily interpret. (I have to report regretfully, also, that some of the files were

lost in the theft of Mr. Walters's automobile.) What individual institutons
sent varied considerably. But we did receive large numbers of course syllabi
(some very detailed, day-by-day or week-by-week), policy statements,
sketches of purposes for curricula, assignment sheets, and in some cases letters
from the director of composition or the department chair describing the writing curricula, and sometimes its evolution, at his or her school. As a result,
we have a large body of information; the findings that follow are based on
some 240 full responses to our inquiries.

Our technique of collecting data, obviously, makes interpretation necessary and misinterpretation and underinterpretation or overinterpretation quite
possible. We were "constructing" the assorted texts sent to us, trying to "read"
them in light of the purposes of the inquiry. We took the chance of error in
reading. My research assistant or I or both of us read the files sent to us and
noted the presence (or absence) of numerous features of the curriculum; as
we proceeded, we added features to look for and reexamined curricula we
had previously studied in order to note for each institution each feature we
focused on. By the time we were close to completion, we were looking at
or for some eighty features of each curriculum.

We recognized, of course, that not only might we misread the documents
before us, but also we might have in our hands unrepresentative documents:
the syllabus sent to us, for example, might in theory guide the teaching of a
newcomer to the staff while more experienced teachers freely departed from
it, or it might apply quite closely to the sections taught by some instructors
but not to sections taught by others. Classroom practices of different teachers,
we recognized, may well go beyond and differ from what one might infer
from the syllabus; attention to such matters as "audience" and "invention,"
discussed below, may well be greater than what the syllabus implies or promises. The syllabus or plan, also, is not necessarily frozen; at the very moment
when we were reading a set of documents representing an institution, the
curriculum or teaching practices at the institution might be changing. Hence,
I am careful not to claim that our findings concerning each of the characteristics
we looked at have anything approaching precision. For this reason, as well as
to avoid anesthetizing the reader with rows of neat, seemingly finite numbers,
I report the findings mostly in large fractions with relatively few specific
percentages. Using these cautions, I am reasonably confident that this discussion presents an essentially fair picture of the curricula in writing in our
colleges. I received word of a few curricula that are distinctive; they are not
included in the generalizations reported here.

From the extended examination of all these data, what emerges? Several
perceptions, on which I will try to elaborate in what follows. First, substantial
diversity: curricula in writing are diverse in focus and strategy; the Ford program officers' inability to find a "center of gravity" in our field is amply
sustained. Second, *formalism*, if that is the word: a predominant emphasis on

teaching forms of writing, patterns of arrangement, compliance with formal requirements (in paragraphs and sentences).

Third, *indifference to the discovery of data and ideas based on data*: except in assignments for the so-called research paper, about which I have written at length elsewhere ("The Research Paper"), curricula tend not to reveal attention to helping students find, interpret, and evaluate data and develop ideas based upon knowledge—ideas, that is, not recoverable by such search procedures as "brainstorming" and "freewriting." (In individual teachers' classroom practices, of course, which the data sent to us do not reveal, this omission may possibly be repaired.) Fourth, *indifference to quality of thought*: most of the curricula we studied did not pay much visible attention to the quality and cogency of reasoning, the adequacy of data cited, the defensibility of assertions made, and ways of strengthening all these in students' writings. Again, classroom practices and instructors' comments on students' writings—which we had no chance to examine (as Kitzhaber did in his well-known study thirty years ago [*Themes, Theories*])—may address this imbalance. But only a minority of syllabi hinted that quality of thought is a central concern of the curriculum or the actual teaching.

Fifth, *inattention to what a completed writing might do to/for readers*: a majority of the curricula we looked at seemed not to give much attention to the *effectiveness* of completed writings in adding to the reader's store of information, inducing belief in an assertion, evoking feelings, or prompting action. (The people at Ford were much concerned that writing programs in colleges contribute to heightening the quality of public, civic discourse.) Despite some attention to "audience," the curricula seemed not to be concerned with the ultimate readers of writing, not to be concerned with the probable impact of the completed writing on readers outside of the people in the immediate classroom. Indeed, I came to suspect that much of the instruction in writing in first-year courses limited its focus to the formal, and maybe the stylistic, characteristics of the text in process and those of the completed text. Even courses that highlight the so-called writing process—which claim to move attention away from the "product" to the "processes" by which the final text comes into being—appear, from the way their syllabi are constructed, to put their emphasis on the felicitous carrying on of the process to the completion of a text that is pleasing to the writer, the other members of the class, and to the teacher. But if we are, as many of us claim to be, teachers of "rhetoric," we are presumably concerned with judging the credibility, cogency of thought, appropriateness of ethos, and force of expression in the texts composed in our classes. In courses where the faithful completion of a "writing process" and the pleasingness of the crafted text claim, by implication, the teacher's and the students' principal attention, the student may well not confront this central question: will this text, this act of discourse, accomplish its work effectively with the readers I envisage for it?

Sixth recurrent feature: *inattention to theory*. Except in discussions of the so-called writing process, and except for the willingess of some courses to incorporate a version of "collaborative learning," we had difficulty discovering in the documents we studied any direct attention to theoretical investigations or research findings about discourse or teaching that might underlie the curriculum. (Not that one wants teachers to present first-year students with the controversial intricacies of rhetorical theory, but some reflection of recent advances in thinking about discourse and about composing might be expected in statements about policy or course objectives. The "Rigid Rules and Inflexible Plans" identified by Mike Rose in the thinking of many students [and many faculty] were still alive and well in writing curricula when we conducted the survey.) Almost any curriculum is grounded in one theory or another and may reflect implicitly, if not explicitly, findings from research. Where the "composing process" was highlighted, that emphasis almost surely reflects attention to research findings. But one might hope that teachers would more than occasionally bring other such theories to the surface of their own (and perhaps even their students') consciousness, instead of allowing them to remain unexplored. Perhaps the fruits of research are so unfocused that course directors are not sure what to take from them into their courses. Perhaps teachers assume that textbooks, which, as I will note below, drive many curricula, will articulate the underlying theory adequately. But textbooks are often slow to incorporate new insights from research.

And seventh, in many ways the most disturbing finding of all, *indifference to evaluation*: I saw hardly any syllabi that discussed in any detail the goals of the institution's curriculum, the specific role of the writing course within that curriculum, the specific goals of the writing course(s), the criteria by which teachers would discover whether the course's goals were being met, ways of discovering whether indeed the students were achieving the goals set for them, or ways of determining whether the writing curriculum as a whole was accomplishing its purposes. Furthermore, given the diversity of the textbooks used and the readings assigned, one might almost say that each teacher is enacting a nearly idiosyncratic curriculum. Therefore, one might at least expect that some guidance would be given to the instructor in evaluating his or her own curriculum. Not so. Few syllabi gave instructors any guidance in how to measure the success of what they were doing, unless one wants to argue that having instructors read portfolios of each others' students—in the relatively few colleges where that practice was followed when we took our survey—might lead to such evaluation. But I've seen little evidence, in my subsequent studies of how portfolios are used, that they contribute much to evaluation of curricula. (Subsequent to the completion of my survey, the concept of the "teaching portfolio," in which teachers compile and reflect upon docuents they use in teaching and keep logs of their teaching, has emerged conspicuously, thanks in large part to the work of Pat Hutchings of the American Association for Higher Education. But my survey turned up no instances in which teaching portfolios played a central role in the operation of the writing program. And teaching portfolios might not get at the value of the curriculum for the institution's goals.) We are a profession, I sense, that does not even try to hold itself or its members accountable for achieving their own defined instructional goals, though in this respect we are, to put the point gently, not unique. We do not examine ourselves. First-year English is a major *un*evaluated enterprise in American higher education.

What, then, are some of the details of what we did find? Some 35 percent of the curricula we looked at are "textbook-driven": the instructor is expected, at least on the printed syllabus, to take the student almost chapter by chapter through the textbook, thus implying to the students that whatever partitioning of the act of writing and of composition as a field of study the textbook adopted is the one the students should learn and adopt. It might be useful to examine the preferred textbooks in writing courses and their assertions/ assumptions about writing. But such an examination is beyond the scope of this chapter.

Roughly 30 percent of the institutions rest some part of the curriculum in composition on assignments in literature; 25 percent (some of which may be in the previous 30 percent) build instruction around literary genres. Also, in a majority of curricula, the instructor is expected to use, in some combina- tion, a reader, usually of essays (55 percent), a textbook on rhetoric (60 percent), and a grammar handbook (55 percent). Further, the curricula in over half the materials we examined organize assignments according to familiar formal sequences: students are taken, one by one, through "modes" or "forms" of discourse (36 percent), or "methods of development" (37 percent), as if writers in the act of writing are concerned principally to contribute a specimen to a taxonomy of discourse. Also, direct attention to grammar and syntactic form characterizes well over half the syllabi we studied, with 30 percent focusing directly on grammatical categories (though only 7.5 percent teach sentence combining—arguably a way of making familiarity with grammar contribute to composing).

But "invention," in some ways the most important act in the rhetorician's repertoire, appeared neglected. Apparently fewer than 10 percent of the curric- ula teach students to employ the classical *topoi*. The percentages of programs that visibly teach students even the newer invention strategies of brainstorm- ing, freewriting, mapping, cubing, and so on were each well under twenty at the time of the survey. Tagmemic rhetoric, admittedly a difficult inventional heuristic to teach, was hard to find in our curricula; probably fewer than 10 percent of the institutions we looked at taught those procedures. The search for information, if that can be called a heuristic, appeared central in fewer than a quarter of the curricula, except in the assignment for the single "research paper."

Dispositio, the second of the central three acts in classical rhetoric, is for the most part in the curricula we looked at taught through instruction in the types and patterns of discourse and through instruction in the forms of the paragraph. Looking at *elocutio*, we found that serious attention to "tone of voice" (6 percent of responses) and "style" (25 percent) is largely missing; some syllabi' urge students to develop their "voices," though it is not clear what guidance is given for the creation of those voices. It appears from the curricular emphases and textbooks used that half of the institutions insist on syntactic correctness as a chief virtue of style.

Some 30 percent of the curricula we examined teach the "writing process," but 55 percent pay attention to revision. Quite a few of these programs take pride in being up-to-date in their teaching because they teach a "process" curriculum, though these curricula seem inattentive to the probability that different writers follow different processes in composing and that all writers may follow different processes in composing in different circumstances. (I view attention to "writing processes" as chiefly just the stretching out, and highlighting, of several acts that most writers regularly perform, quickly and perhaps subconsciously, as parts of the act of writing. There is nothing new in recognizing that writers go through processes while composing.) The call for teaching one central activity in many writers' processes, "revision," often with the aid of peers (28 percent of syllabi refer to inviting "peers' " comments), has reached over half of the institutions, as noted (and probably, in the actual teaching of the classes, more than half). The syllabi featuring "revision," however, leave in doubt how writers can "detect" the need for revision and then can evaluate their strategies for revising, once they have, perhaps with the aid of fellow students, "diagnosed" the difficulties that revision should try to correct. (I use here the terminology from Linda Flower and her associates' article, "Detection, Diagnosis, and the Strategies of Revision.") The same syllabi leave in doubt how the effectiveness of the revised piece emerging from the composing process might be judged: is the possible effect on readers in a human, maybe public, context to be taken into account? And we wondered in how many programs the "writing process" is rolled up with teaching emphases coming out of varied (maybe incompatible) theories, as at one well-known liberal arts college where the first semester of the writing course begins with drills on the sentence and the paragraph, moves for three or four weeks to the "writing process," and concludes with three or four weeks on various modes of discourse. What message about the acts of writing does such a curriculum send to students? Attention to form dominates the advice about revising that we saw, not the need for ideas, data, evidence, clear reasoning, convincingness, and effectiveness in context. (Only 37 percent of the syllabi indicate that attention is given to the quality of students' ideas.) Yet isn't it the final presentation of data (from whatever sources), the interpretation of data, the use of the data as evidence, the reasoning from principles and data (not overlooking the vigor of language and tightness of structure) that evoke for readers the impression of a piece's "overall effectiveness" and thus influence most readers' judgments of, and responses to, what they read?

If these findings suggest difficulties with instruction in writing around the country, and they do, an explanation may lie in the statistics we compiled about the status and probable preparation of those who are teaching the first-year courses in writing. The returned questionnaires amply confirm what many of us have known or guessed for years: that most of the teaching of writing in our colleges and universities is done by part-time, nontenure-eligible, or nontenured staff, especially in the larger four-year colleges. It is not hard to infer—especially since these data were collected six years before this chapter reaches print, when there were fewer graduate programs for people wishing to prepare for the profession of the teaching of writing—that most of these part-time and temporary teachers have had little formal, extended study of theories about discourse, language, and composing, and, except in staff training programs at institutions that offer them, have had little study of the teaching of composition, either. If first-year writing courses are staffed heavily by teachers with little training, one can easily see why these teachers rely on textbooks, familiar and easily grasped taxonomies of form, and imperfectly thought-out generalizations about the "composing process" to guide their work. It would not be surprising if these teachers had had no opportunity to explore various procedures for invention, such as applying tagmemic theory and searching for, interpreting, and evaluating data in different fields; or to consider ways of applying rhetorical concepts such as ethos and tone; or to think about how to estimate the probable reception of writings by ultimate readers and the possible responses of such readers as they deconstruct writers' texts. We could hardly expect underprepared teachers to teach much other than the mostly traditional curricula we discovered.

But, as I have mentioned, when I prepared in 1990 to report on our analyses of the curricula we learned about, I recognized that in a changing field, four- or five-year-old data might not give the firmest basis for generalizing about the state of instruction in writing in American colleges and universities. Some follow-up to the initial investigation was essential. In the fall of 1990, therefore, I sent to all of the 240 institutions that had responded earlier (with more than just the questionnaires about staffing) a further inquiry, asking them to tell me about any changes that had taken place in their writing programs since they had responded to my initial request for information. I suggested that if there had been no important changes in instruction in writing on their campuses, they did not need to reply. Some forty institutions responded this time, many to say simply that nothing had changed, some to give minor changes in goals, syllabi, or textbooks. The responses did not significantly change the general findings about curricula in writing that I have reported on earlier pages. I think that these generalizations, offered with the tentativeness that I suggested earlier, probably hold essentially true in 1993.

But one feature of these responses to the follow-up study was striking. Several institutions, without being asked specifically about the subject, reported with pride, some in detail, about "writing intensive" courses that had been or were about to be put into place on their campuses. They said that their institutions were moving toward recognition that teaching writing, or at least extending what students were able to do in their writing, was coming to be perceived widely on campus as the responsibility of faculty in the academic disciplines. These unsolicited comments were the most informative features of replies to the follow-up inquiry.

The earlier inquiry had brought some reports of efforts to connect writing with the academic disciplines. Some of these efforts, as my research assistant and I came to call them, were "inwardly directed" (17 percent) (the disciplines furnish some of the materals and assignments for use in the writing course); and some of them "outwardly directed" (8 percent: probably too low a figure) (writing was being incorporated into the work of academic disciplines). But the number of such reports had been small, partly because in planning the initial letter of inquiry we had not thought to ask for information about such developments; these scattered reports did not affect the generalizations about institutions' primary writing programs discussed earlier here. In the fall of 1990 these earlier reports, taken together with the proud reports of colleges and universities moving to locate much of the responsibility for evoking writing outside the department of English, suggested a trend worth exploring.

Accordingly, in the spring of 1991, I decided to explore the trend. I sent a one-page questionnaire (one page, in order to simplify the act of responding and increase the likelihood of response) to each of the colleges and universities that had *not* responded to inquiries during the first (1986) part of my study. (For this investigation I did not go back to institutions surveyed in 1986. One has to avoid overburdening chairs with questionnaires, and I had useful information about post-first-year writing from many of the institutions that had responded to the first study.) This questionnaire invited respondents to indicate very quickly whether an institution

- requires an advanced course in writing taken after first-year composition;
- requires students to pass an examination in writing after the first
year;
- gathers and evaluates portfolios of student writing after students
have completed the first-year course (i.e., in the second or later
years);
- requires of students that they take after the first year one or more
courses in which they have to complete one or more writings outside of class;
- expects students to complete writings outside of class in courses
after the first year, even if there is no formal requirement of a
"writing emphasis" course;
- expects to put into place a requirement in writing to be met after
the first year;
- offers "faculty development" programs to promote the use of
writing in the disciplines (i.e., operates a program to assist faculty

in seeing the value of including writing in their courses; in recognizing how they might include writing in their courses; in coming
to feel comfortable assigning writing; and in reading thoughtfully
and responding constructively to students' writing).

Although the questionnaire asked only for brief responses to the several questions, it invited respondents to amplify their responses if they so wished and
to enclose with the returned questionnaire any materials (course descriptions,
summaries of programs, and the like) that might help me to understand the
details of the requirements in writing on their campuses. I came to call this
questionnaire my survey of "extended attention" to writing, and in what
follows I report, essentially, the kinds and amount of extended attention to
writing in the colleges and universities identified in my survey.

The survey demonstrated, perhaps most importantly, that at least half
of the responding institutions now have in place some procedure for giving
extended attention to writing, beyond the student's first-year writing course
(if, indeed, there is a first-year writing course; several institutions reported
offering no such course). Furthermore, many of the institutions that do not
now have a formal program in place report either the intention to install such
a program or the general expectation that students will write regularly in
most or all of their courses. (Several institutions without what we might call
formal requirements of extended attention to writing sent me detailed accounts
of their curricula, making it clear that in many or most of their courses students
do write frequently.) And while not every institution requiring extended
attention to writing has in place a faculty development program (only three-
fifths have such a program), many institutions that do not claim to have in
place a plan for extended attention to writing do operate a faculty development
program to help faculty members come to understand how they can extend
students' abilities at writing and use writing assignments to help students learn
in their courses.

From replies to the specific questions on the "extended attention" survey,
I draw the following conclusions. Only a small number of institutions (7
percent) rely on postfreshman (e.g., junior level) examinations as the only
way of giving extended attention to writing. And a smaller number (3 percent)
rely exclusively on advanced courses specifically in writing to assure that
students obtain extended practice in writing. Asking for portfolios after the
first-year course has caught on at only six or seven of the responding institutions (maybe 1.5 percent) as a way of assuring that students extend their
practice in writing. Three or four other institutions (some responses were
ambiguous) use portfolios in combination with other means of giving extended
attention. Roughly a quarter of the responding institutions report using "writing intensive" or "writing emphasis" courses (as defined on the questionnaire)
as the sole means of assuring extended attention, but well over a third report
using a combination of procedures: an advanced course in writing and/or an

examination along with a requirement of writing in an academic course (or courses). And most institutions that require writing intensive courses—obviously not the best designator—do arrange programs to help faculty come to understand how to use writing in their teaching. Several of these institutions sent descriptions of their faculty development programs, and I hope to inquire later of these and other institutions how they lead faculty to participate in these programs. For clearly students cannot be invited to extend their abilities at writing unless faculty are willing and able to help them do so. And faculty will usually give that help only if they are convinced that they have the time to do so, know how to do so, and will from some source (if only their professional consciences) be rewarded for their efforts. Some faculty, of course, as one of my colleagues notes, can lead students to strengthen their abilities at writing by requiring students to write and by making comments that do no more than signal dissatisfaction with the student's work or note that the writing is inadequately clear. But for large numbers of faculty, confidence in their ability to make wise assignments for writing and give constructive readings of students' work comes only with helpful guidance from experienced teachers of writing and as a result of exchanges with colleagues in other disciplines about examples of students' writing.

What comes across to me most strikingly from the two studies is that the fresh thought being given today to strengthening students' abilities as writers is occurring for the most part in the plans for bringing writing into academic disciplines—for making writing a concern of the entire university. One can find pockets of liveliness (and I did) in the theorizing and practice of first-year writing courses, but there is also a good deal of repetitive sameness for all the apparent diversity of subject matters, strategies, and texts in first-year writing courses. On the other hand, many institutions appear to be rethinking what students should do with writing after the completion of first-year composition and are coming up with new plans. Many colleges that are not now asking of students extended attention to their writing are planning to do so; they are discussing possible approaches. But if such discussions are happening in first-year writing programs (and they may be), I did not hear of many of them.

We confront, then, a body of first-year writing programs across the country in which a substantial majority exhibit one or more (usually quite a few) of the following characteristics: a heavy emphasis on the teaching of form (in sentences, in paragraphs, in whole essays); relative *in*attention to processes of substantive invention—gathering, interpreting, evaluating information, and reconstructing that information into new wholes; lack of visible attention to quality of reasoning and to what makes for forceful arguments on behalf of cogent ideas; an excess of emphasis on the "process" of composing, to the neglect of how one appraises the force and efficacy of a finished piece (i.e., appraises how well that piece might do its work with a reader or readers outside the classroom); a perhaps undue emphasis on the responses of inexpert fellow students to writers' drafts; a general lack of concern for the rhetoric of discourse—for why people compose, whom they address, what they do when they address readers, and how they can judge what they write. And we confront a profession not yet ready to commit itself to defining carefully its goals in teaching and to finding out in a systematic and serious way whether its courses are attaining those goals.

Furthermore, we continue as a profession to place the burden of doing most of our teaching on apprentices without substantial training, apprentices who often lack a clear understanding of who they are as teachers or of what they are teaching, and who may well be in the process of deciding that the teaching of writing is not the professional path they wish to take. In the festschrift for William Irmscher, *Balancing Acts*, Christine Farris essentially confirms these impressions (though she may not have meant to do so) with her reports of her conscientious and considerate efforts to help beginning graduate assistants start to understand—*while* they are teaching—what it means to be a teacher of writing. Farris's essay brings to a focus, for me, a central question: given the shortcomings I observe in so many curricula for writing and the inexperience of many faculty (as teachers, not just as teachers of writing), is the writing course as we now know it a justifiable *requirement* for all students (except maybe for an exempted few) in our colleges if that writing course is not taught by well-prepared, experienced teachers familiar with the theory and research on the teaching of writing? Even if one still answers that question "yes" (and I would incline to answer it "no"), would one answer "yes" to this question: ought the first-year course, as we know it, to be the *only* course in the curriculum where students are required to write and receive guidance in writing? I would answer this second question unequivocally "no."

There are, to be sure, formidable barriers in the way of making writing an all-university requirement. Many faculty will not ask for writing, they say, for numerous reasons: they do not themselves write and they lack confidence in *themselves* as writers; they lack the time to read the students' writing; the writing is so poor that they cannot read or understand it; there is no support for their spending the time needed to read the writing; they are not comfortable talking about writing; they do not know how to assign writing; they have too much material to cover to permit them to talk about writing; and so on. And probably no faculty will participate 100 percent, or 75 percent, or maybe even 66 percent in efforts to make writing an all-college requirement. Furthermore, there is no guarantee whatsoever that placing responsibility for much of the college's teaching of writing on faculty in the disciplines will bring greater benefits than locating that responsibility mostly in courses carrying the title "composition" (or "rhetoric" or "writing"). But many institutions *are* engaging faculty in the effort, and many, as the responses to the second survey show, are operating programs—essential if faculty in the disciplines are to help students extend their abilities at writing—to assist faculty across the campus in becoming more comfortable asking students to write in a variety of forms appropriate to their fields.

Consider the advantages of asking students in all disciplines to strengthen and extend their abilities at writing by composing within those disciplines. First, the teachers, though they may be inexperienced in the teaching of writing and not altogether comfortable with such teaching (limitations they may share with any number of the teaching staff in first-year writing), are in most cases warmly interested in and familiar with their subject areas, able to guide students in gathering and interpreting data for discussion in their writing, able to display and encourage mastery of the kinds of thinking and reasoning that are honored in their particular fields, and able to judge the quality of a student's observations, inferences, and arguments. They are thus in a position (as were the cooperating faculty from the various disciplines studied by Barbara Walvoord and Lucille McCarthy in their research study, *Thinking and Writing in College*) to respond as professionals in their fields to the writings submitted by students.

Second, teachers in academic fields who are willing to teach with writing but have little or no experience in doing so can perhaps be helped to assign, read, and respond to student writing in their fields more easily than inexperienced teachers of English can be helped to understand the essential principles and operations of discourse in a discipline outside English and to adopt the frames of reference within which the scholar in that field responds to writing in that field. There are exceptions, of course: the Brown University Writing Fellows Program helps undergraduates learn enough about central ideas and ways of seeing data in the various disciplines so that they can help students with their writing in those disciplines. But the writing fellow is a teacher's helper; the drafting and administering of assignments and the final evaluation of the student's work is the responsibility of the course instructor.

Third, students, when writing within a discipline, gain practice in addressing, and possibly even influencing the thinking of, a reader familiar with their subject. In James Britton's terms, the student has the opportunity to write as a "participant" in a potentially significant activity—an opportunity the student usually does not have in the first-year writing course, where some, perhaps many, assignments limit the student's role to that of "spectator": one who contemplates an experience and reflects upon it without being a part of it (97–125). Furthermore, in the role of participant, the student may have more of a chance, through writing, to engage in the important work of gathering and evaluating information about current practices or conditions and predicting the results of actions that might be taken—work that the student (especially one enrolled in a course in literature taught with writing) may not undertake much in first-year English.

Fourth, within discipline-centered courses, writing (as a way of learning and communicating) may be an activity in which the student is ready to engage because he or she is more aware of the value of writing as a means of practicing the discipline. Richard Light, director of the Harvard Assessment Seminars, reports just such increased recognition of the value of writing in courses students take in their chosen fields after the first year.

Finally, if the instructor in a discipline assigns writing and reads it at least to form an overall impression of its effectiveness, the student is writing and getting responses. And to have students continue writing after the first year is almost surely essential if they are to retain whatever abilities they have as writers. Like many abilities, the ability to write weakens if not exercised; the student who, completing a composition course, sighs with relief at not having to "worry" any more about writing is probably someone whose writing may weaken over time, as did that of some students discussed in Kitzhaber's study of writing at Dartmouth.

The arguments that favor a requirement of writing in the academic disciplines, of course, do not necessarily demonstrate the inappropriateness of requiring all students to take a first-year course in writing. One might argue— I have heard it argued, though never demonstrated—that the opportunity to write under the watchful eyes of intelligent people, however inexperienced, is important for students even if the teacher is not familiar with the workings of discourse or with ways of gathering data and constructing thought in the field under discussion, and even if that teacher is not a perceptive reader of academic prose. (This argument, I think, poses a question that is open to investigation. But, as noted earlier, our profession does not evaluate its work; it does not examine the impact of its instruction on students as they proceed through their college careers. And one might guess that the impact of instruction could well depend on the alertness and perceptivity of the teacher as maker of assignments and as reader of texts.) I have heard it argued that if the requirement of a first-year course in writing is dropped, there will be no chance to improve the teaching of writing in that course so that the course will become more valuable. That argument comes to me without much power, because so few changes now seem to be in process in first-year writing, and our profession has had so many years in which to decide upon and inaugurate such changes.

My own recommendation at the moment would be to place first-year students in a discipline-centered writing course, taught by faculty in the discipline, instead of in a "generic" writing course, unless the teachers of writing on the campus are well prepared and experienced and are perceptive readers. Critics will be quick to point out the demands that such a course would make on teaching staff, though some of those demands might be met by reducing the number of staff teaching the generic writing course and using funds thus released to make teaching loads more reasonable for faculty who commit themselves to asking students for writing. But where to locate instruction in writing, of course, is not an either/or question; faculties may well want to retain some sort of instruction in essential *activities* of writing early in the student's career, while assigning major responsibility for evoking effective written communication to courses in the disciplines. They may want to link discipline-centered courses with instruction and guidance in writing, as has been done at several institutions. (At one four-year college in CUNY, first-level courses in some disciplines were at one time connected with study labs for the practice of reading and writing, for students designated "underprepared.") Faculty can devise several curriculum plans for instruction in writing and support of students' writing and can evaluate the suitability of each within the institution's overall goals. This chapter is in part an invitation to faculty to engage in that activity of invention.

Regardless of the outcome of the argument against *requiring* a first-year course in writing (there is no suggestion here that such a course not be offered to students who elect to take it), I think that the need for extended attention to writing—the need for using writing to teach, and the need for broadening and widening students' powers to deal in writing with complex subjects—after the first year course now amounts to a moral imperative. In many of today's first-year writing courses there is too much diffuseness, too little attention to ways of gathering data, generating ideas, and developing thought, too little attention to fundamental problems of addressing readers effectively, and too much inexperienced teaching for the course to stand as the only instruction in writing our students receive.

If a liberal education seeks, at least in part, to develop students who understand what it means to have ideas, to support those ideas cogently, to develop them amply, and to express them to readers forcefully, then in such education writing must be a part of every course or tutorial the student takes. It is, I think, a university's moral obligation to enact the central importance of writing as the means by which human beings construct their reality, learn, and share their learning.

Acknowledgments

I want to thank the following people for their helpful readings of an earlier draft of this chapter: Vincent Gillespie and Ross Winterowd (editors of this volume), Christopher Thaiss (George Mason University), and especially my colleague and friend Judith Entes (Baruch College, CUNY). Dr. Entes has given me highly perceptive readings of this chapter and of other essays on related issues.

Works Cited

Britton, James. *Language and Learning*. London: Allen Lane/The Penguin Press, 1970.

Farris, Christine R. "Critical Reflection, Change, and the Practice of a Theory of Composition." *Balancing Acts: Essays on the Teaching of Writing in Honor of William F. Irmscher*. Ed. Virginia A. Chappell, Mary Louise Buley-Meissner, and Chris Anderson. Carbondale: Southern Illinois UP, 1991. 97–110.

Flower, Linda, et al. "Detection, Diagnosis, and the Strategies of Revision." *College Composition and Communication* 37 (1986): 16–55.

Hutchings, Pat. *The Teaching Portfolio*. Washington, DC: American Association for Higher Education, 1992.

Kitzhaber, Albert. *Themes, Theories, and Therapy: The Teaching of Writing in College*. New York: McGraw-Hill, 1963.

Larson, Richard. "The Research Paper in the Writing Course: A Non-Form of Writing." *College English* 44 (1982): 811–16.

Light, Richard J. *The Harvard Assessment Seminars: Second Report*. Cambridge: Harvard University Graduate School of Education and Kennedy School of Government, 1992.

Moffett, James. "Learning to Write by Writing." *Teaching the Universe of Discourse*. Boston: Houghton Mifflin, 1968. 188–210.

Rose, Mike. "Rigid Rules, Inflexible Plans, and the Stifling of Language: A Cognitivist Analysis of Writer's Block." *CCC* 31 (1980): 389–401.

Walvoord, Barbara, and Lucille McCarthy. *Thinking and Writing in College*. Urbana, IL: NCTE, 1991.

9   **Impediments to Change in Writing-Across-the-Curriculum Programs**

Richard E. Young

I

I WOULD LIKE TO USE AS A POINT OF DEPARTURE A STORY TOLD TO the anthropologist Edward Hall by John Evans, who was at one time a superintendent of the Northern Pueblo Agency and who as a young man spent many years among the Taos Indians. The Taos Indians, Hall says,

> are a very independent people who carefully guard all their culture from the white man. They even make a secret of how to say "Thank you" in Taos. This makes it exceedingly difficult for the government representatives whose job it is to work with them. According to Evans, there had been some difficulty finding an agricultural extension agent who could work with the Taos. Finally a young man was chosen who liked the Taos and who was careful to approach them slowly. Everything went along very well and it seemed that he was, indeed, the right man for a very ticklish job. When spring arrived, however, Evans was visited in Albuquerque by the agriculturist, who was wearing a very long face. Evans asked, "What's the matter with you? You look depressed." His visitor replied, "As a matter of fact I am. I don't know what's wrong. The Indians don't like me any more. They won't do any of the things I tell them." Evans promised to find out what he could. The next time there was a council meeting at Taos he took one of the

older Indians aside and asked him what was wrong with the tribe and the young man. His friend looked him in the eye and said, "John, he just doesn't know certain things! You know, John—*think.*" Suddenly Evans understood. In the spring the Taos believe that Mother Earth is pregnant. To protect the surface of the earth they do not drive their wagons to town, they take all the shoes off their horses, they refuse to wear hardsoled shoes themselves. Our agriculturalist had been trying to institute a program of early-spring plowing! (78)

Evans is, of course, talking about a clash of cultures, of shared beliefs, attitudes, and social patterns that shape our lives in pervasive and unsuspected ways. We see in his story an important characteristic of culturally shaped behavior: the beliefs that drive the behavior are often tacitly held and the behavior is often habitual. The beliefs go without saying. The silences, what isn't said, what it's felt doesn't need to be said, may be more important than what is said. Culture, says Hall, "is a mold in which we are all cast, and it controls our lives in many unsuspected ways" (38). However, difficulty in identifying and articulating cultural beliefs and patterns of behavior does not render them any less influential; in fact it may make them more potent since their tacit nature makes them more immune to examination and revision. The difference in the beliefs and practices of the outsider and of the insider can function like an invisible wall between the participants that precludes cooperation.

I want to assume here that the university community has its own characteristic culture—though perhaps cultures may be more accurate, since there are probably several grouped together in a university, despite its name. Or if not *culture* as Hall uses the term, something very like it. If that is the case, then outsiders trying to introduce new beliefs and practices that are inconsistent with the well-established and widely shared beliefs and practices of the community are likely to find themselves in the position rather like that of the young agriculturist—up against substantial resistance that they may well sense but not understand and that subverts their efforts to bring about change.

Those working on writing-across-the-curriculum (WAC) programs have often noted conflicts over tacit assumptions and experienced similar consequences in their dealings with colleagues.[1] For example, Deborah Swanson-Owens in her recent article "Identifying Natural Sources of Resistance: A Case Study of Implementing Writing Across the Curriculum" describes the way her efforts at cooperation with two high-school teachers in a WAC program were subverted by basic differences in educational assumptions. She reports that despite what appeared to be a genuine willingness to cooperate with her, the teachers resisted such standard practices of WAC as collaborative learning and writing to learn. Rather than trying to account for the resistance in terms of differences over specific teaching practices, Swanson-Owens looked to what she characterized as underlying conditions that influence instructional practice. "Because," she says, "these conditions qualify the very process by which curricular goals are accomplished, they are a potential source of resistance. Ostensibly, these conditions must either be met or altogether changed if the [proposed new] curricular system is to be productive from the point of view of the practitioner" (91).

The underlying conditions she describes as divisive include beliefs held by herself and the two teachers, Jack and Naomi, about the source of new knowledge, about the nature of the learning process, and about how instructional goals are specified. In regard to beliefs about the source of new knowledge, she says,

> Jack believes that meaning and thus the source of new knowledge resides in the text. For Naomi, new knowledge develops from new experiences, experiences which are generated and monitored by the teacher. The fact that both teachers believe the source of new knowledge lies somewhere outside the students helps to explain why each felt the need to provide much of the content and control the structure of the writing tasks. (91)

Swanson-Owens, however, in her suggestion that they make use of writing-to-learn techniques, was working out of quite different underlying beliefs. "Unlike either of these teachers," she says,

> I consider the students as much a source of new knowledge as the materials and activities themselves. Believing that new knowledge is conditioned by old knowledge, I felt that the writing tasks should provide less structure for and ask for more personal analysis from the students—that freedom to generate meaning rather than re-produce it would encourage students to use more complex thinking skills and, in the process, generate new knowledge. For me, then, learning depends on—and thus should emphasize—the students' interpretation of the materials. (91)

In generalizing about the study, Swanson-Owens remarks that

> those concerned with effective implementation of writing across the curriculum need to look closely at the ways in which such reform efforts interact with the practical knowledge or conventional wisdom that guides teachers' responses to such initiatives. Without such an understanding, it is easy to overestimate the fit between outsider and insider perspectives, a miscalculation which has doomed many reform efforts. (71)

A close examination of the beliefs held by faculty in virtually any WAC training workshop would quite likely reveal comparable disagreements.

I introduce Swanson-Owen's work as a way of clarifying the kind of problem I want to talk about. Her study is a persuasive elaboration of what it means to presume too much in our collaborations with our colleagues; and what she has to say is clearly of considerable interest to anyone working in a WAC program. However, to the extent that the conflicts she describes are clashes between individual beliefs only (i.e., not the shared beliefs of entire groups), they are not quite what I have in mind. For they do not *necessarily* challenge the basic concepts of writing across the curriculum, only particular efforts to establish particular programs. In contrast, where conflicts arise over basic assumptions that are widely shared in academic communities—that is, in a way analogous to the clash of beliefs held by the agricultural agent on the one hand and by the Taos community on the other—the situation becomes much more problematic for the educational innovator.

II

Consider the belief that issues of linguistic form and convention can be sharply separated from issues of knowledge and social context. It is a position that we might call *Ramistic dualism*, after one of its early and most influential proponents (Ong 161). It is an important belief in the sense that it reflects a basic philosophic issue, the relation between language and thought; it is also important because it provides a foundation for other rhetorical beliefs and practices. But like so many fundamental beliefs, it is usually tacitly held, unarticulated and even unacknowledged until something, like a conflict of the sort Swanson-Owens describes, leads us to attend to it.

One common form the belief takes, though not the only one, is what Karen LeFevre calls the "copy theory" of language. "With this view," she says, "language is thought to be a copy of inner thought or pure ideas, which may or may not occur in linguistic form. Language is what we use to capture thought and report results" (101). We can often see the influence of the belief in our casual conversation and in our comments to students: we speak of thinking before writing, of putting ideas into words, of not saying what we mean, about having good ideas but not being able to express them, of language being the clothes of thought, and so on— all of which imply the possibility of sharply separating language and content. Having been taught well, our students share the belief with us. In an article appearing in a 1912 issue of the *English Journal* (the belief was well established even then), John Cunliffe tells a story familiar to any teacher of English about a student in his literature course who objected to being penalized for careless writing, the student protesting that "I thought it was an examination in literature. I didn't know it was an exercise in composition. I don't call that a square deal" (Combies 83).

Slevin, Fort, and O'Connor observe that

> in the eyes of many teachers, the ultimate goal for student writing
> is to make the writing, to some extent, "unimportant." What teach-
> ers want in "good" writing is unobtrusive, transparent prose that

does not get in the way of the perception of the truths being written about.

. . . Fundamental to this view is the separability of "writing"
from content and the assumption that there is neutral prose. Such
an attitude is common, perhaps a defining characteristic of most academics' views of writing. (11)

The "ultimate goal for student writing" may seem commonsensical and,
hence, incontestable. But we might keep in mind Clifford Geertz's definition
of common sense; it is "not what the mind cleared of cant spontaneously
apprehends [but] what the mind filled with presuppositions concludes" (Russell, *Writing* 17).

The belief is implicit even today in many of our composition texts and
handbooks, with their decontextualized advice on good writing. One might
argue that it is also present in the ubiquitous compendiums of readings for
freshman composition. For the assumption that language and content are
separable does not imply that writing can be taught without some sort of
content. Instead, in writing programs governed by this dualistic conception
of writing, content takes on an instrumental role, becoming simply something
to write about rather than the motive for writing. It is not something the
writer uses his art to convey; it is something the writer uses in order to
acquire his art. That would explain the wide variation in readings from one
composition course to another. The only requirements the teacher places on
the subject matter for the course are that it interest the student and that it can
be understood in a short time, so that it doesn't get in the way of the real
business of the course—which is teaching writing. The assumption implies
no necessary links between linguistic forms and content: the same rhetorical
skills can be cultivated no matter whether one writes about personal experiences, King Lear, or who gets the kidney machine.

Not surprisingly, the assumption that language and content are separable
is implicit in the freshman composition course itself, which typically precedes
and is separate from study in the disciplines. As David Russell remarks in his
history of writing in the disciplines,

when late-nineteenth century educators cast about for ways to solve
the "problem" of student writing, they eventually settled on a single freshman course of about fifteen or thirty weeks (successor to a
very different rhetoric course in the old liberal curriculum). Though
it was taught in many ways to students of every kind, freshman
composition almost always treated writing as a generalizable elementary skill, independent of disciplinary content. The course focused
on mechanical skills: correct grammar, spelling, and usage necessary for transcribing preexisting, fully formed speech or thought
into correct written form. (*Writing* 7)

This highly reductive conception of rhetoric instruction has proven to
be enormously advantageous to English departments, since teaching it requires

no professional qualifications other than the ability to write standard edited English. The conception has allowed English departments to use the course as the principal means of support for graduate students specializing in literary studies; the grad students need no special training prior to going into the writing classroom since they already possess a high level of literacy. The economic value of the course to graduate programs coupled with the minimal requirements for teaching it offer at least a partial explanation for the course's remarkable durability in the face of a long history of attacks on its ineffectiveness (Greenbaum). Another result of the split between language and content has been to devalue the study of writing, since it reduces writing to little more than a concern for the proprieties of standard edited English; with that devaluing has come the familiar political configuration in English departments with the literary faculty dominating the teachers of writing and controlling the reward system.

To try to introduce and sustain innovative writing practices and programs in academic communities where practices incompatible with it are widespread would appear to require that we change the assumptions on which they rest. This is likely to be a difficult task if the assumptions are as fundamental and widespread as the one I have been discussing, though probably not an impossible task. But it becomes much more difficult when we realize that the belief that issues of writing and linguistic convention can be sharply separated from issues of knowledge and social context has been so thoroughly institutionalized that changing it would appear to require changes in the structures of the academic organization itself, not to mention all the practices that have grown up around it.

In her discussion of the Cooperation Movement, a WAC-like educational movement that was popular early in the century, Patricia Combies remarks that

> the movement in which the composition teacher taught writing while the content came from other disciplines separated content and form. The work was seen in two distinct pieces. Language, rather than being a vehicle for thought or communication, was seen as an ornament added after one had invented the content. An outgrowth of this view of cooperative English was that the composition teacher was often seen as an editor, who corrected papers for other classes for form. As early as 1914, C. S. Duncan wrote that members of other departments, feeling unable to correct the language problems, have demanded that the English department correct the papers. He claimed that if English teachers served only as editors, then content and form were definitely seen as separate entities. . . . The danger of this "handmaiden" view of composition is that it devalues any study of writing in itself. Writing becomes identified not so much with cogent thinking as with technical efficiency, thus destroying the original goal of the program. (87)

The point I am trying to make in this discussion of Ramistic dualism is that the belief permeates the academic community and gives shape and meaning to many of its organizational structures, policies, and practices. That is, the belief functions in academic life much as the belief of the Taos community functions in their cultural practices. It seems safe to say, then, that any proposal for writing instruction that rests on beliefs incompatible with those of the prevailing system is in for trouble.

III

Let me push my argument a bit further. About four years ago as part of a WAC project, Lili Velez and I began working on writing problems with Linda Kauffman, a senior lecturer in biology who taught the year-long laboratory course for upper-level biology students at Carnegie Mellon University. Kauffman's students, like so many in the university community, professed the sort of dualism I have been discussing. Hence we thought we should expand their awareness of the uses of language by proposing changes in Kauffman's teaching methods, which would show students the power of language to elicit new ideas and enhance learning in the discipline. So Velez and I proposed introducing into her course one of the characteristic techniques of WAC pedagogy, the journal. We asked Kauffman whether she already required students to keep some sort of journal or notebook. (In true missionary fashion, Velez and I were trying to introduce new practices by grafting them on similar but already well-established ones.) When she said that her students were required to keep a record of their lab work in a notebook, we suggested that the functions of the notebook be expanded to include what the WAC literature associates with the epistemic uses of language (see, for example, Fulwiler, "Personal Connection"; Kalmbach, "Laboratory Reports"; and Selfe and Arbabi). These include using the journal as a place to identify and explicate problems as they arise in the student's thinking, to speculate about them, and to carry on a dialogue with teachers.

Kauffman's reply was dismaying. She said that while the suggestion was not unreasonable, the lab notebooks of professional researchers are often used in patent applications and in product litigation and hence are controlled by strict conventions. Her students' notebooks had to be string-bound; the pages had to be numbered before they were written on; ink had to be used, not pencil; and lines had to be drawn through any blank space at the end of pages—all this so that no undetectable alterations could be made after the original entries. Since Kauffman was trying to teach her students how to behave like professional biologists, our proposal to adapt their notebooks to new uses, no matter how reasonable it seemed, was simply inappropriate. The problem was not that keeping journals in Kauffman's class was necessarily a bad idea; even if the students had to keep two separate journals for different pedagogical purposes, it might well be a profitable activity. The problem for

Velez and me was that we began to think that we did not know enough about rhetorical practices in biology to make useful suggestions. We were beginning to experience the Taos syndrome. That experience led to abandoning our missionary attitude and assuming the role of the anthropologist. With that new role came an intense effort to understand the rhetorical practices of that particular disciplinary community.

When Kauffman talked about writing and writing instruction, she, like her students, appeared to be drawing on the tradition of rhetorical dualism. But when she talked about teaching biology and the language practices of biologists, another, contrastive conception of the relation of language and content seemed to be invoked—what might be called *rhetorical monism.*[2] In monistic conceptions of rhetorical behavior, content plays an intrinsic role in writing since it shapes and in turn is shaped by linguistic and rhetorical choices. When a monistic view of the relation of language and content appears in course work, it is likely to be in advanced courses in the disciplines where writing is seen as part of the professional training of the student, not as a separate educational goal. In such courses, content is seen as inseparable from language; thus it constrains writing and makes a difference in what particular writing skills are learned. To teach the subject matter of a discipline is, in effect, to simultaneously teach languaging about the discipline; and, perhaps also true, to teach languaging in the discipline is to teach the subject matter of the discipline, though that road to disciplinary competence is not often taken.

As was the case with the dualism noted earlier, the monism here is accompanied by a characteristic set of practices. For example, rhetorical monism tends to encourage not the formal teaching of writing but informal learning. We can see the process of learning rhetorical skills, as distinguished from teaching them, in the following taped interview with one of Kauffman's students:

> B[ill]: The next year, though, I plan on taking . . . two classes in
> the spring which are graduate-level courses. The whole theme is
> to read [a report] and discuss it, . . . be able to critique them
> . . . you know, if what you see is wrong with that approach,
> [the] conclusions, [the] capabilities of their methods from the
> data, results. . . . And essentially it's just like a round table. Peo-
> ple sit there, they've read them, give their ideas. . . . We've
> done that a little bit in the classes this semester . . . where he
> had a paper that he wanted everyone to read. Everybody read
> it, and myself and somebody else, one other person . . . talked
> about, which makes you kind of feel pretty stupid because if no
> one else wants to say anything . . . whereas in graduate courses
> that's what you're really wanted [to do].
>
> V[elez]: Do you think that the situation of those round table classes
> are comparable to the kinds of the discussion you might have at
> a lab meeting? Were you looking for research procedures . . . ?

B: Our lab meetings, you have a lab meeting followed by a journal article. Lab meeting people come in and discuss the results . . . where to go next, what everyone thinks. . . . And then after we do have a journal [club] where somebody's read a paper and he gets up and essentially outlines it, and starts discussing it, and people, if they have questions they'll ask you, and if they have thoughts, so, it's not quite a round table discussion. . . .

V: Is that a function of your group . . . ?

B: Uh-huh, well it's essentially, it forces people not to get hooked into just [one way of thinking], it keeps their eyes open so they're not ignorant of what's going on. And sometimes you're forced to read a section of the paper that you're not comfortable with, so you have to go back and read it. Now the previous papers, you get a feel for it.

The focus of such critical activity is not on the discourse as a rhetorical act but on the relation of the method to the data and the conclusions drawn from the data.

One important way biology students learn the rhetorical practices of their discipline appears to be by criticizing the arguments of scientific reports. When we asked Kauffman how biologists acquired their rhetorical skill, she replied that "these kinds of [rhetorical] skills [that enable students] . . . to read them [i.e., scientific articles] effectively, summarize them effectively, write them up effectively, and find them in the library are things which they're expected to be able to do, and I, for the life of me, don't know how they learn how. I really don't." That is, she was participating in an educational practice characteristic of instruction in the disciplines without realizing what assumptions drove the practice. I don't want that to sound condescending; I didn't realize it either until I began trying to tease out the presuppositions that were operating in her class.

In our collaboration with Kauffman, Velez and I were the writing teachers; she was a biology teacher who had her students doing biology. Surprisingly, her students wrote as much in a semester as ours did. If we can generalize from our experience with this course to the discipline as a whole, we can say that in doing biology students learn, almost as an afterthought, to be rhetoricians in biology. At least many of them do. Not much is heard from those who never acquire the rhetorical skills, since they leave the discipline. One of the great disadvantages of this informal method of cultivating rhetorical skill is that it presents the student with a sink-or-swim situation.

Traditional writing programs, based on Ramistic dualism with freshman composition at their center, take their shape from the need to cultivate writing skills in novices. Disciplinary education, on the other hand, in which a rhetorical monism is assumed, takes its shape from the practice of experts and pays little attention to the needs of novice students trying to enter a new discourse community. In the university, the two systems exist in a reasonably stable and complementary relationship, dualism underpinning the freshman service courses offered by the English department, monism underpinning the upper-level courses in the disciplines. Kauffman's expression on different occasions of both dualistic and monistic views only reflects the beliefs and practices of the larger community.

IV

In a survey of 194 writing-across-the-curriculum programs, C. W. Griffin observes that "most have something in common—the premises on which they are based" (402). He lists three:

1. Writing skills must be practiced and reinforced throughout the curriculum, otherwise they will atrophy, no matter how well they are taught in the beginning. . . .
2. To write is to learn. . . .
3. Since written discourse is central to a university education, the responsibility for the quality of student writing is a university-wide one. (402–3)

As is no doubt apparent, none of the principles listed by Griffin is consistent with traditional principles and practices the academic community has developed to teach students to write. That is, the notion that writing skills must be practiced and reinforced throughout the curriculum is inconsistent with concentrating writing instruction in the freshman year. Writing to learn is inconsistent with the notion that writing follows learning. The notion that responsibility for the quality of student writing is a university-wide responsibility is inconsistent with the English department's proprietary claims on courses in writing as well as the educational practices in the various disciplines.

However, such inconsistencies are likely to come to our attention not in disputes over fundamental issues in rhetorical theory but in disputes over particular practices. For example, in his article "The Politics of Research," James Kalmbach discusses a questionnaire circulated at Michigan Technological University by a curricular policy committee opposed to the WAC program. "During the five years of the program," Kalmbach remarks,

> the Humanities Department had gradually shifted from a product to a process orientation in the teaching of writing. If the committee, none of whom had ever attended a workshop, could demonstrate that we weren't doing a good job of teaching freshman composition or that the faculty wasn't satisfied with the new process approach to teaching writing, then it could, by implication, discredit the writing-across-the-curriculum program.
>
> I had seen an early draft of the questionnaire and it had a lot of problems. . . .

The original draft of this questionnaire had stated as its formal objective:

> The purpose of this questionnaire is to solicit the views of the academic faculty on the goals and objectives of Freshman English.

The real objective of the questionnaire, however, appeared just a few lines later:

> Some persons have expressed concern that the new focus advocated in the writing across the curriculum program on "expressive writing" (personal letters, diaries, journals, and reflections in which grammar, spelling, word usage, and overall structure are deemphasized) is consuming time and effort which might be better allocated to "transactional writing" (formal reports, themes, and term papers in which grammar, spelling, word usage, and overall structure are emphasized).

> . . . The single-minded focus of the original draft questionnaire on the mechanical elements of composition had brought a strong protest from our department. We all agreed that mechanical correctness was important, but we felt that our writing program encompassed other things as well. Later versions of the questionnaire were fairer, but certain questions had a habit of reappearing unchanged no matter how hard we objected. (217–18)

The fundamental beliefs are there and at work in the conflict, but the debate is conducted on a less fundamental level.

V

The psychologist Paul Watzlawick has noted two kinds of systemic change:

> one that occurs within a given system which itself remains unchanged, and one whose occurrence changes the system itself. To exemplify this distinction in more behavioral terms: a person having a nightmare can do many things *in* his dream—run, hide, fight, scream, jump off a cliff, etc.— but no change from any one of these behaviors to another would ever terminate the nightmare. *We shall henceforth refer to this kind of change as first-order change.* The one way out of a dream involves a change from dreaming to waking. Waking, obviously, is no longer part of the dream, but a change to an altogether different state. *This kind of change will from now on be referred to as second-order change.* (Watzlawick, Weakland, and Fisch 10–11)

The mistake the young agricultural agent made in proposing spring plowing to the Taos community was to assume that he was proposing a first-order change; to the Taos it was a second-order change. To the agriculturist, spring plowing appeared to be a modest and desirable alteration of a conventional agricultural practice. To the Taos, it threatened the community itself, and they responded accordingly.

As we become more familiar with the history of cross-disciplinary writing education in this country, we see that the writing-across-the-curriculum movement is only the most recent, although the most formidable, of a series of similar educational experiments that began about a century ago. During that time scores of WAC-like programs were developed around the country. What should give us pause for thought is that not one of those programs has survived. Undoubtedly there are many reasons for their disappearance. But I suspect that a fundamental one is a failure to understand what we are up against, which is more than the normal inertia of the institution. When we introduce WAC principles and practices into the university community, we are proposing a second-order change, that is, as I have tried to suggest, a change in the shared beliefs, attitudes, and social patterns that shape our lives in pervasive and unsuspected ways.

Notes

1. See, for example, Fulwiler ("How Well"), Hairston, Heller, Kalmbach ("Politics"), Maimon, McCarthy, McLeod, Russell ("Writing," "Romantics"), and Young and Fulwiler.

2. Louis Milic notes a similar theoretical inconsistency on the same issue with many English teachers (277).

Works Cited

Combies, Patricia. "The Struggle to Establish a Profession: An Historical Survey of the Status of College Composition Teachers, 1900–1950." Diss. Carnegie Mellon U, 1987.

Fulwiler, Toby. "How Well Does Writing Across the Curriculum Work?" *College English* 46 (1984): 113–25.

———. "The Personal Connection: Journal Writing Across the Curriculum." *Language Connections: Writing and Reading Across the Curriculum*. Ed. Toby Fulwiler and Art Young. Urbana, IL: NCTE, 1982. 15–31.

Greenbaum, Leonard. "The Tradition of Complaint." *College English* 31 (1969): 174–87.

Griffin, C. W. "Programs for Writing Across the Curriculum: A Report." *CCC* 36 (1985): 398–403.

Hairston, Maxine. "Some Speculations About the Future of Writing Programs." *WPA: Writing Program Administration* 11.3 (1988): 9–16.

Hall, Edward T. *The Silent Language*. Greenwich, CT: Fawcett-Premier, 1961.

Heller, Scott. "50 Lecturers Lose Their Jobs in a Dispute over How—and If—Writing Can Be Taught." *Chronicle of Higher Education* 17 (Apr. 1985): 23–24.

Kalmbach, James R. "The Laboratory Reports of Engineering Students." *Writing Across the Disciplines: Research into Practice*. Ed. Art Young and Toby Fulwiler. Upper Montclair, NJ: Boynton/Cook, 1986. 176–83.

——. "The Politics of Research." *Writing Across the Disciplines: Research into Practice.* Ed. Art Young and Toby Fulwiler. Upper Montclair, NJ: Boynton/Cook, 1986. 217–27.

LeFevre, Karen Burke. *Invention as a Social Act.* Carbondale, IL: Southern Illinois UP, 1987.

McCarthy, Lucille Parkinson. "A Stranger in Strange Lands: A College Student Writing Across the Curriculum." *Research in the Teaching of English* 21 (1987): 233–65.

McLeod, Susan. "Defining Writing Across the Curriculum." *WPA: Writing Program Administration* 11.1–2 (1987):19–24.

Maimon, Elaine P. "Cinderella to Hercules: Demythologizing Composition Across the Curriculum. " *Journal of Basic Writing* 2.4 (1980): 3–11.

Milic, Louis. "The Problem of Style." *Contemporary Rhetoric: A Conceptual Background with Readings.* Ed. W. Ross Winterowd. New York: Harcourt, 1975. 271–95.

Olson, Gary A., and Joseph M. Moxley. "Directing Freshman Composition: The Limits of Authority." *CCC* 40 (1989): 51–60.

Ong, Walter. *Rhetoric, Romance and Technology.* Ithaca, NY: Cornell UP, 1971.

Russell, David R. "Romantics on Writing: Liberal Culture and the Abolition of Composition Courses." *Rhetoric Review* 6 (1988): 132–48.

——. "Writing Across the Curriculum and the Communications Movement: Some Lessons from the Past." *CCC* 38 (1987): 184–94.

——. *Writing in the Academic Disciplines, 1870–1990: A Curricular History.* Carbondale, IL: Southern Illinois UP, 1991.

Selfe, Cynthia L., and Freydoon Arbabi. "Writing to Learn: Engineering Student Journals." *Writing Across the Disciplines: Research into Practice.* Ed. Art Young and Toby Fulwiler. Upper Montclair, NJ: Boynton/Cook, 1986. 184–91.

Slevin, James, Keith Fort, and Patricia E. O'Connor. "Georgetown University." *Programs That Work.* Ed. Toby Fulwiler and Art Young. Upper Montclair, NJ: Boynton/Cook,1990. 9–28.

Swanson-Owens, Deborah. "Identifying Natural Sources of Resistance: A Case Study of Implementing Writing Across the Curriculum." *Research in the Teaching of English* 20 (1986): 69–97.

Watzlawick, Paul, John H. Weakland, and Richard Fisch. *Change: Principles of Problem Formation and Problem Resolution.* New York: Norton, 1974.

Young, Art, and Toby Fulwiler. "The Enemies of Writing Across the Curriculum." *Programs That Work.* Ed. Toby Fulwiler and Art Young. Upper Montclair, NJ: Boynton/Cook,1990. 287–94.

10 No Longer a Brand New World
The Development of Bibliographic Resources in Composition

Paul T. Bryant

AT THE 1973 ANNUAL MEETING OF THE CONFERENCE ON COLLEGE COMposition and Communication in a keynote address later published in *College Composition and Communication*, I complained that composition teachers, particularly those who wrote about composition and the teaching of composition, were not building on what had gone before. We were, I said, too often like the goose, for whom, according to barnyard lore, it is a brand new world every morning. Like geese we seemed to have no memory, no ability to learn from experience. We were not profiting from knowledge gained and tested by our predecessors, as do scientists, nor were we working from any shared artistic tradition, although the teaching of composition can be approached both as a science and as an art. In issue after issue of our journals, one could read the same hortatory—or self-congratulatory—accounts of individual classroom techniques, what Stephen North has since dubbed "practitioner lore" (23). Year after year, at meetings like those of the CCCC, one could hear the same "innovative and exciting new ideas" described, giving the eerie sense of being caught in a time warp that kept replaying the same events. Indeed, as the immortal Berra is supposed to have said, it was all too often "déjà vu all over again."

What was needed, I said, was a greater sense of continuity and development among composition teachers and researchers. For objective, empirically verifiable knowledge there should be some sense of linear progress, building on the knowledge already gained, rather than endless repetitions of the same experiments. For those aspects of composition more associated with art than with science, there should be awareness of the techniques and traditions that have already been established. The same techniques should not have to be discovered—and hailed as innovative—several times every generation.

One step toward such goals, I suggested, was the development of bibliographic resources for composition and the teaching of composition. With adequate bibliographic "control" of the field, there would be no excuse for moving endlessly in intellectual circles. Every teacher, every scholar and researcher, would have a clear responsibility for awareness of what has gone before, and every journal editor would require that such awareness be displayed in any article accepted for publication. Bibliographic control would promote genuine progress in the field by giving us a readily available means of learning from each other and from the past.

Response to my complaint and plea has been mixed over the years since. Stephen North has called it a harsh assessment of practitioners (326) and "professional self-flagellation" (332), saying I accused composition teachers of being simple-minded and malevolent (327).[1] Patrick Scott calls it "the classic protest" against excessive reliance on local practitioner lore rather than published scholarly research ("Bibliographic Resources" 91).

There were two immediate responses to my remarks in the form of bibliographic projects. Before the 1973 meeting was over, Gary Tate had begun to plan his *Teaching Composition: Ten Bibliographic Essays* (vii–viii). Richard Larson, by whose invitation I had made my presentation, was discussing the selected bibliography he soon thereafter began publishing annually in *College Composition and Communication*, covering 1973–1978. Composition was preparing to take useful steps toward greater academic respectability and a basis for building on knowledge already gained. These were not to be the definitive resources I envisioned, but they did further the process of accustoming composition teachers and researchers to the idea of developing a knowledge community—a discipline.

My concern, of course, was hardly new. It may have provided the tiny bit of irritant that prompted Tate and Larson to produce their particular pearls of bibliography, but others had already expressed similar concerns, and other significant responses had been made. Indeed, I acknowledged as much in my paper, citing both Robert Gorrell's article "The Traditional Course: When Is Old Hat New" and Richard Jordan's "An Interview with Ben Jonson, Composition Teacher" from the October 1972 *CCC* as cases in point ("Brand New World" 30).

Although composition and composition pedagogy have a long and honorable history, often under the rubric of "rhetoric" (see North, Horner), their status as serious academic subjects had been eclipsed in the newly developing English departments in the first half of this century. These departments saw composition not as a potential field for serious research but rather as a matter of "oral folklore" (Scott, "Bibliographic Resources" 73) or "practitioner lore" (North ch. 1), exchanged locally among teachers every day but seldom if ever broadened into the kind of generally held knowledge that can form the basis for an academic discipline. The most common kinds of writing about composition were textbooks and "the hortatory conference paper" (Scott, "Bibliographic Resources" 73).

The founding, in 1949, of the Conference on College Composition and Communication within the already well established National Council of Teachers of English began the development of a professional base for composition as a coherent discipline, but its members were slow to take advantage of this opportunity. As late as 1963, Albert Kitzhaber, as president-elect of NCTE, reproached CCCC for doing no more than holding an annual convention and publishing a "lively journal." In its fifteen years of existence, Kitzhaber complained, CCCC had taken no stands and introduced no order into the "chaos" of college composition. Kitzhaber concluded, "It has not . . . consistently exerted the kind of intelligent and courageous leadership in the profession that alone, I think, can justify its existence in the long run" ("4C" 135).

In that same period, the "communication" movement, given equal billing with composition in the CCCC's title, had come and gone. An effort to reestablish ties with speech and journalism—souls that had strayed from the English fold much earlier—"communication" did succeed, perhaps, in developing stronger connections with the social sciences, but by 1963 this movement was "nearly extinct" (136). The problem was that the CCCC had no "mode of inquiry" or real definition of a discipline through which order and direction could be achieved (North 15).

In the 1950s and 1960s, nevertheless, scholarship and writing about composition began to change, with or without leadership from the CCCC. Some of the stimulus for change may have been increasing attention to student writing skills by those outside of English departments. Some may have come from the alarm bells rung by English scholars like Albert Kitzhaber in his *Themes, Theories, and Therapy*. Some may have come as a result of action by the federal government in such programs as the National Defense Education Act (North 9–17). Certainly academe in this country has shown a marked willingness to adopt federal educational priorities if they are accompanied by federal funds. Whatever the complex sets of stimuli may have been, in the 1950s and 1960s composition began its development from a "service" subject, teaching based on practitioner lore, to a recognizable discipline with a formal research base.

Such changes take time, making it difficult to assign particular dates and occasions to their advent, but if we want a milestone to indicate the "birth" of "modern composition," perhaps the year 1963 will serve as well as any (North 15). That was the year in which *Research in Written Composition*, by Richard Braddock, Richard Lloyd-Jones, and Lowell Schoer, was published by the National Council of Teachers of English.

This slim monograph calls for composition research modeled on the rigor and methods of scientific research, and it reviews only work that has used the scientific method (1). In that process, a full ten years before my complaint, Braddock, Lloyd-Jones, and Schoer observe that research in composition "has not frequently been conducted with the knowledge and care that one associates with the physical sciences. . . . Not enough investigators are really informing themselves about the procedures and results of previous research before embarking on their own" (5)—this in reference to those investigators whose knowledge-building techniques have gone beyond the "lore" stage. As the scientific method of investigation began to open the possibility for some linear development of knowledge in composition, the need for bibliographic resources was becoming clear. This 1963 review of research was soon supplemented by Arthur Applebee and Judith Langer's *Research in the Teaching of English*, a semiannual listing of research studies and reports since 1967 that continues to be published, providing a bibliographic resource covering most of the years since the 1963 monograph.

Both the virtue and the shortcoming of these bibliographic aids is their selectiveness. They assume the function not of listing inclusively but of selecting, annotating, and, for *Research in Written Composition*, synthesizing. This type of project is of greater use for practicing teachers and neophytes, perhaps, but of less value for the experienced researcher. Researchers and scholars, one hopes, do not need an introduction to the subject and guidance through its intricacies but rather a fuller coverage of all that has gone before.

Tate's *Ten Bibliographic Essays* followed this selective and mediative pattern in the 1970s, also. Published in 1976, Tate's volume contained ten essays by noted scholars and researchers in composition: "Invention: A Topographical Survey," by Richard Young; "Non-Fiction Prose," by Richard L. Larson; "Approaches to the Study of Style," by Edward P.J. Corbett; "Modes of Discourse," by Frank J. D'Angelo; "Basic Writing," by Mina P. Shaughnessy; "The Uses of Media in Teaching Composition," by Joseph J. Comprone; "Linguistics and Composition," by W. Ross Winterowd; "Rhetorical Analysis of Writing," by Jim W. Corder; "Composition and Related Fields," by James L. Kinneavy and C. Robert Kline, Jr.; and "Dialects and Composition," by Jenefer M. Giannasi. The very selection of topics for these essays helped to define the areas of interest and investigation for composition researchers. This volume and its successor became standard references in the field.

"For good as well as ill, the characteristic genre of composition bibliography was set very early, not as a reference listing, but as the discursive review essay" (Scott, "Bibliographic Resources" 73), a format that may not have served researchers fully but that undoubtedly influenced a far wider readership in the field than an inclusive bibliographic listing might have reached. For nonspecialists seeking an introductory grounding in a field that was occupying an increasing share of their teaching responsibilities, this approach was undoubtedly useful. Nevertheless, it carried the hazard of excluding ideas and approaches not approved or considered significant by those who were doing the selecting. However well-intentioned to the contrary, a selector can very easily become a censor of new ideas, albeit an unwitting one.

The "tradition" of bibliographic selection and summary continued, however, with such resources as George Hillocks's *Research on Written Composition* (1986) and Gary Tate's *Twelve Bibliographic Essays* (1987), an enlarged and refined successor to his earlier volume. Hillocks surveys and selects research done since the 1963 report, with emphasis again on empirical or experimental work, and adds his own "meta-analysis" of that work. The newer Tate volume drops two of the essays in the earlier book—on media and on related fields— and adds essays on testing (Richard Lloyd-Jones), literary theory and composition (Joseph Comprone), writing across the curriculum (James L. Kinneavy), and computers and composition (Hugh Burns). The other essays are substantially revised and updated, Andrea Lunsford adds an update to Mina Shaughnessy's "Basic Writing," and an index is added. Again the selection of topics in itself helps to establish foci of attention for scholars.

The Bedford Bibliography for Teachers of Writing, by Patricia Bizzell and Bruce Herzberg, another selective resource, is also now in its third edition (first in 1984) and continues to be of wide popular use among composition teachers. In keeping with its introductory character, this bibliography presents "A Brief History of Rhetoric and Composition," from "Classical Rhetoric" through "Rhetoric and Composition Studies for the 1990s," in the restrictive scope of seven pages, followed by 46 pages of selected bibliography. The bibliography itself is subdivided into six major headings, with subdivisions under each. Although at first glance this set of categories appears not to correspond to the ten (later twelve) in the Tate volume, comparison of the subheadings shows considerable correspondence. Either these bibliographers were beginning to discover generally recognized categories within the field, or they were beginning to fashion them from their own organization of the scholarly literature. Perhaps it was some of both. In any case, form was beginning to emerge. The crystallization of this form may have been an additional contribution, not always recognized, of the work of Tate and of Bizzell and Herzberg.

Even though these selective, mediative, introductory works continue to have great value and popularity, by the early 1980s they were not a sufficient bibliographic resource for a discipline that was developing so rapidly both qualitatively and quantitatively. Based on a comparison of Larson's *CCC* bibliographies with Lindemann's *Longman's Bibliography*, Scott estimates that there had been a tenfold growth in the annual number of publications on composition ("Bibliographic Resources" 75).

Donald Stewart, as chair of the Conference on College Composition and Communication, in 1980 clearly saw the need and appointed a committee to consider the problem of developing a comprehensive bibliographic resource for the field. He asked me to chair that effort.

The committee attacked the problem with enthusiasm and high hopes, and, at least on my part, some considerable naiveté. As a group we were not experienced bibliographers, by any means, and we early seriously underestimated the full scope of the project. We scheduled an open meeting of the committee at the 1981 annual conference, hoping to make it a forum in which we could gauge the needs and interests of composition researchers and teachers. Virtually no one came besides the members of the committee. It was clear that there was not yet a ground swell of felt need for such a resource among composition teachers and researchers.

Even so, the committee pressed on with its efforts, realizing very soon that a comprehensive bibliographic project of the scope and quality that we envisioned would require more resources than we, as a committee, were able to assemble without outside help. After a few efforts among the committee to begin actually assembling a bibliography, or at least to define the nature and range of the bibliography we wished to create, our focus began to change from bibliographic work itself to a search for the support and resources necessary for such a task.

When Erika Lindemann made the committee aware of her projected bibliography with Longman, beginning with 1984 and possibly working backward as well as forward from that year, the CCCC committee turned its attention to an effort to provide retrospective bibliographies before the years to be covered by Lindemann, eventually reaching as far back as 1900. Given the Tate volume and Larson's annual bibliographies in *CCC*, the initial goal was to cover the years 1900 to 1973. This very ambitious project, if completed, would have provided some bibliographic base for composition teachers and researchers in the late decades of the twentieth century.

During the time these ideas were being developed by the committee, I had accepted an administrative position at a different institution and felt it best to leave the chair of the committee. Andrea Lunsford and Robert Connors became joint chairs and very ably pressed the work of the committee forward. Unfortunately, the necessary support for the project was not forthcoming, either from the CCCC or the NCTE or any outside source, and the effort finally died of starvation. That neither the CCCC nor the NCTE saw fit by the mid-1980s to devote some of their considerable publication resources to such a clearly needed, basic professional tool as a comprehensive annual research bibliography when, during that same period, they found it possible to provide significant support to various political and social agendas is regrettable. In what he calls an embarrassing failure of support by our professional organizations, Patrick Scott observes, "Even star-studded symposia about trends in the field are simply no substitute for basic informational services, yet those who take the most active part in conference-based professional organizations like MLA or NCTE have sometimes seemed reluctant to pay more than lip-service to composition's development as a research discipline" ("Bibliographic Resources" 82).

As the need for full bibliographic coverage of work in composition and rhetoric became more and more acute in the 1980s, Patrick Scott attempted both to focus attention on that need and to delineate some of the problems that would have to be addressed if such coverage were to become possible. Pointing out that "orientatory bibliographies" and "research guides" were no longer sufficient for serious research scholars aiming at publication of their studies, he identified four areas of basic concern: (1) field demarcation in what has in this century been an applied field that draws on many others; (2) a generally accepted taxonomy and terminology in a field that has been notably protean, at least partially because of the lack of bibliographic control and intellectual continuity; (3) variability in publication format, purpose, and intended audience, which makes it difficult to provide thorough coverage bibliographically; and, (4) segmentation of those interested in composition into many professional organizations and special interest groups ("Bibliographical Problems" 169–72). Those problems identified by Scott in 1986 continue to present difficulties, although some amelioration has been achieved.

Bibliographic resources in historical rhetoric have often been better developed than for modern composition. To some extent this may be the result of established annual bibliographies in speech, literature, and philosophy, related fields on which historical scholars of rhetoric frequently draw. Two particularly useful resources are Winifred Horner's *Historical Rhetoric: An Annotated Bibliography of Selected Sources in English*, published in 1980, and *The Present State of Scholarship in Historical and Contemporary Rhetoric*, published initially in 1983 with a revised edition appearing in 1990. These volumes, however, are still in the pattern of selection and introduction; they are summaries of "the state of the art" but not inclusive bibliographic resources, although, in his treatment of nineteenth-century rhetoric, Donald Stewart renews the appeal for more scholarly awareness of what has gone before (174–75).

Stewart points out various supposedly "new" ideas of the past decade that can be found in the work of Fred Newton Scott and others in the previous century, and he asks for bibliographies and editions of the works of these scholars. "One has only to compare the quantity of literary criticism developed around comparable nineteenth-century producers of belles-lettres to realize the shallowness of the intellectual soil in which we still work," he concludes (175).

By thus pointing out the possibility of continuity and relationship between current composition studies and the work of rhetoricians of previous centuries, Stewart's and the other essays in *The Present State of Scholarship* have helped to reconnect the long-established field of historical rhetoric with the concerns of modern composition teachers and researchers. This connection is made especially apparent in *The Present State* by the inclusion of James L. Kinneavy's essay on contemporary rhetoric (186–246). Kinneavy deals with and summarizes bibliographic resources from the much broader field of rhetoric, with the teaching of composition included as a subdivision. From this broader context, Kinneavy points out the utility of such bibliographic resources as the annual bibliography in the *Rhetoric Society Quarterly*, the *Index to Journals in Communication Studies Through 1985*, edited by Ronald J. Matlon and Peter C. Facciola, the *Current Index to Journals in Education*, and the resources of the Educational Retrieval Information Centers (ERIC).

Such resources can also be supplemented by the use of the citation indexes in the arts and humanities, the social sciences, and the Greenwood Press "bibliographic sourcebooks," but these still require the scholar to search in many places, with coverages that are sometimes overlapping and sometimes haunted by lacunae that are difficult to detect.

Thus the bibliographic review volumes of the 1970s and 1980s have been useful, but they did not solve the greater problem of bibliographic control of the field, an inclusive annual bibliographic record. A solution to this problem has been made more difficult by the shifting boundaries and range of what was considered to be included in the field. If "composition" meant teaching college writing, the *Education Index* and ERIC covered it reasonably well (Scott, "Bibliographic Resources" 80), but as the subject broadened in ways suggested in the subdivisions of James Kinneavy's essay in *The Present State*, it is far from covered by these sources.

In his 1986 consideration of bibliographic problems in composition, Scott observed that "an academic field is socially, not logically, defined . . . and . . . a composition bibliography only becomes possible as the field itself regains some social coherence and stability in its research paradigm" (174). It does appear that definable research paradigms are struggling to be born in composition (Hairston 85; Bryant, "Written Composition" 43–45), but the various approaches are so different in type and in basic concept that even a bibliographic taxonomy has been very difficult to crystallize out of the flux. For example, some theories are derived from empirical observations and are testable by the scientific method, while others are creative metaphors that provide a way of visualizing a conceptual framework but are not susceptible to any form of objective verification. Further complicating the matter, some of the metaphorical concepts (waves and particles, for example) draw their metaphors from the physical sciences, giving an impression of scientific precision and verifiability where none exists. And of course humanists in general are notorious for using the outdated science of the previous generation, or earlier, as a basis for theories (scientific or not). Note, for example, critical and theoretical references to Freud and Jung by literary scholars long after clinical psychology and psychiatry have gone far beyond their theories, or references by composition scholars to Vygotsky long after cognitive psychologists have superseded his ideas (Bryant, "Written Composition" 43–44).

Projects that develop a basis for bibliographic control of composition will undoubtedly contribute to clarification, and perhaps stabilization, of these paradigms by encouraging the development of a bibliographic taxonomy. Until we have terms on the meaning of which practitioners in the field can generally agree, we have very little basis for comparing one theory, or one set of research results, with another. Even practitioner lore is difficult to pass along to other practitioners (or perhaps I should say practitioner experience is difficult to convert into lore) unless there is some shared sense of the meaning of the terms being used.

By focusing attention on this problem of terminology and forcing some standardization of meanings so that a usable taxonomy can be developed, bibliographers are making a contribution to the stabilization of research paradigms that Scott foresaw in 1986 (174). Still, there may be a basic, often unspoken, barrier to the kind of sharing of knowledge, the cooperative interaction of intellectual development of a field, that characterizes the classic concept of scholarly research. Since much of the research in composition is based on the classroom, and to be of value the results must then be translated back into teaching practice in other classrooms, we need to develop an openness—both in intellectual terms and in social and professional terms—about what we do when we teach composition. There exists now a very strong tradition against such openness. As Louise Wetherbee Phelps has recently observed,

> Even today . . . treatments of practice in composition tend to conceive it in terms of the acts of autonomous individuals who independently plan their courses, make assignments and respond to student writing, interact with students, and so on, as if their classrooms were self-contained worlds. . . . There is an ethic of radical individualism in the teaching philosophy of many academic institutions that discourages classroom visits as intrusions threatening a private space of autonomy, intimacy, and power. (866)

Until we can begin to break down this "ethic of radical individualism," we are not going to learn much from each other. Perhaps by making clear to us how much there is to be learned, the movement toward bibliographic control will actually contribute to the development of knowledge in composition not only by providing us with a useful scholarly tool but also by changing our way of thinking about our work.

Recent emphasis on the classroom teacher as a researcher might seem an effective counter to the problem of radical individualism in the classroom. If the traditional role of the researcher is to develop new knowledge and then to share it with colleagues, the teacher-researcher's classroom would appear to have been opened to the world. Unfortunately, as Lucy McCormick Calkins has observed, too often what is called "research" is an anecdotal "celebration of one teacher's classroom practices and of the way several students responded" (129). Such accounts may be interesting and useful, but they are practitioner lore, not research, and their contribution to a community of knowledge is more limited.

Even with such practitioner lore articles, or perhaps because that is what is too often available, teachers and teacher-researchers still appear to lack a basic imperative to consult the existing community of knowledge as preparation for their own work. As examples of this problem, Calkins quotes Donald R. Gallehr, in the *National Writing Project Newsletter* (1980), as suggesting that composition teachers and researchers do not widely consult previous research: "Teacher/ consultants already know an enormous amount about writing, students, and writing instruction, and their own intuitions and curiosity are their best point of departure" (140). In an earlier article (1976), Lee Odell mentions that a teacher-researcher might begin a project with "a little reading or a conversation with a colleague" (106), but, he concludes, a teacher probably already knows useful things to do. Calkins observes that Odell even omits a literature review from his list of the stages involved in practitioner research (140). If the availability of adequate bibliographic resources can help to over-come this type of "radical individualism," or one might even call it intellectual arrogance or romantic "know-nothingism," which allows the individual teacher to assume that he or she possesses all relevant knowledge and can generate all useful ideas for teaching composition, then the bibliographers will have made a major contribution to helping composition develop toward becoming a respectable academic discipline.

Thus it appears that the field of composition is in a kind of "chicken or egg" relationship with its bibliographic resources, after all. Which must come first—serious, coherent research grounded on previous knowledge and estab-lished theories, or reliable, comprehensive bibliographic resources that give systematic access to that previous knowledge and those established theories? And can either occur before their very presence has established a scholarly community that understands their nature and use? These questions may at first appear to pose a "catch–22" for which there is no reasonable answer. In reality, these questions provide a way to see the problem as sharing some of the characteristics of the process of writing. The development of the academic discipline, and of the bibliographic resources needed to support it, has turned out to be highly recursive. Their development has been parallel and constantly interactive. As more organized research beyond the level of practitioner lore has been undertaken, and as the volume of publication related to composition has grown, the need for bibliographic resources has become greater and more apparent. As more bibliographic resources have become available, researchers have learned more from their predecessors and colleagues and have become more sophisticated in their investigations. Writing teachers and researchers "are increasingly coming to view themselves as simply the most recent genera-tion of serious thinkers about language in use, heirs of the rhetorical tradition" (Bizzell and Herzberg 7). The consciousness of being connected to a tradition is a major step forward.

A simple, rough index of these trends is illustrated by a study of the articles published in *College Composition and Communication*. For the 1970 volume, there were twenty-nine articles carrying 66 citations, for an average of 2 citations per article. Ten years later, the 1980 volume of *CCC* carried thirty-five articles with 337 citations, for an average of 10 per article. In 1990, the journal carried sixteen articles with a total of 614 citations, an average of 38 per article. This shift perhaps reflects the changing nature of the contents, from earlier emphasis on exhortation and practitioner lore to more recent systematic research. It may also reflect greater reference to work in the social sciences. If nothing else, this drastic increase shows that composition scholars are now writing with a much greater awareness of the work of others in the field. This kind of awareness needs, and makes use of, bibliographic resources.

The apex thus far of these years of development is, of course, the work of Erika Lindemann. The Longman bibliographies, beginning with 1984, are "exemplary in their coverage; none of the other general bibliographies equals their comprehensiveness or depth" (Kinneavy 215). In these bibliographies, for the first time, scholars have inclusiveness rather than selection and a clear definition of what is being surveyed—a specific list of the journals that are covered. Annotations are provided, but these are strictly descriptive and not evaluative. Thus the bibliographies provide predictability (clear demarcation of what is being surveyed) and relative objectivity. These bibliographies will provide long-term resources for researchers and teachers, standard reference points that will not go out of date, with assurance that methods and viewpoints outside the bibliographer's own interests have not been arbitrarily excluded. Within the range of publication sources listed, everything is included.

These annual bibliographies should both stabilize and pluralize the field (Scott, "Bibliographic Resources" 84). They should enable scholars to build responsibly on previous work so that it is no longer a brand new world for composition teachers every morning. At the same time, by including the full range of contemporary discussion in composition, they should make known all the variety of ideas available.

This major achievement and contribution to composition studies resulted from the vision, organizing skill, and hard work of Lindemann and the support of a commercial publisher, Longman's, that was apparently more farsighted and aware than our own professional organizations. Now, at last, with the volume for 1987, the Conference on College Composition and Communication, in conjunction with Southern Illinois University Press, has taken over the sponsorship of the project. For the CCCC, it is about twenty years late, but certainly better late than never. This belated acceptance of responsibility for this resource may indeed be a sign of the shifting consciousness within the profession toward greater academic rigor and stability.

With this primary resource well established, the other side of this inter- active equation needs increased attention. Now there is no reason for journal and monograph editors to publish work that does not demonstrate a responsi- ble awareness of the professional literature in the field. Now there is no excuse for failure to distinguish hortatory essays (such as my 1973 comments), anecdotal practitioner lore, and reports of actual research. There should be room for all three types of publication, but the distinctions should be recognized and taken into account.

Some current teachers and scholars may be slow to begin making proper use of this new bibliographic resource, but editors and colleagues can do much to educate them to it. Perhaps most important, and still much neglected, is the education of graduate students soon to be entering the profession. Use of the ample bibliographic resources in literary studies has been a staple of graduate education in English for generations, but similar instruction in composition and rhetoric is still seldom found, even in some of our most progressive research institutions. This, perhaps, is the next major project for those who would make the study of composition and rhetoric a fully developed academic discipline. We have the tools. Now let us make sure that the next generation of composition teachers and scholars are adequately prepared to use them. For the next generation of composition teachers and researchers, it should no longer be a brand new world every morning.

Note

1. Simple-minded sometimes, perhaps, but malevolence has nothing to do with the question and was not even hinted in my remarks.

Works Cited

Applebee, Arthur N., and Judith K. Langer, eds. *Research in the Teaching of English.* Athens: U of Georgia P, NCTE Committee on Research. 1967– .

Bizzell, Patricia, and Bruce Herzberg, eds. *The Bedford Bibliography for Teachers of Writing.* 3rd ed. Boston: Bedford, 1991.

Braddock, Richard, Richard Lloyd-Jones, and Lowell Schoer. *Research in Written Composition.* Champaign, IL: NCTE, 1963.

Bryant, Paul T. "A Brand New World Every Morning." *College Composition and Communication* 25 (Feb. 1974): 30–33.

———. "Written Composition: Progress and the Search for Paradigms." *Consensus and Dissent: Teaching English Past, Present, and Future.* NCTE Yearbook. Ed. Marjorie N. Farmer. Urbana, IL: NCTE, 1986. 35–46.

Calkins, Lucy McCormick. "Forming Research Communities among Naturalistic Researchers." *Perspectives on Research and Scholarship in Composition.* Ed. Ben W. McClelland and Timothy R. Donovan. New York: MLA, 1985. 125–44.

Gorrell, Robert. "The Traditional Course: When Is Old Hat New." *College Composition and Communication* 23 (Oct. 1972): 264–70.

Hairston, Maxine. "The Winds of Change: Thomas Kuhn and the Revolution in the Teaching of Writing." *College Composition and Communication* 33 (1982): 78–86.

Hillocks, George, Jr. *Research on Written Composition: New Directions for Teaching.* Urbana, IL: NCTE, 1986.

Horner, Winifred Bryan, ed. *Historical Rhetoric: An Annotated Bibliography of Selected Sources in English.* Boston: G. K. Hall, 1980.

———. *The Present State of Scholarship in Historical and Contemporary Rhetoric.* Rev. ed. Columbia: U of Missouri P, 1990.

Jordan, Richard. "An Interview with Ben Jonson, Composition Teacher." *College Composition and Communication* 23 (Oct. 1972): 277–78.

Kinneavy, James L. "Contemporary Rhetoric." *The Present State of Scholarship in Historical and Contemporary Rhetoric.* Ed. Winifred Bryan Horner. Rev. ed. Columbia: U of Missouri P, 1990. 186–256.

Kitzhaber, Albert R. "4C, Freshman English, and the Future." *College Composition and Communication* 14 (Oct. 1963): 129–38.

————. *Themes, Theories, and Therapy: The Teaching of Writing in College.* New York: McGraw-Hill, 1963.

Larson, Richard L. "Selected Bibliography of Research and Writing about the Teaching of Composition." *College Composition and Communication* (May 1975–1979).

Lindemann, Erika, ed. *CCCC Bibliography of Composition and Rhetoric [1987–1990].* Carbondale: Southern Illinois UP, 1990–.

————. *Longman Bibliography of Composition and Rhetoric 1984–1985.* New York: Longman, 1987.

————. *Longman Bibliography of Composition and Rhetoric 1986.* New York: Longman, 1988.

North, Stephen M. *The Making of Knowledge in Composition: Portrait of an Emerging Field.* Portsmouth, NH: Boynton/Cook, 1987.

Odell, Lee, "The Classroom Teacher as Researcher." *English Journal* 65 (1976): 106–11.

Phelps, Louise Wetherbee. "Practical Wisdom and the Geography of Knowledge in Composition." *College English* 53 (Dec. 1991): 863–85.

Scott, Patrick. "Bibliographical Problems in Research on Composition." *College Composition and Communication* 37 (May 1986): 167–77.

————. "Bibliographic Resources and Problems." *An Introduction to Composition Studies.* Ed. Erika Lindemann and Gary Tate. New York: Oxford UP, 1991.

Stewart, Donald C. "The Nineteenth Century." *The Present State of Scholarship in Historical and Contemporary Rhetoric.* Ed. Winifred Bryan Horner. Rev. ed. Columbia: U of Missouri P, 1990.

Tate, Gary, ed. *Teaching Composition: Ten Bibliographic Essays.* Fort Worth: Texas Christian UP, 1976.

————. *Teaching Composition: Twelve Bibliographic Essays.* Fort Worth: Texas Christian UP, 1987.

11   On Institutes and Projects

Richard Lloyd-Jones

ANYONE MODERATELY FAMILIAR WITH EFFORTS TO IMPROVE THE QUALITY of writing in the schools knows something about the National Writing Project. James Gray, its founder and director, was given the Distinguished Service Award of the National Council of Teachers of English in 1990 in large part because he (and others) nurtured the Bay Area Project until with aid from the National Endowment for the Humanities it spread across the nation under the more inclusive name. The National Writing Project is now a fixture on the educational scene.

In essence, a college—more honestly, a person affiliated with a college—sponsors and directs a graduate program for teachers who wish to become more effective in teaching composition in the schools. Formats vary. Some projects look like regular in-service training, some like regular summer school courses, some like extension offerings, some like old-fashioned literary clubs. Some stress what the instructor has to offer, some are writing workshops, some emphasize advanced study by professional teachers, and some offer mixtures with still other variations according to local conditions. But they all represent commitments of colleges to the schools, they all stress the value of writing in the schools, and they all imply that better qualified teachers are the key to school reform.

Probably most people not affiliated with departments of English imagine that these are self-evident truths and assume that school policy generally is derived from them. By the 1950s, at least, leaders among teachers of English knew better about such "self-evident" truths, for after World War II policy and practice had fallen far behind events. These reformers began a series of conferences and programs that eventually established the climate for the National Writing Project as well as for some of the key elements of its formats in other contexts.

Trying to put a date to the beginning of any movement is an arbitrary act of a writer for managing discourse. For convenience I'll take the Basic Issues Conference of 1958, for that assembly of representatives from the National Council of Teachers of English, the Modern Language Association, the College English Association, and the American Studies Association clearly provided a watershed response to perceptions of confusion about what English was and how it should be redefined to fit the postwar era.

It was hardly the first time the schools were mixed up about English. The confusions had deep roots. In a different metaphor, departments of English had mixed parentage. College people often cite relationships with oratory and rhetoric to emphasize their broad reach into socially oriented discourse. Others stress connections with theology and the training of the clergy, or note how upper-class literature was used to substitute for religion in emphasizing value and morality. Still others, especially in the schools, point out that English teachers have been the ultimate naturalizers of immigrants: the school anthologies of readings used in the early years of the Republic emphasized patriotism and pragmatic virtue, the search for an "American" voice was insistent, and the night school class for immigrants learning English became a staple narrative setting later on. College people also cite a pragmatic variant in the post–Civil War Morrill Land Grant Act, which created advanced training for those interested in agriculture and the mechanic arts and made instruction in writing an issue for the intelligent but unlettered person. A parallel political pressure was created by the open community colleges in the 1960s and early 1970s when the disenfranchised were encouraged to find the language that would help make them upwardly mobile in the mass society.

But as a practical matter, academic prestige in almost all of this century has been given to teachers of literature. Teaching writing—reading papers—is hard work, fit only for blue collar academics. One cannot depend on yellowed lecture notes. Literature provides an Arnoldian substitute for religion, a classroom opportunity for lots of minor sermons and major wit, and a general kind of cultural one-upsmanship—the first function of any literary canon. The way faculty members got ahead in colleges was to cheat the composition students and serve literature, and teachers knew they had succeeded when they no longer taught composition at all.

The value system was well established by the end of the Great War, and the sudden expansion—doubling—of colleges immediately after World War II made it possible for most regular faculty members to abandon composition because there was a shortage of people to teach literature. A concomitant development was the creation of freshman "programs" for composition staffed by temporaries, which in turn led to the creation of the Conference on College Composition and Communication primarily as an aid to the people who had to direct such programs. (Communication courses combining writing and speaking had been popular in speeded-up officer training programs during the war and spread to regular curricula as an efficient way to prepare students for the practical world. They also were administratively convenient for departments of speech.)

The combination of low prestige for composition teaching and even lower prestige for the academic study of rhetoric in the first half of the century meant that little useful training was available for school teachers. They had to depend on watered-down versions of nineteenth-century texts appropriate for finishing-school Americans, for first-generation college students, and for immigrants. Much of the effort was devoted to emphasizing socially correct idioms and manuscript propriety, although the better texts offered canned organizational systems and polite manners. It might be called stenographers' English. Even that limited achievement suffered as schools and colleges moved throughout their curricula more to mass teaching and mass testing, for essays remain essentially handwork and the discrete responses on multiple choice tests are graded by machine. Implicitly the act of writing is separated from the acts of discovery and learning; it is relegated to mere "writing up" of results. The more language is treated as a mass production product, the less attention is paid to what is actually being said.

This oversimplified sketch suggests the challenge that faced teachers of English in the 1950s—at least as understood by college teachers active in professional organizations viewing the work of the schools. The issues addressed at the Basic Issues Conference were basic indeed. How were schools to find enough people well trained to teach what the public and the colleges expected? How were they even to define what they promised to do? Indeed, the conferees asked, "What is English?" Their answer in schematic terms: literature, linguistics, and composition—the tripod model. The Basic Issues report still asked far more questions than it answered (in some ways the report looks like the study questions at the end of chapters in some textbooks), and practical actions lay ahead, but its many questions removed any pretense that the old way was the right way. Although some college departments had been called English Language and Literature, few offered more about language than a narrow version of philology, and Albert Kitzhaber would soon demonstrate that in only a few did composition have an explicit presence.

For this story I now turn to the Commission on English of the College Entrance Examination Board, because under the leadership of Floyd Rinker and with money from five different foundations the commission brokered promises from twenty universities to offer institutes for improving the professional knowledge and skills of teachers in the schools. Departments of English at the college level were preparing to bypass colleges of education in order to improve the schools. Officially the commission's brochure listed four purposes for the institutes: to improve the academic preparation and teaching of 900 carefully selected teachers of English in the schools, to amass samples of excellent teaching materials, to engage university faculties more actively and more realistically in teacher training, and to prove the feasibility of similar institutes, to be supported by grants from foundations or from the federal government in 1963.

The mixture of participating institutions has the diversity of a sound political "slate": Cornell, Duke, Harvard, Indiana, NYU, Ohio State, Penn State, Rutgers, St. Louis, Southern Illinois, Stanford, SUNY-Albany, Tulane, UCLA, Michigan, Nevada, Pittsburgh, Texas, Washington, and Wisconsin. Perhaps it should have been expected that the overall results as later reported masked differences in effectiveness from campus to campus because those differences were hidden in statistical aggregations that protected the weak.

The proposed format for the institutes was built on the tripod—courses emphasizing "current thinking" in each of the three areas with a synthesizing workshop to pull it all together. The faculty would be selected by the chairs of the participating departments. Each institute would be allowed to invite up to forty-five participants who had training, experience, and interest in teaching college preparatory students; the participants would receive stipends of $350 for taking part in a five- to eight-week program, depending on where it was offered. The idea was that these 900 teachers would reach 100,000 students the following year and that the program would inspire copies all over the nation. Such arithmetic betrays the quantitative optimism of people writing proposals to grantors who look for demonstrable effects, but it also suggests that the college people intended to alter school programs by changing school teachers. The official evaluating team was to be led by John Gerber of Iowa, the founding chair of the Conference on College Composition and Communication and soon to be for one year the official part-time consultant on English for the U.S. Office of Education. (There was a four-year period during which even the Office of Education admitted that subject matter specialists might know something useful about their fields in a way important to *education*.)

In the summer of 1961, each of the participating universities sent three representatives (one for each leg of the tripod) to Ann Arbor for a three-week meeting to design the institute courses for the following summer. Helen White chaired the sessions on literature (although Walker Gibson later remembered that Harold Martin of Harvard took charge), Nelson Francis the sessions on linguistics, and Albert Kitzhaber the work on composition. There was to be a synthesizing workshop to develop teaching materials, but it was to be left for planning on each site, perhaps because education as such didn't have a constituency in the tripod (people from English education were not much involved in the institutes and often were objects of scorn for professors of English), perhaps because it implied relationships among the three legs and thus couldn't be isolated, perhaps because college people didn't think in terms of curricular goals.

By way of temporal perspective, Kitzhaber was then working on gathering the data that would appear in *Themes, Theories, and Therapy* and demonstrate how much the colleges had abandoned composition, and Richard Braddock of Iowa and his NCTE Committee on the State of Knowledge about the Teaching of Composition were hard at work on material that would surface in *Research in Written Composition* and demonstrate how little about teaching composition was being discovered by traditional but inadequate social science research methods. That is, the era that Stephen North in *The Making of Knowledge in Composition* identifies as the beginning of composition research had not yet quite begun.

At the planning conference, the development of the literature course caused little fuss. The New Criticism was sufficiently dominant that it could allow a few nods to other "approaches" without being threatened. The linguistics group was expected to tear itself apart, for the fashionable structural grammars were the focus of fury by those who viewed with alarm anything perceived as a threat to "standards" and the still newer generative/transformational grammars were edging over the horizon to baffle the traditionally trained English teacher. In fact, the linguistics people had so many exciting ideas to present that they seemed to work out their differences easily. Probably it was the peace of a prosperous and growing economy, for they would soon have grants under the Defense Education Act and from various other scientific grantors, and many of those linguists then lost in subsections of Departments of English would acquire departments of their own.

The epic battle of the planning conference was among the twenty people who dealt with composition. In the end they could not agree on a single syllabus and so created two courses for use the following summer. The 1963 evaluator's report from Gerber described one course as "essentially subjective and experiential, stressing the roles of the writer." The other course, more traditional, was "basically diagnostic, stressing the art of writing." By 1977 Walker Gibson, who with Scott Elledge of Cornell led the battle for the first course, recalled the passion of the debate with enthusiasm but politely dismissed the issues as products of the moment; yet he speculated that the rebels who designed the first course were outraged by the traditionalists' "dreary dependence of the Four Modes of Discourse" and their "refusal to rely on student experience for one's main subject matter." Ten of the institutes (including the ones at Cornell and NYU, Gibson's university) used the new program, nine the more traditional one, and Southern Illinois designed some sort of fusion. The official report suggests that the schoolteacher participants were about equally pleased or displeased with the two courses, although the teams of visiting evaluators found the new course more interesting. Later follow-up interviews suggested that traditional approaches had been more helpful once teachers had returned to their schoolrooms, perhaps mostly because the schools still had traditional programs and nothing they had learned really threatened the status quo.

Composition teachers owe much to Gibson and through him to Theodore Baird and Elledge even if they have chosen other directions for their own work. No matter how unresolved the planning differences were, the mere fact of a course with serious intellectual claims to challenge the traditional paradigm established a context for revisionism.

Gibson, with a new M.A. from the Iowa Writers Workshop and poems published in *The New Yorker*, came to Amherst in 1946 hoping to teach creative writing but (happily) was driven by Baird into freshman composition. One can see in Gibson's later course assignments traces of Baird's preoccupation with Platonic definition. Such preoccupation also appears in other descendants of Baird, notably William Coles and John Butler, but Gibson seems more aware of the limitations of Socratic verbalizing and more in touch with literary playfulness. Elledge perhaps contributed an Aristotelian bias. Gibson's later *Seeing and Writing* stands as a post-Amherst testament to the expanded vision (as well as a personal version of the insights of the planning conference). It had only two printings (unlike his popular revision of *The Macmillan Handbook*), but it suggests what grew out of the CEEB course.

Given such classical background, the inclusion of Plato's *Phaedrus* in the training of composition teachers might be expected, although some participants seem to have been offended by that and by the emphasis on the writer's voice. Still another symptom of Gibson's contribution to the planning sessions is to be found in *The Limits of Language*, an anthology he had at hand during the Ann Arbor sessions and shared with Elledge. This collection of thirteen excerpts from writers and philosophers about language shows a twist toward French existentialism, quite current at the time, and far more emphasis on the degree to which human personality imposes itself on perception and limits what one can "really" say. On the surface it seems another attempt to enlist "science" in the cause of vague humanism, for a number of the writers are scientists (William James, Albert North Whitehead, James B. Conant, Herbert J. Muller, Percy W. Bridgman, and J. Robert Oppenheimer), but they are also the theorists most engaged in defining the essence of "being." The real message of the collection is that surfaces are only surfaces, and meaning is a complex relationship among many variables. The book went through five printings in its first five years.

The linguists at the CEEB planning conference were being amused by drafts of Martin Joos's *The Five Clocks*, a document on style and discourse theory that also deals with the interaction of form and context. The surface of Joos's book is that of a literary essay with an insistently present narrator, embedded narratives, apparent digressions, and lots of metaphor. The burden of the lay is to describe style in terms of degrees of intimacy suggested by linguistic forms and explicit elaboration of content. The underlying model is that of the normal bell-shaped curve where the midrange describes the language patterns in ordinary civil and responsible discourse between actual strangers who act as friends. Quite evidently the book emphasizes social contexts and personal vision.

Both books turned up as texts in subsequent institutes, and although neither directly addresses what teachers should do on Monday, both redefine how one looks at form. Both ultimately emphasize the role of the speaker/ writer. Although more participants from the traditional course found their course "useful," participants in the personal course claimed in follow-ups more often to have changed their own courses, used sample exercises from the instructors, and altered their attitudes and procedures as a result of the experience. One even made his students read the *Phaedrus*. In a real sense the new theories led to revised curricula, but still, the course was not as immediately "useful" in the ordinary school context.

The issue I understand from the creation of the two institute composition courses is that the new course argued for the instability of form, the contingency of meaning in context, and the general exploratory nature of all statements. The "traditional" course was better than a "course in secretarial correctness," but it was still based on the certainty that knowledge could be exactly revealed in natural language and in mathematics. One assumed with Plato that the name was the essence of the thing and with Lord Kelvin that what existed could be measured, could be shown objectively. Since these concepts represented the dominant assumptions of American education, it struck the reviewers of the institutes as less fresh, but also more useful. The issues dividing the two courses are first principles from which curricula and courses may be derived, but they are not the immediate concern of classroom teachers. It is hardly any wonder that people back in the classroom found the traditional course more helpful in meeting the day-to-day demands of a traditional view of language, even though people from the new course claimed to have changed more. Perhaps more revealing is a comment from the evaluators exhorting future institute teachers to offer real graduate work, not just an annotated freshman course. This suggests that implicitly, at least, they recognized that serious study of discourse was needed and possible.

Those familiar with later developments in teaching composition know that the issues are not dead. Much of the later use and misuse of expressive writing and of the reintroduction of "rhetoric" are allied to these issues. Without raising any questions of "influence" one can speculate on how Ken Macrorie or James Britton would have been perceived, or whether Dudley Bailey's *Essays on Rhetoric* or Francis Christensen's *Notes Toward a New Rhetoric* or James Kinneavy's *A Theory of Discourse* or W. Ross Winterowd's *Rhetoric: A Synthesis* or Edward P.J. Corbett's *Classical Rhetoric for the Modern Student* or *Rhetoric: Discovery and Change* by Richard Young, Alton Becker and Kenneth Pike would have gained acceptance without the larger audience being built by the institutes. Kenneth Burke, I. A. Richards, C. S. Lewis, Herbert Read, Wayne Booth, M. H. Abrams, or others would have made their ways because they were perceived as literary critics even when writing on subjects of interest to rhetoricians, but people who made careers of teaching composition needed the status conferred by the tripod and confirmed by the "new" course of the institutes.

The immediate evaluation of the institutes appeared in 1963 and could not deal with such long-range trends, and yet it is instructive in relation to the four main goals. The first goal separated academic preparation and teaching skills while citing them as part of one goal, and Gerber applauded the intention of treating them both as central to the profession. One might even imagine that they are crucially interactive, especially in teaching composition, but the common separation of English departments from schools of education suggests otherwise. In all twenty institutes only four faculty members were specialists in English education (one was Louise Rosenblatt at NYU), and four others were high school teachers hired on an extramural basis. (NYU also had one of the high school teachers as well as Gibson.)

Among the participants, 43 percent seemed to believe that the institutes provided great intellectual growth, but only 25 percent applied such a term to their improvement as teachers. Yet the exit opinionnaires from all participants, post-institute interviews from sixty of them, and evaluations made by the visitors rated the teaching they received in all three areas as excellent or better in most instances (the linguists came off the worst, but that may be because some people reacted to the social science methodology and the implied threats to everything they thought they knew about language).

Perhaps given the perception that the courses had little influence on teaching, it is not startling that the workshops produced little of interest by way of teaching materials and thus did not satisfy the second goal of the institutes—that of providing samples of excellent teaching materials. Some teachers, conscious that they were being paid $350, did prepare documents, but the evaluators recommended elimination of the goal. In theory the workshops had separate "instructors" (maybe the term is a giveaway about why they didn't prove to be workshops), but in all but two the director of the institute or one of the other instructors simply took on the workshop as well. The workshops were given the back of the hand in the programs, and perhaps it was unrealistic in an overloaded format to expect teachers to be ready to use new ideas even as they were acquiring them. Furthermore, a newly informed teacher carrying a partially worked-out class plan is not in a strong position for changing school routines.

Directing the institutes was not always taken seriously, either. Seventeen of the directors were freed from other departmental teaching, although they served on committees. Only two of the directors appointed their own staffs, and seven had no voice at all in the choices. Only six of the directors had had high school teaching experience of any kind, many were overloaded, and few had enough clerical help. Few seemed aware of the emotional stress on participants and how much directors might need to deal with practical problems of displaced adults suffering drastic role changes in a classroom. In short, the institute experience was in some ways grand but in other ways hand-to-mouth.

The third goal was also viewed as unfulfilled, for department chairs had not as a group paid much attention to whom they assigned the teaching, and departments as a whole took little responsibility for the work, even to the extent of acknowledging its existence during a department meeting. To be sure, some individuals were very much influenced. The report claimed that some college teachers experienced an "epiphany" in realizing that professors of English could actually help in training teachers, and among those individuals are people who led the process of change in teaching composition in subsequent years, but overall they observed that the old, snobbish attitude prevailed. Viewed from a perspective later than 1963, the stimulation of leadership in the universities might be described as an unacknowledged success of the institutes.

Aside from the immediate intellectual effect of the composition course, the format of the institute is also important in an operational sense. In its fourth goal the CEEB expressed the hope that the pattern would be repeated with other funding, and so it was in 1964 under the aegis of the National Defense Education Act. (The federal Department of Education and the NEH came later.) To be sure, even with a stipend, two-thirds of the CEEB Institutes had not drawn the quota of forty-five participants; only a few had been desperately short, but most really didn't "choose" the participants. The classroom educational "leaders" who had been expected to enroll were in short supply, and yet the evaluators had been unanimous in urging that the pattern be copied.

So it is to be expected that at first the new law asked colleges to copy the CEEB Institutes; later, variations were invited. From the outset the federal intention was to alter practices in the schools. To some extent this meant improving individual teachers and their preparation, but it also meant changing curricula. The institutes were expected to prepare people to develop and work with new programs. The workshops were not eliminated in the NDEA patterns; indeed, they were emphasized in grant proposals, but I don't know of evidence that they were generally more successful for the NDEA than they had been for the CEEB. Participants didn't see themselves as affecting the "system," and college English teachers often didn't really know much about it.

For many people, the real emphasis was in correcting perceived weaknesses in the system of training teachers by providing more sophisticated knowledge of the content of the three areas of the tripod. In one of the variations, for example, since it came to be perceived that a very large proportion of those teaching English in the schools had only undergraduate minors in English, institutes were created to fill in gaps of knowledge. Many of these minimally prepared people were primarily teachers of other subjects, did not want to be English teachers, and simply filled out their loads with a class or two, an indication that school administrations assumed that almost anyone could teach English. They came to institutes at least in part to satisfy certification mandates·for additional college credit in an inexpensive way. As had been quietly implied in the evaluation of the original institutes, no mere institute could make up for the lack of undergraduate background. The problem of ill-prepared teachers had less to do with the qualifications of teachers than with the judgment of administrators, and I suspect (mostly on hearsay evidence) that these institutes died of their own futility. But the underlying assumption in such institutes was that the problems were personal rather than structural and intellectual.

Other variations of the basic pattern were more important to composition teachers and to the profession. Two such offerings will serve to illustrate. They were developed at Iowa to influence the real decision makers the CEEB had hoped to attract. One form by Richard Braddock foreshadowed dissemination elements of the National Writing Project; another by Carl Klaus addressed problems of intellectual leadership. Both dealt only with composition, but for the most part as a leg of the tripod. Still, concentration invited thoroughness and commitment and promised new courses as well as new people.

Braddock had been engaged in negotiations with the other three graduate institutions and the twenty largest high school districts in Iowa to create an Advanced Standing Program in composition to counterbalance Advanced Placement Programs in literature. Braddock had just founded *Research in the Teaching of English*, an indication of his dual concern in research and teaching, in curricular development based on sound knowledge and careful identification of goals. As chair of the University of Iowa's freshman composition program, he had perceived that students sought credit for the university's composition course on the basis of what was essentially an AP literature course taught in the high schools for college credit. He believed that the state should develop a network of parallel high school courses in composition and had for a year and a half been arranging for exchange visits between high schools and colleges as well as for a number of discussions among administrators to press the proposal.

One of many organizational problems faced in the discussions was to describe what was an acceptable college course and to certify teachers as qualified to teach such courses, and the NDEA Institutes offered a solution, for the federal administrators were especially interested in programs that had curricular implications. Dissemination of research knowledge was the key. Each of the state's four graduate programs in successive years would offer a federally financed institute to certify advanced standing teachers, who would then with financing from the local districts design appropriate courses just as competent college teachers designed their own courses. The teachers would thus be subsidized in acquiring higher personal market value in their own job searches, and acceptable courses could be created without interfering with the rights of school districts. That finessed problems of planting new curricular ideas into established school structures.

These Advanced Standing Institutes dealt entirely with different approaches to teaching composition and designing courses, Braddock himself leaning toward an emphasis on public issues but his colleagues taking other routes. Essentially the courses in the summer sessions represented the best mixtures of theory and teaching practice current at the time and (like the original institutes) had a goal of improving the writing of the teachers without actually making a separate place for a graduate level writing course. The workshop became a synthesis that allowed teachers to design the course they would teach at home and thus had a more immediate cause for being. On the surface it was just a matter of using the summer to plan the work for the fall. By the fourth year the federal funding had dried up, but the program itself was well-enough established to survive at least in skeletal form for twenty more years, and its implicit emphasis on the responsibility of "superior" teachers for the curriculum was to be picked up later by the Iowa Writing Project.

Klaus's variations were more intense because they always were edging toward new formulations of theory and practice with an overriding concern for what would happen in new classrooms. Each institute was something of an emotional happening, and all emphasized the arts of writing and teaching. He had been first to design an all-composition format for the NDEA to serve department chairs and curriculum directors. That first offering still had discrete graduate courses with relatively isolated instructors, but each subsequent variation became more nearly a merged experience (whatever the transcripts might show) with all of the instructors usually present and participating and classes extending far beyond the classroom into the dorms and parties. Linguistics became less and less emphasized as such and yet more pervasively a part of discussions of style and meaning. Gibson's *Seeing and Writing* often became a basis for discussion both of craft and of how a concern for epistemology was basic to teaching writing. The "traditional paradigm" was constantly in question. Perhaps most importantly the writing of the registrants was a primary text both for what it said and how it said it. These were to be communities of writers, so implicitly the teachers were viewed as "masters" of writing who would later have "apprentices." They were also communities of administrators who would change whole school districts, so current scholarship about the teaching of writing was part of the substance of the institutes, but the real model was the Iowa Writers Workshop and the vision was of variables in language and situation as opposed to forms and classifications.

The vision that dominated these institutes sent many of the participants back to graduate school, often to deal with literary nonfiction as well as with specialties in the teaching of composition. Klaus himself went on to other visions and left this format to Clarence Andrews, who managed two institutes somewhat more directed to visions of business, journalism, and administration. This alteration provided a milder atmosphere, but out of the transactional conviviality came the pragmatic idea of dissemination by forming an organization of high school chairs within the NCTE, the Conference for Secondary School English Department Chairpersons. These were people who wanted academic leadership to come from those trained in the disciplines as well as in school administration. It is now called the Conference on English Leadership.

The ultimate in Klaus's experiments with the institute format came in 1979 and again in 1980 with two six-month Institutes for Directors of Freshman Composition in Colleges financed by the NEH. Participants were selected competitively not only on their own qualifications but also on the basis of institutional type, commitment, and geographical location. College administrators were expected to visit the institutes for their own edification and to commit resources to the programs at their schools. Institute faculty members were expected to serve as consultants for participant colleges. The institute regimen was not merely to offer pleasant academic leaves for directors but also to leverage change in college programs.

During the spring semester of each year there were four "courses": one was explicitly a graduate writing course taught in an open-ended workshop format by Cleo Martin (who had taught in several earlier institutes), two others taught by me, David Hamilton, and Paul Diehl dealt with more conventional scholarly readings assumed to be the property of Ph.D. specialists in composition but with a twist toward involving scholars from other academic disciplines, and one was a colloquium in curricular planning led by Klaus.

Perhaps the most telling example of how the outsiders affected the insiders is that of James Van Allen, the astronomer who described the Van Allen belts. He saw the writing—the translating of knowledge from mathematics and graphics into English—as an important part of the discovery process, not just a "writing up." But anthropologists, historians, mathematicians, and artists had their say as well in revealing processes of symbolization. It was much more than just "writing across the curriculum," although it was that, too. The combination of academic courses was designed to encourage people to think in terms of the goals of the entire college curriculum as much as of the goals of a composition course as such.

Klaus's colloquium on designing courses and on general problems of curriculum design was a second segment in the plan of the institute. At first Klaus had considered a course dealing with style and the essay, areas of study dear to his own scholarly mind, but he was persuaded to shape a summer colloquium more immediately directed to translating the insights of the regular courses into academic action. The colloquium ran through the summer session, which was devoted primarily to specific planning of materials for home department use, and it sustained the sense of community effort established during the first four months. This was a variation of the workshops that had failed in the CEEB Institutes for school teachers and had been at best marginally successful even in the specialized composition institutes.

The six-month format allowed time to combine reading the academic materials and practicing writing in the context of discussions about designing programs. The summer workshops with their specified work goals really put the emphasis on program reform. Some of the materials of those workshops appear in *Courses for Change*, which Klaus edited with Nancy Jones; the collection later won the MLA Shaughnessy Prize as a contribution to teaching. Like the Klaus institutes for school people, the NEH Institute was an emotional hothouse as people dealt with role changes in becoming students again and with constant challenges to their accepted notions, but it also became a community of scholars, and individuals went home with the plans and knowledge to bring about changes. They were subsequently identified as research associates of the Iowa/NEH Institute.

By 1980 the Bay Area Project had been well tested and the NEH funding for expansion had been authorized. That history is well documented in National Writing Project publications, and during the 1980s the project spread to almost every state. The exception was Iowa, where a slightly different model appeared outside of the National Writing Project, although it was originally suggested by it. The two systems are compatible and indeed are yoked in current federal legislation, but the differences are instructive.

The Iowa Writing Project is the child of James S. Davis of the Grant Wood Area Educational Agency, an intermediate school district providing various kinds of educational services—including in-service training—to districts in its area. At the same time that Klaus was planning the Iowa/NEH Institutes, Davis with funding from the research section of the Iowa Department of Education came to the University of Iowa to work out credit and staffing for a three-week project to be managed by school people and to draw participants from the entire range of the schools. (This *is* an issue, for high school teachers are sometimes as sniffy about elementary teachers as college teachers are about both; a secondary agenda in all Iowa projects is to breach the status walls that separate teachers of English.) Davis's intentions fit neatly with Klaus's, to change individuals and affect schools. He wanted the initiative to remain with school people as people in control of their own destiny.

Half of the day for the three weeks was to be devoted to academic study; the other half was to be a writing workshop for the participants themselves. Cleo Martin, who represented the interests of the University of Iowa, gave form to the writing workshop and emotional warmth to the entire endeavor. For a huge proportion of Iowa teachers of writing, Martin was to become the emblem of how writing affected individuals and how much each person was responsible for the work of the whole group. Davis organized the academic part of the program, building a substantial library with a wide range of appropriate readings but heavily weighted toward James Britton, Nancy Martin, Donald Graves, Donald Murray, and "whole language" advocates. After four years the "research" funding for the Iowa projects ran out, but by then individual school districts were so much pleased with the results that funding is now provided in small amounts from many budgets.

In a decade, IWP grew to forty and more sessions offered each summer all over the state. Each fall participants (and usually, the first time at least, their immediate administrators) gather in Des Moines just after the Iowa Council meeting to exchange experiences and writing as well as to carry on more usual professional refreshers. The sharing of writing in manuscript and in many ephemeral booklets, promoted in the Martinesque courses, is now a part of the English-teacher scene and betokens emotional sharing as well as academic support within a professional association.

Soon those who had completed one summer's work wanted more, so three follow-up courses (or levels) were created, each a bit more directed toward classroom research into one's own practice and then toward more elaborate projects with broader implications in school districts and beyond, but each still inviting lots of writing. Many of the participants have been stimulated to return to graduate school for advanced degrees, primarily in English education or in educational administration. Several have written dissertations evaluating different effects of the Writing Projects. Some of these graduates go back to the school classroom, but more go on to curriculum management and teacher training and thus alter school programs even more. More than 5,000 teachers in this small state have taken part in the projects, so it is possible to visit a school building in which almost all of the teachers and some of the administrators have been in one at least. That shapes how composition is valued and taught, but especially in elementary schools it has altered how any academic decision is made. People who have taken part in the project simply think of themselves as competent to make professional judgments and are more likely to challenge building administrators about curricular matters.

For such success Davis and Martin, by providing models and organization, deserve much credit, but it is also important to note the force of emphasizing the teacher as a writer—the master-apprentice model—and as a professional with the obligation to make real decisions about education. The program has retained its strong emphasis on drawing its leadership from people who are teaching in the schools at all levels; the University of Iowa serves primarily as an enabler—and even then most of the red tape is handled by the Grant Wood Area Educational Agency. Yes, teachers need more knowledge about composition, but they also need the rewards and obligations of controlling their own classrooms. That has been one of the subtexts of adjusting the top-down model of education to a more participatory model, so that the schools rather than the university have the initiative in operating the projects. To a large extent they are reaching for the goal that was ignored in the CEEB operation and stressed ineffectively in the NDEA programs. These projects, which honor professionalism at every level of education, have worked through the competence of individual teachers to design curricula.

Other threads can be woven into this story of how the institutes and projects have affected the teaching of composition, for in the third of a century that has passed since the Basic Issues Conference, much has changed in education generally and in teaching composition specifically. But it is easy to over-look these programs that were essentially oral, and much of the exchange of ideas in this period has been oral or bureaucratic. Here the reports, ephemeral documents, memoirs, and other materials created at the same time offer symp-toms of what was a messy, shifting, uneven series of personal encounters. At times connections seem to be quite accidental, results serendipitous. The early stages have less structure than a cocktail party conversation.

Yet, the basic institute idea looms behind the most important devices for dissemination of new ideas about teaching composition and, I suspect, directly but less evidently behind much of its scholarship. In the colleges we are now able to be "professional" and "scholarly" about composition and literacy because the climate has been changed in important ways by what the CEEB Institutes set in motion. The National Writing Project can be effective in part because its methods were tested and its audiences were prepared in subsequent variations on the basic pattern.

Acknowledgments

A conventional notes section would not be helpful in explaining the sources of the comments in this chapter. This essay is in substance my own memoir of my participation as teacher and administrator in many of these efforts after 1963, but I owe much of the specific data to materials from the files of John C. Gerber, Walker Gibson, Carl H. Klaus, and James S. Davis. They wrote proposals and reports and kept better notes than I have, but the story as I have told it is mine and subject to the limits Gibson laid out by proxy in the selections he presented in *The Limits of Language*.

Part 3
Reinterpreting the Context

12 Phantastic Palimpsests
Thomas De Quincey and the
Magical Composing Imagination

William A. Covino

THE REFORMATION OF RHETORIC THAT OCCURS BETWEEN 1500 AND 1700 is an effort to reconstitute the method and expression of intellectual inquiry as a stable scientific relationship between subject and object. For students of English rhetoric, the most famous or infamous reformation manifesto is Sprat's *History of the Royal Society*, in particular his warnings against the licentious imagination that invents an unverifiable reality and against stylistic amplifications that ambiguate true knowledge:

> The Ornaments of speaking . . . are so much degenerated from their original usefulness. . . . they give the mind a motion too changeable, and bewitching, to consist with *right practice*. Who can behold, without indignation, how many mists and uncertainties, these specious *Tropes* and *Figures* have brought on our Knowledge? (112, emphasis in original)

> The *Poets* began of old to impose the deceit. They to make all things look more venerable than they were, devis'd a thousand false *Chimeras*; on every *Field*, *River*, *Grove*, and *Cave*, they bestow'd a *Fantasm* of their own making. . . . And in the modern *Ages* these *Fantastical Forms* were reviv'd. . . . But from the time in which the *Real Philosophy* has appear'd, there is scarce any whisper remaining of such *horrors*. . . . The course of things goes quietly along, in its own true channel of *Natural Causes* and *Effects*. (340, emphasis in original)

With the association of figurative language and witchery and the counterposition of "real philosophy" to chimeras and phantasms in these passages, the Society impugns rhetoric and magic together. Within the seventeenth century establishment of official science and official religion, "the imagination is particularly dangerous when it allows an individual to create a phantasm and impose it on the world for reality" (Vickers 60).

Belief in the reality of phantasms, belief in a dynamic cosmology of phantasmic spirits and powers, had informed Western thought and defined the nature of the imagination since antiquity (Couliano 3–27). This magical imagination allows for infinitely variable combinations and correspondences, informing the "changeable" intellect that Sprat fears. Marsilio Ficino, a fifteenth century neo-Platonic philosopher of both magic and rhetoric, associates phantasy with rhetoric as he reiterates the belief expressed as early as Gorgias's "Encomium of Helen" that the orator and the magus are similar figures. Ficino's perfect orator must accommodate his discourse to the multiplicity and changing dispositions of each human soul, and the magus must accommodate any invocation to the daily shifting positions of the stars and the changing human behaviors incited by the heavens. In his commentary on Plato's *Phaedrus*, Ficino says:

> The perfect orator must know that any human soul is intrinsically
> and naturally multiple (for it has reason, imagination, sense, and
> the powers of wrath and desire); and, likewise, that various souls
> use their various powers as much as possible and differently among
> themselves and are differently affected; and, again, that some of
> their differences are derived from the differences of their bodies.
> Moreover, he ought to know what kind of mental disposition is
> moved by what kind of discourse and accommodate his discourse
> to each one, just as a musician must bring various harmonies to var-
> ious things. (*Marsilio Ficino* 204)

For Ficino, this definition of rhetoric also applies to magic. Writing on celestial magic, Ficino warns that even the slightest change in heavenly constellations affects both human behavior and the powers that magical discourse can invoke, to emphasize that the magical universe—like the rhetorical one—is "intrinsically and naturally multiple" (*Three Books on Life* 3.21.69–74).

By the end of the seventeenth century, the Royal Society's victory over the phantasmic/rhetorical imagination was complete (Vickers 62; Covino 54–55). In this chapter, I first look backwards from that victory, establishing the interpenetration of magic and rhetoric by noting their common dependence upon a phantasmic imagination. In general, I propose that a magic world populated by myriad phantasms offers the possibility for *phantasy*, for an imagination consistently engaged in varieties of transfiguration that we might associate with both magical and rhetorical invention.

I then look forward from the Society's victory, to the romantic revival of magic. The romantic fascination with the magical imagination is explicit in Blake's visionary poetry, Wordsworth's and Coleridge's conjunction of the natural and the supernatural in the *Lyrical Ballads*, Percy Shelley's faith in the power of language and mind over cultural and political "matter" in *Prometheus Unbound*, *The Witch of Atlas*, and *A Defense of Poetry*, and Mary Shelley's portrayal of a magical world ravaged by a monster of science in *Frankenstein*. (See Anya Taylor for a discussion of magic in Coleridge, Wordsworth, Keats, Shelley, and Byron.) The return to medieval landscapes, so characteristic of romantic writing, signals a return to prescientific conceptions of the imagination as a potent creative power. Thomas De Quincey is the romantic prose writer who constantly associates himself with magical intellection. Continuing my attention to De Quincey as a renegade rhetorician (*Art* 108–20), I will focus here on the elements of phantasy in his *Suspiria De Profundis*, which De Quincey calls a mode of "impassioned prose ranging under no precedents that I am aware of" (*Writings* 13.4) and which exhibits the romantic fascination with intercourse between the spiritual and physical, dream and reality, with the interplay of rhetoric and magic. De Quincey represents a belief in writing as the medium for *participation in a magical dialectic of natural sympathies*.

The Composing Memory

Memory and rhetoric are allied processes, most commonly discussed together to emphasize memorization as an important skill for the orator. For the ancients, however, memorization is one use of memory but does not indicate its whole operation. A full assessment of the nature of classical memory reveals that, first of all, memory relies upon the communication between body and mind-soul, via an incorporeal *pneuma*, or spirit, made of the same material as the stars and serving as the vehicle for *phantasms*, which are translations of exterior sensations into the inner, mystical, imagistic language of the mind-soul. Ioan Couliano summarizes this conception of memory, which predates its most-cited exponent, Aristotle, and prevails—*mutatis mutandis*—as a medieval model of the mind for Augustine, Albert the Great, Roger Bacon, Thomas Aquinas, and the medieval encyclopedist Bartholomaeus Anglicus:

> The messages of the five "external" senses are transported by the spirit to the brain, where the *inner* or *common* sense resides. The action of common sense . . . occupies the three cerebral ventricles: the anterior, seat of the imagination; the median, seat of reason; and the posterior, seat of memory. Imagination translates the language of the senses into fantastic language so that reason may grasp and understand phantasms. The data of imagination and of reason are deposited in the memory. (11)

Couliano stresses that "*the phantasm has absolute primacy over the word*, that it precedes both utterance and understanding of every linguistic message"

(5, emphasis in original). In other words, human language is a secondary representation of phantastic language: the "world" that constitutes our fundamental lexicon is magical. To study the discoursing intellect is to study its interaction with a cosmology of phantastic sense-images; such is the common study of prescientific philosophers, rhetoricians, physicians, and magicians. Through the Renaissance, all prevailing models of the mind presume that one cannot understand without phantasms (Yates 71; Kristeller 234–38; Couliano 6–13). As Gianfrancesco Pico della Mirandola explains in his representative 1500 treatise *On the Imagination*, phantasy is the "one, single power of the sensitive soul" that infuses imagination, common sense, and memory and ministers to "both the discursive reason and the contemplative intellect" (35–37). Further, "the life and actions of all animate beings are in great part ruled by phantasies" (39).

One cannot read or write without phantasms. This point is central to Mary Carruthers's *The Book of Memory*, which is sure to become a standard guide to the classical and medieval composing imagination. As Carruthers explains, reading was considered a visual act that also relied on phantasms: "whatever enters the mind changes into a 'see-able' form for storing in memory" (18). In her discussion of the interior senses described by Aquinas in the *Summa Theologica*, Carruthers notes the interaction of the composing imagination with the retentive imagination:

> Four powers are described: common sense; the fantastic (imagination: "as it were a storehouse of forms received through the senses"); the estimative; and the memorative. . . . In his "De potentia animae," cap. 4, Thomas defines the powers more particularly, enumerating five this time: the *sensus communis*; *phantasia* (retentive imagination); *imaginativa* (the composing imagination); *aestimativa seu cogitativa* . . . ; and *memorativa*. But the composing imagination (*imaginativa*) is elsewhere combined with *imaginatio* (or *phantasia*) and called simply *phantasia seu imaginatio*. (51)

For the ancients, a complex and unsettled faculty psychology describes a dynamic interplay of spirits and sensations, memory and imagination, reading and writing. Within the prescientific conception of a sympathetic universe, human intellection is a constellation of processes and powers in which the images of phantasy "are being formed at every moment" (Kristeller 237) and in which the phantastic pneuma transmits the book of the universe, writing on the soul the "seals and characters" of the terrestrial and celestial worlds (Berman 74–75; Thomas 190, 223).

The images of phantasy are understood in terms of contemporary writing technology, often described as imprints on a wax surface. With attention to Plato, Aristotle, Cicero, Quintilian, Aquinas, and Augustine, Carruthers concludes that "the metaphor of memory as a written surface is so ancient and so persistent in all Western cultures that it must, I think, be seen as a governing model or 'cognitive archetype,' in Max Black's phrase" (16). Consequently, the activity of rhetoric is a replication, or redirection, of the phantastic imagination. For Aristotle, the *topoi* that inform rhetorical invention are regions in the mind where arguments are stored as *phantasmata* for ready application (Aristotle 163b; Carruthers 29). And for Quintilian, "the greatest part of rhetorical activity involves the [phantastic] functions of the sensory soul, forming, combining, reacting to, storing, and recollecting sense images" (Carruthers 206).

Through the Middle Ages, rhetorical invention—and for the most practiced intellects, formal composition as well—was a process allied to reverie, in which the writer searched the places of memory in an exercise that "corresponds to what Aristotle calls the 'deliberative imagination,' a combination of *phantasia* with *dianoia*, or the power of constructing with conscious judgment a single image out of a number of images":

> So the act of invention, carried out by cogitation, was thought to be one of combining or "laying together" in one "place" or compositive image or design the divided bits previously filed and cross-filed in other discrete *loci rerum* when preparing to speak, and its close kinship is apparent to the technique of memorizing texts according to their *res*, which one would then shape into words to suit a particular occasion.
>
> For composition is not an act of writing, it is rumination, cogitation, dictation, a listening and a dialogue, a "gathering" (*collectio*) of voices from their several places in memory. (Carruthers 197–98)

De Quincey's Palimpsest

As David Masson points out in his 1890 introduction to volume 13 of De Quincey's *Writings*, a volume that Masson titles "Tales and Prose Phantasies," De Quincey dissociates both "rhetorical prose" and "prose phantasy" from "the ordinary jog-trot prose which suffices for business-documents, books of information, etc." (5). Masson correctly notes that for De Quincey, rhetoric is "the art of conscious playing with a subject intellectually and inventively," and phantasy is a product of "solitary self-musing" or "long nocturnal reverie" (13.5–7). He compares De Quincey's phantasy to Bacon's "feigned history" (13.6) that is, as Bacon explains in the *Advancement of Learning*, "extremely licensed, and doth truly refer to the imagination . . . [which may] make unlawful matches and divorces of things." Such lawlessness is a necessary expression of the human spirit, "the world being in proportion inferior to the soul; by reason whereof there is, agreeable to the spirit of man, a more ample greatness, a more exact goodness, and a more absolute variety, than can be found in the nature of things" (2.4.1).

De Quincey begins his phantastic meditation on imagination, addiction, childhood, and death, the *Suspiria De Profundis*, with appreciation for the art of phantastic reverie, which has disappeared amidst the "fierce condition of eternal hurry" in his own time:

> Among the powers in man which suffer by this too intense life of the social instincts, none suffers more than the power of dreaming. Let no man think this a trifle. The machinery for dreaming planted in the human brain was not planted for nothing. That faculty, in alliance with the mystery of darkness, is the one great tube through which man communicates with the shadowy. And the dreaming organ, in connexion with the heart, the eye, and the ear, compose the magnificent apparatus which forces the infinite into the chambers of a human brain, and throws dark reflections from eternities below all life upon the mirrors of the sleeping mind. (88)

The faculty of dreaming "suffers from the decay of solitude" that defines modern life. Solitude is a necessary condition of the dreaming imagination, which for De Quincey corresponds to the composing imagination. When he is "lying awake, unable to sleep," De Quincey's memory for long unread verses begins to "blossom anew": "I become a distinguished compositor in the darkness, and, with my aerial composing stick [both a printer's tool and, in this context, a kind of magic wand], sometimes I 'set up' half a page of verses, that would be found tolerably correct if collated with the volume I never had in my hand but once" (116–17). De Quincey attributes this capacity to a faculty higher than the retentive memory, which surveys topics through an associative magic and exercises "an electric aptitude for seizing analogies, and by means of those aerial pontoons passing over like lightning from one topic to another" (117). De Quincey follows the ancients with his recognition that invention involves recourse to a phantastic inner sense. His is a composing posture similar to that of Cicero's Crassus, who lies in silent meditation for two hours before delivering his final speech in *De Oratore* (3.5.197); such mental composition was regarded by Cicero and Quintilian as a skill more advanced than composing in writing. In Book 10 of the *Institutio Oratoria*, Quintilian describes an accomplished rhetor not unlike De Quincey's "distinguished compositor":

> For there are places and occasions where writing is impossible, while both are available in abundance for premeditation. For but a few hours' thought will suffice to cover all the points even of cases of importance; if we wake at night, the very darkness will assist us, while even in the midst of legal proceedings, our mind will find some vacant space for meditation, and will refuse to remain inactive. . . . At length, however, our powers will have developed so far that the man who is not hampered by lack of natural ability will by dint of persistent [practice] be enabled, when it comes to speak-

ing, to rely no less on what he has thought out than what he has written out and learnt by heart. (10.6.2–4)

Quintilian's rhetor here exercises the capacity to associate "vivid conceptions" (*rerum imagines*), which Quintilian equates with the Greek *phantasiai* (10.7.15; see also Carruthers 206).

De Quincey's phantasy requires, in the first place, a "constitutional determination to reverie," but such determination is forcibly distracted by "the continual development of vast physical agencies" (De Quincey, *Suspiria* 87), that is, nature-perverting, chaos-producing modern machines that represent, throughout De Quincey's work, "the stresses of external experience inimical to an introspective consciousness" (De Luca 89). In an increasingly crowded, mechanistic world, De Quincey fears that "the action of thought and feeling is too much dissipated and squandered. To reconcentrate them into meditative habits, a necessity is felt by all observing persons for sometimes retiring from crowds" (*Suspiria* 88).

In this world of inexorably decaying solitude, De Quincey clears a space for imagination and writing with opium. The *Suspiria De Profundis* is his admission that the addiction is permanent (91) and that it helps him "to dream more splendidly than others." Finding himself in an age where mechanical progress has displaced visionary scope, De Quincey recognizes that there is no longer—as in the prescientific past—a societal appreciation for reverie as a common habit of mind. He praises opium (while mourning his addiction) as an antisocial technology that maintains the composing imagination, creates a network of associations among the present and the past (among supernatural and natural spirits and powers), and activates the mind as a magical surface, as a palimpsest.

A palimpsest is a writing surface, usually wax or parchment, which has been reused, on which erased manuscripts are still visible beneath the newest writing. Before paper was introduced to the West in the late Middle Ages (Gaur 46–47), palimpsests were commonly used for composing in writing. De Quincey recounts the discovery by medieval chemists of a way "to discharge the writing from the [parchment] roll and thus to make it available for a new succession of thoughts" without completely erasing what had been previously written, so that "the more refined chemistry" of De Quincey's age could "restor[e] all below which they had effaced" (*Suspiria* 141). This is modern chemical magic that surpasses the thaumaturgical claims of a Paracelsus, that "by our modern conjurations of science, secrets of ages remote from each other have been exorcised [summoned] from the accumulated shadows of centuries" (143). The restored palimpsest that De Quincey imagines reveals a history of the human imagination: "In the illustration imagined by myself, from the case of some individual palimpsest, the Grecian tragedy had seemed to be displaced, but was *not* displaced, by the monkish legend; and the monkish legend had seemed to be displaced, but was *not* displaced, by the knightly romance. In some potent convulsion of the system, all wheels back into its earliest elementary stage" (145–46). A succession of texts is transformed by the "witch" of chemistry (143) into a simultaneity of texts. This magical process is an analog to human intellection:

> What else than a natural and mighty palimpsest is the human brain?
> Such a palimpsest is my brain; such a palimpsest, O reader! is
> yours. Everlasting layers of ideas, images, feelings, have fallen
> upon your brain softly as light. Each succession has seemed to bury
> all that went before. And yet in reality not one has been extin-
> guished. (144)

Locating the individual within the "everlasting" suggests, as De Luca notes, that the dreamer/writer "houses the infinite in his own finite corporeality, and it raises the substance of his experience" so that "the history of the individual imagination is thus a microcosm of the history of imagination in general" (60, 75). Writing is thus participation in a "giant composite form" (74) consti-tuted by natural and supernatural objects and powers and infinitely larger than the individual himself. In reverie, which is for De Quincey necessarily maintained artificially—with opium—one composes the giant self.

The "aerial compositor" enacts the translation of phantastic language into human language, as De Quincey demonstrates in the section on "Levana and Our Ladies of Sorrow," a dream-legend of dark goddesses: "Mighty phantoms like these disdain the infirmities of language. They may utter voices through the organs of man when they dwell in human hearts. . . . *They* wheeled in mazes; *I* spelled the steps. *They* telegraphed from afar; *I* read the signals. *They* conspired together; and on the mirrors of darkness *my* eye traced the plots. *Theirs* were the symbols,—*mine* are the words" (149). This description of the translating imagination recapitulates the ancient presupposition of the primacy of phantastic language, while it also exemplifies the worst fears of Sprat and the Royal Society, the replacement of determinate reality by phantasms, which is, effectively, the transformation of reality into a giant self, a cosmology of phantasms. In his essay on "Style," De Quincey associates such a self with "subjective science," which takes thought in the only direction "that open[s] an avenue at once to novelty and to freedom of thought" (*Selected Essays* 222):

> Such a science is found in the relations of man to God,—that is in
> theology; in the determinations of space,—that is geometry; in the
> relations of existence or being universally to the human mind,—
> otherwise called metaphysics or ontology; in the relations of the
> mind to itself,—otherwise logic. . . . In this present world of the
> practical and the ponderable, we so little understand or value such
> abstractions, though once our British schoolmen took the lead in

these subtleties, that we confound their very natures and names. (220–21)

This is another one of De Quincey's attacks on a modern age that has abandoned a sympathetic universe of infinite imaginative (and for the dreamer, palpably real) resources for mechanistic virtues that dissipate novelty and freedom of thought. Passages such as this, in concert with the claims for phantastic intellection in the *Suspiria*, inform De Quincey's persistent recollections of a past in which the "technology" of composing was founded on theories of phantasy, enacted in the strata of both the mental and scribal palimpsest. Such composing, because it is fundamentally associative, requires a sympathetic universe, and it is the loss of that universe that—for romantics like De Quincey—changed for the worse prevailing conceptions of the composing imagination. As Berman concludes, "What was ultimately created by the shift from animism to mechanism was not merely a new science, but a new personality to go with it" (113). He summarizes that lost personality which the romantics would recreate:

> The world [before the seventeenth century] was seen as a vast assemblage of correspondences. All things have relationships with all other things, and these relations are ones of sympathy and antipathy. Men attract women, lodestones attract iron, oil repels water, and dogs repel cats. Things mingle and touch in an endless chain, or rope, vibrated (wrote Della Porta in *Natural Magic*) by the first cause, God. Things are also analogous to man in the famous alchemical concept of the microcosm and the macrocosm: the rocks of the earth are its bones, the rivers its veins, the forests its hair and the cicadas its dandruff. The world duplicates and reflects itself in an endless network of similarity and dissimilarity. (74)

While prescientific rhetoric entails the *trained capacity for phantastic reverie*, the romantic rhetoric that De Quincey represents entails a *nostalgia for phantastic reverie* and for the sympathetic universe such reverie requires. But phantasy, like rhetoric, has "silently faded away before the stern tendencies of the age" (De Quincey, *Selected Essays* 97), so that practicing it in the nineteenth century requires determination and drugs.

The Reappearance of Phantasy?

When Roland Barthes defines the postmodern text as "a galaxy of signifiers" in which "the networks are many and interact" (5), he is answering the Royal Society's appeal for a singular "right practice" by conceiving writerly intellection as phantasy. Barthes's galaxy is populated by *lexias*, units of reading whose interaction creates a "density of connotations" (13) within this magical cosmology of signifiers:

The text, in its mass, is comparable to a sky, at once flat and smooth, deep, without edges and without landmarks; like the sooth-sayer drawing on it with the tip of his staff an imaginary rectangle wherein to consult, according to certain principles, the flight of birds, the commentator traces through the text certain zones of read-ing, in order to observe therein the migration of meanings, the out-cropping of codes, the passage of citations. (14)

Lest we presume—taking leave of De Quincey—that opium is the last, best inducement of a phantastic composing imagination, I cite Barthes here in order to mention that a postmodern conception of writing as the open, magical play of signifiers, coupled with computer technologies that make it possible to migrate from citation to citation, meaning to meaning, may constitute new possibilities for phantasy.

In *Writing Space*, Jay Bolter argues that the computer can call up a network of sympathetic universes: "The computer is the ideal technology for the net-working of America, in which hierarchical structures of control and interpreta-tion break down into their component parts and begin to oscillate in a continu-ously shifting web of relations" (236). The computer, in this conception, becomes a reverie machine, a box of *lexias*-as-phantasms, an artificial intelli-gence that—although it represents the epitome of scientific achievement in this century—has reached a stage of advancement at which it can replicate the prescientific composing imagination.

If we reconceive the history of the composing imagination in phantastic terms, as I have attempted here, it would seem that the technology for its reenchantment has indeed appeared on the scene, or if you will, the screen. The electronic page is the new palimpsest, the computer network a participatory cosmology, and hypertext—the simultaneous display of topics, graphics, glosses, digressions, and drafts that comprise the writer's working "mem-ory"—is the postmodern grammar of phantasy. As George Landow explains, a hypertext is a "docuverse" in which memory, imagination, reason, and intellect merge in the act of phantastic travel among *lexias* (see especially 42). As such, it may reawaken the Royal Society's fear, that stable, consensual knowledge will vanish at the keyboard of the phantastic, postmodern, giant self.

Works Cited

Aristotle. *Topics. The Complete Works of Aristotle.* Ed. Jonathan Barnes. Princeton: Princeton UP, 1984. 2:167–277.

Bacon, Francis. *The Advancement of Learning.* Ed. G. W. Kitchin. Totowa: Rowman, 1974.

Barthes, Roland. *S/Z.* Trans. Richard Miller. New York: Hill, 1974.

Berman, Morris. *The Re-Enchantment of the World.* Ithaca: Cornell UP, 1981.

Bolter, Jay. *Writing Space: The Computer, Hypertext, and the History of Writing.* Hillsdale: Erlbaum, 1991.

Carruthers, Mary. *The Book of Memory: A Study of Memory in Medieval Culture.* Cambridge: Cambridge UP, 1990.

Cicero. *De Oratore (On Oratory and Orators).* Trans. J. S. Watson. Carbondale: Southern Illinois UP, 1970.

Couliano, Ioan. *Eros and Magic in the Renaissance.* Trans. Margaret Cook. Chicago: U of Chicago P, 1987.

Covino, William A. *The Art of Wondering: A Revisionist Return to the History of Rhetoric.* Portsmouth: Heinemann-Boynton/Cook, 1988.

———. "Magic and/as Rhetoric: Outlines of a History of Phantasy." *JAC* 12.1 (1992): 349–58.

De Luca, V. A. *Thomas De Quincey: The Prose of Vision.* Toronto: U of Toronto P, 1980.

De Quincey, Thomas. *Selected Essays on Rhetoric.* Ed. Frederick Burwick. Carbondale: Southern Illinois UP, 1967.

———. *Suspiria De Profundis. Confessions of an English Opium Eater and Other Writings.* Ed. Grevel Lindop. Oxford: Oxford UP, 1985. 87–181.

———. *Writings of De Quincey.* 1890. Ed. David Masson. AMS, 1968.

Ficino, Marsilio. *Marsilio Ficino and the Phaedran Charioteer.* Ed. and trans. M. J. B. Allen. Berkeley: U of California P, 1981.

———. *Three Books on Life.* Ed. and trans. Carol V. Kaske and John R. Clark. Binghamton, NY: Center for Medieval and Early Renaissance Studies, 1989.

Gaur, Albertine. *A History of Writing.* London: British Library, 1984.

Gorgias. "Encomium of Helen." Trans. Rosamond Kent Sprague. *The Rhetorical Tradition: Readings from Classical Times to the Present.* Ed. Patricia Bizzell and Bruce Herzberg. Boston: St. Martin's, 1990. 40–42.

Kristeller, Paul Oscar. *The Philosophy of Marsilio Ficino.* Trans. Virginia Conant. Gloucester: Peter Smith, 1964.

Landow, George. *Hypertext: The Convergence of Contemporary Critical Theory and Technology.* Baltimore: Johns Hopkins, 1992.

Pico della Mirandola, Gianfrancesco. *On the Imagination.* Trans. Harry Caplan. New Haven, CT: Yale UP, 1930.

Quintilian. *The Institutio Oratoria of Quintilian.* Trans. H. E. Butler. Cambridge: Harvard UP, 1922.

Sprat, Thomas. *History of the Royal Society.* Ed. Jackson Cope and Harold Jones. St. Louis: Washington UP, 1958.

Taylor, Anya. *Magic and English Romanticism.* Athens: U of Georgia P, 1979.

Thomas, Keith. *Religion and the Decline of Magic.* New York: Scribner's, 1971.

Vickers, Brian. "The Royal Society and English Prose Style: A Reassessment." *Rhetoric and the Pursuit of Truth: Language Change in the Seventeenth and Eighteenth Centuries.* Brian Vickers and Nancy Streuver. Los Angeles: Clark Memorial Library, 1985. 3–76.

Yates, Francis. *The Art of Memory.* Chicago: U of Chicago P, 1966.

13   Voice as Echo of Delivery, Ethos as Transforming Process

Theresa Enos

REHISTORICIZING THE NEGLECTED ART OF DELIVERY CAN HELP US SEE THE connections between this fifth art of classical rhetoric and the concept of voice and ethos in contemporary rhetoric. As Kathleen Welch argues, making connections between presenting a self in speaking and presenting a self in writing can help us illuminate twentieth-century conceptions of ethos (139). Central to the new rhetorics as well as classical rhetorics is ethos as the most powerful persuader, the interiorizing of the writer's presentation of a discourse. But our new rhetorics call for a reconceptualization of the notion of ethos. Both new criticism and postmodernism make it impossible to say about the author of a text, "This is someone who is telling the truth"—indeed a momentous change. Reconceptualizing ethos will allow us to see that through the text the writer is asking for assent, not presenting the "truth." Textual knowledge comes not so much *from* the text but rather someone speaking *through* the text. Ethos, then, becomes part of the whole rhetorical strategy; it is that set of values that we can find coming through the immediate text. The main shift is from presentation of truth to facilitating the acceptance of belief.

Voice and ethos are common terms in rhetoric and composition, yet perhaps no terms are harder to define—unless it's the word *rhetoric* itself. What I'd like to explore here is that orphaned delivery, detached from its sister arts for most of its history, is one reason for our present-day difficulty with concepts of voice and ethos. To do this I'll offer an historical sketch of delivery, moving from its classical treatment to the prominence given it by the Elocutionary Movement in the eighteenth-century and then its apparent demise in the twentieth century. What I hope to do by charting delivery's rise and fall is to suggest that we can better understand the concept of voice in written discourse by recognizing it as an echo of the past's art of delivery.

Classical Conceptions of Delivery

The importance of delivery is evident in what we know of Sophistic rhetoric, that strand of rhetoric that now resides in the new rhetorics: Because we cannot rationally know truth, it is one's presentation of ethos, not just logical presentation, that is the most powerful persuader. Rhetoric creates belief, not "truth." The Sophists' method was to imitate those orators whose speeches were the most effective in bringing about belief or action, and delivery was the primary instrument, thus foregrounding the character of the speaker (see G. Kennedy 25–26, 40).

Aristotle, like other classical rhetoricians, admits that delivery is of great importance but, like most other classical rhetoricians, dismisses the subject in a few sentences. Dividing delivery into voice and volume, pitch and rhythm, he thus related delivery to the whole idea of style as concrete presentation versus abstract formulation. In effect, then, Aristotle unites delivery and diction, bringing them into the province of style, mentioning, however, that there was no treatise on matters of voice.

Cicero renamed delivery *actio*, saying that it produces the same effects as acting. In giving over three-fourths of *De Oratore* to elocution, Cicero stressed the importance of the orator appearing to his listeners to be the sort of man that he wishes to appear. Equating delivery and voice, Cicero says, "To effectiveness and excellence in delivery the voice doubtless contributes the most, the voice, I say, which, in its full strength, must be the object of our wishes; and next, whatever strength of voice we have, to cherish it" (3.60). Quintilian also equates delivery with voice, giving to voice the power to conciliate, persuade, and move (11.3.154).

The author of *Rhetorica ad Herennium*, while arguing that no one of the five arts of rhetoric is the most important, puts delivery before style and memory in his system of persuasion, stressing that an "exceptionally great usefulness resides in the delivery" and that none of the five arts is of value without delivery (qtd. in *Readings from Classical Rhetoric* 168). *Rhetorica ad Herennium* considers delivery, also equating it with voice, from three aspects: volume (gift of nature), stability (training), and flexibility (variance in intonation). This last aspect, flexibility, is classified into three parts: conversational tone (relaxed and closest to daily speech), tone of debate (energetic and argumentative), and tone of amplification (exhortatory, either of wrath or pity). The author of *Rhetorica ad Herennium*, aware that he is undertaking the great task of "trying to express physical movements in words and *portray vocal intonations in writing,"* is not altogether confident that it's even possible to treat such matters in writing. However, he is sure of one thing: "Good delivery ensures that what the orator is saying seems to come from his heart" (*Readings from Classical Rhetoric* 169, 171; emphasis mine).

The later Ramian classification placing invention and arrangement under philosophy and style and delivery under rhetoric had the effect of separating delivery from style. Ramus divided style into tropes and figures, delivery into voice and gesture. Perhaps because of the ascendancy of print, he had little to say about delivery (or memory), and this too may have led delivery, along with its sister art, memory, to be orphaned.

Although classical rhetorics didn't give us a *theory* of delivery, they did give it prominence, even foregrounding it as the art all else depended on. But after giving delivery prominence, for the most part the classicists went on to discuss the other arts of rhetoric. Delivery was a matter of voice, primarily meaning diction, that is, choice and arrangement of words.

The Elocutionary Movement

Not until the eighteenth century did delivery, as the nexus of theory and practice, receive the emphasis that the earlier tradition said it should have, even though no real rules had ever been established. With Campbell's *The Philosophy of Rhetoric*, elocution was reabsorbed into style. To Campbell "eloquence" meant those stylistic qualities by which the discourse adapted to its desired effect. To Hugh Blair, echoing Gorgias, Isocrates, Cicero, and especially Quintilian on eloquence (see G. Kennedy 236), nature/nurture both are necessary for improvement in eloquence. The orator must have natural talent for it to be much affected and improved by the practice of the art of rhetoric. Personal character, knowledge of subject, and imitation all are important, but Blair was against "mechanical" style—practice coming out of an overly prescriptive methodology—in which he included delivery. By this time rhetoric had pretty well been integrated into writing about literature, and this set the stage for the Elocutionary Movement.

By the second half of the eighteenth century, interest in elocution surged. Thomas Sheridan, the most recognized of the eighteenth-century elocutionists, gave the emerging movement *applied* voice and gesture, believing the need was great for expressing ideas orally and hoping to "lift oral English to the high status level enjoyed by written English" (Golden, Berquist, and Coleman 218). The emphasis on delivery, associated primarily with Sheridan's application, was rather shallow, although for the first time its methodology was based on theory. In Sheridan's methodology survived the Sophistic strand of classical rhetoric, the movement underscoring the consequence of the speaker's achievement (G. Kennedy 228).

The prescriptive methodology of the Elocutionary Movement turned more and more to the science of gesturing. Gilbert Austin's *Chironomia* reduced delivery to a consideration of gesture, fifteen chapters of this curious work detailing position of the feet, arms, hands, head, eyes, shoulders, and body. Wilbur S. Howell comments on this detrimental attention to such mechanical rules of gesture:

> Voice and gesture seem much more trivial when studied by them-
> selves than they are when studied within the context of the best pos-
> sible conceptions of invention, arrangement, and style. It was the
> solidest virtue of Cicero's and Quintilian's rhetorical writings that
> they saw delivery as an activity allied with but never separable
> from, the speaker's need to know his subject, arrange it properly,
> and to give it effective expression. Indeed, Cicero and Quintilian
> had learned this virtue from Aristotle, and the lesson should never
> be forgotten. (18)

The mechanical rules of gesture were also soundly criticized by Whately in *Elements of Rhetoric,* who argued for the need for a natural mode of delivery instead of a prescriptive system that promoted artificiality.

The treatment of delivery, especially in the latter half of the eighteenth century, was tied essentially to *actio,* to the oral voice. Left to itself, we can see how *elocutio* tended inevitably toward an art of display, consisting of training and frequent practice in the management of the voice and gestures. The classical concept of voice as establishing one's ethos was thus shallowly appropriated by the elocutionists; classical concepts of delivery echoed only faintly.

Classical Concepts of Ethos and Voice

To Aristotle, ethos denotes the sum total of a person's moral qualities (see 2.1.5–7). The orator persuades by moral character when the speech is delivered in such a manner as to render the speaker worthy of confidence. But this confidence must be due to the speech itself, not to any preconceived idea of the speaker's character. To Aristotle, moral character constitutes the most effective means of proof. To this he adds goodwill and the very quality of goodness. The content a given, the understandable focus is not on what one is saying but on how one is saying it. Of course, such a focus has in part led to the pejorative sense of rhetoric as stylistic ornamentation over content.

Michael Halloran, however, has deepened this familiar Aristotelian theory of ethos I've sketched, showing how the classical concept of ethos is argument from authority, the argument that says, "Believe me because I am the sort of person whose word you can believe" (60). Ethos in the classical tradition means a depiction of the conventional self rather than the private self, the ideal orator of classical times, the "good man skilled in speaking," who embod-ied the cultural values of the time. Aristotle, as well as other classical rhetori-cians, believed that a person achieves this ethos of convention through the process of habituation. One becomes virtuous through performing virtuous actions. One's "right" character is formed through this process. Halloran's example: "To achieve courage, an aspect of *ethos*, I must act courageously over and over again until it becomes quite natural for me to act in a courageous fashion. When I have the habit of courage, I have the virtue of courage as part of my character" (61). Halloran's point is that through rhetorical pedagogy, through practice, an ethos can be interiorized not only by choosing ethical modes of action but also by schooling in "proper rhetorical habits" (61). These habits of course come from playing the role, from working with style, from awareness of voice. This may seem a "calculated ethos" in contrast to the modern concept of ethos, which stresses an evocation of the private more than the public character.

Twentieth-Century Concepts of Ethos and Voice

By the end of the 1930s, the teaching of voice in the elocutionary style for the most part had disappeared. Even though emphasis was on style, primarily "correct" style, delivery and voice had little place in the writing classrooms in American schools. However, voice and persona were easily understood terms in the interpretation of literary texts. Voice had been separated from the classical concept of ethos.

Indeed, as Roger Cherry points out, ethos and voice in this century have not been "subjected to careful examination. . . . Neglect of self-representation in the study of writing is curious given the almost universal significance attached to the self-as-speaker and self-as-writer" (252). Furthermore, Cherry argues that the concepts of ethos and persona are commonly conflated. Aristotle's *Rhetoric* identifies the characteristics of ethos that lend credibility to the speaker: practical wisdom, good moral character, and goodwill toward the audience. The problem with substituting the persona for ethos is that persona has come to us from a literary rather than a rhetorical tradition. Persona, from its initial meaning of "theatrical mask" or "role," accounts for this "disjunction between an author and the author's presence in the literary text" (Cherry 256–57). Literary theory, most especially poststructuralist theory, holds that "authors can never really be said to be present in the literary text, that it is essential to distinguish between the voice or persona of the literary work and the historical author who created it" (257). The author cannot actively be present in the literary text; he or she is present only indirectly, that is, only through a mediated persona.

But ethos in rhetorical theory is paramount; the speaker in a text needs to project the three qualities of good sense, moral character, and goodwill in order to achieve credibility and thereby effect persuasion. Therefore, in rhetorical theory, ethos and persona, if not absolutely equivalent, are closely interrelated. Walker Gibson in *Persona: A Style Study for Readers and Writers* makes this argument, showing little distinction among ethos, persona, and voice.

Cherry, however, places ethos (the writer's real self) at one end of a continuum and persona (the writer's fictional self) at the other. Through ethos writers gain credibility through practical wisdom, moral character, and goodwill; through persona they create the role appropriate to the discourse community in which they are operating.

Although Cherry is careful to stress the interaction of ethos and persona, he argues for the usefulness of distinguishing between them, saying in his proposed continuum that "*ethos* would reach farther toward persona than would persona toward *ethos*" (269). I would, however, reverse the movement and argue that ethos emerges from voice. The classical concept of delivery as the art of speaking what the speaker means, and what the speaker *is*, shifts to a concept of the speaker's character as instrumental in facilitating the acceptance of *belief*, not "truth." The inventive universe of style subsumes ethos and voice.

Style as Verbal Mansions

Just as concepts of ethos and voice are sources of confusion, so is the concept of style. Like the word *grammar*, style causes problems because of its different levels of definition. We easily accept its definitions of personal expression that sets one writer's verbal idiosyncrasies apart from another's and conventionality of technique as taught by most handbooks ("be clear," "be correct," and so forth). The eighteenth-century biologist Buffon's often-quoted "style is the man himself," while encompassing both these accepted definitions of style, comes closer to a definition of style I want to explore further as I try to show how ethos emerges from voice—rather than vice versa—according to the stylistic mansions one builds in a discourse.

The Greek word for style, *lexis*, seems best to capture Buffon's familiar definition of style, encompassing all its definitions into one word. In *A Sense of Style*, Jane Blankenship explains how *lexis* carries with it "the three connotations of thought, word (*logos*), and speaking" (1). This last connotation, speaking, is the "expression" of logos; thus I'd argue that this especially is the element of voice. This definition of style, encompassed in *lexis*, best captures its comprehensiveness, its power as a way of looking at things: "Style is what we see, our vision, and *how* we see, our means/mode of vision" (Ullman 201).

That there are differences between one's ethos in speech and writing is understandable. As Robert Connors points out, even if the speaker is unknown to the audience, "the speaker is surrounded by a far richer context for establishing [ethos]. Nonverbal methods of procuring a favorable *ethos*—manner of dress, personal appearance, types of gesture—are available to the speaker, as are the purely verbal methods: tone of voice, richness and loudness of speech, speed of delivery" ("The Differences" 285). In comparison the writer has few tangible factors to use in creating ethos. (The manuscript itself, font type, page format, and the like is also a means of ethical appeal, as Connors points out in "*Actio*: A Rhetoric of Manuscripts.") "Unseen by the reader, left to show a personality only through the product, the writer is in a position of fewer but more controllable possibilities . . . [of] style and . . . the sort of argument he or she chooses to use" (285).

But even Aristotle told us that language intended for the ear differs from language intended for the eye:

> Compared with those of others, the speeches of professional writers sound thin . . . those of the orators, on the other hand, are good to hear spoken, but look amateurish [to] a reader. This is because they . . . contain many dramatic touches, which, being robbed of all dramatic rendering, fail to do their own proper work, and consequently look silly, thus strings of unconnected words, and constant repetitions of words and phrases, are very properly condemned in written speeches: but not in spoken speeches—speakers use them freely. (197)

Aristotle here is contrasting the oral with the literary in terms of grammatical structure. Our oral speech is chiefly formulaic while in literary texts there is little formulaic composition. Oral is typically nonperiodic, proceeding in an adding or cumulative style. On the other hand, literary composition tends to be more periodic. Oral composition generally uses well-established themes and ideas that can be placed in standard patterns. Literary composition uses typically newer themes or combines older themes in ways more novel than in oral composition.

However, though the distinctions between actually speaking and writing suggest incompatible differences, we can compare two kinds of written discourse, a speaking style and a writing style, as Walker Gibson does in *Persona*. (Also see Enos, "Ethical and Stylistic Implications in Delivering Conference Papers.") And it is by an examination of the speaking style of written discourse that I will argue for a twentieth-century concept of delivery: a transforming ethos where we see, and share, the process of transformation taking place. The twentieth-century concept of voice echoing from the art of delivery particularly includes the *conscious* selection of *patterns* that project an ethos. Such stylistic, *rhetorical* choices are, like voice in the ancient art of delivery, stylized verbal *forms*. And the form, I would argue, is closer to the structure of narrative— as Jim Corder keeps telling us—than to analysis or argument as a *presentation*. Rhythmic patterns are paramount, for the conscious re-forming of stylistic patterns shapes not only language use but also meaning. This narrative style, or speaking style, of writing as opposed to a literary style of writing groups words in order to enhance rhythmic patterns (see Gibson; Gregg 74).

Ethos as Transforming Process Through Voice

Although I would not go so far to say that voice in traditional rhetorics is akin to lines being drawn on some ethical Etch-a-Sketch, the concept of voice has changed in the movement from classical to elocutionist to modern rhetorics. The main shift, of course, is from presentation of truth to facilitating the acceptance of belief. And the idea of voice as the art of "speaking what you mean and are" is still valid, though I would argue here for a shift to make the concept better fit into the underriding philosophy of the new rhetorics: Instead of seeing voice as the kind of "proof" that character projects in discourse, voice emerges through the discourse as a way of becoming, knowing. That is, it leads to what I'm calling a transforming ethos.

But voice has had shifting connotations even within the twentieth century. When expressionistic rhetoric was in full flower during the 1960s and 1970s, voice was its most important quality. If someone isn't persuaded that one speaks the truth, it's because the speaker hasn't given the "authentic" sign. By the end of the 1970s, however, as cognitive theories of composition began taking center-front, the attention to style/voice had dwindled. By the latter part of the 1980s, increasing attention was being focused on the new rhetorics in English departments. (In speech communication, however, the attention to the shift from persuasion to identification in Burke's sense of the term was pretty much in full swing in the 1950s. Burke's theory of identification is based on the philosophical basis of style. A writer, as a symbol-using animal, uses linguistic strategies, to give signs to the reader that some characteristic of the writer is similar to or identifies with some characteristic of the reader, thereby achieving what Burke calls identification. And for Burke, persuasion can be effected only through the "strategy" of identification.)

One of the terms used to distinguish the new rhetorics from other modern rhetorics is *epistemic*. That term underscores the idea that through the intersubjective clash of ideas and the inclusive, transactional, dialogic nature of the new rhetorics, discourse creates belief much more than truth. Epistemic rhetoric is a way of knowing, but the awareness of that process of change is crucial. The audience of epistemic discourse has to be acutely aware of this change through transforming ethos in order for persuasion to take place. Furthermore, transforming ethos demands the process of dialogic action.

Though too often we think of prose as being written in silence and read by its readers in silence, we do know there is a voice there, and this voice is an essential part of the discourse. As readers, we see, but, consciously or not, we hear too, and it is by this "hearing," this dialogical quality that most strongly touches us and moves us to join the writer, to open ourselves up to the writer's "courtship," as Burke calls the process of achieving identification, and thus move toward *being* persuaded.

Ong says about this dialogic process: "Every human word implies not only the existence—at least in the imagination—of another to whom the word is uttered, but it also implies that the speaker has a kind of otherness within himself . . . voice is the foundation for role playing among [us] in the sense that the use of voice and its understanding . . . forces [us] to enter into others" (88). Neither the writer nor the reader can really "emit" words unless either one is at the same time "receiving" them. Ong points out that "speaking and hearing are not simply operations." They are entangled in that each exhibits "a dialectical structure which mirrors the mysterious depths" of a person's style. As the writer composes thoughts in words, he or she "hears these words echoing within . . . and thereby follows his [or her] own thought, as though he [or she] were another person." Conversely, the reader repeats the words he or she hears and "thereby understands them," as though this reader were two persons. "This double and interlocking dialectic . . . provides the matrix for human communication. The speaker listens while the hearer speaks" (83).

This language activity is dialogic in nature; the center of emission is a receiving center, a tool. Berlin says such activity is social-epistemic rhetoric, one emphasizing the interaction of subject-writer-reader with language as the agent of mediation: "Meaning comes about as the external world, the conceptions the writer . . . brings to the external world, and the audience the writer . . . is addressing all *simultaneously* act on each other during the *process* of communicating. The result of this dialectic is unpredictable, providing for *creativity* and accounting for the *inevitability* of change" (167, emphasis mine).

All of this, of course, comes out of the inventive universe of style. Ong says voice offers semantic stability by bonding meaning and intention. But at the same time "it disrupts that stability by making linguistic usage distinctive, personal, idiosyncratic" (78). Figurative language also brings instability; however, figures differ from voice: "Whereas figures breach the relationship between signifiers and signifieds, voice heals the breach. In a linguistic universe of semantic instability, readers and hearers perceive intended meanings in figurative language because rhetorical voice makes them understood" (qtd. in W. Kennedy 78). Writers shape their personal voices by lexical choices, syntactic combinations, figurative language, and devices of rhythm, pacing, and tone. Voice functions to highlight linguistic traits that establish the writer's character. But the individuality of any voice is not just idiosyncratic; it is rather a sharing in the discourse of others through conventions and ritual (W. Kennedy 86). Voice's dialogic quality prompts the reader's creative participation with the writer. Voice frames shared meanings; thus ethos grows out of voice. The beginning of this process, of course, is the Burkean notion of identification wherein opposites are reconciled through voice.

The shift in rhetoric from persuasion to identification elevates ethos. Furthermore, ethos cannot be separated from audience consideration because part of the ethical appeal is one's stance, a textual manifestation of an attitude and what Aristotle calls goodwill, the benevolent attitude of the writer toward readers. Neither can ethos be separated from the writer in that the writer has to evidence reasoning power, common sense, and control over the subject matter. And, of course, the speaker's presence reflects character and moral values. While in pathos and logos attention is primarily focused on the listeners, in that an emotion is elicited from them or a process of syllogistic thinking is initiated, in ethos the appeal shifts toward the writer. Still, effective persuasion arises from the union of writer and reader; the opening up of a world holding within it values that both participants adhere to underlies the whole concept of ethos (see Enos, " 'An Eternal Golden Braid' ").

Epistemic rhetoric perhaps more than any other modern approach foregrounds style in a holistic way because its focus on writing as a way of knowing requires interaction of writer, subject, and audience through language. Style in this framework means that we can never dissociate our very selves from the ways in which we open up our views of reality onto the written page.

Analyzing Ethos Through Voice: An Application

Why *do* we listen to some and not to others? To learn about the voice that speaks to us, that invites us to begin the process of self-persuasion, we must turn to style, which emanates from one's inventive universe. Burke has told us, "Only those voices from without are effective which can speak in the language of a voice within" (39).

Because Jim Corder's essays always exemplify a writer speaking and because they always are precisely worded, intellectual explorations or expositions, I would like to offer a brief essay of his and then try to show what makes his voice so distinctive. Those familiar with Corder's writings know that his usual subject is ethos, but no one, as far as I know, has analyzed Corder's own ethos by studying his rhetorical choices that create identification and thus persuasion.

Corder's style is new rhetorical rather than in the oral tradition because he is not so much concerned with "winning" an argument as he is in presenting himself through voice so as to establish an ethos he hopes others will share, will identify with. I hope to show the importance of audience in the realization of the transforming ethos, for a large part of Corder's effectiveness is the sense that he is *talking* to us, an audience he believes is committed to the speaker/writer's values, to his logos and pathos.

Indeed, all of Corder's writing is faithful to spoken form. Much, if not most, of the success of his writing depends on the voice element we hear. If we analyzed as we read, we would notice the numerous rhetorical sentence patterns, the harmony of vowel sounds, of pitch changes, of rate, of pausing, of climactic movements. We may not be aware of all this going on when we read Corder, but we can feel the inner voice's presence. What we do see is the voice riding above the material; what we do see in the discourse is first the finding of a voice and then the unfolding of the thinking on the page itself. What we end with is a realization of voice as the vehicle for a transforming ethos.

Lest I be criticized for attempting yet another stylistic analysis so pervasive in literary interpretation, let me offer Ross Winterowd's argument for doing such work as he himself quotes Bruner:

> For this reason, stylistic exercises can never be "mere" exercises in style. More dramatically stated: manner controls matter. "It has

been remarked that words are invitations to form concepts. It can
equally be said that the combinatorial or productive property of language is an invitation to take experience apart and put it together
again in new ways. . . . I am urging, in effect, that in some unknown but considerable measure, the power of words is the power
of thought." (Winterowd 164; Bruner 105)

Here is Jim Corder's essay.

Humanism Isn't a Dirty Word

Along the way—I like to think it's been sporadic rather than habitual—I've been called a number of things that I took to be uncom-
plimentary. The young man on the back of whose head I broke my
nose in a collision at first base all those years ago in high school
was uncommonly colorful in his address to me. A certain Lieuten-
ant Jackson, somewhat later, was consistently deprecatory, but
nearly always dull in his accounts of my character and behavior.
Others—who have not been able to know how dear, bright, and
cuddly I'm likely to be—have been sometimes imaginative, sometimes repetitious in their denunciations, their remarks calling God's
doom down on me, or classifying me with animal or anatomical
imagery.

I never expected, however, to be called a "secular humanist."

I don't guess I knew I was one, in the first place.

In the second place, I don't guess I ever expected anyone to think
of calling someone else a "secular humanist" in ordinary conversation. I'm more than a little surprised that the term ever got to be
common, much less vituperative.

Yet the phrase has become common. Particularly in the last year
or so. I think I have not seen or heard the phrase used by people
who might accurately be called "secular humanists" as a way of
identifying themselves. Instead, the phrase is almost invariably used
as if in condemnation of the pursuit of false gods and the practice
of subversion, if not heresy. Occasionally, it appears to be enough
for those so minded to charge those they disapprove with mere "humanism," but if the judges are severe and passionate and the sins to
be denounced are scarlet, then the amperage and magnitude are increased with the addition of the modifier, "secular."

The phrase seems to be used in attack most often by those who
seem surest they are right about most things. Wray Herbert, in a report of the American Association for the Advancement of the Humanities, reports that beginning in 1978:

> The religious Right has since launched a systematic attack—
> spearheaded by the Moral Majority—on what it calls "secular
> humanism," a heretical and morally destructive philosophy,
> Fundamentalists claim, that is being taught in the schools, col-
> leges, and universities and through the media.

Tim LaHaye, in his book, The Battle for the Mind, argues that
275,000 secular humanists have "conspired to control public debate

in the United States." His long list of "secular humanist" organizations includes all public schools, colleges and universities, the American Civil Liberties Union, government bureaucrats, all unions, the
National Organization for Women, the Supreme Court, and the
Ford, Carnegies, and Rockefeller Foundations. . . .

Among some groups, the phrase "secular humanism" is already a
standard, non-controversial form of denunciation. If one is of a particular kind of attitudinal persuasion, it appears, then one can without examination or debate denounce certain kinds of dissidents as
"secular humanists" and expect the judgment to signify wickedness
and corruption. (Unfortunately, I should add, recent attacks on "humanism" and "humanists" have often, in confusion, included denunciation or repudiation of the "humanities," the distinction apparently making no impression on the attackers, many of whom in
fact take issue with the humanities as well as with humanism.)

But "humanism" isn't a dirty word, even if it is preceded by the
dreaded modifier, "secular."

For that matter, it seems pretty silly to me to attribute class
names either to others or to oneself. If you label all members of
some group with a class name, just as sure as taxes some maverick
in the group will turn up who doesn't fit, and there you are. If you
label yourself (choose any label—humanist, linguist, biologist, anar-
chist, member of the Moral Majority), then just as sure as taxes
someone wiser will show up and point out your failure to measure
up to the standards of the class label. It seems, at any rate, a vain
and prideful thing to attribute to oneself a class name, and besides,
I'd always thought that it was probably better to be *found* moral
than it is to *call* oneself moral.

The term "humanism" with its modifier "secular" doesn't, at any
rate, seem to me to signal anything all that scary. I don't know that
I fit the category. I'd about as soon, in fact, not fit *any* category.
Some humanists reject the supernatural in any form. I probably
don't belong with them. I've seen children grow and people love
and so am perfectly glad to believe in magic in this world and out.
Beyond that, I'm inclined not to talk publicly about my religious
beliefs. People tend to look at a fellow peculiarly if they discover
that he thinks God lives on top of the Double Mountains in West
Texas, so I'll just quietly be my own priest, thank you.

Otherwise, the term "humanism" taken alone signifies a variety
of honorable things, depending upon how one defines it and what
context one locates for it. To be a "humanist," for example, could
mean to associate oneself with the great scholar-thinkers of the Renaissance to whom the modern world owes both its modernity and
its precious connections with the past. To be a "humanist," for another example, could mean to associate oneself with the distinguished line of Christian humanists that includes T. S. Eliot and
other remarkable people.

I'm glad enough simply to take the term at its most literal level,
where it signifies "the character and quality of being human." What
more could one ask, even if one wishes to preserve a religious con-

text at all times? We are "fearfully and wonderfully made," the Psalmist says; we are "the marvelous works of God." We have, despite every woe and depravity, all reason to celebrate our own "humanism" in the literal sense I have suggested:

> When I consider thy heavens, the work of thy fingers, the moon and the stars which thou hast ordained;
> What is man that thou are mindful of him? and the son of man, that thou visitest him?
> For thou hast made him a little lower than the angels, and hast crowned him with glory and honour.
> Thou madest him to have dominion over the works of thy hands; thou hast put all things under his feet:
> All sheep and oxen, yea, and the beasts of the field;
> The fowl of the air, and the fish of the sea, and whatsoever passeth through the paths of the seas.

And Christians, of course, make the most striking claim of all for "the character and quality of being human" when they worship God become man to act specifically in history, thence forever.

As for the modifier "secular," I find no shame in that, either. Taken literally, it means "of or pertaining to this world or the present life, temporal, worldly." The protestations of those who are vain and public about their piety notwithstanding, none of us anywhere has any claim to be otherwise. We are of this world, and temporal, regardless of what we may wish to proclaim in some prideful posturing. We *are* secular, whatever our yearnings.

I can understand, I think, the threat that something called "secular humanism" might pose to any who need a clear-cut, dualistic picture of the world to carry around for comfort. However, if I'm allowed to have *my* definition, the phrase "secular humanism" can be taken as a way of naming our hope for being fully human—not more than human, which we can't be, not less than human, which means becoming animals or things. All we can be is human, and always secular. We are, Pope says, "Placed on this isthmus of a middle state," beings who are "darkly wise and rudely great." "Born but to die, and reasoning but to err," we are, Pope goes on:

> *Created half to rise, and half to fall;*
> *Great lord of all things, yet a prey to all.*

In *this* world we are, regardless of the name we claim, responsible for ourselves. In *this* world, we are:

> *Sole judge of Truth, in endless Error hurl'd:*
> *The glory, jest, and riddle of the world!*

And isn't that a wondrous marvel?

The voice at first we think is tentative, but then we realize Corder projects an *assured* voice, as he argues through definition, developed by example, illustration, quotations. The essay is a classic treatment of argument through authority as Corder effectively brings in some great thinkers, the Bible (ironically, given the attack he's responding to—a strategy so powerful that it is one of the most effective refutatios I've seen), other Christians who were also scholars, T. S. Eliot, Alexander Pope, and the like.

The beginning humorous anecdote not only establishes identification but also shows, at first, the author to be rather timid, not the "secular humanist" boogeyman (notice that someone's head didn't break his nose but that *Corder's* nose was at fault: "The young man on the back of whose head I broke my nose . . ."). Also the two asides—the interruptors that foreground the inner voice—establish a reflective mind at work and start us on our way toward seeing, and identifying with, Corder's transforming ethos. Throughout the essay in fact, Corder's asides, his personal hedges, particularly characterize his style: "I like to think," "I'm likely to be," "I don't guess," "I'm more than a little surprised," "I think," "as if," "appears," "seem," "I'd always thought," "I'd about as soon," "probably," "inclined," "I'm glad enough." One important effect of the many interruptions and hedges is to slow down the reader, to create a reflective aura, to invite the reader to *think*, to share an intellectual surety with the audience.

The liberal use of other repetitive devices (the asides themselves create a rhythmic pattern) not only gives the reader time to think *with* the writer but also brings about cohesiveness. Many of the sentences Corder uses are based on repetition: anaphora, epistrophe, epanalepsis, anadiplosis, polysyndeton.

Interesting is that from the self-effacement at the beginning, tentative almost to the point of being timid, the voice gains momentum and strength till it becomes forceful—an earned force, I'd say. Notice the force and straightforwardness here, reinforced by the hard alliterative *ps* and the balanced, rhythmic syntax:

> As for the modifer "secular," I find no shame in that, either. Taken
> literally, it means "of or pertaining to this world or the present life,
> temporal, worldly." The protestations of those who are vain and
> public about their piety notwithstanding, none of us anywhere has
> any claim to be otherwise. We are of this world, and temporal, re-
> gardless of what we may wish to proclaim in some prideful postur-
> ings. We *are* secular, whatever our yearnings.

This voice is not seeking so much to disprove the fundamentalists' charge or even to convince them otherwise. Much of the charm and beauty of Corder's ethos is that he writes to a reader who agrees with his position (though Corder would probably prefer the word *narrative* instead of *position*), and he takes pleasure in their *mutual* awareness of the inanity of those detractors. Vincent Gillespie, in a recent letter, captures Corder's voice best:

The beauty of the essay is that he [draws the reader into this mutuality] with such grace, charm, and a reasonable degree of satire: he uses his detractors' "text," the Bible, to underscore their error and makes excellent use of Pope (a "secular humanist" if there ever was one) to show the vanity of their position. And he does so gently. And Corder knows that the satire must be reasonable, that is, not harsh, because both writer and reader realize that his detractors are not significant within the valorized world they share. To come down too hard would detract from the charm of his *voice*.

The essay, I think, illustrates voice as transforming ethos because of stylistic choices and representative anecdotes/examples that enable Corder to engage with the reader in dialogue. Voice as transforming ethos demands this dialogic action, where both writer and reader are aware of, and enjoy, the engagement.

Maybe, as Donald Stewart (whose ideas gave me the impetus for this essay and whose writings have always projected the "authentic voice") has been telling us for years, we should, first, tell our students to find a voice, *then* think. Can we show them that their essays, even "academic" essays, can be, as Corder's are, affirmations that rest on demonstrated openness and comprehensiveness—all this expressed by a transformed voice that seeks identification without sacrificing conviction?

Acknowledgment

I wish to thank Vincent Gillespie for his helpful comments on an earlier version of this paper. Vince was especially helpful as I struggled to capture what Corder was trying to do in the essay.

Works Cited

Aristotle. *The Rhetoric of Aristotle*. Trans. W. Rhys Roberts. New York: Modern Library, 1954.

Berlin, James A. *Rhetoric and Reality: Writing Instruction in American Colleges, 1900–1985*. Carbondale: Southern Illinois UP, 1987.

Blankenship, Jane. *A Sense of Style*. Belmont, CA: Dickinson, 1968.

Bruner, Jerome S. *Toward a Theory of Instruction*. New York: Norton, 1966.

Burke, Kenneth. *Rhetoric of Motives*. 1950. Berkeley: U of California P, 1969.

Cherry, Roger D. "*Ethos* Versus Persona." *Written Communication* 5 (1988): 251–76.

Cicero. *De Oratore*. Trans. H. Rackham. 1942. Cambridge, MA: Harvard UP, 1982.

Connors, Robert J. "*Actio*: A Rhetoric of Manuscripts." *Rhetoric Review* 2 (1983): 64–73.

———. "The Differences Between Speech and Writing: *Ethos, Pathos*, and *Logos*." *College Composition and Communication* 30 (1979): 285–90.

Corder, Jim W. "Humanism Isn't a Dirty Word." *This Is TCU* 24.2 (Nov. 1981): 10–11.

Enos, Theresa. " 'An Eternal Golden Braid': Rhetor as Audience, Audience as Rhetor."

A Sense of Audience in Written Communication. Ed. Gesa Kirsch and Duane H. Roen. Newbury Park, CA: Sage, 1990. 99–114.

———. "Ethical and Stylistic Implications in Delivering Conference Papers." *Journal of Teaching Writing* 5 (1986): 113–20.

Gibson, Walker. *Persona: A Style Study for Readers and Writers*. New York: Random, 1969.

Golden, James L., Goodwin F. Berquist, and William E. Coleman. *The Rhetoric of Western Thought*. 4th ed. Dubuque, IA: Kendall/Hunt, 1989.

Gregg, Richard B. *Symbolic Inducement and Knowing: A Study in the Foundations of Rhetoric*. Columbia: U of South Carolina P, 1984.

Halloran, S. Michael. "Aristotle's Concept of *Ethos*, or if Not His Somebody Else's." *Rhetoric Review* 1 (1982): 58–63.

Howell, Wilbur S. "Sources of the Elocutionary Movement in England." *Quarterly Journal of Speech* 45 (1959): 1–18.

Kennedy, George A. *Classical Rhetoric and Its Christian and Secular Tradition from Ancient to Modern Times*. Chapel Hill: U of North Carolina P, 1980.

Kennedy, William J. "Voice as Frame: Longinus, Kant, Ong, and Deconstruction in Literary Studies." *Media, Consciousness, and Culture*. Ed. Bruce E. Gronbeck, Thomas J. Farrell, and Paul A. Soukup. Newbury Park: Sage, 1991. 77–89.

Ong, Walter. "Voice as Summons for Belief." *Literature and Belief*. Ed. M. H. Abrams. New York: Columbia UP, 1958. 80–105.

Quintilian. *Institutio Oratoria*. Trans. H. E. Butler. 4 vols. Cambridge: Harvard UP, 1920–1922.

Readings from Classical Rhetoric. Ed. Patricia P. Matsen, Philip Rollinson, and Marion Sousa. Carbondale: Southern Illinois UP, 1990.

Rhetorica ad Herennium. Trans. Harry Caplan. Cambridge, MA: Harvard UP, 1954.

Ullman, Stephen. *Language and Style*. New York: Barnes & Noble, 1964.

Welch, Kathleen E. *The Contemporary Reception of Classical Rhetoric: Appropriations of Ancient Discourse*. Hillsdale, NJ: Lawrence Erlbaum, 1990.

Whately, Richard. *Elements of Rhetoric*. Ed. Douglas Ehninger. Carbondale: Southern Illinois UP, 1963.

Winterowd, W. Ross. "Style: A Matter of Manner." *Quarterly Journal of Speech* 56 (1970): 161–67.

14   Threes

Victor J. Vitanza

> *In many languages of the world counting has never been developed. In some languages of New Guinea . . . people . . . count: one thing, two things, many things, and then must stop; one man translated his counting system into Pidgin English for me as one fellow, two fellow, plenty fellow.*
>
> — *K. Pike*, Linguistic Concepts

> *Who is the third who walks always beside you?*
> *When I count, there are only you and I together*
> *But when I look ahead up the white road*
> *There is always another one walking beside you*
> *Gliding wrapt in a brown mantle, hooded*
> *I do not know whether a man or a woman*
> *—But who is that on the other side of you?*
>
> — *T. S. Eliot*, The Waste Land

IA. Some Preliminary A/topoi

> *. . . during his seminars Lacan sometimes mused about how high his analysands could count.*
> — *S. Schneiderman*, Jacques Lacan

MY CON/FESSIN'. THIS IS A THIRD ARTICLE IN A TRILOGY OF ARTICLES. Hence, "threes." The other two articles, whether they get written or not—and it persistently seems less important that they do—are entitled respectively "Neo-Momism" and "Trees." The "Neo-Momism" article, with its paracritique of a feminism, has been pre/saged in *Finnegans Wake*: "I am not leering, I pink you pardons. I am highly sheshe sherious" (570). The "Trees" article, with its paracritique of a Cartesian, Chomskian, phallologocentric view of language and rhetoric, has also been pre/saged in *Finnegans Wake*: " 'Tis a tree story" (564) based on an "adamelegy" (77) in the "root language" (424).[1]

This third article, "Threes," is at times planned for a general academic audience, though at other times the language is quasipoetic (or quasipsychoanalytic?, or quasinoisesome?), for which I will not and, anyway, cannot apologize. (Like some of the pre-Socratics, I [too] don't mind hiding some of what I have to say. [Compare Plato, *Theaetetus* 180c–d]. I am a *cacographist*. I would turn the reader into an *epigraphist*. But then, really, who is doing the hiding? What language is all about is a site of a loss [*fort*] and then a site of appearance [*da*]. But what this third article is all about is an attempt, however, to get beyond the negating conditions of *fort/da*, to get, instead, to the affirmative conditions of the possibilities of pastiche and farce.) Though planned for a general academic audience, the hoped-for audience is especially rhetoric and written and speech communication theorists and pedagogues, who are not One but a radical *Many*. As Robert Connors says, "our discipline . . . is spinning centrifugally to pieces" (232). I would insist on and incite further its spinning, spinning, spinning. (Oh noisesome, impatient audience.) It is spinning to pieces. To pastiche(d) . . . subject effects.

Purposes, Without Apologies. In "Threes" I wish to suggest a way in which rhetoric—in its broadest possible sense—has ac*count*ed for itself, especially in its (e.g., Brian Vickerian) defense of itself. I would claim, in the simplest terms and only in passing, that rhetoric has counted-itself-into-being just as traditional philosophy has. It has insisted on a certain unity (logos, ratio, reason, rationalism), however, that has been, and continues to be, purchased at the expense of the excluded other. For the most part philosophy has counted itself as either *One* (as perfect unity) or allegedly *Two* (as contraries, binaries), while "philosophical rhetoric"[2] has counted itself as *Two* (e.g., as counterpart to Aristotelian dialectic). Almost without exception, however, philosophical rhetoric has only deflected its penchant for *One*, or a One as homogenized/systematized *Many*, and, therefore, has deflected, or systematically excluded, wild (noisesome) sophistics.

And what might these excluded and wild sophistics (*Letteraturizzaziones*) become?[3] What do I have in (or mostly out of) mind? I have specifically in mind Michel Serres's notion of "the excluded third." He writes: "*To hold a dialogue is to suppose a third man* [sic] *and to seek to exclude him*; a successful communication is the exclusion of the third man. The most profound dialectical problem is not the problem of the Other [as interlocutor], who is only a variety . . . of the Same, it is the problem of the third man [the excluded Other]. We might call this third man the *demon*, the prosopopeia of noise." And again Serres writes: "Dialectic makes the two interlocutors play on the same side; they do battle together to produce a truth on which they can agree, that is, to produce a successful communication. In a certain sense, they struggle together against interference, against the demon, against the third man. Obviously, this battle is not always successful. In the aporetic dialogues, victory rests with the powers of noise" (67; Serres's emphasis). And what are the political implications of such an exclusion? Serres suggests that "we" would have a city/*polis* (like an ideal Republic) "maximally purged of noise" (68). (Or maximally purged of ethical-political resistance!)

Another purpose of this article, therefore, is to help locate not only how philosophical rhetoric has accounted for itself (which I see as being cryptomonistic, and as overly operational and rationalized) and not only how philosophical rhetoric has become the hegemonic rhetoric that determines what counts as and for *The* History of Rhetoric, but also to help locate how we—the insatiable ones—might resist and disrupt and, finally, dis/locate *The* dominant discourse, might perpetually disrupt it so much so that rhetoric and written and oral communication would no longer be a discipline or metadiscipline, but—yes, yes, yes, and I will incite it repeatedly—become a *nondiscipline*, for what Foucault would see as a nondisciplinary, noncarcerial society. In speaking of *The* History of Rhetoric, what I would call for, here then—in its being written, rather perpetually rewritten—is the nondisciplined (nonnegated), free flow of (libidinalized) desire. (I have previously discussed this notion under the rubric of the "antibody rhetoric" [see "Critical Sub/Versions"]).

> . . . *to reinvent history as the history of desire*. . . .
> —*M. Pierssens,* The Power of Babel

And so really, what am I alluding to here in my thinking about history and rhetoric and discipline? if not counterviews of language themselves! What is wanted (I am going to insist and incite) is a paratheory of language that would be *a libidinalized* (perhaps *Marxist*) view of language, such as is expressed by N. O. Brown in *Life Against Death,* when he says that "language is an operational superstructure on an erotic base" (69). This libidinalized, or erotic, base might also be called "desire," but a desire based not by and on negation, exclusion (lack), but on affirmation (excess). Like Blake, I desire exuberance.

An Interruption, on Negation. Let us look at this problem of negation more closely, for it must be seen for what it is (and will have been) before we can make our move toward affirmation and away from a perpetually dark, negative future. (However, we will be moving not merely from negative to affirmation, but to a third term called *nonpositive affirmation*.) Perhaps the best way to understand negation is to relate it to our teaching. When we teach students (and we do so, so innocently) how to define (limit) some thing, we are teaching them to think in terms of the negative; that is, we teach them (it is part and parcel of the genre of teaching) to say what "some thing" is by virtue of what this so-called "some thing" is not: hence, we have definition (meaning, rationality, community) by ill virtue of negation, with a *species* being placed within a *genus,* and then the *species* being *differentiated* from all other *species* within the same *genus* (compare Burke, *Grammar of Motives* 23–25). We foster in students' minds, then, the illusion/delusion that, by employing this dialectical, definitional process, they ideally or actually come to know "some thing." It is an insidious and invidious procedure by difference/exclusion.

But really, how is this bad? And if bad, how bad? If time and space permitted, I would give a genealogy of the negative. Instead, I will speak without transition or without plodding development of the wreck. To wit: Genus-cide. As Theodor Adorno has warned us, "[As] early as Plato, dialectics [*diaeresis*, definition] meant to achieve something positive by means of negation" (xix). Dialectics by negation led, Adorno more pointedly argues, quite logically to Auschwitz: "Genocide is the absolute integration [totality]. It is on its way wherever men [*sic*] are leveled off . . . until one exterminates them [excludes them] literally, as deviations [*differentiae*] from the concept of *their total nullity* [species-genus]." And then Adorno concludes: "Auschwitz confirmed the philosopheme of pure identity as death" (362; emphasis mine). Let us remember that not only Jews and Gypsies and Polish people were systematically excluded—given this mode of knowing—but also women and gays and hermaphrodites. The contemporary feminist Catherine Clément writes: "Somewhere every culture has an *imaginary zone* for what it excludes, and it is that zone we must try to remember *today*. This is history that is not over" (Cixous and Clément, *Newly Born Woman* 6; first emphasis mine). And again Clément says: "The same goes for women as for madmen; in a *manifest* position of exclusion, they keep the system together, *latently*, by virtue of their very exclusion" ("Enslaved Enclave" 134; Clément's emphasis). Today, in the midst of rampant nationalism, *ethnic cleansing* is practiced. But besides certain human beings, certain aspects of language itself are excluded. Julia Kristeva writes: "We have [a] Platonistic acknowledgment on the eve of Stalinism and fascism; a (any) society may be stabilized *only* if it *excludes* poetic language." And then: "The question is unavoidable: if we are not on the side of those whom society wastes in order to reproduce itself, where are we?" (*Desire in Language* 31; emphasis mine). And so, how would we now teach, if teach at all?

More than anyone else, our contemporary "teacher" Kenneth Burke has struggled with the overly moralizing character of the negative, has attempted to move from the overly exclusionary starting point of a Parmenides/Plato to a less exclusionary point of a neo-Aristotelian view (or, more accurately, an inclusion of both views as separate but complementarty attitudes/motives). It would appear, therefore, that "Papa" would be an includer.[4] (And it would appear that many of us would teach as he teaches, with an attempt to move toward a better life.) Burke, too, however, practices an exclusionary pedagogy by inventing out of the dangerously moralistic negative. He says (from Bergson) that though there are no negatives in nature, the negative presents itself as an inescapable product of our symbol systems. In his famous "defintion of man [*sic*]" Burke defines "man," in part, as "inventor of the negative" and goes so far as to say perversely that the negative itself " 'invented' man" (*Language* 9). Now, where are we?

I think that Burke—who employs invention by negation, while he is aware of its many problems—raises for us the continuing specter (haunting possibility) of the negative. To be sure, he has his solutions to the problem (those of "attitudinizing" or "perspectives by incongruity"), but they do fall short of what others would both need and desire—which would be simply to work from the nonpositive affirmative. Whereas Burke dismisses "Grand Papa" Nietzsche as being in the cult of the primitive positive (see *Language* 419–79)—and this is the point at which I differ from Papa quite dramatically cum farsically in this familial squabble—I would pursue, quite illegitimately, Nietzsche's joyful affirmations; I would pursue "the excluded third" (Serres); pursue "desire in language" (Kristeva). As Nietzsche says, "Excess reveal[s] itself as truth" (*Birth* 46). Therefore, I and you cum eventually "we" will have been dispersed.

In what follows, therefore, I am going to (a) examine three different aspects of counting: the first based on Oneness; the second, on a multiplicity that is systematized/homogenized; and a third, on a radical multiplicity that resists and disrupts systematization/genus-species analytics. (Hence, we will have counted one, two, and excessively "some more.") I am going then to (b) propose, in passing, a paragenealogy of this third (position of "some more"). And finally, I am going to (c) examine and propose, more particularly, a third (subject) position in relation to a concept of ethics and ethos, a third (subject) position whose desire is not negated by, say, Aristotelian virtue, Kantian duty, or Benthamian utility, but one cum a radical many that takes the shapes of free-flowing libidinalized desire. And I am going to do all this with a special emphasis (though ever incipiently) on writing histories/hysteries of rhetorics.

IB. I Love (Eros, Desire) You, but First Let Us Count (Discount) the Ways!

Both Plato (Socrates) and Aristotle speak directly on the subject of desire—for example, Plato in the *Phaedrus* (in relation to nonlover, evil lover, and noble lover) and in the *Symposium* (in relation to Socrates' renderings of Diotima's teachings concerning love's appetite for the beautiful and good [201d–212b]), and Aristotle in the *Metaphysics* (in relation to "all men by nature desire [have an appetite] to know" [980a]). The best Aristotelian example, for my purposes here, however, is found in the *Nicomachean Ethics*, especially in relation to how Aristotle (and traditional philosophy) thinks that desire must be controlled by reason. Aristotle writes, "In general the desiring element in a sense shares in [the rational principle], in so far as it listens to and obeys it; this is the sense in which we speak of 'taking account' of one's father or one's friends, not that in which we speak of 'accounting' for a mathematical property" (1102b 29–33). But to be sure, this mathematical (abstractly rational) dimension of both Plato's and Aristotle's thinking comes into play, specifically in relation to our desire of and appetite for the true, good, and beautiful.

I myself desire to follow this (paralogical, pastiche-like) line of thinking and the relationships between "taking account" and "accounting for." I am very interested in *how far philosophers* (who have shaped our attitudes toward [philosophical] rhetoric) *can count.* Let us take, therefore, two more, but elaborated, examples (one from Plato, another from Aristotle), which are by now fairly famous, so that we might get on to a discussion of "threes" (or an uncertain, Sophistic way of thinking about dis/counting).

> Stranger: . . . *among things that exist we include number in general.*
> Theaetetus: *Yes, number must exist, if anything does.*
> —Plato, Sophist

Ac/Counting for Plato. The first example is from the *Parmenides* (132a–133d), in which there is a discussion of ideal forms, whether there be One or Two or Three. Parmenides is addressing Socrates in the give and take discussion and concludes that there must be only One: "Otherwise a second form will always make its appearance over and above the first form, and if that second form is like anything, yet *a third.* And there will be no end to this emergence of fresh forms" (133a; my emphasis; compare *Sophist* 237d–238d). The problem here, of course, is that of infinite regress, which becomes dis/solved in a dialogic relationship by merely excluding the possibility of the third form. It is, however, not only a problem for establishing ideal forms but also of our own existence. (The ontology-epistemology [ethical] link is strong.) Plato's strategy becomes, then, the exclusion of *the third person* so as to maintain, as Adorno, Clément, Kristeva say, our *identity.* (This problem of infinite regress is a problem in post-Cartesian thinking that revisits us today as the problem of "the third man"; I am thinking, for example, of Fichte and Marx, and of Lacan and Derrida [see Dews, *Logics of Disintegration*], as well as of Bertolt Brecht and Orson Welles and their cohorts.)

Ac/Counting for Aristotle. The next example is from Aristotle, who is equally concerned with whether there is One, Two, or Three. How Aristotle counts is difficult to determine, but he tells us quite explictly in the *Physis* (Book 1, ch. 5–6) that he counts *Two* (as "contraries") and *Three* (as "substratum"), but "neither One nor Innumerable" (189a). (This "Three" is not the *Three* that I will eventually speak of; it is important to realize, in addition, that Aristotle says there cannot be a *Four*-plus, or an "innumerable" [189a 20].) Therefore, seemingly, Aristotle counts *Two, Three.* But let us not be fooled: Aristotle is playing a shell game with only *One* primary pea, if any at all. His notion of counting to *Three* (as "substratum") is a generic synthesis/unity of the prior *Two* (the "contraries"); it is a *Three* cum "One" that is "differentiate[d] . . . by means of contraries, such as density and rarity and more and less" (189b 9–10). Hence, while agreeing to the possibility of *Twos,* he still has his crypto-*One,* which he calls a *Three.* Moreover, he says, "it is impossible that there should be more than one primary contrariety" (189a 20–25), thus emphasizing Unity/*Oneness* again. Which gets us to Aristotle's *Analytics*, in which he favors *One*/Certainty (a closed logic, though based on the contraries of the law of noncontradiction). And which gets us to the *Rhetoric*, in which he develops a system based on *Many*/Probability (an open logic, but nonetheless still highly systematized, based on the same law).

My whole point—that which I have been preparing the way to drift up to—is that we must have yet other, third ways of counting. In dis/order to let be written hysteries of desire in language, in rhetorics, in dis/order to get to these other ways—so that we might tap into still other ways in dis/respect to *The* History of Rhetoric—we must dis/engage in a . . .

Dis/Counting and Re/Counting (of) the Sophists. Running irradically, discontinuously, sub/versively parallel with Plato and Aristotle are the Sophists, who, I *could* venture to say, generally counted to *Two* by way of *dissoi logoi*, or antilogic (see Kerferd ch. 6). But to say that this so-called group—what I would call, at best, *a molecular agglomerate* (my concept of a Third) group (see Schiappa; compare Vitanza, "Neopragmatism")—counted to *Two* would have, at best, only heuristic value, would be an admission that they, too, counted-themselves-into-being just as traditional philosophy has. (To be sure, the Sophists are often dis/counted, mis/appropriated in this manner.) The narrative of traditional history writing—that is, the metanarrative of cause and effect and of birth and enlightenment and of accountability—however, is inappropriate for telling the *parastory* of the Sophist. Why? Because what desires to be told cannot be told/expressed in this overly privileged, all too exclusionary narrative (see Kofman). What the Stranger in the *Sophist* says is ironically relevant here: "One cannot legitimately utter the words [that would make the counternarrative possible], nor speak or think of that which just simply is not. It is unthinkable, not to be spoken of or uttered or expressed" (238c; compare Wittgenstein, *Tractatus* prop. 7). And so, we will have to find, as Jean-François Lyotard says, a new idiom for what desires to be said about a re/counting (of) the Sophists, and then we will have to bear witness to it, though it is denied, even forbidden (see *The Differend*). And so, let us ("some more" of us) be about our (libidinalized) business.

To be sure, historians write of the "First" and "Second" Sophistics (see Kennedy; Bowersock), and I have written of the "Third" (see " 'Some More' Notes" and "Neopragmatism").[5] This sequencing for me, however, is not *One*, *Two*, *Three*, in a continuum on its way to *Six* (Sumerian) or *Ten* (Roman), and so on; instead, this counternarrative movement is to be conceived of as if there were (and there is!) a dis/counting system capable of perpetually dis/informing the traditional narrative scheme by way of *One*, *Two*, and then a deviating *Some/Plenty More*. The "logic" (or rather misology) that informs this movement toward *Some More* is not *logos* (as philosophical dialectic) or *dissoi logoi* (an antilogic) but is a third (nonsynthesized, nonsynecdochic) term, which I have called *dissoi paralogoi* (as paralogy, radical dispersion via the logics of disintegration or contradiction [see "Critical Sub/Versions" and "Concerning a Post-Classical *Ethos*"]). If I were forced (or farced) to find a mis/representative (antidote) who would embody the Sophists, I would not select Protagoras or Gorgias or Aeschines, but Favorinus of Arelate (Gaul), who "was born double sexed, a hermaphrodite" (Philostratus and Eunapias 23; see Vitanza, "Neopragmatism").

Hermaphrodites cause us problems; and "I" cum "we"[6] figuratively would problematize writing *The* History of Rhetoric. As Judith Butler tells us, hermaphrodites (and satyrs) challenge our very sense of order and identity— given our necessity for a disjunctive syllogism—as either "male" or "female"; therefore, we must banish hermaphrodites as well as other physical (and mental) transgressions (see *Gender Trouble*). It *is*, after all, a matter of logic and specifically the law of noncontradiction. Andrea Nye, in her feminist history of logic, discusses Parmenides' poem, and in reference to its "teachings" says, "If a female mixes with a male [i.e., as a hermaphrodite, mixed genders in one], the result is both female and not female, impossible by the rule of noncontradiction" (14; compare Plato, *Symposium* 191d-e; Foucault, *Herculine Barbin* preface). As the "teachings" continue, the situation gets worse for females, who are defined semiotically across the *lack* of not being males. As we know, by definition (i.e., species-genus analytics), freaks—including hermaphrodites, "women"—are imperfections and, therefore, contradict what we take *to be* perfection. To the hermaphrodite as well as the satyr (to contradiction itself, and to its noise), we will return, eternally return, in reference to logic and narrative and especially ethos; but now, what wants/needs to be elaborated is a paragenealogy and a paralocus of Threes, so that we might have a better idea of how resistance and disruption of the dominant discourse (*The* History of Rhetoric) might be realized.

II. A Truncated Paragenealogy of "Threes"

> *Synecdoche is totalitarian.*
>
> —R. Barthes, Rustle

Prayfatio. When I hear and write the word "genealogy," I think (again, ever again) of Burke (his genealogy of the negative, in *Language as Symbolic Action*, ch. 7) and by contrast think of Nietzsche (*Genealogy of Morals*) and Michel Foucault (*Discipline and Punish*). Whereas Burke focuses on the necessity of negation, Nietzsche and Foucault focus on the crippling effects of the negative (overly exclusive) and, consequently, reach for the nonpositive affirmative (overly inclusive). (Whereas Burke attempts to be all-inclusive by accounting for different perspectives by incongruity in his works, so that he might include them all, he nonetheless favors a synecdochic [container-thing-contained] structure to control [via species-genus analytics] those perspectives.

[I have heard him counting: "One, two, three, four, five, perhaps six!"]
Whereas Burke does allow for much babeling [babbling (simply witness his
magnificent critique of Hitler's battle)[7]], he still, nonetheless, grammatizes
these [motives and rhetoric and symbolic of] babeling. I would desire *still
more*, however, and in the mis/form of a paragrammatization [see Pierssens].
Even the great systemizer Saussure, the great excluder, eventually begins to
read and hear paragrams [see Barthes, *Rustle* 42].)

> L'exclusion—*Exclusion*
>> *Utopia (a la Fourier) that of a world in which there
>> would no longer be anything but differences, so that to
>> be differentiated would no longer mean to be excluded.*
>> —*Roland Barthes*, Roland Barthes

Similarly, the word *genealogy* suggests to me *the sign of threes*. Threes,
however, are usually dialectical, with a synthesizing third, which is made
possible by way of negation (repression and oppression), by refining and
purifying. This third in its simplest form is composed of two people excluding
a third person. (Recall Serres's "the excluded third"; recall the process of
definition, species-genus analytics.) This third, then, is the achievement of
integration (community and social-bonds) but by way of segregation (victimage and scapegoating and elimination). The political implications are obviously catastrophic. (Recall Adorno's *Negative Dialectics*.) Threes, however, do
not have to be dialectical, with an exclusionary synthesizing-synecdochic third.
Instead, they can be reconceived as moving from negative and positive to an
all-inclusive nonpositive affirmative. (Another way of making this distinction
is to speak of constructions, negative deconstructions [merely switching binar-
ies], and then affirmative deconstructions [moving beyond binaries].) Nietzsche attempted a non-Hegelian synthesis, which was a movement beyond
(the binaries of) good and evil. His was an attempt to rise beyond a master-
slave morality (dialectic) and thoughts of *ressentiment*; his was an attempt to
self-overcome. He writes in his *Genealogy*: "Slave morality from the outset
says No to what is 'outside,' what is 'different,' what is 'not itself'; and *this*
No is its creative deed. . . . The reverse is the case with the noble mode of
valuation . . . its negative concept 'low,' 'common,' 'bad' is only a subse-
quently-invented pale, contrasting image in relation to its positive basic concept" (36–37; Nietzsche's emphasis). The difference that basically lies in the
distinction between the master-slave morality and a subsequent noble morality
is the difference that exists between *an order* founded on resentment, exclusion,
victimage and an order founded on inclusion and gradation. (Whereas Burke
seeks comedy, with a remaining didactic penchant for tragedy [*Grammar of
Motives*], and whereas Nietzsche seeks to understand and embrace early Greek
tragedy [*The Birth of Tragedy*], I would seek, here, *farce*. Hence, a nonsynthesized three: comedy, tragedy, *farce*.)

Much has been written recently on Nietzsche's unfinished project of revaluing value, and much is beginning to be written on the different ways that both Grand Papa Nietzsche and Papa Burke have dealt with the problem of the "sacrificial negative." It is not my purpose to work out their differences (see Desilet). Of great importance to us here, however, are those (illegitimate) thinkers who have come out of Nietzsche in their attempts to locate third (subject) positions beyond traditional reactive positions and that do not exclude. Therefore, in concluding my *prayfatio*, what I intend to do in the rest of this second section is to serialize, ever briefly, nonsynthesized threes (trinaries). In the remaining section, three, I will then as promised discuss Nietzschean third (subject) positions (a postmodern ethos, or poly*ethoi*) that move beýond (without synthesizing into androgyny) the gender binaries of male-female. (The focus, as usual, though implicit at times, is on writing histories of rhetorics.)

(Nonsynthesized) Threes (Some Paranotes). In his introductory essay to *The Sign of Three*, Thomas Sebeok counts "One, Two, Three Spells U B E R T Y." To the word *uberty* Sebeok adds the word *esperable* so that he might get *esperable uberty*, which he describes as "rich growth, fruitfulness, fertility; copiousness, abundance" (1). As we might expect, Sebeok links this phrase and concept with C. S. Peirce, who in a letter suggested (this is Sebeok's inference and paraphrase) that logicians should "educe the possible and esperable uberty, or 'value in productiveness,' of the three canonical types of reasoning, to wit: deduction, induction, and abduction." Sebeok continues: "It is the uberty, that is, the fruitfulness, of this last type of reasoning that, [Peirce] tells us, increases, while its security, or approach to certainty, minifies" (1). Much has been written about Peirce's obsession with threes; my use of him, however, is only as a stepping-off point in dis/order to discuss a still more abundant "esperable uberty," one cum a radical many that would increase productivity while security-in-certainty or even -in-probability decreases. In other terms, the higher the risk to be found in the third term/concept, the greater possible "returns" (as in the returns of the eternally repressed).

Few philosophers or rhetors obviously wish to take this, or a still more risky, risk, but there is a group (paragroup) of thinkers who have established third (subject) positions in the attempt to escape Hegelian master-slave relationships or morality, in other words, to find a way out of dualities/binaries, or what is better stated as dialectical negation, with, for example, a privileged position (male) over a supplementary position (female). This group desires to shatter the concept of negative containment (genre/gender, synecdoche) and especially *in propria persona*. This group, therefore, searches for ways out by searching for *third* (but nonsynthesized) *positions*. These third positions I would think of as a rich (*esperable uberty*) paraset of *atopia*, a rich paraset of new *de/conceptual* (a neologism: deception [*apate*] plus conception) starting places, which would stand in both opposition and apposition to philosophical-rhetorical (negative) invention.

Roland Barthes. I will begin with Roland Barthes, who more so than any other thinker in this paragroup has developed the idea of a *third (subject) position* throughout his early and late works. The best passage I can find that illustrates, with an appropriate analogy, his search for "threes" is in his autobiography, *Roland Barthes by Roland Barthes*. He writes:

> When I used to play prisoner's base in the Luxembourg, what I liked best was not provoking the other team and boldly exposing myself to their right to take me prisoner [i.e., not be reactive]; what I liked best was to free the prisoners—the effect of which was to put both teams back into circulation: the game started over again at zero [which is another word, as in the phrase "zero degree of writing," for his concept of a third term (see 132)].
>   In the great game of the powers of speech, we also play prisoner's base: one language has only temporary rights over another, all it takes is for a third language to appear from the ranks for the assailant to be forced to retreat: in the conflict of rhetorics, the victory never goes to any but the *third language*. The task of this language is to release the prisoners: to scatter the signifieds, the catechisms. As in prisoner's base, *language upon language*, to infinity, such is the law which governs the logosphere. Whence other images: that of choosing up hand over hand (the third hand returns, it is no longer the first one), that of scissors, paper, stone, that of the onion in its layers of skin without a core. That difference should not be paid for by any subjection: no last word. (50; Barthes's emphasis)

In the autobiography, under the rubric "Dialectics," he again speaks of and to a third term:

> Everything seems to suggest that his [Barthes's] discourse proceeds according to a two-term dialectic: popular opinion and its contrary, *Doxa* and its paradox, the stereotype and the novation, fatigue and freshness, relish and disgust. *I like/I don't like.* This binary dialectic is the dialectic of meaning itself (*marked/not marked*) and of the Freudian game the child plays (*Fort/Da*): the dialectic of value.
>   Yet is this quite true? In him, another dialectic appears, trying to find expression: the contradiction of the terms yields in his eyes by the discovery of a third term, which is not a synthesis but a translation: everything comes back, but it comes back as Fiction, i.e., at another turn of the spiral. (68–69)

Then from "Dialectics" he moves to the contrary rubric "Aesthetics," in which he searches for a name for the kind of writing (from a third position) he dis/engages in. (The movement to a third position is usually toward the poetic as, for example, toward epideictic.)[8] We can see here the impact of Kant's three critiques, with the *third critique* on judgment/aesthetics being the most prominent. Barthes writes that "he attempts to compose a discourse which is not uttered in the name of the Law and/or of Violence: whose instance might be neither political nor religious nor scientific; which might be in a sense the remainder [the excluded] and the supplement of all such utterances." He asks: "What shall we call such discourse? *erotic*, no doubt, for it has to do with pleasure; or even perhaps: *aesthetic*" (84; compare *Pleasure of the Text* 18, 55).

Barthes has discussed, in other possible ways, his understanding of a third (language) position. See his "The Third Meaning," in which he discusses three levels of meaning in film: The *informational*, the *symbolic*, and "a *third meaning*—evident, erratic, obstinate, . . . I am unable to give it a name" (*Image/Music/Text* 53; emphasis mine). Or see his third (reading) position, in which he is neither *mad* nor *sane* but *neurotic* (*Pleasure of the Text* 6). Or see his discussion and distinction among *topia* (being "pigeonholed"), *utopia* (being reactive), and *atopia* ("drifting") (*Roland Barthes* 49). Or see his discussion and use of the three parts to Fourier's "Tree of Happiness," in which Fourier distinguishes among *lustful-ness*, *group-ness*, and *serial-ness*, the latter of which includes three ways of resisting, disrupting, transgressing the dominant discourse (*Sade/Fourier/Loyola* 100–101). Or see his discussion of a "third semiological chain" as a locus for resisting "mythifying" (*Mythologies* 135). Or see his history of writing, in which he discusses "a third term, called a neutral term or zero element [the middle voice]: thus between the subjunctive and the imperative moods" (*Writing Degree Zero* 76). The examples continue throughout his work.

Others. But along with Barthes, there are numerous others who have found third (subject) positions for both people and ideas. I herefrom list them, with pertinent references.

- instead of *master* versus *slave* relationships, Georges Bataille (like Nietzsche) goes on to a third (subject) position of *"sovereignty"* (*Inner Experience*; see Derrida, *Writing and Difference* ch. 9);
- instead of *active* (sadism) versus *passive* (masochism) voices, Lacan (at times, a hysteric) speaks in the hysterical *"middle voice"* (see E. White, *Kaironomia* part 2; C. Scott, *The Question of Ethics* ch. 2, sec. 2; also compare Clément, *Lives and Legends* for Lacanian *mi-dire*, "mid-speak," 59–60; Barthes's "zero degree of writing");
- instead of "male" versus "female" positions, Monique Wittig speaks of the "lesbian" subject position (see Butler, *Gender Trouble* 111–16), or Brown speaks of the "hermaphroditic" position (*Love's Body* 84; compare Barthes, *A Lover's Discourse* 226–28), or Butler speaks of a radical mutiplicity of sexes/genders, or Lacan, S. Zizek, and feminists speak of the hysteric position;
- instead of *encoder*, *decoder*, and *referent* (and code/signal) as a communication model, Lacan speaks variously of *imaginary*, *symbolic*, and *the real* (and the field of language) as a miscommunication

model (see Zizek), which can be (and always already is) employed to resist and disrupt the dominant discourse (the *real* is that which cannot be represented in the symbolic, except by way of a stand-in, or "a little object other");

- instead of *coding* (territorializing) and *recoding* (reterritorializing, as a Marxist attempt, in order to make the world a better place), Deleuze and Guattari *decode* (or deterritorialize perpetually, in dis/order to resist and disrupt e/utopian cum dystopian attempts, which only exclude) (see *Anti-Oedipus* and *Thousand Plateaus*);
- instead of *le parole* (individual speech act) and *la langue* (grammar, system), Lacan and Kristeva speak of *"lalangue"* (babel, babble, babylonianisms) as a site of resistance;
- instead of the pre-Socratic and Platonic *One* and *Many* (*Theaetetus* 160d), Deleuze and Guattari speak of a third subject position as "molecular agglomerate" (*Anti-Oedipus* 277–96) and distinguish among *molar, aborescent multiplicities*, and their third position *rhizomatic multiplicities* (*Thousand Plateaus* 33);
- instead of *dialectic* and *negative dialectic* (or *negative deconstruction*), Derrida and Gayatri Spivak speak of and employ an *affirmative deconstruction*, which is a guarding of and a resistance to answering the question (of Being) posed by a negating, exclusionary dialectic (see Spivak, "Feminism");
- instead of the *discipline* and/or *metadiscipline* of rhetoric, I have discussed a *nondiscipline*; instead of *traditional* and/or *revisionary* history, I have written of *sub/versive hystery*; instead of *dialectic* and/or *dissoi logoi*, I have enacted *dissoi paralogoi* (*polylectics*); instead of *philosophy* and/or *philosophical rhetoric*, or *First* and/or *Second Sophistics*, I have described/enacted *Third Sophistic (para)rhetorics* (see "Critical Sub/Versions"; " 'Some More' Notes"; "Neopragmatism"); instead of *sentences* and/or *speech acts*, I have discussed and performed (at times) *theostrick, theatricks* (see "Three Countertheses" and "An Open Letter"); instead of the *individual* and/or the *social*, I have discussed *the social in the individual* (see "Concerning a Post-classical *Ethos*"; "Taking A-Count"); instead of *Grammar A* (Harbrace) and/or *Grammar B* (W. Wethers), I have written in *Grammar Z* (this present article and "Concerning a Post-classical *Ethos*"); instead of speaking always from *Grand Papa Nietzsche* and/or *Papa Burke*, I have (been) spoken from *illegitimacy* (see "Preparing to meet the faces"); instead of *tradition* and/or *countertradition*, I have recently spoken of Foucault's *counter-memory* ("Teaching-Nothing"); instead of *comedy* and/or *tragedy*, I have more recently discussed *farce* (as in *this* "my [Earwicker's] farced epistle to the HE-brews of *The* History of Rhetoric").

In typology—a branch of mathematics—there has been the successful search for a *third object position* in the form of Klein bottle, a typological jar with no inside but an outside. (I mention this latter typological strategy, for it can suggest ways of placing in dispersion synecdochic [negative, container-thing-contained] structures.)

IIIA. Ethos and Genders: From One or Two Genders to an "Excluded Third" of a Radical Multiplicity of Genders cum Poly*ethoi*

> Hegel remarks somewhere that all facts and personages
> of great importance in world history occur, as it were,
> twice. He forgot to add: the first time as tragedy, and
> the second as farce.
> —*Marx*, Eighteenth Brumaire

> Farce is the mode of demystification[;] the tragic mode
> remystifies
> —N. O. Brown, Closing-Time

In this concluding (beginning?) third section, I am going to dis/engage in some (more) farce. As I see it, tragedy is to farce as parody is to pastiche. Each member of this ratio (analogy) has a different epistemology. Tragedy and parody believe in originals, while farce and pastiche believe in copies. Tragedy and parody each signify a dialectical exchange of two (tragedy: two goods in conflict; parody: an original being corrected by way of a satirical other). Farce and pastiche, however, are a signifying chain that is beginningless and endless, therefore, pretty much in a state of middles. Moreover, tragedy and parody only remystify in their attempts to correct what they see as wrong, in their attempts to return "us" back to a locus prior to mystification (parody suffers from nostalgia). Pastiche and farce, however, demystify (perpetually) by way of serialization (*tmesis*) and disruptions/interruptions in their attempts to deliver us from a nostalgic pull toward some transcendental original place or some so-called real (but nonetheless, great-good) place—to wit, paradise.

This distinction will make more and (some) more sense as we proceed toward a discussion of "identity politics/ethics" (a politically fixed ethos), specifically, as we proceed toward a discussion of gender as "male" versus/against "female." (Therefore, whereas we have been focusing previously on logos [ac/counting to destabilized "threes"], we will now focus on ethos [a destablized poly*ethoi* that passes into infinite regress].) While, to be sure, it *is* necessary that feminist rhetoricians reclaim all of the women/"females" who have been systematically excluded from *The* History of Rhetoric, this (my) discussion of gender and of writing histories of rhetorics wishes to move beyond "male/female" altogether, or beyond separate histories of rhetorics, to a third locus for writing *hysteries* of rhetorics, to where there are more than two genders/sexes. In other words, my tactic will be to mis/identify and mis/employ the differences in these two epistemologies (tragedy/farce) in dis/order to get on to third (subject) positions, or to get on to nongeneric poly*ethoi*. ("I" cum "we" are interested in enacting, as I have said repeatedly, "mis/representative antidotes.") The final (beginning?) purpose will be to include particular "personages" in writing the histories/hysteries of rhetorics who,

heretofore, have been systematically excluded. (I am thinking of such personages as "Dora," the "Wolfman," "Judge Schreber," "Antonin Artaud," and
Other so-called hysterics, schizos, crazies! Recall what Nietzsche, Clément,
and Kristeva say about these excluded people and the ideas they mis/represent
and implicitly about their *pharmakonic* value.)

Let us proceed, then, and begin with Nietzsche (who in his last letter to
Jacob Burkhardt wrote, "I am all the names of history" [see *Portable Nietzsche*
686]), which is with whom and where (poly*ethoi*) Judith Butler herself begins
and traces Nietzsche through Deleuze and Guattari, and then through her
own repositioning of gender/sex as neither *nonessentialist* nor *strategic essentialist*
but as loci of *cultural performance*. What I am specifically going to be concerned
with now is how a subject (agent) can be situated outside of gender and sex/
uality, or genus, scene, container (synecdoche)—all of which are, according
to Butler, "political categories" (*Gender* 1). If situated inside genus, there is
only One sex (Lacan), or Two sexes (Capital/ism). But if situated outside, if
situated in the loci of excluded third, then, there are "as many sexes as individuals" (*Gender* 118; compare 6. Also see Barthes, *Roland Barthes* 69). Let's re/
turn to Nietzsche.

And begin with Nietzsche's epistemology, for it is his contrary (anti-
Enlightenment) epistemology that Butler runs with. In *Genealogy of Morals*,
Nietzsche writes of his postepistemology of the "subject," or his rejection of
the metaphysics of substance: "There is no such substratum; there is no 'being'
behind doing, effecting, becoming; 'the doer' is merely a fiction added to the
deed—the deed is everything" (45). In other words, for Nietzsche, there is
no necessary essence/essentialism behind human beings and, more to our point
here, behind "male" or "female." Butler will pick up on the notion of "the
deed [action, performing] is everything."

Deleuze and Guattari—influenced by Nietzsche—work out of the same
postepistemology. There is no necessarily *fixed* essence. For them, "the phallus
is not one sex, but sexuality in its entirety." (Compare Irigaray, *This Sex
Which Is Not One*.) They argue: "Marx says . . . that the true difference is not
the difference between the two sexes, but the difference between the human
sex and the 'nonhuman' sex." For Deleuze and Guattari, "desiring production," pure and simple, produces *molecular aggregates*, which supply an infinite
number of sexes, which might be called " 'nonhuman' sex." This number
($n +$), however, is channeled and controlled by "social production" (i.e., by
capital) so that there will no longer be molecular aggregative representations of
sex but *molar representations*, that is, an "*anthropomorphic* [human] *representation of
sex*": One sex (for Freud, the "female" [the locus of lack] has no sex) or Two
sexes (for the sake of social-molar illusion) (*Anti-Oedipus* 294). Hence, for
Deleuze and Guattari, sexuality is constructed through social-political production.

Butler, like Nietzsche and Deleuze and Guattari, moves beyond a molar/
capitalistic male and female. Gender especially, but sex as well—she has the

hermaphrodite Herculine Barbin in mind—are both simulation/simulacrum without reference or circumference, that is, without "reality" or genus. This is how, working with a postmodernist epistemology, Butler defines "gender":

> Gender ought not to be construed as a stable identity or locus of agency from which various acts follow; rather, gender is an identity tenuously constituted in time, instituted in an exterior space through a *stylized repetition of acts.* . . . This formulation moves the conception of gender off the ground of a substantial model of identity to one that requires a conception of gender as a constituted social temporality. . . . Gender is also a norm that can never be fully internalized; "the internal" is a surface signification, and gender norms are finally phantasmatic, impossible to embody. (*Gender Trouble* 140–41; Butler's emphasis)

With this definition, Butler takes on Fredric Jameson's critique of postmodernism, which he partially achieves across the distinction of "pastiche" and "parody" (*Postmodernism* 16–19). Jameson says that pastiche "is a neutral practice of . . . mimicry, without any of parody's ulterior motives, amputated of the satiric impulse, devoid of laughter and of any conviction that alongside the abnormal tongue you have momentarily borrowed, some healthy linguistic normality still exists." He continues: "Pastiche is thus blank parody" (17). Pastiche, in other words, is a mere copy of a copy, with no socially productive purpose, while parody is a mimicry of an original with the purpose of satirizing to improve. Now whereas Jameson sees pastiche as a failing and parody as a virtue, Butler sees value in reversing (but affirmatively deconstructing) this characterization. It is this reversal that discloses the counterepistemology of postmodernism that Jameson does not recognize and that discloses, more importantly, a paratheory of nonpositive affirmation and of "threes." Let me explain with Butler's discussion of "drag queens," which exemplifies her interpretation of gender.

Relying on the work of the anthropologist Esther Newton (in *Mother Camp*), Butler writes: "The structure of impersonation reveals one of the key fabricating mechanisms through which the social construction of gender takes place. . . . Drag fully subverts the distinction between inner and outer psychic space [synecdoche] and effectively mocks both the expressive model of gender [the so-called stable "I"] and the notion of a true gender identity [negative essence]" (*Gender Trouble* 136–37). Butler quotes Newton: "At its most complex, [drag] is a double inversion that says, 'appearance is an illusion.' Drag says . . . 'my "outside" appearance is feminine, but my essence "inside" [the body] is masculine.' At the same time it symbolizes the opposite inversion; 'my appearance "outside" [my body, my gender] is masculine but my essence "inside" [myself] is feminine' " (137). What we have in the "drag" is *a performance of contradiction and/or paradox.* (Recall the Klein bottle, which has no inside or outside, or has no inside but an outside; and recall the hermaphrodite.)

The two implicit epistemologies that are colliding and in collusion here are *ones* that work from an original that can be copied (or parodied) and *an/other* that plays from a copy that can only be copied (or pastiched, or farced). What the "drag" discloses is "the imitative structure of gender itself—*as well as its contingency*" (137; Butler's emphasis). Butler further explains: "Indeed, part of . . . the giddiness of the performance is in the recognition of a radical contingency in the relation between sex and gender in the face of cultural configurations of causal unities that are regularly assumed to be natural and necessary. In the place of the law of heterosexual coherence, we see sex and gender denaturalized by means of a performance which avows their distinctness and dramatizes the cultural mechanism of their fabricated unity" (138). Hence, whereas Deleuze and Guattari find a virtue in schizo-society—specifically, in its ability to avoid finally being coopted by capital—Butler finds virtue in a schizo-gender and -sexuality. (Butler agrees with Deleuze and Guattari: "There are . . . as many sexes as individuals" [118].) In dis/respect to the whole concept of modernism (which works out of the negative and nostalgically longs to seize the fantasy of the real), the "drag" makes a sham of *identity politics*, of the way that we get politically represented (in *The* History of Rhetoric), while the "drag" simultaneously makes a virtue of postmodern resistances to and disruptions of capital's ready-made agent(s) and agency.

Butler, contrary to Jameson, sees that "there is a subversive laughter in the pastiche-effect of parodic practices in which the original, the authentic, and the real are themselves constituted as effects. The loss of gender norms would have the effect of proliferating gender configurations, destabilizing substantive identity, and depriving the naturalizing narratives of compulsory heterosexuality of their central protagonists: 'man' and 'woman' " (146). (And, in turn, would have the potential effect of proliferating subject positions in dis/order to rewrite *The* History of Rhetoric.) Outside this binary we will have taken a step toward *including* the "excluded thirds," which will have been a means of representing excess. If the strategy of *ex*cluding the third is a strategy of dialectic (the negative), then, the strategy of *in*cluding the third is a strategy of denegating the negative or of libidinalizing dialectic and dialogue. As Butler concludes: "If identities were no longer fixed as the premises of a political syllogism, and politics no longer understood as a set of practices derived from the alleged interests that belong to a set of ready-made subjects, a *new configuration* of politics would surely emerge from the ruins of the old" (149; emphasis mine).

IIIZ. "Where Are We Now?" (Burke) Or, "What Is the Meaning of a Pure Series of Interruptions?" (Barthes)

Moving from A to Z, from grammatical norm to paragrammatical deviation, I have been leading up to a discussion of ethos that would be poly*ethoi* (or polysubject positions) and specifically in dis/respect to writing histories/

hysteries of rhetorics. But not only would the new historians include the heretofore-excluded personages (improper *ethoi* such as Dora and Judge Schreber) in their new histories/hysteries, but also (and now I emphasize in closing) these new hysterians (or schizographers) *would write*—if it can still be called "writing"—*the way Dora and Schreber would write hystery!*

And so, *how* would this "we" write?

When we write, memory and delivery (theater, performance) will be of the utmost importance. We will need Foucault's concept of "counter-memory" (see *Language* 29–52); and we will need Antonin Artaud's "theater of cruelty" (*The Theater and Its Double*). Style, too, will be important. We will need L-F. Céline's "I am not a man of ideas. I am a man of style. . . . This involves taking sentences . . . and unhinging them" (see Kristeva, "Psychoanalysis" 314–15). And arrangement will take the form of a "z." It will be very deviant (Barthes, *Roland Barthes* 91). However, invention, at least traditional notions of invention, will play little part in this kind of writing. But I have already listed at great length the para*topoi* of "threes" (in the second section of this paper). But having attempted to answer this question of *how* would this "we" write, I am well aware that there can be no grammar, only a paragrammar; no rhetoric, only a pararhetoric.

Having somewhat answered the question of *how*, I would now turn to the question of *where* (place, para*topos*), which is a question again of parainvention (para*topoi*), with *where* as a pre/conceptual starting place, certainly not epistemic, but mythomorphic; certainly not synecdochic, but a containerless, free-flowing (fluid) of desire.

A quick answer: as I see them, the choices for an answer, then, are between, on the one hand, the *polis*, which is the site of two speakers in a dialectic/a dialogue excluding a third, the prosopopoeia of noise (Serres), and, on the other, the *pagus* (literally "country"), which is the site finally, after being excluded, to be inhabited by a third. (This site is the uncanny, the unhomely.) What Klein has done to the bottle (remember his topological jar [container] with no inside but an outside), "we" future historians/hysterians must do to the *polis*. What Klein has done to the bottle, we must do to the traditional, exclusionary genre of *The* History of Rhetoric.

A longer answer: We have insisted historically (in writing *The* History of Rhetoric) to maintain a (negating) distance between what is sacred, the *polis*, and what is allegedly profane, the *pagus*. (Some readers may read this *polis/pagus* as a binary; I do not, and for the simple reason that the *polis* is the site of one and two [dialectic] while the *pagus* is the site of three [polylectic, a radical multiplicity]. The *polis* is the site of two people excluding thirds, namely, *pagani*.) The best that the ancient Greeks could do was to deflect the *pagus* via a social structure called the *Areopagus* (a high council of elders). This *Areopagus* deflected the *pagus* by way of being a mediating structure, or a containing "space," between the *polis* and *pagus*. (Compare Godzich's discussion of the functioning of the Greek *theoria*, in his foreword to Paul de Man's

Resistance to Theory.) The *polis* is the place of law (authority by negation, prohibitions, decalogues of all kinds) while the *pagus* (not just the "country") is the un/place of outlawry (beasts, barbarians, pariahs [as in mutations from the norm], political exiles, "crazies") and site of—as a Jürgen Habermas would have it—the *pathos* of ugliness. The *Areopagus* functioned, and still functions, like the virgule between *polis/pagus*, while the *pagus* functions like an "imaginary zone" (recall Clément), or a gulag or septic tank where we can displace or flush away that which would threaten the sacred or so-called political stability. (Whereas both Freud and Lacan said that the unconscious is the most ethical place and there they must go, "I" cum "we," then, must say that the *pagus* is the most ethical place, and there "we" must pre/amble.)

I would, then, when writing histories/hysteries of rhetorics go to and with Jean-François Lyotard's idea of the *pagus*, which is

> a border zone where genres of discourse enter into conflict over the mode of linking. War and commerce. It's in the *pagus* that the *pax* and the pact are made and unmade. The *vicus*, the home, the *Heim* is a [imaginary] zone in which the differend between genres of discourse [or genders] is suspended. An "internal" peace is bought at the price of perpetual differends [phrases in dispute] on the outskirts. (The same arrangement goes for the ego [the subject], that of self-identification.) . . . Joyce, Schöberg, Cézanne: *pagani* waging war among the genres of discourse. (*Differend* 151)

To the list of *pagani*, I would add (some more) Dora, Nietzsche, the Wolfman, Judge Schreber, the Papin sisters, Antonin Artaud, Herculine Barbin, Deleuze and Guattari, A-Mad-Deus, Antonio Salieri (the "patron saint of mediocrity"), and Peter Shaffer.[9]

If we historians *and* hysterians of rhetorics would wage war among the genres of discourse, I would hope it would not be, however, with the purpose of winning so that we might paradoxically all lose. (Again!) If this were our goal, we would of course no longer be *pagani*. I hope that we would go with, but drift beyond, Nietzsche's argument in "Homer's Contest," in which he says, "The contest is necessary to preserve the health of the community," but then Nietzsche "reflect[s] on the original meaning of *ostracism* [which is]: 'Among us, no one shall be the best: but if some is, then let him [*sic*] be elsewhere and among others'" (36). The *health*, however, that I would have for "the [discordant, paralogical] community" finally *cannot be realized across exclusion, as demanded by the principle of negation.* Instead of exiling the despot, therefore, I would *reverse* Nietzsche's suggestion and have us all leave the *polis* (Virgil's *Aeneid*) and dwell, as writers of histories/hysteries of rhetorics, in the *pagus* (Ovid's *Metamorphoses*), which would be to live as elsewhere (in exile) and among (excluded) others. (Compare Deleuze, "Nomad Thought"; and Lanham.)

Notes

1. I have taken great liberties in writing this piece for Don Stewart's festschrift. The topic and the writing are, indeed, "savage" and "wild." (Freud, Lenin/ Althusser, and R. Barthes speak of *such a* practice and writing.) I take this liberty *in style*, however, because Don has previously recognized this *tendency* in my writing, and has referred to me as "Victor Vitanza, that occasional Paganini of the printed page, who employs some of the devices of Grammar B while writing deconstructed prose" (174). If I have previously engaged in Grammar B, I have pointed here toward what I will now call Grammar Z. If construed as impolitic, I would hope that Don (and others) would think of "weav[ing] a circle round [me] *thrice*."

2. I am using this phrase "philosophical rhetoric" to mean an overrationalizing of language. Compare Mason, who has a different notion.

3. I take this word *Letteraturizzaziones* from Kennedy's brief history, in which he defines it as "the tendency of rhetoric to shift its focus from persuasion to narration, from civic to personal contexts, and from discourse to literature, including poetry" (5).

4. This reference to Burke as "Papa" I have previously used on several occasions and make much of it in "Preparing to meet the faces that 'we' will have met." (No doubt, in part, it signals an anxiety of influence, of belatedness.) This reference to "Papa," again, may appear to be an indiscretion of mine or presumption. If so, then so. I am using it/him here as part of trinary thinking. As the reader continues, perhaps this aspect of my use of the en/titlement will become, in part, clear.

5. I am well aware of the recent controversy (e.g., between Edward Schiappa and John Poulakos) about mis/appropriating the Sophists and have written about it in the second chapter of my booklength manuscript on historiography of rhetoric. Moreover, I have put forth my own statement concerning the historiciz- ing of the Sophists in " 'Some More' Notes" and have responded to Schiappa in my "Neopragmatism."

6. This phrase " 'I' cum 'we' " is an idiomatic attempt to enact/perform poly*ethoi*, that is, a third-position, radical multiplicity of voices. I have employed it extensively in my "Concerning a Post-Classical *Ethos.*"

7. See Burke, "The Rhetoric of Hitler's 'Battle,' " in *The Philosophy of Literary Form.* I have made much of Burke's discussion of Hitler's rhetoric in my "Taking A-Count."

8. I see epideictic discourse as a "third" (and closely akin to *Letteraturizzaziones*) in the sequence of three classical speech acts (along with deliberative and forensic). Compare Barthes, *Rustle* 143.

9. For this cast of characters, this litany of profane names, see Freud, *Dora*; Schreber, *Memoirs*; Wolf-man, *The Wolf-Man*; Papin sisters, Clément's *Lives and Legends.* They are all variously discussed by Deleuze and Guattari, *Anti-Oedipus.* And obviously, I am referring to the play/film *Amadeus.*

Works Cited

Adorno, Theodor W. *Negative Dialectics.* New York: Continuum, 1987.
Aristotle. *The Basic Works of Aristotle.* Ed. Richard McKeon. New York: Random, 1941.

Artaud, Antonin. *The Theater and Its Double*. Trans. Mary Caroline Richards. New York: Grove, 1958.

Barthes, Roland. *Image/Music/Text*. Trans. Stephen Heath. New York: Hill and Wang, 1977.

———. *A Lover's Discourse: Fragments*. 1977. Trans. Richard Howard. New York: Hill and Wang, 1978.

———. *Mythologies*. 1957. Trans. Annette Lavers. New York: Hill and Wang, 1972.

———. *The Pleasure of the Text*. 1973. Trans. Richard Miller. New York: Hill and Wang, 1975.

———. *Roland Barthes by Roland Barthes*. 1975. Trans. Richard Howard. New York: Hill and Wang, 1977.

———. *The Rustle of Language*. 1984. Trans. Richard Howard. New York: Hill and Wang, 1986.

———. *Sade/Fourier/Loyola*. 1971. Trans. Richard Miller. New York: Hill and Wang, 1976.

———. *Writing Degree Zero* and *Elements of Semiology*. 1953, 1964. Trans. Annette Lavers and Colin Smith. Boston: Beacon, 1970.

Bataille, Georges. *Inner Experience*. 1954. Trans. Leslie Anne Boldt. Albany: SUNY, 1988.

Bowersock, G. B. *Greek Sophists in the Roman Empire*. Oxford: Clarendon P, 1969.

Brown, Norman O. *Closing-Time*. New York: Vintage, 1974.

———. *Life Against Death*. Middletown, CT: Wesleyan UP, 1959.

———. *Love's Body*. Berkeley: U of California P, 1966.

Burke, Kenneth. *A Grammar of Motives*. Berkeley: U of California P, 1966.

———. *Language as Symbolic Action*. Berkeley: U of California P, 1966.

———. *The Philosophy of Literary Form*. New York: Vintage, 1957.

Butler, Judith. *Gender Trouble: Feminism and the Subversion of Identity*. New York: Routledge, 1990.

Cixous, Hélène, and Catherine Clément. *The Newly Born Woman*. Trans. Betsy Wing. Minneapolis: U of Minnesota P, 1986.

Clément, Catherine. "Enslaved Enclave." *New French Feminism*. Ed. Elaine Marks and Isabelle de Courtivron. New York: Schocken, 1981. 130–36.

———. *The Lives and Legends of Jacques Lacan*. 1981. Trans. Arthur Goldhammer. New York: Columbia UP, 1983.

Connors, Robert J. "Rhetorical History as a Component of Composition Studies." *Rhetoric Review* 7.2 (1989): 230–40.

Deleuze, Gilles. "Nomad Thought." *The New Nietzsche*. Ed. David B. Allison. New York: Delta, 1977. 142–49.

Deleuze, Gilles, and Félix Guattari. *Anti-Oedipus*. Minneapolis: U of Minnesota P, 1983.

———. *A Thousand Plateaus*. Trans. Brian Massumi. Minneapolis: U of Minnesota P, 1987.

de Man, Paul. *The Resistance to Theory*. Minneapolis: U of Minnesota P, 1986.

Derrida, Jacques. *Writing and Difference*. Trans. Alan Bass. Chicago: U of Chicago P, 1978.

Desilet, Gregory. "Nietzsche Contra Burke: The Melodrama in Dramatism." *Quarterly Journal of Speech* 75 (1989): 65–83.

Dews, Peter. *Logics of Disintegration*. New York: Verson, 1987.

Eco, Umberto, and Thomas A. Sebeok, eds. *The Sign of Three*. Bloomington: Indiana UP, 1988.

Foucault, Michel. *Discipline and Punish*. Trans. Alan Sheridan. New York: Random, 1979.

——. *Herculine Barbin*. New York: Pantheon, 1980.

——. *Language, Counter-Memory, Practice*. Trans. Donald F. Bouchard and Sherry Simon. Ithaca: Cornell UP, 1986.

Freud, Sigmund. *Dora: An Analysis of a Case of Hysteria*. New York: Macmillan, 1963.

Godzich, Wlad. "Foreword: The Tiger on the Paper Mat." *The Resistance to Theory*. Ed. Paul de Man. Minneapolis: U of Minnesota P, 1986.

Irigaray, Luce. *This Sex Which Is Not One*. 1977. Trans. Catherine Porter. Ithaca, NY: Cornell UP, 1985.

Jameson, Fredric. *Postmodernism, or, The Cultural Logic of Late Capitalism*. Durham: Duke UP, 1991.

Joyce, James. *Finnegans Wake*. 1939. New York: Viking, 1975.

Kennedy, George A. *Classical Rhetoric and Its Christian and Secular Tradition from Ancient to Modern Times*. Chapel Hill: U of North Carolina P, 1980.

Kerferd, G. B. *The Sophistic Movement*. Cambridge: Cambridge UP, 1981.

Kofman, Sarah. "Nietzsche and the Obscurity of Heraclitus." *Diacritics* 17.3 (1987): 39–55.

Kristeva, Julia. *Desire in Language*. 1969, 1977. New York: Columbia UP, 1980.

——. "Psychoanalysis and the Polis." *The Kristeva Reader*. Ed. Toril Moi. New York: Columbia UP, 1986. 301–20.

Lacan, Jacques. *The Four Fundamental Concepts of Psychoanalysis*. Trans. Alan Sheridan. New York: Norton, 1981.

Lanham, Richard A. *The Motives of Eloquence*. New Haven: Yale UP, 1976.

Lyotard, Jean-François. *The Differend: Phrases in Dispute*. Trans. Georges Van Den Abbeele. Minneapolis: U of Minnesota P, 1988.

Marx, Karl. *The Eighteenth Brumaire of Louis Bonaparte*. New York: International Publishers, 1963.

Mason, Jeff. *Philosophical Rhetoric*. New York: Routledge, 1989.

Nietzsche, Friedrich. *The Birth of Tragedy and the Case of Wagner*. New York: Vintage, 1967.

——. *The Genealogy of Morals and Ecce Homo*. Trans. Walter Kaufmann. New York: Vintage, 1969.

——. "Homer's Contest." *The Portable Nietzsche*. Trans. Walter Kaufmann. New York: Penguin, 1984. 32–39.

——. *The Portable Nietzsche*. Trans. Walter Kaufmann. New York: Penguin, 1984.

Nye, Andrea. *Words of Power*. New York: Routledge, 1990.

Philostratus and Eunapius. *The Lives of the Sophists*. Trans. Wilmer Cave Wright. Cambridge, MA: Harvard UP, 1968.

Pierssens, Michel. *The Power of Babel: A Study of Logophilia*. Trans. Carl R. Lovitt. London: Routledge and Kegan Paul, 1980.

Pike, Kenneth L. *Linguistic Concepts*. Lincoln: U of Nebraska P, 1982.

Plato. *The Collected Dialogues*. Ed. Edith Hamilton and Huntington Cairns. Princeton: Princeton UP, 1987.

Schiappa, Edward. "Sophistic Rhetoric: Oasis or Mirage?" *Rhetoric Review* 10.1 (1991): 5–18.

Schneiderman, Stuart. *Jacques Lacan: The Death of an Intellectual Hero*. Cambridge, MA: Harvard UP, 1983.

Schreber, Daniel Paul. *Memoirs of My Nervous Illness*. 1903. Trans. and ed. Ida Macallpine and Richard A. Hunter. Cambridge, MA: Harvard UP, 1988.

Scott, Charles. *The Question of Ethics*. Bloomington: Indiana UP, 1990.

Sebeok, Thomas A. "One, Two, Three Spells U B E R T Y." *The Sign of Three*. Ed. Umberto Eco and Thomas A. Sebeok. Bloomington: Indiana UP, 1988. 1–10.

Serres, Michel. *Hermes*. Ed. Josué V. Harari and David F. Bell. Baltimore: Johns Hopkins UP, 1982.

Spivak, Gayatri Chakravorty. "Feminism and Deconstruction, Again: Negotiating with Unacknowledged Masculinism." *Between Feminism and Psychoanalysis*. Ed. Teresa Brennan. New York: Routledge, 1989. 206–24.

Stewart, Donald C. "The Nineteenth Century." *The Present State of Scholarship in Historical and Contemporary Rhetoric*. Ed. Winifred Bryan Horner. Rev. ed. Columbia: U of Missouri P, 1990. 151–85.

Vitanza, Victor J. "Concerning a Post-Classical *Ethos*, as Para/Rhetorical Ethics, the 'Selphs,' and the Excluded Third." *Ethos*. Ed. James Baumlin and Tita French Baumlin. Dallas: Southern Methodist UP, 1993.

———. "Critical Sub/Versions of the History of Philosophical Rhetoric." *Rhetoric Review* 6.1 (1987): 41–66.

———. "Neopragmatism, Pragmatics, and *The Differend*: Still Some More Talk about a Third Sophistic." *Rhetoric, Pragmaticism, Sophistry*. Ed. Steven Mailloux. Forthcoming.

———. "An Open Letter to My 'Colligs': On 'Counter'-Ethics, Para/Rhetorics, and the Hysterical Turn." *PRE/TEXT* 11.3–4 (1990): 237–87.

———. "Preparing to Meet the Faces That 'We' Will Have Met." *Writing Histories of Rhetoric*. Ed. Victor J. Vitanza. Carbondale: Southern Illinois UP, 1993.

———. " 'Some More' Notes, Toward a 'Third' Sophistic." *Argumentation* 5 (1991): 117–39.

———. "Taking A-Count of a (Future-Anterior) History of Rhetoric *as* 'Libidinalized Marxism' (A PM Pastiche)." *Writing Histories of Rhetoric*. Ed. Victor J. Vitanza. Carbondale: Southern Illinois UP, 1993.

———. "Teaching-Nothing." Unpublished ms. read at the Issues in Cultural Theory Conference at the University of Texas, Arlington, Feb. 1992.

———. "Three Countertheses; or, A Critical In(ter)vention into Composition Theory and Pedagogy." *Contending with Words*. Ed. Patricia Harkin and John Schilb. New York: MLA, 1991. 139–72.

White, Eric Charles. *Kaironomia: On the Will-to-Invent*. Ithaca, NY: Cornell UP, 1987.

Wittgenstein, Ludwig. *Tractatus Logico-Philosophicus*. 1921. Trans. D. G. Pears and B. F. McGuiness. London: Routledge and Kegan Paul, 1977.

Wolf-Man. *The Wolf-Man*. New York: Basic Books, 1971.

Zizek, Slavoj. *The Sublime Object of Ideology*. London: Verso, 1989.

15 Ecofeminist Poetics
A Dialogue on Keeping Body and Mind Together

C. Jan Swearingen and Diane Mowery

> Bid a singer in a chorus, Know Thyself; and will he
> not turn for the knowledge to the others, his fellows in
> the chorus, and to his harmony with them?
>
> —Epictetus

IN THE FOLLOWING DISCUSSION WE EXAMINE PARALLELS AMONG THE values held by the ecology movement, the images of earth and of women to be found among the early Goddess religions that have been reclaimed within the ecology movement and within feminism (Zawicki), and the paradigms of feminine thinking and writing that have been advanced within American feminism and French postfeminism (Cixous and Clément, Ebert, Worsham). These movements share a group of revisionist values and have generated a number of metaphors for thought and discourse that, we propose, can provide revisionist composition theories and teaching with companionable alternatives to the existing lexicon of terms for the writer and for writing. Process and cognitive paradigms for writing and thinking continue to shift, merge, and diversify in relation to social constructionist, collaborative, heteroglossic, and personal-expressive narrative paradigms. Concepts of the identity of the self, or writing subject, as well as of the nature of written discourse are affected by such shifts.

The ecology movement and the related resurgence of study of early Goddess religions and cultures have been particularly attractive to feminists because of the imagistic grounding they provide for values and patterns of identity, thinking, and writing that are being defended as feminine, or feminist, or both. Current attempts to define a feminist approach to composition theory and teaching (e.g., Clark, Flynn, Lamb, Miller) can benefit from an examination of the values defended by both the ecology and Goddess movements, we propose, because of the high degree of overlap—some might say confusion—among these values and those that are defended within feminist proposals for a feminization of composition studies (e.g., Flynn, "Composing 'Composing' "; Lamb, "Reply" 498–99). It has been argued that the so-called feminization of composition studies is neither inherently nor necessarily feminist (Cosby, "Response" 497; Musgrove "Response" 495) and that it is actually not productive to view it as gendered (Berthoff, "Rhetoric" 285) . Postfeminists have criticized the ecology, Goddess, and feminist composition movements alike on the grounds that they are "essentialist," that is, that they seem to assume or posit as innate precisely those "feminine" traits that many feminists want both women and men to see as culturally imposed rather than biologically determined (Hekman).

After discussing these views, we conclude with an appraisal of these related proposals for introducing gendered models and metaphors into discourse theory. We turn first to an examination of how and why the models of feminine discourse advanced in different ways by Gilligan, by Belenky and her colleagues, and by literary theorists under the heading of writing the body have proved so appealing. Parallel concepts of a harmonic, holistic interdependent feminine nature in the ecology and Goddess movements of the past decade have undergone deconstruction in the hands of postmodern and postfeminist theorists. More recently, similar criticisms have been leveled at feminine and feminist paradigms for writing and composing.

Mowery: The plethora of recent publications explaining, honoring, defending, and promoting the notion of the sacred female or divine ancestress attests to the wide array of modern Goddess movements and to their surge in public appeal, especially for women. Spiritual- and ecofeminists, who are specifically interested in liberating not only women but also the earth and other Others, have, in the past few decades, turned much of their attention toward positing the Goddess as a metaphor, a "sign" for ultimate liberation through "feminization." The Goddess validates an order that is antithetical to the traditionally accepted order of things: it is "earth-centered, not heaven-centered, of this world, not otherworldly, body affirming, not body denying, holistic, not dualistic" (Gadon xii). The Great Mother of all of the universe's re/pro/creative processes, the Goddess affirms the "feminine" side of Western philosophy's gendered dichotomies: body, nature, pathos, mother.

The Goddess's feminist appeal becomes apparent when we consider the powerful effect of myth, metaphor, and ritual on human life. Clifford Geertz, for instance, suggests that "sacred symbols function to synthesize a people's ethos—and their world-view—the picture they have of the way things in sheer actuality are." Religion, he says, "is a system of symbols which act to produce powerful, pervasive, and long-lasting moods and motivations" (205–6). Merlin Stone, a Jungian feminist historian of religion, emphasizes the perceptual aspects of religious symbols. Sacred myths "present ideas that guide perception, conditioning us to think and even perceive in a particular way" (4). Even those who have given up belief in an all-knowing God very likely remain entrenched in the mythic symbolism of God-the-Father because, as Carol Christ suggests, "a symbol's effect does not depend on rational assent, for a symbol also functions on levels of the psyche other than the rational" (274).

The moods and motivations created by Father-God symbolism can have a devastating effect on women's images of themselves. The West's association of women with sexuality and the body has also been an association of women with evil, and the image of the Father-God offers a continual reinforcement of that association. According to Carol Christ, even when a woman is ignorant of the biblical account of female evil, she "acknowledges the anomaly of female power when she prays exclusively to a male God. She may see herself as like God (created in the image of God) only by denying her own sexual identity and affirming God's transcendence of sexual identity. But she can never have . . . her full sexual identity affirmed as being in the image and likeness of God" (275). Mary Daly concurs: "If God in 'his' heaven is a father ruling 'his' people, then it is the 'nature' of things and according to divine plan and the order of the universe that society be male dominated" (54).

In times of crisis, as Carol Christ has pointed out, many women find themselves, despite their intellectual objections, on their knees praying to God-the-Father. Christ suggests that this phenomenon occurs primarily because "the mind abhors a vacuum." Women cannot simply reject patriarchal symbol systems; they must instead replace them with more acceptable ones (275). The Goddess, as a sign of a woman-centered, body-affirming order, fills the void. As Stone suggests, a symbolic order that grows from and is propagated by "a religion in which the deity [is] female, and revered as wise, valiant, powerful, and just" should provide "very different images of womanhood from those which we are offered by the male-oriented religions of today" (5). The Goddess appeals to feminists because She affirms female wisdom, power, and sexuality; She legitimizes woman-as-subject in a phallocracy where the only legitimate subjects have been male.

But She is more than a symbol of simple material liberation for women. In fact, She can be seen as the culmination of modernity's project. Michel Foucault suggests that in the modern episteme, "foundational truths" are viewed as linguistic constructions, rhetorical creations; modernists recognize no prelinguistic point of stasis on which to base any system of order. And yet, they are nevertheless interested in constructing such foundations, in systematizing and structuring a totalization of language games that will lead ultimately to liberation. Motivated by a nostalgic drive for unity, modernists attempt to construct an all-embracing "transformation without residuum" (Foucault 305), a holistic system of order in which nothing is excluded. In this sense, it seems to me that the Goddess is Herself very much a modernist construct. She does not recognize the truth/myth dichotomy. Language, for Her, is self-referential, and it is the language itself, the mood, the rhythm it creates that is important. Rather than laying down laws or establishing creeds, Goddess ceremonies utilize chants and poetry, rhythmic language and rituals that emphasize "what people do—and not what people believe" (Adler 170). "Truth" is understood as a linguistic construction. As

Aidan Kelly suggests, for Goddess proponents, "Everything, even the Great Metaphor of the Goddess, is still only a metaphor" (qtd. in Adler 171–72). She is revered not as a material deity so much as a mythopoetic, socially and linguistically constructed base upon which Her proponents hope a better world might be built, a world that might finally realize an all-inclusive totality devoid of oppression. She represents for them the culmination of modernity's project with a feminist corrective. In fact, it could be said that Her brand of systematization, Her brand of liberation takes the form of "feminization." For Her proponents, She becomes the "total reabsorption of all forms of discourse into a single word," the ultimate "transformation without residuum."

The Goddess is associated with what Riane Eisler calls the "partnership model," a "feminine" model of social relations based on inclusion, on "power-as-linking," on a "win-win" rather than a "win-lose" view of power relations (28). The symbol of the Goddess represents interconnection rather than separation, power together rather than power over. This has, Eisler says, "from time immemorial been symbolized by the circle or oval—the Goddess's cosmic egg or Great Round—rather than by the jagged lines of a pyramid where, as gods or as the heads of nations or families, men rule from the top" (193). Starhawk, a Wiccan high priestess, suggests that the Goddess is a metaphor for "power-from-within," for Being as perpetual regeneration. She advocates a supplanting of "masculine" metaphors of war and domination with "feminine" metaphors of birth and regeneration, webs and weaving, interconnection and nurturing, because when viewed across these "feminine" metaphors "the cosmos becomes a living body in which we all participate, merging and emerging in rhythmic cycles" ("Feminist" 174).

The Goddess symbolizes "connectedness, sustenance, healing, creating" (Starhawk, *Dreaming* 4), an all-inclusiveness that embraces previously excluded others. For Starhawk, Eisler, Gadon, Lerner, Christ, Stone, and other spiritual- and ecofeminists, the sign of the Goddess signifies the ultimate totalization of language games, the ultimate harmonic consensus, the ultimate resolution to conflict. As Christa Wolf has suggested, the Goddess is the sign of an all-in-oneness that does not get hierarchicalized (98). And the mandatory use of the definite article in reference to Her is, as Martin Heidegger likes to say, not no/thing: it implies that She is complete, settled, finished, total. Her proponents tend to view Her as a solid, albeit socially constructed, foundation upon which we might create our own liberation; and they call for a transformation in the form of "feminization," advocating many voices in harmony over one tyrannical voice, sensual experience over disembodied rational thought, the cosmic egg over the hierarchical pyramid.

The very idea of an inverted order of privilege points up the easy reversibility of things and spotlights resources that have long been hidden, silenced, and exiled. The Goddess's greatest gift may be Her signification and legitimation of the "other." But not so that we might blindly leap into it as "The Answer," rather because, in the chaotic moment that Her inversion of Father-God order creates, possibilities that lie outside of binary oppositions get the chance to be dis/covered. Hélène Cixous has suggested that if the traditionally accepted and unquestioned "phallocentric" foundations upon which Truth has been established were exposed as simply one (rather oppressive) option among many, "all the stories would be there to retell differently; the future would be incalculable; the historic forces would and will change hands and change body—another thought which is yet unthinkable—will transform the functioning of all society" (65). In the Goddess's attempts to legitimate the mirror image of Father-God order, to make the weaker side the stronger, She may be capable of inspiring something more than that, something outside of that Father/Mother opposition altogether. And it may be in *this* way that the Goddess's flame could make light the way toward Cixous's brand of transformation, the kind that could create an "uncalculably" less oppressive, because less totalistic, *will have been.*

Swearingen: Sharing with postmodern theory a rejection of "Enlightenment" rationality, postfeminist theory (see Hekman, Ebert, Zawicki) questions not only the modes of speaking and writing that are taught in composition classrooms but also the collective, collaborative, and social constructionist models of thought and discourse that feminist studies have found more comfortable and, experientially, more natural to many women than argument. The patterns of collaborative learning and socially or collectively shaped knowledge are defined by some scholars as themselves "feminine" (e.g., Belenky et al., Lunsford). In a recent response to many of these issues, Donald Stewart proposed, albeit without reference to gender per se, that there is an inherent irony in advocating, on pluralist grounds, more tolerance for arguing controversial issues while at the same time espousing "both consensual and social constructionist attitudes toward language and community and the benefits of collaborative learning strategies" (496). Can there be contention within collaborative paradigms? Does argument preclude consensus? Does consensus forbid argument? One would hope that our knowledge of the history of rhetoric would permit a quick "of course" in answer to the first question and a confident "definitely not" to the second and third. However, doctrinal orthodoxies lurk behind these questions and their answers, some of them tied to gender.

The social and epistemic models of the web of connection and collaborative learning, as well as the image of the stalwart solitary writer forging a way through forests of thought, need not be gendered images; but it is precisely because gender has already become linked to these models as an issue in composition studies that its presence and meanings should be more fully appraised. What can we learn from examining the gendered metaphors that lurk among our diverse, sometimes competing paradigms of cognition, discourse, composing, and writing? Attending to gender can improve our understanding of the appeal of these models and perhaps help reduce some of the tensions that have made both the use and the avoidance of gendered models such vexed choices.

In "The Ecology of Writing," Marilyn Cooper reviewed ecological metaphors for writing and writers as alternatives to the cognitive process paradigm of writing. By emphasizing that writing is thinking, she argued, cognitive process models remove to the periphery social and interpretive interactions that many of us would like to see placed in a more central location in writing theory. "The ideal image the ecological model projects is of an infinitely extended group of people who interact through writing, who are connected by the various systems that constitute the activity of writing" (372). In constrast, the ideal image of the writer projected by cognitive process models "is isolated from the social world." This "solitary author works alone, within the privacy of his own mind" (365). The Cartesian elements in this model are tied to long-standing assumptions about the epistemic value and archival uses of texts and literacy (see Olson, "Mind and Media"; Welch). Heir as well to postromantic notions of expression, individual uniqueness, and creative imagination, the image of the writer projected by cognitive process paradigms isolates the individual while at the same time arms a concept of the author with abilities not to be found in Descartes's arsenal of systematic doubt. "Writing becomes a form of parthenogenesis, the author producing propositional and pragmatic structures, Athena-like, full grown and complete, out of his brow" (366). Paradoxically, such models of writing and writers can replicate the product-centered, isolationist, and individualist values of the current-traditional classroom that they were intended to supplant.

Cooper's essay advocates and exemplifies what Ann Berthoff likes to call thirdness, that is, the representation of thought and language as mediated, irreducibly social, dialectical means for understanding differences—in this case between cognitive process and social models—that incorporates both within an ongoing dialectical third term (e.g., Berthoff, *Sense* 11–27; "Rhetoric as Hermeneutic"). "An ecological model of writing" is one in which "a person is continually engaged with a variety of socially constituted systems. The term ecological is not, however, simply the newest way to say 'contextual' " (Cooper 367). Unlike contextual models that ultimately sustain an emphasis on the isolated product that can be distilled from its context, an ecological notion of writing can emphasize "how writers interact to form systems: all the characteristics of any individual writer both determine and are determined by the characteristics of all the other writers and writings in the systems" (368).

Adapting the ecological model to describe writing and writers entails the adoption of a systemic, holistic model as a governing metaphor, a master trope, a heuristic model (e.g., Rappaport, esp. 223–46) for representing complex relationships and for highlighting features that we want to emphasize or have not amply attended to before. Like contemporary feminist appropriations of the ancient Goddess myths of weaving and giving birth, an ecological model highlights the notion of a web, among its other representations of relatedness, reciprocity, and connectedness. "Anything that affects one strand vibrates throughout the whole" (Cooper 370). Ecological models of the writing process adapt systems-theory approaches for uniting and diversifying the complex relationships among writer and audience and stimulate questions about how writers both invent and talk to their audience/readers (372). Conceding that the ecological model is an idealized utopian construct, Cooper concludes her discussion with a brief consideration of its potential influence upon the ownership and private property concepts of writing products and of ideas more generally. The ecological model "encourages us to direct our corrective energies away from the characteristics of the individual writer and toward imbalances in social systems that prevent good writing" (373).

Since Cooper's essay appeared, several themes touched on in her discussion have taken a quantum leap and now verge on either a paradigm shift or dissolution into chaos. The audience/reader concept has been expansively addressed within reading theory to further establish ties—as well as discontinuities—among writer, reader, meanings, and texts. If a connected web model directs us to see collaborative and interdependent relations, some reading theory directs us once again to the individual as site and origin of textual meaning and emphasizes the indeterminacy of any meaning outside the perceiver/reader/audience. We witness in this an ironic pun on Kenneth Burke's quip that the new criticism had canonized in its notion of the verbal icon authorless books read by no one. Now, in contrast, instead of venerating the text as icon, we have removed all meaning from the text to the reader, creating meaningless texts read differently by everyone. Having long since surpassed the city limits of pluralism, the processes of reading and writing alike are staking out new theoretical and pedagogical territory in relationship to one another and informed by a number of cultural issues, among them gender.

In the search for feminine as well as feminist models of composing, writing, and thinking, we can observe parallels with some of the paradigms described by Cooper under the headings of ecology and ecosystems. A longitudinal study of women's patterns of moral development and ethical reasoning, Carol Gilligan's *In a Different Voice* employs the phrase "web of connection" in all its metaphorical and mythological meanings to characterize her women subjects' ways of making—and ways of seeing themselves as making—highly contextualized, multivariable ethical decisions. This way of reasoning Gilligan contrasts to the pattern found more commonly in male subjects: the "logic of justice," where one rule—such as "it is wrong to steal"—is applied uniformly to the "same" ethical question in different settings. A related study, *Women's Ways of Knowing* (Belenky et al.), draws on Gilligan's notion of the web of connection as well as upon Peter Elbow's model of the doubting game and the believing game to characterize a spectrum of learning styles, among them what the authors term "separated" and "connected" modes of learning and "subjectivist," "procedural," and "social constructionist" understandings of knowledge. Reactions to both of these highly popular studies have charged that they "essentialize" women's characterisitics as if to say that they are innate and universal, despite the fact that both studies carefully qualify themselves as studies of specific groups of women subjects, studies whose research goals were in part to record how it is that the women studied define themselves. By valorizing, or at least by legitimizing the modes of knowing, speaking, thinking, and learning that the women themselves said they were most comfortable with and proud of, Gilligan's and Belenky and her colleagues' studies have been widely acclaimed for reinterpreting and reappraising women's language and epistemology. Criticism persists, nonetheless, grounded most often in claims of essentialism or of excluding men.

Similar objections have been leveled at two related movements: attempts to define feminine modes of composition practice, theory, and teaching (e.g., Flynn, "Composing 'Composing' ") and the burgeoning interest in ancient Goddess religions. Several recent revolutions in composition pedagogy, among them the cognitive process and empowerment models, have overthrown or attempted to overthrow—*subvert* is the word often chosen—

the current traditional paradigm of academic writing. Down with the five-paragraph essay and most formalist, linear, and monologic models for writing, argument, and academic discourse. Though they have not in most cases identified themselves explicitly with gender issues, many of these movements have tried to restore aspects of discourse and language use that were excluded or denigrated in the older, hierarchical systems (but see de-Beaugrande). Many new writing pedagogies favor associative ("natural") rather than linear ("artificial") patterns of thought, encourage uses of narrative rather than expository and particularly argumentative modes, and defend poetic rather than abstract expression. Similarly, feminist theologians and critics of immanent versus transcendent conceptions of deity (e.g., Trible; Pagels, *Gnostic*) have favored collective, egalitarian, nonhierarchical, and participatory patterns of worship and spiritual expression. The recent challenge presented to social constructionist and consensus models within composition theory warrants comparison with parallel objections to nonhierarchical theologies among theologians and religious scholars who object to feminist reinterpretations.

Religious, cultural, and linguistic studies of gender differences in culturally transmitted understandings of power and possession can and I hope will be applied in various ways to the development of new writing pedagogies. For many women in our culture, power is understood as shared, as power *to*, as enriched by collaboration—an understanding that is reflected in the pedagogical goal of empowerment. Men in our culture are encouraged to measure power as power *over*, as control, and as something that exists in fixed quantities such that for one person to have power means for another to lose it (Gadon, Schaef, Tannen). The same set of assumptions has been shown to govern implicit rules of conversational exchange, creating situations in which the meaning of the exchange is entirely different for male and female participants (Gilligan, Tannen). The insights gleaned from these studies have yet to be fully adapted to the situations and issues indigenous to the writing classroom. They bear on many topics, among them argumentation, dialogics, empowerment, identity, subjectivity, voice, social context, and purpose.

Although the ink has barely dried on some of these studies, objections are already being raised in a number of quarters about the prudence and validity of incorporating questions of gender difference into writing theory and pedagogy. A recent exchange between Robert Bly and Deborah Tannen brought together questions concerning gendered language paradigms in our culture and the appeal of the early goddess religions and more broadly of "neopaganism" in today's spiritually bereft culture. Tannen defended the study of difference on the grounds that unless social patterns of gender differentiation that allow men to do things—such as interrupt one another without punishment—that women are not allowed to do, the patterns cannot be revised. She added that any mention of gender, any talk of "women" and "men" introduces the possibility that people will hear the words themselves as accusations (Bly and Tannen 96). Tannen concedes that there is always something dangerous about lumping people together—about saying "women," or "men," or any other group. "One of the worst things people do is to lump other people into groups and to heap scorn on them. That's the opening for all kinds of evil. But I believe that if there are patterns, the danger of *not* identifying them is greater than the danger of identifying them. And it's women in particular who suffer if we don't describe the differences, because we have one standard in this country—and that standard is based on men's way" (94).

The important synthesis of feminism with language studies was inaugurated by Tannen's mentor, Robin Lakoff, in *Language and Woman's Place*. Subsequent studies have documented both the perception and the practice of gender differences in language and its interpretation. When men interrupt or shift topics, it is generally accepted and even valued as a sign of strength and assertiveness; when women do so, they are often perceived as out of place or rude by both men and women. The same behavior means different things. Similar analysis of other marginalized groups reveals parallel practices with regard to some behaviors: underlings defer to their bosses and interrupt them less frequently than bosses do to underlings, but within each of those groups the gender differential also functions.

Establishing ties between empirical studies in language and gender and composition theory and pedagogy has been more difficult than many thought. Not the least of the worries has been the conflation of empiricism with positivism in recent postmodern theory and the resulting charge of "essentialism" leveled at the work of Belenky, Gilligan, and other feminist empiricists. Positivism and feminist empiricism can be distinguished from one another on several grounds. Feminist empiricism challenges the incomplete methods employed by most empiricism, its lack of metamethodological consciousness (Harding 183; Flynn, "Composing 'Composing' " 87). Where traditional empiricism viewed the social identity of the observer as irrelevant, feminist and other culturally sensitive empirical investigators have increasingly dispensed with the view that "facts" are value-neutral found objects in a statis observable reality. Ostensibly, value-neutral research usually reflects the values and interests of dominant cultures—including gender (Flynn, "Composing 'Composing' " 87). This can be readily observed in early twentieth-century anthropologists' preoccupations with sexuality, property, and kinship systems—clearly post-Freudian preoccupations of males in capitalist societies. To many, the very idea of a feminist positivism is an impossibility, a contradiction in terms because a feminist approach is by definition not value-neutral in methods, choices of theories, and observations of facts (87). For the same reason, a feminist empiricism—in composition studies or any other field such as Gilligan's in psychology—must define and defend its methods even as it employs them. Experimental feminism (deBeaugrande 258), in short, is in its infancy.

There persists what can only be called a reluctant hesitation to introduce gender issues into composition studies, and sometimes skepticism or even hostility when overtly feminist or feminization agendas are defined (see George; Flynn, "Composing 'Composing' " 88). Though literary criticism has for some time profited from a growing industry of French-American feminist theories and theorists, the analogs within composition studies have not as quickly materialized (but see Bleich, Miller). Aside from occasional work such as Walter Ong's on "male" agonistic patterns in argumentation (Swearingen), the question of gender, much less an overtly feminist agenda for composition scholarship, languished as a minor area of study until the import of Gilligan and Belenky (see deBeaugrande). The wholesale overhauling of large questions of subjectivity, authorship, knowledge, writing, and literacy that has visited every field in the humanities has affected composition scholarship as well. Ironically, this has occurred just as questions of gender and feminism are achieving their first clear formulations within writing theory and pedagogy. As in other quarters, the charge of "essentialism" has been the first in a series of rebukes, accompanied by "not necessarily feminine" and "not intrinsically feminine" leveled at patterns of thought and forms of discourse alike (e.g., Farrar et al.). Like gender, rationality has been called into question, or placed under erasure, as the deconstructionists like to say it, on the grounds that only a literal-minded essentialism can posit either gender or rationality as in any way innate or intrinsic. Nonetheless, both rationality and gender persist: they appeal as self-images and as vehicles for understanding a number of processes through metaphorically enriched and enriching terms.

Socrates won a prize from the Delphic oracle for being the wisest of all men. Unlike Descartes, he knew that he did not know. In this regard, he might be adopted as a proponent of some of the deconstructions you recommend, or even as a defender of "Goddess" values! Whether under the aegis of the goddess or not, many today share the Socratic belief that it is important to dispel students' dependency upon the notion that teachers have the Truth and that they are expected to find and report the one true Truth (Belenky et al., Bruner). But as we attempt to guide students beyond passive modes of learning, it is crucial that we sustain and defend notions of truths and of epistemologies, the "sense of learning" and "the making of meaning" (Berthoff). Otherwise, we might as well pack up our tents and go home.

Mowery: The terms *sustain* and *defend* make me a bit nervous because I don't think the meaning-making process is ever an innocent one; it's driven by a modernist desire to regroup, to unify, to systematize so that the "bloomin', buzzin' confusion" might once again be masterable. It ends up a political question of who gets to be the subject who knows and who/what gets relegated to object status. I think continuing to question everything—including who might benefit from any making of meaning—while at the same time guarding every question, not letting go "of the questionable character of all things" (Nietzsche 337), might keep us from growing roots in the foundational constructs we utilize (and that utilize us), might prevent us from allowing truths to become as totalistic as Truth.

Swearingen: Experiences, too—all that chaos and "bloomin', buzzin' confusion"— are ideas, and as such both are simultaneously ways of knowing and objects of knowledge. I am reminded of the British Marxist Raymond Williams's *Keywords* here. Under "experience" he notes, as does Gadamer in *Truth and Method*, that the term was not used in the totalized form familiar to us prior to the Enlightenment. It is astonishing to think that up until the 1750s or so people simply didn't think of their "experience" as a source of anything. I find in this a complement to the ideas you develop concerning reality as infinite and constantly changing and of truth and myth alike as metaphors (Berthoff, Richards). That many Goddess proponents openly acknowledge Her as mythomorphic is an important point: aware of Her as a construct, a representation, a self-imaging process, they can dismantle some of machinery that buttresses dogmatic religions—and theories—and uncover these as the emperor who has no clothes. The danger with this dismantling, however, is that in the wrong hands it can turn into dial-a-god. Like anything-goes pedagogies that promote the equality of all interpretations and truths, it can lead into a perverse pluralism that damages precisely those who most need help. You allay this concern with your emphases upon connectedness, shared power rather than power-over, the round cosmic egg rather than the pyramid—of the five-paragraph essay! I think of Don Murray's long-standing objections to argumentation in the writing classroom: "it excludes women." For what is argument if not an "I win; you lose," one-up-one-down (Tannen) paradigm?

Mowery: Recent trends in feminist composition pedagogy do appear to parallel a wider radical/spiritual/ecofeminist movement to reclaim the sign of the Goddess. As a symbol of the "partnership model," of a "power-together" view of social relations, the Great Mother can inspire the dialogic and collaborative interaction feminist pedagogy promotes. Feminist appropriations of the nurturing mother model for the classroom manifest themselves in several ways. The "Great Round," for instance, often takes the form of an explicit rearrangement of the furniture: the chairs are placed in a circle rather than in rows, and the teacher's desk assumes a position within the circle rather than at the front of the room. The "partnership model" takes the form of collaborative work, students combining efforts, talking, brainstorming, and writing together. Arguing and competing are replaced with dialogue, supportive interaction and mediation, through which the students are often expected to come to some sort of consensus. The pedagogue in these classrooms guards against conflict and encourages cooperation. He or she plays the conversation facilitator, the social lubricant, the nurturing mother, who stands ready to affirm collaborative solutions and collective accomplishment. Both the Goddess and these "feminized" pedagogies call for a turn away from the authoritative father and toward the nurturing mother, who, as Lamb suggests, encourages "cooperation, collaboration, shared leadership, and integration of the cognitive and the affective" (11). If Woman is excluded from traditional argument and patriarchal religions, these alternatives, conventionally labeled "feminine," seem to welcome her back.

But, though they are appealing in many ways, I can't help but be a bit suspicious of consensus and harmony: both can be seen as more examples of the drive for a phallic oneness, which always ends up exclusive. Even a win-win solution requires a loser; the "I'm okay, you're okay" scenario only works up against a conception of something that's not okay. Any act of consensus, of gaining a win-win solution to conflict, is simultaneously the successful exclusion of any variable that cannot or will not remain in harmony, "inside the lines," so to speak. Michel Serres says the two winners come together to "do battle . . . against interference, against the demon, against the third man" (67). There is always the "demon," the "noise," the *loser* that must be excluded to stabilize the illusion of consensus and harmony.

It's also important, I think, to remain suspicious of the female pedagogue who plays the role of the gentle teacher-mother. She is, after all, no politically neutral nurturer. She advances the specific agenda of liberating students by infusing them with the power she has assumed. She is a mother-master, a female authority, and her acceptance of the pedagogical position ("subject presumed to know") while draped in the robes of "feminine" nurturance may simply remystify the phallic nature of the pedagogical position itself, a position that cannot be transformed simply by putting women in it. Playing this role without problematizing it traps feminist pedagogues within the very phallic economy they aim to subvert/suplant. Their classrooms can easily become, in the words of Hélène Cixous, "the place of the phallic mother"—something I find quite problematic for women.

Swearingen: The contemporary German poet Heinrich Moller provides a slightly different emphasis: "It is good to be a woman and no victor" (*Quartet*, qtd. in Wolf 296). Serres's model is Schwarzenegger's—and the only alternative would seem to be silence. Whether the question is posed in gender questions or not, we seem to have returned to Don Stewart's comment that you can't have it both ways—increased tolerance for contending arguments and emphasis on nurture, collaboration, and social construction. Your exposition illuminates both a parallelism and a disharmony between some of the values of the Goddess religions and the French theorists who promote writing the body, *l'ecriture feminine*, and *jouissance*. If understood as a dialectical process within an ever-evolving and changing world of discourse, understanding, knowing, and experience, binaries provide helpful heuristic constructs and metaphors. To take them literally, or as essences, is to replicate precisely the top-down, one-up, hierarchical and authoritarian Truth that Father religions and Western philosophy have propounded and that is exemplified by Serres and your vision of the domineering mother-teacher forcing people to engage in harmony.

Mowery: The Goddess in vogue today has, to a large extent, resexualized the Jungian Great Mother archetype (especially as it is manifest in, for instance, Sophia, the knower). The modern-day Goddess inverts the traditional binaries, privileging the "feminine" and privileging the body and sensuality as aspects of the "feminine." But this "feminine" is too often restricted and predetermined by "masculine" parameters; it is the other of the same, the "feminine" defined up against and by the "masculine." Binaries, as you suggest, remain intact here, and the Goddess is a sign of the simple reversal of privilege: from the Father to the Mother, what Baudrillard has called "the phallic fable reversed" (16). I don't think French postfemininists who promote *l'ecriture feminine* are talking about the "feminine" in binary terms. Cixous, for example, says that women who put their faith in mere inversions of privilege will find themselves confined by "the same handcuffs, baubles, and chains. Which castration do you prefer," she asks, "the father's or the mother's?" (263). Cixous and Irigaray, in particular, seem interested in exploring a "feminine" that resists binary restrictions, that is wildly excessive, not the other of the same but radical otherness in itself. It's a third position, outside the binary. Such an undefinable "feminine," though, is probably too radical to be appropriated for the classroom. Lynn Worsham has argued, in fact, that if it were unleashed intact, this radical "feminine" would very likely destroy the university system itself.

Swearingen: We need not always invoke the Goddess, any more than we need always invoke a Father God or employ modes of discourse that some, but not all, regard as masculine or feminine. But gendered metaphors, heuristics, and allusions need not necessarily be avoided either. Without directly alluding to gender issues, Donald C. Stewart chides those social constructionists and proponents of collaborative writing who "adopt a patronizing point of view toward anyone who tries to point out to them that it simply is not possible for some people to work in this way. (This usually comes out in remarks to the effect that those who do not share their position on this issue, simply do not understand it. Quite to the contrary. We have a much different perception of social dynamics than they do)" ("Response" 496). It may in some settings be helpful to identify these "different perceptions of social dynamics" and ways of being able to work during the writing process with gender socialization and to encourage a plurality of understandings of social dynamics and of ways with words as well.

If we want to promote modes of individualism that draw on collective, participatory models of knowing, meaning, and action, we could revive an extended notion of dialectic that would restore the sense of ourselves as "the mediating devices of our own knowledge" (Hegel 97), dialogic dialectical notions that are given exposition in the work of Gadamer and Bakhtin, and for composition, Berthoff, Bleich, and Elbow. Taking responsibility for being the mediating device of one's own knowledge is a demanding task, and for that very reason many are drawn to simpler notions of rigid binaries built into the nature of things or language. If the Goddess runs the risk of becoming yet another mythomorphic orthodoxy, by the same token and with the corrective quality of polyvocality She also has a potential that you nicely sum up under the heading of the future perfect: She can be a sign unto us of what we may yet become.

Works Cited

Adler, Margot. *Drawing Down the Moon: Witches, Druids, Goddess-Worshippers, and Other Pagans in America Today.* Rev. ed. Boston: Beacon, 1979.

Baudrillard, Jean. *Seduction.* New York: St. Martin's, 1979.

Belenky, Mary Field, Blyth Clinchy, Nancy Goldberger, and Jill Tarule. *Women's Ways of Knowing: The Development of Self, Voice, and Mind.* New York: Basic Books, 1986.

Berthoff, Ann. *The Making of Meaning: Metaphors, Models, and Maxims for Writing Teachers.* Portsmouth, NH: Boynton-Cook, 1981.

———. "Rhetoric as Hermeneutic." *CCC* 42.3 (Oct. 1991): 279–87.

———. *The Sense of Learning.* Portsmouth, NH: Boynton-Cook, 1990.

Bleich, David. *Double Perspective: Language, Literacy, and Social Relations.* Oxford: Oxford UP, 1988.

Bly, Robert, and Deborah Tannen. "Where Are Women and Men Today?" *New Age Journal* (Jan./Feb. 1992): 28–33, 92–97.

Bruner, Jerome. *Actual Minds, Possible Worlds.* Cambridge: Harvard UP, 1987.

Christ, Carol. "Why Women Need the Goddess: Phenomenological, Psychological, and Political Reflections." *Womanspirit Rising: A Feminist Reader in Religion.* Ed. Carol Christ and Judith Plaskow. San Francisco: Harper and Row, 1979. 273–87.

Cixous, Hélène. "The Laughter of Medusa." *Signs* (1) 1976: 875–93.

Cixous, Hélène, and Catherine Clément. *The Newly Born Woman.* Trans. Betsy Wing. Minneapolis: U of Minnesota P, 1975.

Clark, Suzanne. *Women Writers and the Revolution of the Word.* Bloomington: Indiana UP, 1991.

Cooper, Marilyn M. "The Ecology of Writing." *College English* 48.4 (Apr. 1986): 364–75.

Cosby, Wayne. "Response." *CCC* 42.4 (Dec. 1991): 497–98.

Daly, Mary. "After the Death of God the Father: Women's Liberation and the Transformation of Christian Consciousness." *Womanspirit Rising: A Feminist Reader in Religion.* Ed. Carol Christ and Judith Plaskow. San Francisco: Harper and Row, 1979. 53–62.

deBeaugrande, Robert. "In Search of Feminist Discourse: The 'Difficult' Case of Luce Irigaray." *College English* 50.3 (Mar. 1988): 253–72.

Ebert, Theresa. " The 'Difference' of Postmodern Feminism." *College English* 53.8 (Dec. 1991): 886–904.

Eisler, Riane. *The Chalice and the Blade: Our History, Our Future.* San Francisco: Harper and Row, 1986.

Farrar, Julie M., Laurence E. Musgrove, Donald C. Stewart, Wayne Cosby, and Catherine E. Lamb. "Responses to Catherine E. Lamb." *CCC* 42.4 (1991): 493–99.

Flynn, Elizabeth A. "Composing as a Woman." *CCC* 39.4 (1988): 423–35.

———. "Composing 'Composing as a Woman': A Perspective on Research." *CCC* 41.1 (1990): 83–89.

Foucault, Michel. *The Order of Things.* New York: Vintage, 1973.

Gadamer, Hans Georg. *Truth and Method.* Trans. Garrett Barden and John Cumming. New York: Seabury Press, 1975.

Gadon, Elinor W. *The Once and Future Goddess: A Symbol for Our Time.* New York: Harper and Row, 1989.

Geertz, Clifford. "Religion as a Cultural System." *Reader in Comparative Religion: An Anthropological Approach.* Ed. William Less and Evon Z. Vogt. 2d ed. New York: Harper and Row, 1965. 204–16.

George, Diana Hume. "The Miltonic Ideal: A Paradigm for the Structure of Relations Between Men and Women in Academia." *College English* 40 (1979): 864–71.

Gilligan, Carol. *In a Different Voice: Psychological Theory and Women's Development.* Cambridge: Harvard UP, 1982.

Gulick, Walter B. "The Bible and Ecological Spirituality." *Theology Today* 20 (Summer 1991): 182–94.

Harding, Sandra. *Feminism and Methodology.* Bloomington: Indiana UP, 1987.

———. *The Science Question in Feminism.* New York: Basic Books, 1986.

Hegel, G. F. W. *The Phenomenology of Mind.* Trans. George Lichtheim. New York: Harper Colophon, 1967.

Hekman, Susan J. *Gender and Knowledge: Elements of a Postmodern Feminism.* Boston: Northeastern UP, 1990.

Kuykendall, Eleanor H. "Subverting Essentialisms." *Hypatia* 6.3 (Fall 1991): 208–17.

Lakoff, Robin T. *Language and Woman's Place.* New York: Harper and Row, 1975.

Lamb, Catherine. "Beyond Argument in Feminist Composition." *CCC* 42 (Feb. 1991): 11–24.

―――. "Reply." *CCC* 42.4 (Dec. 1991): 498–99.

Lerner, Gerda. *The Creation of Patriarchy*. New York: Oxford UP, 1986.

Lunsford, Andrea. "Composing Ourselves: Politics, Commitment, and the Teaching of Writing." *CCC* 41.4 (1990): 71–82.

McDaniel, Jay B. *Earth, Sky, Gods, and Mortals: Developing an Ecological Spirituality*. Mystic, CT: Twenty-Third Publications, 1990.

McFague, Sallie. "Models of God for an Ecological Evolutionary Era: God as Mother of the Universe." *Physics, Philosophy, and Theology: A Common Quest for Understanding*. Ed. Robert John Russell, et al. Vatican City State: Vatican Observatory, 1988.

Miller, Susan. *Textual Carnivals: The Politics of Composition*. Carbondale: Southern Illinois UP, 1991.

Musgrove, Laurence E. "Response." *CCC* 42.4 (Dec. 1991): 494–96.

Nietzsche, Friedrich. *The Gay Science*. Trans. Walter Kaufmann. New York: Vintage, 1974.

Olson, David R. "Interpreting Texts and Interpreting Nature: The Effects of Literacy on Hermeneutics and Epistemology." *Visual Language* 20 (1986): 302–17.

―――. "Mind and Media: The Epistemic Fictions of Literacy." *Journal of Communication* 38.3 (Summer 1988): 27–36.

Pagels, Elaine. *Adam, Eve, and the Serpent*. New York: Vintage, 1989.

―――. *The Gnostic Gospels*. New York: Vintage, 1981.

Rappaport, Roy A. *Ecology, Meaning, and Religion*. Richmond, CA: North Atlantic Books, 1979.

Richards, I. A. *The Philosophy of Rhetoric*. Oxford: Oxford UP, 1965.

Rolston, Holmes. *Philosophy Gone Wild: Essays in Environmental Ethics*. Buffalo: Prometheus, 1986.

Schaef, Ann Wilson. *Women's Reality*. New York: Harper and Row, 1986.

Serres, Michel. *Hermes: Literature, Science, Philosophy*. Ed. Josue V. Harari and David F. Bell. Baltimore: Johns Hopkins UP, 1982.

Shiach, Morag. *Helene Cixous: A Politics of Writing*. Boston and London: Routledge, 1991.

Smith, Carol H. "The Literary Politics of Gender." *College English* 50.3 (Mar. 1988): 318–22.

Starhawk. *Dreaming the Dark: Magic, Sex, and Politics*. Boston: Beacon, 1982.

―――. "Feminist, Earth-based Spirituality and Ecofeminism." *Healing the Wounds: The Promise of Ecofeminism*. Ed. Judith Plant. Philadelphia: New Society, 1989. 173–85.

Stewart, Donald. "Response." *CCC* 42.4 (Dec. 1991): 496–97.

Stone, Merlin. *When God Was a Woman*. New York: Dorset, 1976.

Swearingen, C. Jan. "Discourse, Difference, Gender: Walter Ong's Contributions to Feminist Language Studies." *Media, Consciousness, and Culture*. Ed. Bruce E. Gronbeck, Thomas J. Farrell, and Paul A. Soukup. Newbury Park, CA: Sage, 1991.

Tannen, Deborah. *You Just Don't Understand*. New York: Morrow, 1991.

Trible, Phyllis. *God and the Rhetoric of Sexuality*. Philadelphia: Fortress, 1978.

Warren, Karen J., ed. "Introduction." *Hypatia* 6.1 (Spring 1991): 1–2.

Welch, Kathleen. *The Contemporary Reception of Classical Rhetoric: Appropriations of Ancient Discourse*. Hillsdale, NJ: Lawrence Erlbaum, 1990.

Williams, Raymond. *Keywords: A Vocabulary of Culture and Society*. 2d ed. New York: Oxford UP, 1983.

Wolf, Christa. "A Letter, about Unequivocal and Ambiguous Meaning, Definitions and Indefiniteness; about Ancient Conditions and New View-scopes; about Objectivity." *Feminist Aesthetics*. Ed. Gesela Ecker. Boston: Beacon, 1985. 95–107.

Worsham, Lynn. "Writing Against Writing: The Predicament of *Ecriture Feminine* in Composition Studies." *Conending with Words: Composition and Rhetoric in a Postmodern Age*. Ed. Patricia Harkin and John Schilb. New York: MLA, 1991.

Zawicki, Terry Myers. "Recomposing as a Woman—An Essay in Different Voices." *College English* 43.1 (Feb. 1992): 32–38.

16   Style, Invention, and Indirection
Aphorisms

George Yoos and Philip Keith

NOT ONLY DO WORDS COMMUNICATE BY LEAVING IMPLICATIONS FOR readers to make, but almost everything we do, and how we do it, leaves implications for culturally attuned people to notice our behaviors. If we dress with a red bow tie and green suspenders, we are creating style. If we laugh a great deal, grinning from ear to ear, and sway and rock as we talk, that is style. Such antics are equally possible in how we speak and write. Our manner of presenting ourselves in speech and writing to others is style. Insofar as we consciously and deliberately invent a style of writing, we have indirect control over how people react to us. Insofar as style is such a major factor in communication, by which we control the reaction of others to us, by which others draw implications from what we do and say, it cannot be ignored in our creation of discourse, nor in our assessment or criticism of it, nor in our teaching of it.

Aphoristic remarks are particularly interesting and useful as a stylistic feature of discourse. They mark a style. They direct readers' responses or writers' responses by indirection. And in response to aphorisms, writers can adapt to them as templates of style or can in reaction to them find their own style. Both of us were particularly struck as we were working on this writing project that a great deal of communication, sermons, political oratory, and serious intellectual discussion quite often begins with aphorisms, is generated from aphorisms, and ends in aphorisms.[1]

As coauthors, our relationship has been one of symbiosis and synthesis. Ours is not a common voice but a sharing voice. We want to bring to the attention of our readers some of our separate and exchanged reflections and considerations of the role of aphorisms in communication, and at the same time we wish to illustrate how much of our mutual theorizing about aphorisms emerges in practical applications by one of the coauthors. We are convinced that embodied in the student responses to aphorisms we find in strikingly clear form some of the major problems and issues of contemporary composition pedagogy. Let us then begin our discussion with theoretical issues. This discussion will merge and enter into reflections about practical applications of aphorisms in the classroom.

Some of the theoretical considerations about aphorisms and style are reflected in the difficulties one of the authors has had in interpreting an aphoristic remark of A. N. Whitehead. In his *Aims of Education* Whitehead says cryptically, "Style is the ultimate morality of mind" (24). Note that here there is no question about the meaning of the words that Whitehead uses. Yet, though we know the meaning of these words, we don't know for certain what it is that Whitehead means by them. In this case, knowing the meaning of words is not enough to know *what it is that is being said*, let alone knowing whether or not it is true.

A very important distinction about varieties of style underlies our emphasis of the above phrase *what it is that is being said*. There rests here embedded and conflated in the grammar an important distinction that allows us to distinguish what gives rise to different styles. The *what* and the *it* here refer to what in speech-act parlance are called *utterance acts* and *locutionary acts*. The distinction is the same as that between the words of what is being said and the substance of what is being said by the words. Or, to use old logic terminology, it is the distinction between sentences and propositions. Or, in different terminology, the difference between the words quoted and the paraphrase. Or, pretty much the same distinction between direct quote and indirect quote. But, there is also a third level or sense of "saying something." We say things by indirection or contextual implication. "You said so and so." "No, I didn't say that, but I certainly implied it." Thus, we distinguish three levels or senses of "saying something":

1. What is said *in* words;
2. What is said *by* words directly, literally, explicitly, substantively, as *by* a locutionary act; and
3. What is said by indirection, suggestively, by allusion, figuratively, or by contextual implication.

We need to keep these distinctions separate in talking about style. They tend to be conflated. There is a tendency to think of style simply as a matter of words, that is, of style on the first level. But style is more than the effects of sounds or written words. Note, for example, that voice is a stylistic feature, but there are three levels to stylistic voice: the speaking voice, the voice in the text in direct references and in the self-references to itself, and finally the voice of the implied persona, the voice implied by what the author does and says in a text. Again to illustrate, grammatical parallelism is on one level, clarity is on a second, and irony is on a third. As a final example, rhythm and stress are on the first level, imagery is found on the second, and metaphor operates on the third. From the perspective of the writing teacher, reader and writer must be able to manage language at each level separately and to integrate them at the same time.

Recall as an illustration of the three levels of style Robert Frost's famous one-sentence haiku-like poem, *A Dust of Snow*, an account of how snow shaken from a hemlock tree improves the poet's attitude on a winter day. It is aphoristic: condensed, memorable, and pithy. The style is simple and perspicuous on the first two levels. It is almost monosyllabic, has strong meter, and is strongly rhymed. The style is defined in the simplicity of rhyme, rhythm, and word choices. This simplicity combines with the second-level simplicity of imagery of snow, hemlock tree, and starkly contrasting crow. The imagery of the little dust of now-falling snow is literally carried by the meaning of the words. We find that the third level of style, the effect the imagery has on the lyrical voice, fits well with comparable experiences of our own. We bond with the speaker in his explicit reference to his own feeling, sharing the perspective of seeing "implication enrichment" happen. This is why it is *the way* the crow dusted the speaker rather than the dusting itself that changed the mood and saved the day. In addition, the imagery implies a great deal about the speaking voice in the poem and about the life and state of mind behind that voice. In our reaction to the simplicity of the imagery, we draw all sorts of cosmic implications about beauty and little things. The imagery thus triggers thoughts on life and attitudes about it, about our relationship to the lyrical voice in the poem, and Frost. Such richness of implication is an essential part of the style of the poem.

Here in our discussion of the style of the poem, there is another important consideration we need to attend to. Our interpretation starts with the level of words: words first, imagery second, and implication third. Both in the writing process and in our interpretation of what we read and write, or write and read, words come first. Next comes what we say by the words and then finally the implications that follow from what we say by the words. The failure of E. D. Hirsch to recognize this priority of words to meaning and the priority of meaning to the implications of meaning is what is so faulty about Hirsch's account of expression in the writing process in *The Philosophy of Composition*.[2] Hirsch, in stressing the importance of finding words to say *what we want to say*, is putting the second level of intentions first. In stressing exclusively the values of readability and clarity, his account proves blind to an important fact about language and communication. As Monroe C. Beardsley points out in a review of Hirsch's book, "My own view is precisely opposed—that the revision of a prose passage, if it is helpful, always changes the meaning, and must do so, if the teaching of composition is to have a point" (111). Beardsley's presumption here is that different texts present different meanings and that any paraphrase, interpretation, or commentary would not be able to say the same thing as the original words of the text. We contend, as does Beardsley, that it is the words that are prior in developing meaning and style. A major part of style is sharing the writers' view of their words—what they mean and how they mean. It is this focus on words that makes aphorisms so attractive as a starting point in the writing process. We are starting with words and finding in our words, in response to those words, both a meaning and a style.

To return to Whitehead with these distinctions in mind, any grasp of his remark requires, if we are to get at what he says and the style of it, that we analyze his remark on the three described levels. It would especially require an analysis of Whitehead's context, situation, and knowledge background, and most particularly we would need to see his expectation of the way his readers would see his words. We would need to examine his philosophical views if we are to know what it is that he is saying on the second and third levels. If we are ever to interpret what it is that he is saying, we need especially to frame Whitehead's presumptions. But, finally and importantly, if we are ever to know whether what he is saying is true, we would have to know Whitehead's reasons for thinking that it is so and for thinking that we should see it so.[3] Thus, we need a great deal more than the language code to read Whitehead's remark on style. It is a misconception, then, in speaking about "what is being said" to reduce "what is said" to a simple paraphrase. We need, if we are to write about it, to say a great deal. To arrive at the full scope of the meaning and the implications of what is being said on the level of words, we need to think at length of what is being said on the other two levels. Such a full statement would have to be a complex commentary, both interpretive and evaluative.

If we take the words "Style is the ultimate morality of mind" out of the context of Whitehead's text, as we have done, we have also lost not only the surrounding text but also the context of the text within that text. The loss of both text and context within text makes it especially problematic to interpret Whitehead's remark on the third level. Detached and separable from the text, standing alone like an aphorism, the sentence transposes into an aphorism. But as an aphorism, the remark is murky, obscure, cryptic, very suggestive, deep, and apparently profound. Standing alone, it demands that we think long and hard about it to give it any possible meaning, that we *imagine* complex contexts and situations (though probably not that of Whitehead's text) to frame an interpretation of it. We would need a very lengthy, explorative, interpretive commentary just to begin to make any sense of it. It is thus at the point where we detach a remark from its text, when it stands alone, that we are faced with this need for speculative interpretation. And, we find that apart from the text, independent of text, it is a challenging but compelling task to discover what might be good reasons for the truth of any possible interpretations or constructions of Whitehead's remark on style. It is compelling because however difficult it is to construe the remark, it is almost as difficult to let it go, given its intriguing suggestiveness.

In Whitehead's discussion of education, his remark on style comes almost as a summation after lengthy discussions about important qualities of mind that ought to be developed in education. Yet, it is not simply a summary sentence. It implies more than what was being said previous to it. One of us, after reading all of Whitehead's explanations and amplifications, found for himself no satisfactory interpretation of Whitehead's remark on style, let alone arrived at a satisfactory account of its truth or falsity. Rather, what struck him were the stylistic implications of Whitehead's frequent use of such aphoristic-looking remarks such as the one on style. For him, Whitehead's style tended towards aphorisms, and his aphoristic style had many implications for understanding Whitehead's persona as a philosopher. Ironically, Whitehead's remark on style is self-referential. It calls our attention to "the morality of Whitehead's own mind," the morality of his mind in his style of doing philosophy.

Whitehead's aphoristic style is pretty much in harmony with his epistemology and his way of doing philosophy. Whitehead's aphoristic style expresses his insights about life, God, and nature. Such an aphoristic rhetoric runs counter to much of the rhetoric of contemporary English and American philosophy, and it explains in part the apparent sudden decline of interest in Whitehead as a philosopher during the second half of the twentieth century, for Whitehead's style of putting forth memorable claims in pithy and obscure sentences is no longer considered a stylistically appropriate way of doing philosophy. In contrast, for example, Ludwig Wittgenstein is very explicit about his intentions for his readers in his work. He is not making big truth claims. Not only are his intentions reflected in his tentative and discursive style, but in the *Philosophical Investigations* he asks us in his preface not to use his writing as an excuse not to do our own thinking (x). In contrast, Whitehead tells you what is his *big* truth. What he says appears to be coming down from his mountaintop.

Note this very style in Whitehead's famous definition of religion: "Religion is the vision of something which stands beyond, behind, and within, the passing flux of immediate things; something which is real, and yet waiting to be realized; something which is a remote possibility, and yet the greatest of present facts; something which gives meaning to all that passes, and yet eludes apprehension; something whose possession is the final good, and yet is beyond all reach; something which is the ultimate ideal, and the hopeless quest" (191).

Such a quote from *Science and the Modern World* is eminently detachable from its context. It invites the sort of interpretive discussion that we find in the commentary on it by William Stace in *Time and Eternity: An Essay in the Philosophy of Religion*. It drives Stace's thought about it. What is it saying? Is it true or not? What is implied in such paradoxical language? The quote has style, and it invites style. Such was Stace's reaction to it.

Our contention in this paper is thus that an aphoristic style, such as Whitehead's, has some particular virtues for expression and for the teaching of writing about style. Not only do aphorisms have the value of giving writers a sense of style, but they have what is probably an even greater value in that "aphorisms are tools for invention." They invite creative responses to their meaning and truth. This means, as one of us discovered in his writing classes, that as used in writing assignments, they have a unique value as a diagnostic tool for assessing the stylistic dimension of student writing and reading. Before going into a discussion of what we believe sustains our judgment about these values of aphorisms for the teaching of writing, we want first to investigate their "nature," or better yet, what has been the commonly accepted concept of what an aphorism is.

It is best in our view not to ask, "What is an aphorism?" Rather we should look to the history of the use of the word. *Aphorism* is a historically conditioned term for statements that are terse and memorable. The use of the word nominally begins with Hippocrates' *Aphorisms*. The first aphorism by that name was his famous opening sentence: "Life is short, art is long, opportunity fleeting, experimenting dangerous, reasoning difficult." Traditionally, however, the term has been applied both broadly and narrowly. As expandable, it tends to be generalized to include all sorts of short, memorable statements that would include proverbs, maxims, precepts, epigrams, and wise sayings. Usually aphorism and proverb are overlapping concepts. On the other hand, the word tends to be narrowed to only those remarks that meet a standard of profundity.[4] In this, aphorisms are profound, while proverbs are of the more homely variety. In speaking of aphorism, we favor the broad use of the term that aphorisms are simply any pithy, condensed, suggestive, brief, memorable remark. Yet, for uses in the teaching of writing, we are more interested in the profound ones, for they provoke the most interest in student responses.

If we take the term *aphorism* in its more generic sense, a great deal of what we see going on in communications is aphoristic. The present pattern of news presentation in the mass media of taking out bytes from the speeches of people prominent in the news is "aphoristic." Such quotable, memorable bytes are easy and effective for those wanting to slant the news in intended ways. We especially see this sort of communicative abuse in contemporary political campaigns, where television news spots are manipulated for intended journalistic effects. It seems obvious that this mode of news presentation is actually even affecting speaking styles of candidates whose communications are managed to take advantage of this mode of news presentation and distillation. Speech writing is increasingly controlled by the effort to invent detachable bytes striking and memorable and rich in innuendo. Just as with aphorisms, these bytes use condensation to make the language pithy, ripe with numerous implications, or, if you will, loaded with innuendo for controlling and manipulating listener or viewer responses. Taken in perspective, this contemporary tendency to generate what the latest buzz word describes as "McNuggets" is no more than the language of company and advertising slogans. It is also no more than the ancient traditional rhetoric of the epigram, the epitaph, the proverb, the maxim, or precept. It is the rhetoric of the "old saying," the "old saw."

Historically we have discovered that the first literature was the literature of the aphorism. It was the literature of terse and memorable statements of wisdom and insight evolving out of oral traditions. Such literature predates our own Western literary foundations in Greek literature and the Bible. It characterizes Indian literature in the sutras, which were philosophical tenets stemming from the Vedas. The sutras were intended to serve as aids to memory and as elaboration. Because of their extreme conciseness, the sutras are difficult to understand. Again in the Confucian tradition in China, statements are fragmented and given apart from original contexts. They too are consequently difficult to interpret apart from Chinese culture and language. Note an even earlier historical aphorist. The following is an assessment made by A. T. Olmstead in his *History of the Persian Empire* of the compendium of aphorisms by the storied Ahiquar, "a wise and ready scribe," counselor of all Assyria: "These aphorisms varied with every edition, until the 'Wisdom of Ahiquar,' became a regular compendium of the world's best literature in Aramaic, Syriac, Arabic, Armenian, and Ethiopic. Democritus cites it. Aesop uses it, it was imitated in our present edition of Tobit, the New Testament is filled with its wise sayings, and Jesus of Nazareth condescends to employ it" (324).

Whitehead's writing style tends to strive for similar condensations, for readily detachable, insightful, citable "sound bytes." His aphoristic style tends to arise from the authority of his own thinking and experience. Thus, his sound bytes have all the appearance of *out and out* truth claims. We find that in reading Whitehead we have the same problem we have in reading the Proverbs in the Old Testament, which are advanced as the wisdom of Solomon. There is an alleged certainty or authority about the biblical Proverbs; as God gave Solomon his wisdom, they are the word of God.

Yet this revealed wisdom is problematical. We see the problem of proverbs raised in the opening passage of The Book of Proverbs. Depending upon the translation of the Bible, we find them described as "riddles," "dark," "profound," "deep," "subtle," "words of intelligence with hidden meaning." Such language suggests that it is unclear what truths proverbs communicate. Such suspicions about their meaning and truth invite critical thinking. And, it is this invitation to the reader of a proverb or aphorism to consider their truth that makes aphorisms provocative and an inventional tool for a critical and responsive writer.

We find that aphorisms do not operate simply as *topoi* or as mechanical heuristics reducible to a matrix of questions or an algorithm. Rather they require imaginative thought about what would warrant their seeming truth claims. They drive invention in writer responses to them. Thus, aphorisms are valuable tools to explore and develop certain lines of thought and certain lines of argument. These lines grow out of imaginative reconstruction of contexts, situations, and background knowledge in the student writer. They are lines of thought that would make aphorisms true in the writers' frames of experience. Such rhetorical invention is not systematic. Rather the interpreter and critic of aphorisms subjectively follows the implications of what appears most relevant in the student writer's frame of experience.

One major problem with an aphoristic style is the lack of control over the contextual implications that an aphorism might have for a reader. This difficulty of control is no more than the difficulty any use of figurative language has in controlling a reader's response. To say that "John is a pig," independent of context, might mean that John's sexual proclivities are indecent or that he is a glutton or a cop. It is simply that communicating by indirection, the mode of communication of both metaphor and aphorism, demands that the audience frame and contextualize their interpretation. Thus, it is the seeming relevance of aphorisms to so many contexts and presumptions behind them that makes it difficult not only to interpret them but also to determine their truth. For this reason aphorisms seem always open to question. They generate counter-aphorisms: "A penny saved is a penny earned"; "Penny wise and pound foolish." Note that cynical remarks often contain counter-aphorisms in the ironic implication that plays on an original aphoristic commonplace: "So convenient a thing it is to be a *reasonable Creature*, since it enables one to find or make a Reason for everything one has a mind to do" (Franklin); "A gentleman is never unintentionally rude" (Wilde).

Aphorisms as a result of this shifting pro and con perspective often appear questionable and biased. They seem to be "half-truths." But, what is a half-truth? The notion of a half-truth is an abomination to logicians who live and die by the law of excluded middle, that is, that a proposition is either true or false "at the same time in the same respect" (Aristotle's famous dictum). But there is a third alternative for the logician, namely, that the statement is logically indeterminate. How then is it logically possible to discuss an aphorism as a truth claim if it is logically indeterminate? But logic deals with what in technical jargon is traditionally called *propositions* or *statements*. To use speech–act jargon, what an aphorism says is a function, not just of an utterance act being used to affirm or express a locutionary act (a proposition), but also a function of indirection or of contextual implications—the *way* it says what it says. What is being said by an aphorism is not literally or logically determinate. Rather, what is said is said by indirection. It is left for the reader to infer what was indirectly *intended*, that is, to infer how the writer expected a reader to see *the words meaning* (as a verb) as opposed to *the words' meaning* (as a noun).

It is our contention that we need to pass beyond issues of logic and semantics of a sentence if we are to see how aphorisms function in discourse. We need to examine the rhetorical force of an aphorism. The rhetorical force is assessed by examining the effects of the statement on the reader, but the effects as a function not of the meaning but of the style, of the *way* the statement is to be seen, psychologically speaking, or what Dan Sperber and Deirdre Wilson call in *Relevance: Communication and Cognition* the "cognitive effects." What is important, then, is to show how aphorisms trigger mnemonically complex levels of experience, to see how they are deeply embedded in the cognitive and emotive representations of our psyches. Aphorisms differ in the extent that they attach themselves to or embed themselves in our complex scenarios of past experience. Some are profound. Others border on the trivial.

As Whitehead's style is aphoristic, we can see that detachable quotes from his work are often cited as if they were capable of standing alone. Standing alone they are memorable in the mind of the reader. In other words, as we use the term *aphorism*, an author's style is aphoristic if it is eminently quotable and if the remarks can meaningfully stand alone. However, as an aphorism is didactic, the force of the statement goes beyond its memorability to require persuasiveness grounded in the aphorism's context. But since an aphorism, as "detachable," functions outside of its context, it demands contextualizing by the reader to be operationally persuasive. This problem is endemic when reading Whitehead. As Whitehead in his writing appears to be advancing truth claims, he is not inviting us to spread our thoughts over his words at his expense. He is simply, as in the spirit of the biblical Proverbs, providing us with the "wisdom of Solomon," putting forth truth claims that are not intended to expand beyond any of the immediate implications intended.

But despite Whitehead's didactic intentions, we nevertheless do challenge his aphoristic remarks. They do indirectly provoke in us a reaction to them. Despite the existence of any explicit invitation, such as Wittgenstein's, or that of Richard Rorty, who speaks of philosophy in similar terms as a conversation, we should think that Whitehead as a philosopher would want to offer us a similar invitation to have a conversation with him. This last observation is confirmed in a prefatory remark to *Process and Reality*: "In philosophical discussion, the merest hint of dogmatic certainty as to finality of statement is the exhibition of folly" (ix). What then should be our attitude to the following sorts of aphoristical categorical remarks from Whitehead? Should we treat them as invitations to a conversation?

> The pleasures of philosophy are denied to deity.
> Religion is the last refuge of savagery.
> It is better that a statement be interesting than true.

This last remark brings to mind William G. Perry's anecdote from Whitehead's teaching career at Harvard when a student complained to the philosopher that the student's paper should not have received an A grade since it was nonsense. "Yes!" Whitehead is reported to have replied, "But ah! Sir! It's the right *kind* of nonsense" (318).

Frequently we do find an aphoristic style monologic, sententious, tending towards pomposity. Aphorisms appear merely as didactic, as conversational closures, such as we find at the end of a moral tale or at the end of a lecture. Polonius's speech to his son in *Hamlet* illustrates this stuffy mode of moralizing that we find commonly in lists of aphorisms: "To thine own self be true." But, despite this seemingly "shut up and listen" attitude, we find that aphorisms do dialectically drive thoughts pro and con. They serve as effective tools for invention in composition. An exploration of the implications of an aphorism for a reader is in our view an ultimate act of deconstruction. It sets aside the author's intentions from the focus of a student's consideration. The voice of the aphorism seemingly coming down from on high is neutered. The student in taking it off its pedestal is becoming a critical thinker. For the student it becomes a tool to think with.[5] In addition, it is the nature of most aphorisms that when we think long and hard about them, they suddenly lose that original sense of completeness. They have a down side. They do not fit into our frames of experience. They appear to be false. They suggest their own refutation. They have initiated dialectic.

Aphorisms as statements, detached and stripped of presumptions and contexts, activate interpretations very much like a Rorschach test in driving interpretations of what is representational to the perceiver. Words as Rorschach ink blots invite intellectual and emotionally projected interpretations. Likewise, aphorisms can in a comparable way be used to give us a rough measure of a student's stylistic and inventional maturity, something like a writing-style status exam based upon numerous student responses to the same aphorism.

Interestingly enough, a psychiatrist whom we know (and who requested anonymity) pointed out that a set called the Benjamin Proverbs is used as a "mental status exam." This sort of exam is directed to various intellectual/cognitive areas and permits the examiner to derive a variety of insights in a period of fifteen to twenty minutes.

The Benjamin Proverbs list was used within a more elaborate test for such modalities as reading, arithmetic, spelling ability, fund of knowledge, clarity of stream of consciousness, and orientation with regard to time and person and place. The proverbs were used to get insight into abstracting ability, concretization, and erudition and to spot patterns of trailing off with loose associations. Our correspondent reports that he used the following series of proverbs, having become familiar with response patterns from a thousand or more trials.

1. "When the cat's away, the mice will play": most everyone, he observed, gave the "character disorder" response—when parents or

spouse are away a person will act out, but very few got the dangerous theme that they live in a world that threatens them with being eaten.

2. "Even monkeys fall from trees": he said that perfectionists always identify with this one.
3. "Still waters run deep": he said that this tests emotional aspects of a person.
4. "One robin does not make a springtime": this, he said, tests gestalt ability. To "get it" the respondent would presumably have to recognize the importance of patterns of symptoms rather than single symptoms.
5. "The golden hammer breaks the iron door": this, he said, required a higher class of abstractive ability.
6. "The hot coal burns, the cold coal blackens": this supposedly expressed a valuing of moderation over excess once one saw the situation of managing the heat level in a coal stove (what our correspondent called the "genius question").
7. "Mother fuckers make the best lovers": this was a late addition in our correspondent's repertoire, a "sign of the times" used "to blow open a dependent sexual psychotic."

This testing method corresponds in some interesting ways to how one of us uses aphorisms for writing assessments in his teaching. The testing situation with the aphorisms written on a sheet or on a group of cards calls for with both tester and testee an intense sensitivity to what is being meant "by" what is being said, to a disjunction between meaning and saying. As we shall see, Sperber and Wilson, in their very important book on relevance theory, call this a highly "ostensive-emphatic" situation for discourse that thereby calls on an actively inferential view of style. The "best" response is the response that accommodates the ostensive implications of the test items, that sees the "style" and matches a style to it.

We were very much intrigued by our correspondent's use of the phrase "blow open" with relation to his seventh aphorism, since it makes the aphorism-test process seem much more direct than we see it to be in a classroom application. His method relates more than ours to the internal violence that the crossing of taboo/secrecy wires can set off, but his illustrates the force of the method of indirection in approaching style inferentially. His operational metaphor is more like that of a Mount St. Helens than one we would be more comfortable with—something between a political coup and Pearl Harbor.

For a student who is asked to write in response to an aphorism, aphorisms look like thesis statements without the "development." They thus invite the student to illustrate the aphorism as if it were a thesis (or to illustrate the negative of the aphorism). Secondly, the aphorism gains its force from its "weight" of style. For example, Jules Janin's aphorism, "A woman is much more responsive to a man's forgetfulness than to his attentiveness," persuades (or irritates) not because of the obviousness of the statement—in fact it is verging on the paradoxical or even nonsensical, that is, one may "react" to an action such as forgetting, but one presumably responds to an act of communication. Janin's statement gets its force (both for persuasion and aggravation) from the style—from the exquisite weight of "is much more responsive to" rather than "reacts to," or even "responds to"; of "A woman" rather than "Woman" or "Women"; of "attentiveness" rather than "attention." When we are alive to the style of such an aphorism, we see the speaker (translator) picking his words and are seduced, if you will, into the aphorist's reasoning about the choices. We play the game at a level of inferring both meaning and awareness.

This is a useful game for students to play because the aphorism invites response at various levels of skill and awareness. Mina Shaughnessy's Basic Writing (BW) student, who she describes in *Errors and Expectations* as tending to respond by sentence rather than paragraph, will usually offer general statements of agreement or denial, chunking along like a bicycle between the rails of a railroad track. The "skilled" student, on the other hand, who has become familiar with thesis and development patterns as controlling functions of discourse will (generally trivially) illustrate the truth or the untruth of the literal statement of the aphorism. The advanced student, in contrast, who has managed to learn the processes by which, in William Coles's phrase, he or she can "develop a style to match a style" will respond with a greater subtlety of inference and awareness, both in the understanding of the aphorism expressed and in the language he or she uses. The aphorism exercise, we want to argue, thus creates a framework—one that bridges style and meaning, integrating style in meaning—for encouraging and understanding writing development, since the different responses in a class will illustrate the different levels of language operation among different students and among different performances of the same student.

Writing to aphorisms has been a tradition in the teaching of writing, although if Nan Johnson's underlying assumption in her recent study, *Nineteenth-Century Rhetoric in North America*, is right, the emphasis on imitation in writing instruction as opposed to the earlier emphasis on dialectical operations that aphorisms instigate may indicate some shifts in pedagogical perspective that could well be worth studying. Thus, it is to the dialectical operations stimulated by aphorisms that we look to explore their value in composition pedagogy.

And, when we turn to studying an inferential theory of communication, we see the theoretical justification of our enterprise. For example, an inferential theory of communication looks upon the elements of style as producing effects indirectly through the inferences that audiences or readers have in reacting to the overall pattern of action of an author in a piece of discourse. This is to say that style is a function at least in part of a reader's activity of thought rather than simply the reader's perception of language objects in a text. The appropriateness of the reader's response or reaction to a text, therefore, has to do with that reaction's relevance to the text, context, or situation. Correspondingly, the writer (or speaker) writes (or speaks) with a kind of body-English, to use a pool metaphor. That is to say, that going along with a literal meaning in a text is a sense or intention in the writer that is passed on and picked up in the style, that the reader or listener should see the text as related to things not in the text. A good deal of sophisticated reading of Shakespeare or advertising and listening to conversation or popular music involves a sensitivity to style as a fuzzy envelope or an aura and a willingness to see relevance relations between the text and other things. These relevance relations are inferential and may involve similarities (or identities) but may also include other sorts of connections: contrasts, conditions, consequences, and so forth. The writer (or speaker) is always saying implicitly with every statement that he or she is expecting you to take this text or statement within the context and situation and to assume the connectability of the text or statement to that context—and perhaps others that the author may not have been conscious of, or even have knowledge of.

This quality of pointing to context-thing is called by Sperber and Wilson the "ostensive" feature of communication. The kind of communication that we have been describing as appearing par excellence in aphoristic communication is ostensive-inferential communication. Sperber and Wilson's book is in the line of philosophical/linguistic pragmatics, moving beyond speech-act theory to a broader view of language and cognition. We are not going to go into the full range of implications or applications of Sperber and Wilson but are merely pointing out the importance of their view that inferential processes, looking at style interpretively and holistically (as opposed to objectively and atomistically) as necessarily ostensive and as critical, guide us toward a meaningful understanding of highly developed skill in reading and writing performance. Sperber and Wilson see their work as concerning primarily the processes by which people understand oral (or visual) communication: Melissa says she has a headache and Shane walks into the kitchen and takes down a frying pan because he knows that she means she cannot cook tonight. However, we hold that the kinds of understanding operations Sperber and Wilson are discussing are of equal importance to a meaningful understanding of mature developments in written literacy.

In discussing how aphorisms function in discourse as apparent truth claims, the nature of their truth requires some further definition. This is particularly true given the tendency of aphorisms to operate frequently with opinions that many readers would presume to be false, as seems to be the case with Whitehead's already-cited remark, "It is better that a statement be interesting than true." It is offered to our apprehension as readers when we take up the ostensive seriousness and give full attention to the possibilities' inferrable relevancies. To assume, as Whitehead seems to assume, that such offering is the only way to transmit real knowledge is to be operating with an essentially Platonic epistemology—that the truth cannot be directly stated

but only apprehended directly by the mind through its own reasoning properties and activities. Whitehead's style is thus probably best defended as being
about as good as you can get in embodying a process of communication that
does not formulate truth but that invites by its indirection our confirmation
of its insights by intuition. From this perspective, Whitehead's aphorism can
be seen as the aphorism of all aphorisms because it enacts the whole aphoristic
process.

Note that this sense of things is at play in Whitehead's own amplification
of his aphorism, "Style is the ultimate morality of mind": "Where, then, does
style help? In this, with style the end is attained without side issues, without
raising undesirable inflammations. With style you attain your end and nothing
but your end. With style the effect or your activity is calculable, and foresight
is the last gift of gods to men. With style your power is increased, for your
mind is not distracted with irrelevancies, and you are more likely to attain
your object. Now style is the exclusive privilege of the expert" (24).

Style is in these terms the ostension-envelope of the statement that controls
the way the reader perceives it—that is, to recall Frost's poem, the *way* the
author wrote it. Note that Whitehead's final amplifying aphorism, "Now
style is the exclusive privilege of the expert," is equivalent to saying that the
relevance to an expert determines the appropriateness of inference.

One may not be too far off base then in seeing Whitehead's style as
rhetorically akin to that of Janin's aphorism that was used in class to drive
student responses. Our review of student responses to "A woman is much
more responsive to a man's forgetfulness than to his attentiveness" illustrates
rather well a range of style articulation, creating indeed a simple but useful
essay scale. As we have suggested, it enables us to create a stylistic measure
of maturity in student writers. The examples we are working with here are
ten-minute responses to an aphorism the students in an advanced composition
class saw for the first time, so the writing needs to be understood as "shaping
at the point of utterance" discourse, in James Britton's terms, rather than
discourse shaped by revision and an elaborated sense of audience. We are
using such specimens because they reflect a verbal world closer to the invention
process in which the aphorism plays.

The first example represents a fairly characteristic Basic Writing level of
performance.[6]

> I think this statement is true, but I also think it can go both
> ways. In fact, I think it can be related to anyone (children in-
> cluded). It's easier to find fault with people than good, and there-
> fore we become a lot more assertive towards people when they ne-
> glect to do something due to forgetfulness, than becoming grateful
> to a person for remembering.

The first sentence makes two starts, and the second a third ("I think . . . ,
but I also think. . . . In fact I think . . ."). The third sentence is an attempt

to translate the aphorism, but the difficulties with syntactic control over parallel patterns is symptomatic of the degree to which the writer's energy is going to control the, language and thought for himself rather than carrying any ostensive force for the reader. The ostension here is working very much within a test/instruction mode: the focus is on summarizing "accurately" and displaying rather than using the logical connective "therefore." To a significant degree, this writing is style-less in Whitehead's terms.

That the second example in response to Janin's aphorism has a good deal more can be seen immediately:

> We think this statement is very true. Women, as a whole, have very good memories. We remember birthdays, old songs, dances, anniversaries. We never forget what someone wears or what we wore. Now I know men don't have terrible memories, but there must be something genetically predisposing them to be so forgetful. Sometimes it seems as if they are forgetful on purpose. Women expect men to remember the same things they do. This will never be possible for we are much too different. I think women are much more prone to remembering details while men remember events as a whole.
>
> A man's forgetfulness has lead [*sic*] to the downfall of many relationships. If anyone ever discovers the cause or develops a cure, they surely will save the world.

The most striking feature is the sense of cohesion: where the first sample has the feel of a bicycle on railroad ties, the second has a self that controls the sentences. It makes its first explicit appearance in the "we" of the third sentence and is sustained with the humorous hyperbole of "there must be something genetically predisposing them to be so forgetful" and "If anyone ever discovers the cause or develops a cure, they surely will save the world." The shift from natural genetic interpretation to disease interpretation makes us infer ostensiveness, or in Whitehead's sense, style at work. Once one becomes aware of this aspect of the student example, the final two-sentence paragraph takes on the quality of an aphorism itself. Not a great one, perhaps, but a real one, nonetheless. This raises an issue about pedagogical objectives that we will be taking up in other responses to different aphorisms.

In a last example of a response to Janin, a somewhat lengthy one, the issue of ostension and the inferential style becomes quite complex:

> Janin's statement at first seems kind of strange, but after taking a closer look at it, I believe it does hold *some* truths. But it is demeaning to women, because it makes them sound like—well—bitches. And being a woman, I don't take it too kindly, for it does *not* state a complete truth.
>
> Yes, one can say that a woman responds to a man's forgetfulness. When a man forgets something, her response is anger, frustra-

tion and other feelings. But that does not mean one can say that a woman responds *more* to forgetfulness than to attentiveness. Women like attention, and when they finally receive it, they respond in a more agreeable fashion. Women may not show their response as clearly as a response to forgetfulness because they might not want to appear like they easily melt at the hands of a man. Their responses are on the inside, and if a man is lucky enough, they may show their response on the outside!

Men just notice negative responses easier than positive responses! And if Janin is a male, he definitely has reason to believe his statement is true. So, depending upon the gender of the person reading this statement, they may take it in different ways. As a woman, I can be insulted. If I were a man, I could be very agreeable to this statement. In either case, both men and women are justified in their responses.

What is interesting in this is the mixture of styles, or, to put it more precisely, the use of one style to control another. In the first paragraph, one sees the writer cross-checking her own perspective to achieve "academic balance," that denial of the personal that a good deal of writing teaching aims to teach. The second explains the woman's perspective in a way that counters Janin's aphorism. The third paragraph makes the effort to strike a balanced view through the control of the terms *reason* and *justified*.

We put this paragraph third in our "writing assessment" scale because it involves reaching beyond the natural voice and creates a framework for learning a style to match a style. One part of any writing teacher would probably be bothered by the last sentence's effort to earn a claim about justification. The term isn't earned, to be sure, but its use defines a more substantial field for discourse.

Aphorism response writing has the advantage of baffling the algorithmic habit by creating a writing environment that is dialectical and multidimensional. This can be seen in our second response set, using the following aphorism of Chekhov: "The stupider the peasant, the better the horse understands him." Auden and Kronenberger place this (with heavy ostensive force) in the category of "Education." The implication there would seem to be that education is bad for the peasant. In a recent quarter, one of us used this aphorism as an exercise in a freshman-level class several weeks after the class had read Chekhov's story "Misery," a sketch of an old and sickened horse-cab driver deeply mired in poverty in Moscow who, we eventually discover, is grieving for the death of his son but cannot get any of his passengers to listen to his story, so he ends up telling it to his horse while looking forward to his own failing. The aphorism also has some inferrable reverberations for students themselves since in a fall-quarter English class, the word "stupid" points to the great dark cave of anxiety for most college freshmen. Sperber and Wilson point out how frequently the purpose of communication is not to provide information but to modify the cognitive environment of the reader

(46). The contextualizing information above all relates to ways this modification can take place and thus trigger responses, hopefully not of a Mount St. Helens intensity. The student writing rather consistently shows efforts to come to terms with this sort of stimulation.

Here are three reactions to the Chekhov aphorism.

> A man who is extremely stupid may seem like a lesser man, and since it is believed by many that we descend from animals, we are indeed animals. Perhaps, then, he is less man and more animal, which enables the horse to better understand those who are considered lesser. However, not knowing much about horses, I really don't know if this is a likely conclusion.

> I think the Russian philosopher was trying to get the point across that horses understand simple commands. For that matter, it could be aimed at people in general. One doesn't need to be a scholar or expert in a certain area to give directions or be a good leader. Sometimes the stupidest person can be the best leader simply because his/her directions or orders are more easily understood and are said in the simplest way possible. A person could be the smartest person in the world but if he can't be understood or followed easily then what good is all that knowledge.

> This seems on the surface to be a pretty dumb statement. How could a peasant's IQ have anything to do with whether a horse reacts to the reins? Horses only understand what people want in limited ways. As a matter of fact, in my experience with horses, they seem intentionally dumb. I've heard of horses that are highly responsive to subtle cues, but that takes training—of the sort peasants hardly seem capable of. But Chekhov seems to be suggesting something else, that the less rational and sophisticated a person is, the more he can relate to his horse, and in that way, the more the horse can feel comfortable with him. That makes a certain kind of sense—and suggests that the "understanding process" is more complex than one usually thinks.

The first is styleless railroad-tie writing again, in which the writer verbalizes "out" without getting essay-wise and finally ends by denying the basis of what he has said at the start. The second finds a style in a populist anti-intellectual pose. Notice how the writer moves quickly through horses to a world-frame in which the dumbest leader is best because he uses simple language. We can say that philistinism masked as pragmatism is intellectually dishonest, but it involves an act of mind that is in terms of language and thought construction an advance over the first.

The third is, as many readers may have guessed, a kind of trick, since it was written by the class instructor, though at the same time and under the same situational constraints as the students. The style is characterized by a macrostrategy that begins with "on the surface" and balances that with "But

Chekhov [really] seems to be suggesting something else" and shades the overall meaning as making "a certain kind of sense." It also moves directly and systematically to illustrations in ways that might well surprise us in student writing, especially at a freshman level. Compared with the second response, it suggests a writer more attentive to his own meaning-making, or meaning-discovery.

These three responses offer a kind of a vector moving from sentence-limited focus to paragraph- or discourse-limited focus to a reactive focus. We would not want to suggest that this should be understood as the only value or growth vector in writing. Obviously, this is just one of many ways to relate exploratory written responses like this, and other vectors based on more formal or conceptual criteria can be equally useful or valuable.

Not only does this writing component provide a shared experience in the prior reading assignment, but the value of the instructor in participating in this shared exercise reduces student anxiety about his or her relationship to the instructor. It removes the instructor from a distant pedestal and places the writer in the center of the student's efforts. Moreover, instructor participation in a shared exercise as in this case has the advantage of giving students an audience for a transactional writing exercise. Students were not writing for themselves as in the usual journal exercise, nor were they writing as is quite typical in composition to the instructor as their sole audience, but rather they addressed the writing group as a whole, of which the instructor was a part. Consequently, the specific aphorism-induced response in these exercises had a well-defined audience built into it. It is noteworthy, then, that such exercises can give students the opportunity to move toward a mature style of transactional writing.

As a final example of aphorism-driven exercise, we want to discuss aphorisms that run counter to the students' belief systems. The aphorism used was Nietzsche's: "Shared joys make a friend, not shared sufferings." This was a rather nasty setup for college freshmen from central Minnesota, imbued as they are with the fear of negativism. We expected that it would be very hard for some not to have their minds possessed by such clichés as, "Friends must be for the bad times as well as the good." Consequently, we believed they would have a lot of difficulty not being unbalanced by Nietzsche's refusal to collapse the dichotomy and would say that both shared joys and shared suffering can contribute to friendship. That is to say, I suppose, that it is hard for students to see the cynicism of the aphorism productively.

The first student response provides us with a good illustration of this point:

> By saying this, I think Nietzsche is making a statement about human nature. He is saying that people are more likely to become friends with the people that they have positive experiences with rather than the people they have negative experiences with. On the

surface, this may seem good, but is it really best to only be friends with the people that share the good times? All people will have some bad times in their lives and will the people that have been called "friend" still be there when these bad times come? I think sharing both the joy and the suffering makes true friends. A true friend will be willing to share the bad times and help you through them just as much as they will be happy to share your good times.

The writer here sees the "realism" in the aphorism and puts it in probabilistic terms. But then she switches to value terms and makes the move of "becoming her own grandmother," so to speak, arguing virtue with a rhetorical question ("is it really best . . . ?"). The class environment for the writer as a writer has become a kind of dorm-room bull session, where what is inferred—or ostensively put forth here—is a church-retreat community against which the evil of the pragmatic world is measured.

> I assume that Nietzsche believed that to have a person as a friend, one must share many happy experiences with that person. He also possibly believed that friendships could not endure moments of suffering. I feel that a friendship is bound to last longer if there are many happy, easy times. But true friendships, the ones that last a lifetime, are made stronger and able to endure shared suffering and hardship. If a friend isn't able to stand by through the suffering then that person doesn't deserve the important title of friend.

(One might be reminded of Franklin's remark that the way to make a person your friend is to get him to do a favor for you.) This response uses an Aristotelian *topos*—the more, the less—to redefine Nietzsche's concept of friendship into a stronger concept that is stronger for having survived hardship. This does not get trapped in ostensive assumptions in the way that number one did. This difference is important and may well get missed if one worries only about details or specifics. Both one and two are equally general, but two has a commanding point to work from.

> I believe Nietzsche was trying to make a positive statement. By saying what he did, I got the message that he meant that a good, happy experience is one that would make the difference in a friendship. A negative experience may have a tendency to create tension therefore in some cases pull friends apart. He goes about saying this by making a comparison. He uses his positive vs. negative conflict in the context that many of his readers can relate to. Just about everyone has had at least one joy and one suffering that they have experienced with a friend. Therefore, it is a statement that a wide variety of people can easily call to mind.

This is an interesting example of freshman-level discourse analysis. The student made the freshman English communication process explicit (or ostensive), defining the message in terms of "makes a comparison," "uses his positive vs. negative conflict in the context . . . readers can relate to." This is a classical example of how formulaic writing can baffle authentic reaction. The ostension here is based on a kind of testing context—the student wants to be a good student by using the right language, and this gets in the way of making plausible sense.

> There is a cynical truth in Nietzsche's aphorism. Relationships are based on successes. When someone gets fired from a job, fails a course, or screws up in some other way, some embarrassing way, personal relationships seem to retrench, and that can add to the pain of failure. Friendships are often anchored in auras. A lot of what they do is provide status. In some ways, isn't it true that the friendships that make us most comfortable, even happy, are those that don't cost us anything, but give us acknowledgment, status, rank? We have to manage them with joy, optimism, and energy. That seems to define social relationships that I see among most high school kids I see. But such relationships are maintained at a high cost none the less.
>
> Kids do commit suicide when the cost of maintaining illusions becomes too much. Nietzsche may be saying that friendships will always be limited—that that is the human condition. Or he may mean that there is something between people that goes beyond friendship. Who knows? That is the puzzle of the aphorism.

This is, of course, another teacher's effort. Part of what controls the effect is the rhetoric, perhaps, an obvious effort to map onto student-talk in order to appeal to students when on a class discussion sheet. Then, it models elaboration, redefinition, and turns the whole idea ostensively to relate to the student audience by analyzing their world. You might even say it is trying for the aphoristic—rather awkwardly we must admit—in the epigrammatic condensation of "Friendships are often anchored in auras," a phrase that pretty clearly aims to be "difficult," to demand thought. But even such writing in such a framework can be illuminating and educational.

In a chapter such as the present one, we cannot illustrate any results of the use of aphorisms as an inventional strategy beyond brief exercises. We leave it to our readers to expand and amplify on the variations we have illustrated that extend beyond one and two paragraphs. Obviously when using Sperber and Wilson's principle of relevance in interpretation, one finds that implications tend to diminish and trail off into what our psychiatrist acquaintance called "loose associations." To use aphorisms to drive lengthy inventive developments obviously would give diminishing returns. But, as just illustrated, aphorisms bring to mind other closely related aphorisms that in turn can generate theme upon theme for a respondent. Aphorisms imply counteraphorisms, which add to the complexity of the response. Such aphoristic dialectic invites argument and counterargument. Thus, the measure of any aphorism's depth, profundity, or insight is in part a measure of the degree that the aphorism spawns relevant implications that confirm or disconfirm its truth about our experiences and become the right "way" or even "the right kind of nonsense."

Aphorisms and insights without amplification are intellectually dissatifying to mature minds. At first sight aphorisms appear simply as "nuggets" of distilled wisdom. But, we soon find that they rest superficially upon surface descriptions of life experiences. It is the perception of this superficiality, this inadequacy as truth claims, that makes aphorisms effective in driving students beyond surface descriptions of life experiences. Such experiences of aphoristic superficiality illustrate to students that striking and memorable phrases and sentences without development and amplification is an empty style. It is a style of empty slogans, sound bytes, and proverbs. "The future is ahead of us." "A life without goals is aimless." It is the rhetoric of "jobs," "quotas," "flag," "a thousand points of light," and "a new world order." The student contrasts such an empty rhetoric of slogans and sound bytes with a style of developed and elaborated thought. The student sees that a developed and elaborated style deals more adequately with the complexities of life's experiences. Students thus come to see that "the ultimate morality of mind" demands an elaborated and developed style. Such a style is "the privilege of the expert." It is indeed "the ultimate morality of mind."

But note, that in making our summation on the value of aphorisms in the teaching of style, how we too have returned to aphorisms, to an aphoristic style. We see the value of aphorisms in their refocusing and encapsulating thought. "Aphorisms without development and amplification are empty." "Expert knowledge is knowledge of complex contexts of thought." "A mature style returns to aphorisms." We end here with aphorism upon aphorism. To reuse once again I. A. Richards's aphoristic phrase, aphorisms as we have been using them are "tools to think with."

Notes

1. Any useful collection of aphorisms should include the following: Erasmus, *Adagia*; La Rouchefoucauld, *Maxims*; collections of proverbs by John Heywood (1549), and Florio (1578), and William Hazlitt (1869); Paul Rosenzweig, *Book of Proverbs*; W. G. Smith and F. P. Wilson, *The Oxford Dictionary of English Proverbs*; John Simpson Franklin, *The Concise Oxford Dictionary of Proverbs*; Ambrose Bierce, *The Devil's Dictionary*; Mark Twain, "Pudd'nhead Wilson's Calendar"; Auden and Kronenberger, *The Viking Book of Aphorisms*. For foundational commentary on aphorisms, one can start with Aristotle's discussion of maxims in the second book of the *Rhetoric*, and Coleridge's *Aids to Reflection*.

We shall be showing that many aphorisms are simply detached quotes from contexts of writing. In this connection, it is interesting to note a comment made by Justin Kaplan, the editor of the most recent version of *Bartlett's Quotations*. He said in a recent interview on public television that over the years, *Bartlett's*

Quotations has been used mainly by writers and speakers to discover and generate what they have to say.

2. Hirsch elaborates his notion of the necessity of synonymy in chapter 4 of *The Aims of Interpretation*.

3. Watzlawick, Beavin, and Jackson have an interesting angle on this view of style that they bring from their work in family therapy. They see communication happening in terms of Person X understanding statement A in terms of how it implies Person Y is seeing Person X, and the way it implies Y seeing X seeing Y, and the way it implies Y seeing X seeing Y seeing X, and so forth. This also shows some common ground with Walter Ong's notion of the reader in the text in "The Writer's Audience is Always a Fiction."

4. See, for instance, Auden and Kronenberger's foreword to *The Viking Book of Aphorisms*.

5. Another remark reported to be made by Whitehead by way of Charles Hartshorne, a student of Whitehead, to one of us exemplifies how the richness of a suggestive or pithy remark can drive thought. Hartshorne heard Whitehead say [an indirect quote]: "It was better to think of force vectors not as adding up into a predetermined resultant force as they come together externally at a point, but rather as having their tails tied together internally within an agent."

The implications of this remark should be obvious to anyone who knows a little something about force vectors. For such a context of knowledge the remark is both pithy and profound. It is a transforming perspective in cosmology. Characteristically Whitehead was trying to give us a physical cosmology that has a place for agency in the world. The world would not be just a nexus of external forces impinging on one another where there is no place for free choice. The future in such an image of the world would not be predetermined by a concatenation of external forces impinging on points. It would involve agents generating events and occasions by bringing forces together at impinging points of connection. It would involve subjective aims controlling the outcome of events or occasions. All these implications follow not just from what we happen to know of Whitehead's metaphysics but from a little knowledge of statics and dynamics. Obviously the implications we have shown when fitted into larger generalities and frames of knowledge open up multitudinous lines of thought. Indeed the remark treated as aphoristic is food for thought.

Yet, despite its enormous suggestiveness for anyone interested in physical cosmologies, *is it true*? What would make it true? Aphorisms at their best are very much like Whitehead's reported remark—highly suggestive, implying profound truths about the world and life and what is important in it. They at first seem to have a sense of completeness of vision of things in them.

6. A side effect of working with style-focused writing is that the notion of developmental categories become somewhat fuzzier. Advanced students do a good deal of work in BW modes when lacking style control. This reminds one of the limitedness of Shaughnessy's *Errors and Expectations* in addressing the phenomenon of style, precisely because, for all of the depth and ingenuity of Shaughnessy's understanding of sentence error, the book lacks the depth of understanding of style that research in pragmatics is providing.

Works Cited

Auden, W. H., and Louis Kronenberger. *The Viking Book of Aphorisms*. New York: Viking, 1966.

Beardsley, Monroe. "Review of E. D. Hirsch *The Philosophy of Composition.*" *Rhetoric Society Quarterly* 8.3 (Summer 1978): 109–13.

Coles, William E., Jr. *The Plural I—and After.* Portsmouth, NH: Heinemann, 1988.

Hirsch, E. D., Jr. *The Aims of Interpretation.* Chicago: U of Chicago P, 1976.

———. *The Philosophy of Composition.* Chicago: U of Chicago P, 1978.

Johnson, Nan. *Nineteenth-Century Rhetoric in North America.* Carbondale: Southern Illinois UP, 1991.

Kaufer, David. "Review of *Relevance: Communication and Cognition.*" *Rhetoric Society Quarterly* 19.2 (Spring 1989): 171–72.

Olmstead, A. T. *History of the Persian Empire.* Chicago: U of Chicago P, 1948.

Ong, Walter, "The Writer's Audience Is Always a Fiction." *PMLA* (Jan. 1975): 9–21.

Perry, William G. "Examsmanship and the Liberal Arts." *Examining in Harvard College: A Collection of Essays.* Cambridge, MA: Harvard College, 1963. Rprt. in *The Norton Reader.* 8th ed. New York: Norton, 1992. 318–28.

Shaughnessy, Mina. *Errors and Expectations.* New York: Oxford UP, 1971.

Sperber, Dan, and Deirdre Wilson. *Relevance: Communications and Cognition.* Cambridge, MA: Harvard UP, 1986.

Stace, Walter. "What Religion Is." *Time and Eternity: An Essay in the Philosophy of Religion.* Princeton: Princeton UP, 1952. Rprt. in *Harper and Row Reader.* Ed. Wayne Booth and Marshall Gregory. New York: Harper and Row, 1984. 605–9.

Watzlawick, Paul, Janet Beavin, and Don Jackson. *The Pragmatics of Human Communication.* New York: Norton, 1967.

Whitehead, Alfred N. *The Aims of Education.* New York: New American Library, 1949.

———. *Process and Reality.* New York: Macmillan, 1969.

———. *Science and the Modern World.* New York: New American Library, 1949.

Wittgenstein, Ludwig. *Philosophical Investigations.* Oxford: Basil Blackwell, 1958.

Contributors

Contributors

James A. Berlin is professor of English at Purdue University, where he teaches courses in the theory and history of rhetoric. He is the author of *Writing Instruction in Nineteenth-Century American Colleges* and *Rhetoric and Reality: Writing Instruction in American Colleges, 1900–1985.* He has also edited, with Michael Vivion, *Cultural Studies in the English Classroom.*

Paul T. Bryant is professor of English and dean of the Graduate College at Radford University. He is author of *H. L. Davis,* editor of *From Geography to Geotechnics,* coeditor with Donald C. Stewart and Patricia L. Stewart of *The Eclectic Reader,* coeditor with David Mogen and Mark Busby of *The Frontier Experience and the American Dream,* and author of essays on Western American literature, composition and rhetoric, and nature writing. He has served as president of the College English Association, president of the Conference of Southern Graduate Schools, chair of the National Council of Teachers of English Commission on Composition, member of the NCTE editorial board, member of the Conference on College Composition and Communication and Western Literature Association executive committees, chair of the CCCC Braddock Award Committee, and member of the WLA Don Walker Prize Committee. His current research interests include nature writing and Western American literature.

Robert J. Connors is an associate professor of English at the University of New Hampshire. He is the author of a number of articles on rhetorical history and theory. With Lisa Ede and Andrea Lunsford, he coedited *Essays on Classical Rhetoric and Modern Discourse.* He coauthored *The St. Martin's Handbook* with Andrea Lunsford and *The St. Martin's Guide to Teaching Writing* with Cheryl Glenn and edited the *Selected Essays of Edward P.J. Corbett*. In 1982 he was given the Richard Braddock Award by the Conference on College Composition and Communication for the article "The Rise and Fall of the Modes of Discourse" and in 1985 was corecipient of the Mina P. Shaughnessy Award from the Modern Language Association for *Essays on Classical Rhetoric and Modern Discourse*. His current projects include research on genre in student writing, a study of student spelling patterns, a long essay on patriarchy and the feminization of rhetoric, and a book on current-traditional rhetoric in its cultural and historical contexts.

Edward P.J. Corbett began his teaching career at Creighton University in Omaha, Nebraska, where he served as director of freshman English and, during his final year there, as president of the Nebraska Council of Teachers of English. In 1966, he joined the staff of Ohio State University, and in 1991, he retired as professor emeritus of English. During his tenure at OSU, he served for five years as director of freshman English; as president of the Ohio Council of Teachers of English; as chairman of the Conference on College Composition and Communication; as editor of the journal *College Composition and Communication*; and as chair of the College Section of the National Council of Teachers of English. Among his many published books are *Classical Rhetoric for the Modern Student*, *The Little English Handbook*, *The Elements of Reasoning*, and *Selected Essays of Edward P.J. Corbett*. His *The Essay, Old and New*, coedited with Sheryl L. Finkle, was published in 1993. Corbett was granted the Ohio State University Distinguished Scholar Award and the Distinguished Service Award from the National Council of Teachers of English, and in his final year of teaching, he was elected to an honorary membership in the OSU chapter of Phi Beta Kappa.

William A. Covino is associate professor of English at the University of Illinois at Chicago, where he teaches in the graduate program in language, literacy, and rhetoric. His articles on rhetorical theory and history have appeared in several journals, and his books include *The Art of Wondering: A Revisionist Return to the History of Rhetoric* and *Forms of Wondering: A Dialogue on Writing, for Writers*. He is currently completing a book on the interrelationship of rhetoric, magic, and literacy.

Theresa Enos, founder and editor of *Rhetoric Review*, teaches in the graduate program in rhetoric and composition at the University of Arizona. Besides publishing in various journals on rhetorical theory, she is the editor of *A Sourcebook for Basic Writing Teachers* and *Learning from the Histories of Rhetoric: Essays in Honor of Winifred Bryan Horner*. She has coedited with Stuart C. Brown *Defining the New Rhetorics* and *Professing the New Rhetorics*. She currently is working as general editor of the *Encyclopedia of Rhetoric* and is writing a book, interweaving statistical analyses and personal narrative, on gender and disciplinary bias in rhetoric and composition.

Vincent Gillespie is associate professor and assistant head of the Department of English at Kansas State University. He was a department colleague of Donald Stewart for all but thirteen years of Stewart's professional life. Gillespie received a B.A. from Sterling College and both an M.A. and Ph.D. from the University of Kansas. His teaching specialties have been in technical writing, rhetoric and composition, folklore, and American literature. He has taught at the University of Kansas, Emporia State University, Dartmouth College, and since 1966 at Kansas State University. He has served as assistant head for twelve years and was director of the Composition Program from 1974 to 1981. Gillespie was research associate with Albert Kitzhaber for the Dartmouth Study of Student Writing, was director of the three-year NEH Kansas Writing Improvement Program, and during the years of his active involvement in the Conference on College Composition and Communication delivered numerous papers on composition and program administration.

Lawrence D. Green is associate professor of English (Rhetoric-Linguistics-Literature) at the University of Southern California. He translated and edited *John Rainolds's Oxford Lectures on Aristotle's "Rhetoric."* His essays on the use of enthymemes in composition have been widely cited. His current focus is on the history of rhetoric and the cultural history of composition and rhetoric.

Winifred Bryan Horner is the Lillian Radford Chair of Rhetoric and Composition at Texas Christian University. Her book, *Nineteenth-Century Scottish Rhetoric: The American Connection,* was published in 1993. She has also published a number of articles on the teaching of rhetoric at the universities of Edinburgh, Glasgow, and Aberdeen. She is currently working on an edition of selected writing from three nineteenth-century Scottish rhetoricians: George Jardine, Edward Edmondstoune Aytoun, and Alexander Bain. She has published six books and numerous articles on the history of rhetoric and composition.

Nan Johnson is associate professor of English at Ohio State University, where she teaches the history of rhetoric, rhetorical theory, critical theory, and writing. She is the author of *Nineteenth-Century Rhetoric in North America* and numerous book chapters, articles, and reviews on nineteenth-century rhetoric and general topics in the history of rhetoric and composition. Currently her research focuses on the popular rhetoric movement in nineteenth-century America and cultural attitudes in this period regarding rhetorical performance and gender.

Philip Keith is currently coeditor of *Rhetoric Society Quarterly*. He has published articles and reviews on various subjects in rhetoric and at its margins. He has taught English at Swarthmore College, Washington and Lee University, and, since 1977, at St. Cloud State University, where he is professor of English and has served as composition director, writing-across-the-curriculum director, and general education assessment coordinator.

Richard L. Larson is professor of English and associate of the Institute for Literacy Studies at Lehman College of The City University of New York, where, in addition to undergraduate courses in writing, he teaches graduate courses in the English language and in the teaching of writing in college. He is a past chair of the Conference on College Composition and Communication and a past editor of the journal *College Composition and Communication*. He has written numerous essays about the teaching of writing and the preparation of teachers of English and a monograph, *The Evaluation of Teaching: College English*.

Janice M. Lauer is professor of English at Purdue University, where she directs the graduate program in rhetoric and composition. She is coauthor of *Four Worlds of Writing* and *Composition Research: Empirical Designs* and author of articles on writing as inquiry, composition as a discipline, and invention. For thirteen years she directed a national summer rhetoric seminar on current theories of teaching composition. She has been chair of the College Section of the National Council of Teachers of English, member of the executive committee of the Conference on College Composition and Communication and of the Modern Language Association's discussion group on the history and theory of rhetoric, and member of the board of directors of the Rhetoric Society of America. She is editor of the rhetoric and composition entries for the *Encyclopedia of English Studies and Language Arts*. Current research interests include historical studies of invention, persuasive writing as inquiry and critique, and pedagogies of invention.

Richard Lloyd-Jones of the University of Iowa led the program in advanced expository writing and nonfiction for twenty years, chaired the Department of English for nine years, directed the School of Letters for ten years, and taught in numerous summer institutes. He chaired the Conference on College Composition and Communication in 1977 and was president of the National Council of Teachers of English in 1987. He received the Distinguished Service Award of the Iowa Council, the second Francis Andrew March Award of the Association of Departments of English, and first Exemplar Award of the CCCC. He coauthored *Research in Written Composition*, coedited the statement accompanying *The Students' Right to Their Own Language*, codesigned Primary Trait Scoring, and collaborated on *Democracy Through Language*, the report of the English Coalition Conference.

Diane Mowery is a Ph.D. candidate in humanities at the University of Texas at Arlington. Her areas of concentration are rhetoric and composition and critical/cultural theory. Her most recent work focuses on postmodern/ postfeminist critiques of modern–day Goddess movements and of feminist composition pedagogy. She is currently the editorial assistant for Victor J. Vitanza's *PRE/TEXT: A Journal of Rhetorical Theory*.

C. Jan Swearingen is professor of English at the University of Texas at Arlington and graduate advisor for a collegewide, rhetoric-based Ph.D. program. She is author of *Rhetoric and Irony: Western Literacy and Western Lies* and editor of a forthcoming collection of essays on language and religion, *The Word: Studies in the Language of Religion and the Religious Meaning of Language*. Her recent articles and chapters focus on theories of narrative, dialogue, rhetoric, and interpretation in related fields; theorizing approaches to women and the feminine in classical literature; and ideologies affecting educated women and the education of women from antiquity to the present.

Victor J. Vitanza, associate professor of English at the University of Texas at Arlington, is the editor of *PRE/TEXT* and the director of the Center for Rhetorical and Critical Theory. He has two forthcoming edited books, *Writing Histories of Rhetoric* and *PRE/TEXT: The First Decade*. He is presently completing a book tentatively titled *Negation, Subjectivity, and the History of Rhetoric*.

W. Ross Winterowd, founder of the graduate program in rhetoric, linguistics, and literature at the University of Southern California, is now hard at work on a history of English department humanities from the Enlightenment to the present, accounting for the exaltation of "imaginative" literature and the virtual banishment of history, biography, autobiography, and the essay from the canon; for the ghettoization of composition/rhetoric; for the stigma placed on questions about the uses of literature; for the servile status of those interested in the art of teaching; and for the scorn with which members of the literary establishment view the common reader.

George Yoos is professor of philosophy at St. Cloud State University. He has been editor of the *Rhetoric Society Quarterly* and has been an active promoter of the Rhetoric Society of America since its beginning in 1968. At present he is associate editor of the *Quarterly*. He is author of a number of articles and book reviews on diverse topics in aesthetics, rhetoric, argumentation, informal logic, philosophy, speech, reading, and composition. His major interest is philosophy of communication.

Richard E. Young is professor of rhetoric and English literature at Carnegie Mellon University. From 1978 to 1983 he was head of the Department of English at Carnegie Mellon, during which time he oversaw the development of its graduate programs in rhetoric. His continuing research interests have been rhetorical invention, research methodologies, and the pedagogy of writing. At present he is working on problems of language learning in undergraduate education.